"Status quo national security perspectives of the
security focus that is integral to the Women, Pe.
edition of *Women, Peace and Security*, Johnson-Freese provides compelling evidence demonstrating that women's participation and voice in national security produce tangible impacts such as lowering violence, creating lasting peace agreements, lowering corruption, developing more trust in governments, and improving health and education outcomes. Women, Peace, and Security is a vital security topic – not just a social justice issue – that treats women as security agents rather than victims or bystanders and demands women be integral to security-related decision-making."

Captain David G. Smith (USN Ret), PhD, *Associate Professor in the Johns Hopkins Carey Business School and co-author of* Good Guys: How Men Can Be Better Allies for Women in the Workplace and Athena Rising: How and Why Men Should Mentor Women

"I hear your skepticism: what's the point of considering gender in national security spheres? Read this WPS introduction and you too will be convinced that a gender-inclusive foreign policy is the only way forward. Without a gender perspective, we cannot make sense of women suicide bombers; the roots of misogyny in domestic terrorism and cyber violence; why peace agreements that involve lead women negotiators last longer; and how women's insecurities will be foundational to numerous future state stability threats, especially for a warming world in which women lack insufficient power to achieve resilience for themselves and their families. If lasting peace is your aim – whether you work in government, development, nonprofit, or the armed forces – you need this overview to understand why international security theory must be redefined using a rigorous application of a gendered lens."

Maryruth Belsey Priebe, *Pacific Forum, Director for Women, Peace and Security Programs and Senior Fellow*

"Joan Johnson-Freese significantly expands the scope of Women Peace and Security with this insightful book on how women in national security roles make a profound difference in constructing sustainable outcomes. This treatment of WPS expands the author's first groundbreaking book with new insights on a women's roles in the media, the military, and at the diplomatic negotiating table."

Kitty Pilgrim, *Journalist, Author*

"This volume contributes to an ever-growing body of research linking gender inequality with violence and conflict, and gender equality with greater peace and stability, and as such places gender equality as central to human and national security. Joan Johnson-Freese lays out a compelling argument for how to use the WPS framework to advance peace by using gender equality as an integral vehicle of transformative change. The reading is both critical and forward-looking and recognizes that the first step is looking internally – not externally."

Heather Huhtanen, *Gender Expert, Geneva, Switzerland*

"Joan Johnson-Freese simultaneously educates policymakers and practitioners that gender equality is a critical dimension of security while empowering these same actors to achieve better security outcomes through their heightened awareness. The reader is treated to an interdisciplinary feast of gender and feminist theory explored and applied in a security context. Her wide-ranging case studies illustrate the phenomenal power the gender lens can wield to understand war, conflict, development, and politics. *Women, Peace and Security* fills a critical curriculum gap across all dimensions of security studies."

Marybeth Peterson Ulrich, *General Maxwell D. Taylor*
Chair of the Profession of Arms, US Army War College

"This publication represents a significant contribution to the ongoing discussion on Women, Peace and Security, and moves the debate beyond the confines of the United Nations and embeds it in practical security considerations that governments must grapple with on a daily basis. It exposes the bias that still exists towards the involvement of women in security discussions, operations, and activities, and makes a strong case for women as positive actors in guaranteeing security at the community, state, regional, and international levels; and not merely as beneficiaries of security."

Rocky R. Meade, *Chief of the Jamaican Defense Force*

Women, Peace and Security

This book offers an accessible overview of the issues related to the Women, Peace and Security (WPS) global agenda. This new edition has been updated and includes new chapters on WPS and Environmental Change and on WPS in Regional and Security Organizations.

The second edition explains Women, Peace and Security as a security framework, different though related to both gender equality as a social justice issue or a Diversity, Equity and Inclusion issue. Within the context of the changing nature of warfare, a complex and volatile global political climate, and through consideration of empirical evidence, it examines the definitions, theoretical underpinnings, and methodological challenges associated with implementing WPS. It then discusses with more specificity violence against women, women civilians in war, the role of women in peacemaking, women in the military and in development, and women politicians, with new material on environmental change and on regional and security organizations. Examples and case studies draw from Africa, Asia, the Middle East, Europe, and North and South America. The need for more sex-disaggregated data on every topic is emphasized throughout, necessary to both demonstrate relationships between gender and security and to identify solutions to problems. The book concludes with a look to the future and number of action items from the macro to the micro level.

This book will be of much interest to students of peace studies, security studies, gender studies, and IR, as well as professional military college students.

Joan Johnson-Freese is Senior Fellow, Women in International Security and Professor Emeritus, Naval War College, Faculty, Harvard Extension & Summer Schools. She is author of several books, including *Educating America's Military* (2012), *Space Warfare in the 21st Century* (2016), and *Women vs. Women* (2022).

Women, Peace and Security

An Introduction

Second Edition

Joan Johnson-Freese

LONDON AND NEW YORK

Cover image: 'For a Better World' – Anne Sibireff

Second edition published 2024
by Routledge
4 Park Square, Milton Park, Abingdon, Oxon OX14 4RN

and by Routledge
605 Third Avenue, New York, NY 10158

Routledge is an imprint of the Taylor & Francis Group, an informa business

First edition published by Routledge 2019

British Library Cataloguing-in-Publication Data
A catalogue record for this book is available from the British Library

Library of Congress Cataloging-in-Publication Data
Names: Johnson-Freese, Joan, author.
Title: Women, peace and security : an introduction / Joan Johnson-Freese.
Description: Second edition. | New York : Routledge, 2024. |
Includes bibliographical references and index.
Identifiers: LCCN 2023029478 (print) | LCCN 2023029479 (ebook) |
ISBN 9781032537528 (hbk) | ISBN 9781032537504 (pbk) | ISBN 9781003413417 (ebk)
Subjects: LCSH: Women and peace. | Women and war.
Classification: LCC JZ5578 .J64 2024 (print) | LCC JZ5578 (ebook) |
DDC 303.6/6082–dc23/eng/20230809
LC record available at https://lccn.loc.gov/2023029478
LC ebook record available at https://lccn.loc.gov/2023029479

ISBN: 978-1-032-53752-8 (hbk)
ISBN: 978-1-032-53750-4 (pbk)
ISBN: 978-1-003-41341-7 (ebk)

DOI: 10.4324/9781003413417

Typeset in Times New Roman
by Newgen Publishing UK

Contents

Acknowledgments

Women, Peace and Security (WPS) is a multidisciplinary field both a mile wide and a mile deep. Nobody is an expert in all aspects, and certainly not me. That leaves me reliant on the hard work and research of the many individuals working on aspects of WPS to build and present an overview of the subject matter material, or at least as much of an overview as one can do in 130,000 words. I continue to be dazzled by their scholarship, commitment, and professionalism, and thank each and every one for their efforts. For this second edition, discussions with Samantha Turner, Tahina Montoya, Duilia Mora Turner, Marigo Dulaku, Heather Huhtanen, Katherine Lucey, Greta Holtz, Jim Minnich, Kitty Pilgrim, and Saira Yamin were especially helpful.

Working with Harvard for now almost 20 years has been gratifying for both its faculty support, including a research assistant, and for allowing me to teach some really amazing students. I am very grateful. Cara Condit, you've been a great help as my research assistant. Thank you for proofreading and commenting on draft chapters from your legal background. Most of all, though, it is the students that I want to acknowledge and thank. Chuck Houston, Ashley Kelso, Melissa Deehring, and Maryruth Belsey Priebe, you were all students who transitioned to being remarkable WPS teaching assistants. Chuck and Melissa, it was great working with you on WPS articles as well. Alexandra Islas, your social media work on my behalf and WPS has been outstanding, and it was a pleasure to help you launch a publishing career too! Among most recent students I'd like to thank, Dr. Staci Emerson for her insights on women's mental health issues, Jon Ratchick for his work on WPS and Professional Military Education, Jeff Lockwood for his work on Kurdish women's forces, and Cathleen Pearl for introducing me to the Female Tactical Platoon program. Their work sparked me to look into areas I might not have otherwise. And there are so many other students whose questions, thoughts, and papers pushed me to be a better researcher and teacher. I'm not going to try to name everyone because I don't want to leave out even one name, but I hope you all know who you are.

I'd also like to thank Ariela Blatter, Karin Johnston, and Roksana Verahrami at Women in International Security (WIIS). Working with them and WIIS is a privilege. And Blaire Harms and Nick Tomb at the Institute for Security Governance in Monterey – you run a fantastic program. I am always pleased and grateful to be a part of your WPS work, as I always learn something new.

I'd also like to thank the many WPS class guest speakers who have given of their time so generously. Listening to them is, again, a learning experience for me as well as the students and I'm very appreciative.

Responsibility for the views and material in this book is, of course, fully mine.

Finally, thank you to my family. You support me always, even when, as two-year-old Alice says, "Bagga needs a minute."

Abbreviations

ABA	American Bar Association
AFRICOM	US DOD Africa Command
AI	Artificial Intelligence
AIDS	Acquired Immunodeficiency Syndrome
ASEAN	Association of Southeast Asian Nations
AU	African Union
BPD	Borderline Personality Disorder
CAF	Canadian Armed Forces
CEDAW	Convention on the Elimination of All Forms of Discrimination Against Women
CIHR	Canadian Institutes of Health Research
CLA	Constitutional Loya Jirga (Afghanistan)
CRA	Colombia Reintegration Agency
CRSV	Conflict Related Sexual Violence
CRVAW	Conflict-Related Violence Against Women
CST	Cultural Support Team
DDR	Disarmament, Demobilization and Reintegration
DHB	US Defense Health Board
DHS	US Department of Homeland Security
DOD	US Department of Defense
DOS	US Department of State
ELN	National Liberation Front (Colombia)
EU	European Union
FAO	Food and Agriculture Organization
FARC	Revolutionary Armed Forces of Colombia
FGM/C	Female Genital Mutilation/Cutting
FFP	Feminist Foreign Policy
FMLN	Farabundo Marti National Liberation Front (El Salvador)
FTP	Female Tactical Platoon
GAO	Government Accounting Office
GBV	Gender-Based Violence
GENAD	Gender Advisor
GDP	Gross Domestic Product
GFP	Gender Focal Point

GIWPS	Georgetown Institute for Women, Peace and Security
HIV	Human Immunodeficiency Virus
HBS	Harvard Business School
IADB	Inter-American Defense Board (of the OAS)
ICC	International Criminal Court
ICRC	International Committee of the Red Cross and Red Crescent
ICT	Information and Communications Technology
IDF	Israel Defense Forces
IDP	Internally Displaced Person
ISIL	Islamic State of Iraq and the Levant (also called Daesh)
ISIS	Islamic State of Iraq and Syria
IPV	Intimate Partner Violence
IR	International Relations
ITU	International Telecommunications Union
ISIS	Islamic State of Iraq and Syria
LGBTQ+	Lesbian, Gay, Bisexual, Transgender, Queer, Plus
MAMA	Mobile Alliance for Maternal Action
MEL	Monitoring, Evaluation and Learning
MDG	Millennium Development Goals
MGI	McKinsey Global Institute
MIT	Massachusetts Institute of Technology
NAP	National Action Plan
NATO	North Atlantic Treaty Organization
NGO	Nongovernmental Organizations
NIWC	Northern Ireland Women's Coalition
NorAF	Norwegian Armed Forces
NOW	National Organization for Women
PME	Professional Military Education
PTSD	Post-Traumatic Stress Disorder
RAP	Regional Action Plan
SAE	Special Area of Emphasis (US DOD)
SDF	Syrian Democratic Forces
SDG	Sustainable Development Goals
SDO	Social Dominance Orientation
SEWA	Self Employed Women's Association
SSE	Solar Sister Entrepreneurs
STEM	Science, Technology, Engineering and Math
TiP	Trafficking in Persons
UK	United Kingdom
UN	United Nations
UNDP	United Nations Development Program
UNESCO	United Nations Educational, Scientific, and Cultural Organization
UNFPA	United Nations Population Fund
UNHCR	United Nations High Commissioner for Refugees

UNICEF	United Nations Children's Fund
UNSCR	United Nations Security Council Resolution
US	United States
USAID	US Agency for International Development
WASP	Women Air Force Service Pilots (US)
WISTAT	Women's Indicators and Statistics Database
WHO	World Health Organization
WHRD	Women Human Rights Defenders
WIPNET	Women in Peacebuilding Network (Liberia)
WPS	Women, Peace & Security
YPG	People's Protection Unit (Kurdistan)
YPJ	Kurdish Women's Protection Unit

Introduction

As a social science, there are very few the-Earth-is-round-like "facts" associated with international relations. There are many theories, perspectives, and endless opinions (opinion being the lowest form of knowledge), but few facts. There are, however, areas of consensus demonstrated by empirical research. States are important global actors. There has been a rise in populist-nationalism over the past decade. Globalization has had profound effects on the economies of many countries. All of these aspects of international relations are largely accepted as fact and standard fare in introductory International Relations (IR) courses. What is not standard fare in IR courses is considering the state of gender relations in a country, though it is an equally important consideration as state sovereignty, populism, globalization, and so forth. Gender is not included because rather than its importance being seen as a consensus view, it is, as I've been told many times, considered simply opinion. But that is wrong. Researchers have been empirically testing the effects of gender equality within and among countries on security-related issues for decades and the results are clear. Gender matters.

As Harvard Professor Dara Kay Cohen and Cornell Professor Sabrina Karim point out in a 2022 article, however, it is rarely considered.

> Research on these questions branched in new directions in the early 2000s when quantitative scholars, analyzing large cross-national data sets, demonstrated a statistically significant correlation between sex and gender inequality – measured a variety of ways – and the probability of interstate war and civil conflict, even controlling for many other factors known to be associated with the onset of violence. This core result has been replicated many times: nearly a hundred studies indicate some type of link between sex and gender inequality and violent outcomes. Scholars characterize the relationship between sex and gender inequality and war as "well established," and a "near-consensus." Yet despite the overwhelming evidence, it has not been widely embraced in the international politics literature; instead, it has been relegated to a specialized group of IR scholars, whose work is rarely integrated into major IR theories.[1]

The neglect of sex and gender in IR studies must change. Ignoring gender in IR studies leaves the field incomplete through neglect of a critical component.

While there are some specialized university courses (often within gender studies programs) with titles such as "International Relations through a Feminist Lens," "Global Feminism: Race and Gender in International Relations," and "Feminism and Critical IR Theory," which cover gender relations as related to international relations, that feminist lens, and thereby gendered relations, is not standard fare in university survey courses at the undergraduate or graduate level, or anywhere in high school courses or in government-administered and funded educational programs such as Professional Military Education (PME). Not covering the perspectives,

DOI: 10.4324/9781003413417-1

knowledge provided by, and issues associated with half the global population leaves a huge knowledge gap for future practitioners of international relations, global politics, security studies, and many other related subject matter monikers. It is important as well for students in other fields who become part of the general public, thereby influencing public views of what is important and consequently, public policy. That must change.

Feminist writer and political science professor Cynthia Enloe lamented how easily gender politics was dismissed by security practitioners in her book *Bananas, Beaches, and Bases* (1989). "Despite the remarkable activist engagement that has generated today's multi-stranded transnational women's movement," she wrote, "many journalists (and editors who assign their stories), foreign-policy experts, and policy decision makers remain oddly confident in their dismissal of feminist ideas."[2] She further argued that women's voices needed to be heard in IR studies, but her voice was largely drowned out within that male-dominated academic field, her colleagues then focused on the Cold War.

Enloe suggested several reasons for gender marginalization at that time. First, feminist considerations were categorized as a "special interest" rather than an integral part of international relations. When that is the case, women are granted no real role in international relations but instead are viewed as mindless victims or commodities, such as sex workers, service workers, home workers, and child bearers. Second, it was assumed that what happens to women is private/domestic/cultural and what happens to men is political/military/security, and those categories of issues are unrelated. For example, not supporting women in the workforce was dismissed as not related to economic development issues that might spur conflict between nations, and not having legislation criminalizing rape was not seen as signaling permissiveness regarding violence. Third, issues such as the treatment, or mistreatment, of women had been considered related to culture and therefore too difficult to tackle as part of foreign policy or international relations. That's especially ironic given that some countries haven't seen trying to export democracy to communist or authoritarian countries as "too difficult." And so, gender equality was seen as a lost cause or a bargaining chip at negotiation tables. Finally, gender-equality issues were considered as part of a social justice agenda, rather than a power and security agenda. Sadly, too little has changed in the 30 plus years since Enloe was writing. But consideration of gender-related issues unveils power structures and challenges across all areas of international relations.

Even the language of international relations inhibits women's involvement. Commonly used concepts such as rationality, objectivity, and power – mostly in coercive, military terms – are considered masculine, whereas empathy, subjectivity, and cooperation – including diplomacy and arms control – are considered feminine. Consequently, "feminine" policy alternatives such as diplomacy and arms control are too often dismissed as soft. That was certainly the case for the decades that I researched and wrote about space security issues in conjunction with the military. There, the heavily male-dominated field consistently saw technology and the weaponization of space to be the answer to every question – with "how to win a space war" the primary question asked. Subsequently, arms control and diplomacy were curtailed, though technology had been repeatedly shown ineffective or even counterproductive in addressing space-security issues. While "how to win a space war" is an important question, so too are "how does the United States (US) prevent a space war?" and "how can the US address the inherently multinational issue of space debris?" But those questions require diplomats, not warriors, and individuals don't join the military to be diplomats.

Human security deals with issues directly related to individuals, as opposed to geopolitical, state security. The spindle/spear stereotypes that represent men protecting and providing for women, while women stay home and care for the family have been globally enculturated as fact through families, religions, public institutions, the arts, and popular culture for a very long time. More than 30 years since Enloe wrote, the spindle/spear stereotype and the idea that human security largely deals with "women's issues" to which women should be relegated still prevails, in some cases due to bias, in others simply to inertia and ignorance. Education can help change that.

Certainly, strides have been made toward breaking the spindle/spear worldview of gender. Women serve as government officials, lawyers, judges, doctors, heads of corporations, fighter pilots, construction workers, and so forth around the globe. But there are still over millions of school-age girls not attending school, sometimes because of being banned from education. Mothers working outside of the home are also still primarily responsible for homemaking chores and childcare as well in most countries. The World Health Organization (WHO) estimates that one in three women globally have been subject to either physical and/or sexual intimate partner violence or non-partner sexual violence over the course of their lifetime, and 45% of women globally cannot make their own decisions about sexual and reproductive health.

Topics taught in IR classes have evolved. Once focused primarily on geopolitics, power, and diplomacy, in various ways and degrees, now considerations such as development, economics, the environment, religion, and food security, and perhaps most recently health security, have been added. Part of that evolution stems from the changing nature of defining security. Traditional definitions of security focused on "national security" issues – those related to states, defense, and the military – but even in this resurgent era of geopolitics, issues related to individuals, including health, food, the environment, education, and so on are increasingly included.

Women are "involved" in security-related issues from the micro, family level, to the macro, national and global level, negating the idea that there is such a thing as "women's issues." The Covid-19 pandemic clearly pointed out the critical role that women play in the workforce. Globally, women comprise the majority of frontline healthcare workers. In many families, women's jobs were revealed as more security related than those of their male spouses. Women needed to go to work, and to do so, they needed childcare, exposing childcare as a family issue. Additionally, their often-frontline role put women at increased risk of exposure, and of mental health issues. And just as healthcare is a security issue, so too is food production and distribution, and in many countries more women than men work in the agriculture sector. The spindle/spear dichotomy was never really the case – women have worked inside and outside of their homes throughout history – but globalization and the interconnected nature of society and societies have stripped away the last vestiges of that myth. Unfortunately as well, women are too often involuntarily drawn into the "spear" realm of politics.

In the first two decades of the twenty-first century, most wars were fought within nations rather than between nations, and when they were between nations, they were most often border wars. Consequently, battle zones have included streets, villages, and cities, and civilians – especially women and children – have been plunged into the thick of the fighting. Women are disproportionately affected through issues including displacement, gender-based violence (GBV), a rise in child marriages, and disrupted access to reproductive healthcare, but are excluded from peace negotiations, thereby leaving the issues disproportionately affecting women out of the negotiations. While the US, China, and Russia are focused on Great Power Competition (now referred by the US as simply Strategic Competition to allow for inclusion of countries like Iran and North Korea), Russia's incursion into Ukraine and conflicts in other areas evidence that deep civilian impacts from conflicts are still widespread. Rape, including what has been characterized as "systematic rape," has been widely reported as being carried out by Russian troops against Ukrainian women, and more than seven million Ukrainians have been displaced, over half of those women, children, and marginalized populations.

The Women, Peace and Security (WPS) framework is a first-of-its-kind in its recognition of the integral role that women play across the board in security-related issues, and calls for women's voices to address those issues. A word of note: Though United Nations Security Council Resolution (UNSCR) 1325 is often referred to as the Women, Peace and Security *agenda*, I suggest a better alternative is the Women, Peace and Security *framework* as too many times I've been told by individuals in security fields that the word "agenda" implies a devious scheme or plot. Words can influence how individuals accept or reject information. Once during the many years I worked on space security issues, I insisted that two very bright, young Czech political scientists not use the term "manifesto" in the title of a paper they were authoring for an organization I worked with, as in the US, manifesto is a negatively "loaded" term associated with communism. Similarly, WPS faces enough acceptance hurdles without adding one that can be easily avoided.

WPS is not a petition for gender equality as a social justice issue, though the oppression of women certainly is a social justice issue. In 2009, husband and wife writers Nicholas Kristof and Sheryl WuDunn called the fight against gender inequality the "paramount moral challenge" of this era, equivalent to the abolishment of slavery in a prior era, in their book *Half the Sky*. Unfortunately, however, those who benefit from gender inequality are not swayed by calls for social justice. They may in fact actively resist any change from the status quo. WPS, the focus of this book, is a call for recognition that gender equality is good for men, women, boys, and girls in that it increases the potential for stable, thriving environments at all levels of security analysis, articulates barriers to achievement, and stipulates what needs to be done to achieve gender equality, thereby strengthening human and subsequently national security.

It should be noted that neither UNSCR 1325 nor any of its follow-on resolutions specifically mention lesbian, gay, bisexual, transgender, queer or questioning, and more (LGBTQ+) individuals. But there is a clear intent to broadly define gender in considerations of "gendered perspectives," within the WPS framework. The peace process in Colombia, for example, included a gender subcommittee involving LGBTQ+ organizations, and the LGBTQ+ community is referenced multiple times in the final version of the peace agreement. Canada's 2017–2022 National Action Plan to implement UNSCR 1325 specifically pledges to pay attention to the LGBTQ+ community and asylum seekers. A 2022 United Nations (UN) report on protection against violence and discrimination based on sexual orientation and gender identity reflects increased attention to issues specific to LGBTQ+ and gender-diverse persons. The WPS framework is constantly evolving, and striving to be inclusive.

The first edition of *Women, Peace and Security: An Introduction* was published in 2018 and much has changed since then. After two decades, US troops left Afghanistan in 2021. Though the protection and empowerment of women was part of the George W. Bush administration's rationale for being there, and the US is the first and only country to make implementation of the WPS framework a legislative mandate, women were largely absent from the negotiating table before the US left, and the rollback of women's rights there began almost immediately. Men and women took to the streets in Iran after the sudden death – murder – of Mahsa Amini in 2022, subsequent to her being arrested by the morality police for violation of the country's hijab laws. Women's rights have regressed in countries ranging from Myanmar, with pro-democracy women there targeted at unprecedented levels with doxxing and hate speech, to the United States with the stunning 2022 reversal of *Roe v. Wade* by the US Supreme Court. The unprovoked Russian invasion of Ukraine in February 2022 thrust not just soldiers but also boys, girls, civilian women, and all vulnerable populations into a conflict marked by homelessness and the weaponization of rape.

Throughout this second edition, it is stressed that there is no such thing as "women's issues," and how that characterization is a detriment to gender equality and security. Further, it is not enough to have women at the table where security decisions are made; they must have a voice. If international relations is a field of study to determine best routes to long-term international stability, then women must be included. Things must change.

Chapters 1 through 5 in the book cover fundamental terms, concepts, and frameworks relevant to Women, Peace and Security, as prerequisites for fully understanding the specific areas of application covered in Chapters 6–12. Chapter 13 offers recommendations for moving WPS implementation forward. The need for more sex-disaggregated data on every topic from gender-based violence to allocation of supplies in relief and recovery plans to global mediation and negotiating teams is emphasized throughout, necessary to both demonstrate relationships and find solutions to problems.

Chapter 1, "A place and a voice at the table," focuses on establishing Women, Peace and Security as a security topic rather than a social justice topic, through the presentation of women as security agents rather than victims or bystanders, and through explaining the importance of having women part of security-related discussions and decision-making. The four pillars of the WPS framework are introduced and challenges of implementation presented. The need for and challenges of obtaining sex-disaggregated data are also explained.

Chapter 2, "The role of feminist theory," explains and considers feminism and feminist theory in the development of the Women, Peace and Security framework, including the definition and discussion of key terms such as intersectionality, agency, sex, and gender. Power hierarchies are discussed, as well as how power is taken, given, and fought over between the sexes, including over reproductive rights. It also covers the differences and similarities between Feminist Foreign Policy and Women, Peace and Security as alternative but broadly overlapping frameworks for addressing gender biases and prejudices, toward a more secure world.

Chapter 3, "Patriarchies," begins to unpack the linkages between many seemingly disparate acts against women as part of a larger, systemic effort by a patriarchy that has historically made customs, policies, and laws to benefit themselves and to subordinate women. The chapter also explicates, based on empirically supported analysis, how that subordination hurts internal and external security. Power is at the heart of all political struggles, and those who have it are not going to willingly give it up without being convinced that there is a better way to achieve their goals and that power is not zero-sum. Also considered in the chapter is the role that women too often play in the perpetuation of the patriarchy.

Chapter 4, "Prejudice and enculturation," addresses the challenges of bias and prejudice against women that Women, Peace and Security is seeking to address to allow inclusive diversity to flourish. Inclusive diversity is defined, discussed, and a case is made for the importance of its presence in security-related decision-making. The negative effects of the objectification of women and the various avenues of enculturation for gender stereotyping are considered in the chapter, as well as discussion of how various masculinities factor in gender relations.

Chapter 5, "Gender-based violence," begins by examining the horrific breadth and depth of gender-based violence (GBV). It then proceeds to discuss the "normalization" process that not only allows acceptance of violence against women and men based on their gender, but in too many cases supports the continuation of it. Abatement strategies are examined as well as the challenges to those strategies. Finally, short descriptions of the reasons behind and challenges presented in trying to address female genital mutilation, acid attacks, honor killings and sex trafficking are presented as forms of GBV.

Chapter 6, "Women and development," begins by establishing that development is a clear factor in security. Development is then put into the context of the UN Sustainable Development Goals and national security. The three dimensions of gender equality are considered in relation to development, including the importance of reproductive rights. Finally, the "aid" versus "investment" debate and the role of technology in women's economic development is explained, and examples of success stories regarding women's economic development are provided.

Chapter 7, "Gender, the environment, and climate change," is a new chapter in this second edition. It deliberately follows the chapter on development to explicate that advances made in development can be quickly wiped out by climate instability as a "threat multiplier." That is, all the challenges presented in other chapters can and are being exacerbated by changes in the climate. The gendered effects of climate change are presented as well to point out the necessity of gendered responses, as well as how genders react differently to solutions in areas like recycling. The global threat to environmental activists is also discussed, before giving consideration to why and how it is necessary to plan for a very different future, specifically focusing on the protein part of the food chain as exemplary.

Chapter 8, "Women in conflict," surveys the different roles that women play in different types of conflict, from protests in Iran, to the plight of the Rohingya minority in Myanmar, to war zones. Rape as a strategy and a tactic of war is also explained, again driving home the fact that gendered violence is a tool in warfare, and that since women are the primary targets, they need to have a voice in strategizing for its abeyance. The role – good and bad – of UN peacekeepers is also considered in conjunction with why more women peacekeepers are said to be needed. How women adapt to often suddenly becoming the head of their households, and to life in refugee camps is also examined.

Chapter 9, "Women and peacemaking," looks at why the inclusion of women in mediations and peacekeeping talks results in demonstrably higher rates of peace treaties holding at the conclusion of negotiations and why, nevertheless, women's inclusion is still by exception rather than as a rule. The various formal and information avenues of participation that women have used toward stopping the violence in their countries is examined, with lessons learned gleaned in example cases from Liberia, Northern Ireland, and Colombia.

Chapter 10, "Women in the military," examines the expanded and critical roles that women have played at the frontlines of the battlefield and both the structural and cultural barriers they have and often continue to face. Two very different models of women currently serving at the frontlines in Syria and Ukraine are also presented, as well as a discussion of women in the military in ostensibly "progressive" countries, Israel, Norway, Canada, and the US. Finally, the situation faced by women warriors when they leave the battlefield is discussed, as the equality and acceptance often found when countries have a united front against an aggressor often fades when the women warriors go home.

Chapter 11, "Women political leaders," begins with a short consideration of the fight that women faced even getting the right to vote, let alone compete for leadership positions, and then considers what women leaders bring to leadership positions different than men. How perceptions of leadership qualifications work differently for women than men are then considered, along with roads to leadership traditionally accessible to women, including the roles that quotas often play. And finally, the how and why of women often falling harder and faster from public grace is examined, reaching back to cultural considerations for answers.

Chapter 12, "Women, peace, and security in security organizations," directly reminds readers that Women, Peace and Security is a framework for individual, community, national, and global security by looking at how five international organizations charged with security considerations are implementing its principles. The North Atlantic Treaty Organization, the African Union, the

Association of Southeast Asian Nations as and the Organization of American States, and the European Union are presented as examples of challenges faced in trying to implement a framework that challenges the status quo.

Chapter 13, "Moving forward," suggests what will be needed to move the Women, Peace and Security framework forward, especially 1) mainstreaming knowledge of the framework, 2) focusing on both internal and external components of the framework rather than (more often than not) primarily external components and assuming all is well (or acceptable) internally, and 3) moving beyond performative allyships. This last chapter also, as throughout the book, highlights the need for more and better gender-differentiated data.

There is a plethora of outstanding edited volumes, articles, and papers on individual parts of the Women, Peace, and Security framework. I will provide a list of selected foundational and more recent ones at the end of each chapter. But the intent in this book is to address the subject as a whole, stressing the value of inclusive diversity and consideration of gendered perspectives, and showing the links between the individual parts.

A gender lens requires looking at a situation from two angles: through one lens, we view the realities, needs, perspectives, interests, status, and behavior of men and boys, and through the other we view those of women and girls. Combined, they help us understand gender dynamics and prove a comprehensive view of a situation of society.[3]

Bringing the two lenses together provides strategic bifocals through which to more clearly see the world. And make no mistake, once the relevance of gender equality to security is recognized, it can't be "unseen." This survey book is intended to offer those bifocals.

Notes

1 Dara Kay Cohen and Sabrina Karim, "Does More Equality for Women Mean Less War: Rethinking Sex and Gender Inequality and Political Violence," *International Organization* 76 (Spring 2022): 415–416.
2 *Bananas, Beaches and Bases*, 2nd ed., University of California Press, 2014, 13.
3 Rick Barton and Cindy Y. Huang, "Creative Solutions for Crisis Response and Stabilization: The Power of a Gendered Approach," *Women on the Frontlines of Peace & Security*, NDU Press, 2014, 26.

1 A place and a voice at the table

Beyond a social issue

This is a book about security, not social justice. It is a book that illuminates what traditional international security and security studies has too long ignored – that gender equality matters as a factor in internal state stability and external relations, and that women are agents of security, not bystanders or victims. As former president of the Republic of Kosovo Atifete Jahjaga has succinctly stated, "The security of the woman is the security of society."

UNSCR 1325 (2000), outlining the Women, Peace, and Security (WPS) framework, was a landmark resolution in its recognition of the important, active roles that women play in peace and security affairs. It is built on four pillars relating to women's roles: participation, protection, prevention, and relief and recovery.[1]

- Participation – Full and equal participation and representation at all levels of decision-making, including peace talks and negotiations, electoral processes (both candidates and voters), UN positions, and the broader social-political sphere.
- Conflict prevention – Incorporation of a gender perspective and the participation of women in preventing the emergence, spread, and re-emergence of violent conflict as well as addressing root causes including the need for disarmament. Addressing the continuum of violence and adopting a holistic perspective of peace based on equality, human rights, and human security for all, including the most marginalized, applied both domestically and internationally.
- Protection – Specific protection of the rights and needs of women and girls in conflict and post-conflict settings, including the reporting and the prosecution of sexual and gender-based violence, and domestic implementation of regional and international laws and conventions.
- Relief and recovery – Access to health services and trauma counseling, including for survivors of sexual and gender-based violence.[2]

Subsequent UN resolutions have increasingly focused on definitional specificity regarding responsibilities and goals, and calls for implementation accountability.

It is important to note here that there is some debate on whether UNSCR 1325 and the subsequent resolutions, particularly those related to conflict-related sexual violence, are binding in international law.[3] While most experts say that UNSCR 1325 is binding because it authorizes acts that are *intra vires* (within the power) of the UN Charter and other international laws, there is no enforcement mechanism and so it is generally considered to have no binding force under international law. However, the broadly recognized and repeated WPS principles and the state- and institution-based actions conducted in the fulfillment of the WPS agenda indicate some

DOI: 10.4324/9781003413417-2

international obligation.[4] Whether legally, politically, or strategically imposed, these obligations are resourced and executed differently across national, regional and international organizations.

Together, the WPS pillars aim to facilitate both inclusive diversity and consideration of gendered perspectives in decision-making regarding matters of peace and security. Inclusive diversity involves both quantity and quality. That is, it requires not only demographic diversity, which provides women and minorities a place at the table, but also a voice at the table. It is important to understand as well that WPS is not a Diversity, Equity and Inclusion (DEI) initiative; rather, it is a peace and stability initiative with a DEI component. A gendered perspective recognizes that policies and programs affect men, women, boys, and girls differently. NASA's 2019 scheduled all-female spacewalk had to be cancelled because there was only one spacesuit small enough for the women astronauts. No one had considered that women's body types differ from men. A range of items such as spacesuits, crash dummies, CPR mannequins, and police vests that don't account for women's smaller body sizes or breasts are by default built to accommodate men's sizes and therefore do not work well, or at all, for women. Conversely, programs intended to help sexual assault victims, mostly women, can inadvertently neglect to consider male victims. All genders must be considered in policy and planning, men and women, boys and girls, and at-risk populations within them, including LGBTQ+. Through the inclusion of women's voices and consideration of gendered perspectives, UNSCR 1325 recognizes and seeks to strengthen women's roles in security-related discussions and decision-making, toward an overall more stable and peaceful world.

The link between gender equality and security has been firmly established. Political scientist Mary Caprioli's groundbreaking 2000 *Journal of Peace Research* article titled "Gendered Conflict" prompted a body of quantitative research examining the relationship between gender inequality and armed conflict. Caprioli's study empirically tested the relationship between domestic gender equality and state militarism. The findings substantiated the theory that gender equality has a pacifying effect on state behavior at the international level. Building on Caprioli's work and that of others, Texas A&M professor Valerie Hudson and a team of multidisciplinary researchers employed both rigorous statistical analysis and in-depth case studies in their book *The First Political Order* (2020), to study the link between gender equality and national security. The study found that if a nation scores high on gender inequality it was: more than twice as likely to be a fragile state; more than three times the chance of having a more autocratic, less effective and more corrupt government; and more than one and a half times the chance of the country being violent and unstable.[5]

Now decades of research has established that in nations with gender inequality and subsequent high levels of gender violence in the home, violence becomes established as the de facto method of problem-solving overall. Relations in the home are the first political order upon which larger, societal orders build. The link between domestic/culturally-related violence and broader/national security-related violence leads to some interesting questions regarding what constitutes a violent society and what are useful indicators of a violent society. Gun ownership? Prevalence of violence in popular video games and television/movies? Domestic violence rates? Mass violence events? What is known is that autocratic nations and failed states with high levels of gender inequality are more likely than full democracies to experience intra- and interstate conflict, whereas democratically governed nations are both safer for women and experience lower levels of intra- and interstate conflict.

Security is more than men with guns talking to other men with guns, and ignoring that reality can be costly. Security has been primarily associated with power, and power is considered masculine. Facts and issues regarding women's roles in societies – so-called women's issues – are treated as social issues, not issues relating to security. But there is no such thing as "women's issues." That can't be said too often. Issues including conflict, food shortages, healthcare, and climate change affect men, women, boys, and girls, though differently. Labeling something a "women's issue" has been a way to sideline the issue and an excuse for excluding women from discussions and decision-making labeled as security-related. However, national security is predicated on the ability to identify and mitigate all threats to the safety, security, and functioning of a country, great and small, domestic and foreign. The reality is that no country can defend itself from every threat, but not including and welcoming half the population into the identification and mitigation of threats inherently creates serious national security vulnerabilities.

Canadian Joy Buolamski was a Black woman researcher at the Massachusetts Institute of Technology (MIT) Media Lab when she discovered that the facial recognition software she was using didn't recognize her face. Some Black faces were recognized by the software as gorillas or other primates. The problem was that the artificial intelligence (AI) had been taught to recognize only part of the spectrum of facial structures and skin tones. Only about 12% of machine-learning researchers are women, and only a small portion of those Black. AI is only as good as those teaching it. "Who codes matters,"[6] Buolamski has pointed out. Now, imagine if the military was relying on AI technology in a national security crisis to identify someone who had been left off the facial recognition spectrum. Bias has been found in other areas of machine learning as well. Amazon had to scrap its algorithm-based recruitment tool when it was found to eliminate all women applicants. Whether AI, space, cyber, or another potentially disruptive technology, omitting the involvement of half the population in its development and utilization inherently diminishes its capabilities. In the case of AI as well, since it is made by humans, it internalizes the same biases found in its developers and society, which means gender bias. Yet women in security fields have already demonstrated their value.

Women in the intelligence community, field operatives and analysts, have long played a significant role in security matters. Women have acted as field operatives – as spies and in helping spies – since Biblical times, as described in the book of Joshua. They have acted as code breakers, linguists, and analysts. Before women were allowed into combat positions in the United States, many women in the military chose the intelligence field, feeling it was there that they could be closest to the fight and make valuable contributions. Women intelligence analysts in the military and in civilian agencies have been involved in developing widely used threat assessments used in decision-making. Whether gender-related issues are regularly considered as factors in those intelligence assessments is, however, less clear but equally important, as inclusion requires knowledge and use of WPS principles by women and men within internal organizations charged with assessments. And to make another point that can't be said too many times, gender expertise is an analytic competence not a physiological trait. Raising awareness among the entire population and in professions is needed, including the media as it presents security-related events and policies to the public.

The media sets the agenda for what is important and what is not for the public. The media can shape public opinion regarding government actions involving security, violence, and war as righteous or wrongheaded. It also frames events – a protest, for example – as good news or bad, and can change the narrative on a subject, including on subjects like women as political leaders. Unfortunately, however, women are underrepresented in political reporting and as often as not, the media perpetuates stereotypes of women. Women editors and correspondents can push for more gender-related stories ignored by men and for more coverage of women in politics. In conflict zones, women correspondents consider conflict in terms of human costs more often than their male colleagues, They are also generally fearless.

New Zealand-born CNN camerawoman Margaret Moth, easily identifiable by her jet-black hair and thick black eyeliner, carried a 55-pound camera on assignments across the globe. In July 1992, she was shot in the face while filming in Sniper Alley in Sarajevo. Despite her severe injuries and consequently her blurred speech, she was back working in Sarajevo six months later, joking that she returned to look for her missing teeth. Former CNN Moscow bureau chief Eileen O'Connor covered the Russian coup that ousted Boris Yeltsin from inside the Russian White House, reporting live on everything from the chaos among the coup organizers to (correctly) identifying Russian military hardware in the streets.

Women journalists also have been targets of violence when covering stories, sometimes by the nature of the gender-related issues they are covering. Chinese #MeToo journalist Xueqin (Sophia) Huang disappeared on September 19, 2022, one day before she was to board a plane for the United Kingdom (UK), accused of inciting subversion of state power. Russian journalist Anna Politkovskaya, a critic of Vladimir Putin, was poisoned in 2004, recovered, but was then shot and killed in an elevator in her apartment block in Moscow in 2006.

Women also play important roles in countering violent extremism. Most terrorist organizations are not state sponsored, but rather are comprised of individuals recruited from communities. While poverty does not cause terrorism, poverty provides a petri dish within which radicalization can more easily take root. Therefore, it is in the interests of all countries to work with communities to strengthen civil society, economic opportunities, and promote generally stable conditions. Further, while women have been involved in terrorist organizations, as mothers, wives, daughters, and sisters, women also have unique access within families and communities to abate terrorism through offering training on how to discuss terrorism with family, friends, and the broader community; on how to recognize signs of radicalization and proclivities for violence; and offering resources to turn to if women suspect that individuals or groups are planning terrorist attacks.

In the Kenyan city of Garissa, a group of women, part of a network called Sisters Without Borders, have worked with the police to prevent at least two verifiable Al-Shabaab attacks. The women are from different ethnic and political backgrounds but agree that it is in everyone's interest to counter extremism. They understand the local triggers of radicalization and can use that knowledge both in stemming radicalization and in working with the Kenyan authorities to stop attacks. Human security efforts are preventive medicine.

Women are the members of the population most closely connected to human security issues, including food production and feeding families. According to the Rome-based Food and Agriculture Organization (FAO), in 2022, 2.3 billion people (or about 30% of the global population) were moderately or severely food insecure in 2021, an increase of over 350 million since 2019. Women make up 48% of agricultural employment across low-income countries. Yet they face greater constraints than their male counterparts in owning land, and in accessing essential resources, services, technology, market information and financial assets, and consequently are underrepresented in local institutions and governance mechanisms, and so have less decision-making power. They face excessive work burdens and much of their labor goes unpaid and unrecognized. An FAO study has determined that if women in rural areas had the same access to land, technology, financial services, education, and markets as men, agricultural production could be increased and the number of hungry people reduced by 100–150 million. Women's labor, their ability to stretch and utilize resources, and to prioritize spending makes a global difference.

Equal rights for women does not mean fewer rights for men; it's not a pie. Including women in security-related discussions and decision-making is additive; it enhances the potential for development of successful strategies, policies, and programs. Therefore, it is important to understand what women add.

What women bring to the table

Strategy is developed based on goals (ends), achieved through different approaches to achieving those goals (means), and specific methods of implementation (ways). Strategy development takes place within external considerations of resources (there is an adage that only poets develop strategy without a budget). Three external elements are key to strategy development: resources, an assessment of the security environment where the strategy will be executed (as complete as possible), and considerations of risk. A schematic of strategy development by Naval War College professors Derek Reveron and James Cook is illustrative.

It is important to note that the process is not linear – one and done – it must be constantly reassessed according to changes in the goal, resources, commitment, lessons learned, and other factors. For example, the official reason (goal) for the US invasion of Iraq in 2003 was to pre-empt Iraq's development or use of a nuclear weapon, and the military was charged with that responsibility (means) through both Shock-and-Awe airstrikes and then ground troops (ways). When no nuclear weapons were found, the goal changed to deposing Saddam Hussein and that was quickly accomplished by the military. The ends/means/ways were in alignment. Then, however, the goal changed to be the democratization of the country, but the means to accomplish the goal did not, though militaries are ill-equipped tools of democratization. Further, the US military initially was operating without a full understanding of the Sunni-Shia conflict, which put it at a significant disadvantage in developing a post-Saddam stabilization strategy. The end-means-ways were no longer in alignment and environment was not fully understood.

Strategy development, or decision-making, references identifying the best means and ways to achieve long-term, or big, goals. Strategic decision-making describes the process of understanding interactions between or among decisions and the potential impact on an organization's ability to gain an advantage or achieve its goals. The true power of strategic

Figure 1.1 Strategy development.

Source: Joint Force Quarterly

decision-making is said to stem from being able to make the right decision at the right time. Who is involved – the individual people – in both strategy development and strategic decision-making makes a difference.

Women add different information and knowledge than men throughout the strategy development and decision-making processes. Women know things. They often have different daily activities and life experiences than men in some areas are the most familiar with local environments because they walk daily for water, firewood, and other resources. During the 2006 peace negotiations in Darfur, for example, male negotiators deadlocked over the control of a particular river, water being a precious and often scarce resource in the region, until local women, who have the experience of daily fetching water and washing clothes, pointed out that the river had dried up. Expanded information inherently enhances the ability to assess a security environment.

Additionally, women add different conflict resolution options to discussions and decision-making. The most-often-used male options for conflict resolution are compete and avoid. Women add collaboration and compromise to those options as their favored approaches to goal achievement. Achieving a goal can be very different than simply "winning" a competition.

Women also communicate differently than men, focused on building relationships, developing big picture views and being good listeners, whereas men exercise dominance through language, speak literally, and use conversation to gather and dispel information. Including women in discussions and decision-making thereby allows the presentation of more information, differing perspectives on that information, and consideration of more options for conflict settlement.

The most often forgotten part of strategy development and strategic decision-making is consideration of risk. Leaders must take risks, but those risks must be prudently taken. Prudence means keeping focused on goals and understanding what is important to achieving them, and being able to exercise self-discipline by reason. It is not hesitation, moderation, indecisiveness, or being risk-averse; rather, it is keeping ego and temperament in check. Women have long been shown more prudent and less reckless when it comes to risk-taking than men,[7] with that prudence often considered as a feminine weakness.

However, America's first president, George Washington, often spoke of and is quoted on the importance of prudence to leadership: "Much is to be done by prudence, much by conciliation, and much by firmness." Noble Prize winner and the first democratically elected president of Poland, Lech Wałęsa, also recognized the value of prudence: "I will talk and act, not on my knees, but with prudence." More recently, US Congresswoman Nancy Mace said: "We should use prudence when making decisions as to what is best for us, our families and our communities based on the information we have." Retrospectively, it is clear that prudence was ignored before the United States invaded Iraq in 2003, in favor of hubris, power, and revenge. Christine LaGarde, president of the European Central Bank, pointed out that if it had been the Lehman Sisters rather than the Lehman Brothers running that financial institution, it would be a different world today, with fewer people still suffering and smarting from personal financial loss and anger over the bailout of "too big to fail" banks.[8] Women bring more prudence to the table.

Finally, inclusivity avoids the danger of groupthink. Groupthink is the sociological phenomenon that occurs when a group reaches a consensus without critical reasoning, without a complete consideration of consequences or of alternatives. Most often, it occurs through a common desire of the individuals to maintain internal group harmony. Individuals, especially if they are a small minority, will even sometimes base their decisions out of eagerness to be accepted within the group. Groupthink is considered a factor in US failed decision-making regarding the Japanese being able to catch the United States by surprise with the bombing of Pearl Harbor, the failed Bay of Pigs invasion of Cuba during the Kennedy administration, and the 2003 US invasion of Iraq. More diverse voices offer more perspectives.

It is important to recognize as well that what women can add to security discussions and decision-making is relevant to all environments across the security spectrum, from irregular warfare and civil conflicts to geopolitics. Great power competition is actually about the rise in parity among competitors. The "edge" that the United States has held over competitors, for example, has become smaller. Consequently, "wins" can be by very thin margins. No country can afford to discount or squander any advantages it might have. Implementation of the WPS framework is intended to capitalize on advantages offered by 50% of the population and to offer more options to policy and decision makers.

The United Nations reports that when women are included in peace processes, there is a 20% increase in the probability of an agreement lasting at least two years and a 35% increase in the probability of an agreement lasting at least 15 years. The increase in the potential for a more lasting peace is attributed to women raising and insisting that root causes of the conflict be addressed at peace talks. Former US Ambassador to Angola Donald Steinberg has talked about his experience in 1994 peace talks toward ending two decades of civil war in Angola. Women played no role in the negotiations. The Lusaka Protocol that resulted was primarily focused on men pardoning men.

> The peace accord was based on 13 separate amnesties that excluded the possibility of prosecution for atrocities committed during the conflict. One amnesty even excused any actions that might take place six months in the future. Given the prominence of sexual abuse and exploitation during the conflict, including rape used as a weapon of war, these amnesties meant that men with guns forgave other men with guns for crimes committed against women.[9]

Issues like clearing land mines in frequently traversed areas and offering assistance to rape survivors were ignored. Angola went back to war in 1998. Women are included in peace processes less than 10% of the time.

The term "social contagion" refers to the spread of behaviors, emotions, and attitudes through groups or networks. The idea that security is a man's purview has spread over a long period of time, with subsequent behaviors that while not shown especially effective, have considerable inertia. Those ideas, however, must be overcome if nations are to truly move beyond the idea that security is merely the absence of active conflict. Gender and security specialist Dr. Carol Cohn succinctly states the problem.

> These ideas are deeply embedded in the national security discourse, where they underlie core assumptions about what makes us more secure, and what counts as "rational," "self-evident" and "realistic" in security policy. In doing so, they act as a preemptive deterrent to thinking complexly, creatively and truly realistically about security.[10]

Additionally, feminist international relations theorist J. Ann Tickner pointed out in the 1990s that negotiations are often hampered by the projection of stereotypically masculine characteristics onto state behavior whose success as international actors is largely measured in terms of their power capabilities and capacity for self-help and autonomy. The benefits of including women for what they bring to negotiation tables have been demonstrated.

Updating UNSCR 1325

Implementation of the WPS framework will not solve all security problems. But given the rather dismal state of international relations at present, incorporating an empirically tested approach to decision-making seems well worth the undertaking.

Since its passage in 2000, nine supporting resolutions have been added to supplement UNSCR 1325.

- UNSCR 1820 (2008) recognizes sexual violence as a weapon of war and calls for troop training to prevent sexual violence, and the deployment of more women peacekeepers.
- UNSCR 1888 (2009) mandates women and children are protected from sexual violence.
- UNSCR 1889 (2009) recognizes the barriers to women's participation in peace processes and calls for indicators to track progress regarding their inclusion.
- UNSCR 1960 (2010) calls for an end to sexual violence in armed conflict and provides for measures aimed at ending impunity for perpetrators of sexual violence, including through sanctions and reporting measures.
- UNSCR 2106 (2013) stresses accountability for perpetrators of sexual violence in conflict, as well as women's political and economic empowerment.
- UNSCR 2122 (2013) positions gender equality and women's empowerment as critical to international peace and security, recognizes the differential impact of all violations in conflict on women and girls, and calls for consistent application of WPS across the Security Council's work
- UNSCR 2242 (2015) establishes the informal experts group (IEG); addresses persistent obstacles in implementing the WPS agenda, including financing and institutional reforms; focuses on greater integration of the agendas on WPS and counterterrorism and countering violent extremism; and calls for improved Security Council working methods on women, peace, and security.
- UNSCR 2467 (2019) positions conflict-related sexual violence as firmly rooted in the broader women, peace, and security agenda; stresses justice and accountability efforts; calls for support and protection to women's civil society organizations; and calls for attention to children born of rape.
- UNSCR 2493 (2019) calls for full implementation of all previous resolutions on women, peace, and security; requests the UN to develop context-specific approaches for women's participation in all UN-supported peace processes; and urges member states to ensure and provide timely support for the full, equal, and meaningful participation of women in all stages of peace processes, including the mechanisms set up to implement and monitor peace agreements.

Resolutions 1325, 1889, 2122, and 2242 address issues related to women's inclusion in conflict prevention and peacemaking. Resolutions 1820, 1888, 1960, and 2106 address issues related to the prevention of and response to conflict-related sexual violence (CRSV). Resolutions 2242 and 2493 address the continuing gap between rhetorical support for WPS and actual implementation, including within the UN.

There has been a discouraging record of adherence, for example, regarding the UNSCR 1325 requirement that women be included – participate – in peace negotiations. A Council on Foreign Relations report titled "Afghanistan 2020" states that women were present in an official capacity in only 2 of 23 rounds of talks between the Afghan government and the Taliban. Women often play important roles in "Track 2" backchannel diplomacy events and in mass action campaigns, and that should not be discounted, but women need to be at the negotiating table as well. There has been a clear gap between WPS aspirations and reality.

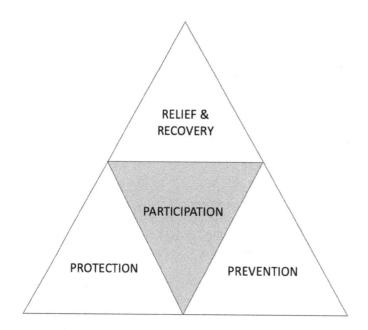

Figure 1.2 Concentric WPS triangles.

Source: Author's Creation

While all WPS pillars are considered essential and of equal importance, clearly "participation" is essential to and touches upon all.

Regarding conflict prevention, political scientist Valerie Hudson has posited that the gender relations within a society are akin to canaries in a coal mine, with poverty, malnutrition, poor health, turbulent violence, and extremism the canaries indicating the state of gender relations and strong indicators of national stability or instability. Heeding and addressing those indicators can, therefore, prevent conflict. Analyst Brenda Oppermann has categorized women's active agency in pre-conflict, ongoing conflict, and post-conflict activities as hawks, doves, and canaries. Hawks are those women who foment violence and aim to destabilize societies. Doves are those who work for peace and stabilization. Canaries are those who serve as warning signs of instability and pending conflict. She argues that a better understanding of these roles would benefit those involved in stability operations. Attorney and WPS analyst Melissa Deehring has pointed to Afghanistan as an example of where instability could have been anticipated were data available for analysis, and that analysis was actually used in planning.[11]

The "protection" pillar has sometimes been misconstrued. Its wordage specifically refers to protection from gender-based violence in conflict and post-conflict zones – and accountability for those who perpetrate those acts – and more generally that women cannot participate in security-related discussions, decision-making, policymaking, and conflict prevention if they fear leaving their homes. It does not substitute the protection of women as an alternative for the empowerment of women, though it sometimes seems interpreted that way. The George W. Bush administration viewed the protection of women in Iraq and Afghanistan as important and was very vocal on that issue, but was less assertive about empowerment.

The relief and recovery pillar recognizes that when guns stop firing, traumatized citizens, many of them victims of gender-based violence, are left in the wake and require treatment. A mental health study[12] conducted on Syrian women refugees in Turkey, for example, found post-traumatic stress disorder (PTSD) prevalent, with neither enough funding nor trained professionals available to provide necessary treatment. Too often, that situation is the norm.

WPS implementation

Implementation of the Women, Peace, and Security framework is left to individual nations through National Action Plans (NAP). NAPs vary considerably regarding focus, timelines, content, monitoring, and evaluation plans and budgets. As of February 2023, 105 countries have adopted NAPs, constituting 54% of UN member states. Fifty-four countries have developed one NAP; 27 have developed two; 17 have developed three; and six countries are on their fourth NAP. Unfortunately, however, 33% of the NAPs are outdated, having expired in 2021 or before. Regional Action Plans (RAP) have also been developed for organizations including the African Union (AU), the European Union (EU), the Association of Southeast Asian Nations (ASEAN), the League of Arab States, and the North Atlantic Treaty Organization (NATO), again though, some have expired without renewal. Additionally, there has been and continues to be a gap between rhetorical support for UNSCR 1325, and actual support, as evidenced by budgetary commitments.

Every year the UN Security Council hosts an "Open Debate" on WPS in October. At the 2019 annual event, 140 nations requested time at the podium to speak out in support of the program. Talk is free and an opportunity to gain status international status and legitimacy. Yet less than 25% of those states with NAPs have been willing to commit budgets to implement them, and clear data on budget amounts are difficult to come by. UN reports consistently state lack of funding as an obstacle in implementing UNSCR 1325 even in developed nations.

In the United States, WPS was not funded in the National Defense Authorization Act until FY2019, and then in the amount of $4 million out of a $1.3 trillion budget. If you believe that you can identify an organization's priorities by its budget, that relatively small amount is not an encouraging indicator. For comparison, an oft-cited 2015 *Military Times* article stated that the military spends some $84 million annually on erectile dysfunction drugs such as Viagra and Cialis. WPS funding was doubled in the Department of Defense (DOD) budget in FY2021, to $8.25 million. But to be clear, prioritization for funding is a function of political will. The primary obstacles to WPS implementation at national levels are lack of support for civil societies' initiatives and failure to recognize and accept the importance of WPS application in practice.

Each country's process and experience with implementing its NAP will differ. To use the United States as an example, the United States passed its first NAP in 2011, perhaps not surprisingly while Hillary Clinton served as secretary of state. Positive movement toward implementation requires a champion, though even under Clinton's tenure WPS tenets were too frequently overridden by realpolitik. The NAP was updated and renewed in 2016. But a precursor to budgetary deficiency was a lack of knowledge within security communities that such a framework existed or that United States had committed to support.

A 2016 survey conducted in the United States by the New America Foundation asked the question "How much do national security practitioners consider the ways policies and programs impact men and women differently?" It was answered through a series of in-depth interviews, focus groups, and surveys regarding how the US national security community and elite influencers (from the federal executive branch, Congress, think tanks, media, business, labor unions, religious organizations, and interest groups) "understand the WPS agenda and perceive its core intellectual constructs." The conclusion reached was: not very much.[13] In fact, basic knowledge about issues, terminology, and how to make the case to others regarding the importance of WPS was found significantly lacking. Consequently, it is not surprising that use of a WPS "lens" among US security practitioners has been missing.

The United States became the first country to make implementation of the Women, Peace, and Security framework the law of the land when Congress passed the Women, Peace and Security Act of 2017, signed in 2018 by President Donald Trump. In 2019, the US National Strategy on Women, Peace, and Security was released, tasking four federal departments with implementation: the Department of Defense, the Department of State (DOS), the US Agency for International Development (USAID), and the Department of Homeland Security (DHS). Additionally, four lines of effort were identified in that strategy.

- Seek and support the preparation and participation of women in decision-making processes
- Promote the protection of women's and girl's human rights
- Adjust US international programs to improve equality and empowerment outcomes for women
- Encourage partner governments to adopt similar focused plans.

Consequent to that strategy, budgetary allocations began to be made.

The White House Fact Sheet: *U.S. Government Women Peace and Security Report to Congress*, released in July 2022, reported on actions taken and funding spent. In FY 2021, the DOD spent, for example, $5.5 million to establish policies and programs to advance implementation of WPS, hire and train qualified personnel, and integrate WPS into relevant training curriculum and professional military education. The DOD also initiated use of $3 million from the International Security Cooperation Programs funding to conduct security cooperation programs with other countries that incorporate gender analysis and advance women's participation in defense institutions and national security forces. While progress was noted across all agencies charged with implementation, it was inconsistent. For example, compared to the $5.5 million spent by DOD, DOS invested $110 million, and USAID $239 million for WPS execution indicating significantly higher organizational investment.

Globally, Gender Advisers (GENADs) and Gender Focal Points (GFPs) (or similar designations) within implementing organizations are key components of WPS implementation. GENADS are responsible for facilitating implementation of the WPS framework within organizations. They are accountable for assuring that both inclusive diversity and consideration of gendered perspectives are included in plans, policies, and practices, supported by GFPs. Challenges encountered by GENADs and GFPs include positions going unfilled or filled by individuals without sufficient rank or knowledge to be able to be effective, working without a clear and robust policy framework to guide their work, dealing with senior leadership that sometimes does not fully understand or embrace WPS, and experiencing lack of access to senior leadership on a regular basis, and budget. Funds are needed to, among other things, train more, and better train both GENADs and GFPs.

It is important to note that implementation of WPS has both internal/inward-looking and external/outward-looking components. The focus of many NAPs from developed countries is considered largely outward-looking, framed to guide peacebuilding assistance efforts. Inward-looking NAPs have been considered to be largely from countries emerging from conflict, assisted by the UN and donor nations. That differentiation, however, is too essentialist regarding NAP importance to furthering gender equality. Regarding developing countries, it is wrong to view all developing countries as passive recipients of NAPs. That view merely reinforces the North-South binary, and is incorrect. Nigeria's NAP, for example, has an external component due to its role in peacebuilding.[14]

In some cases and countries as well, WPS is seen as largely reflecting goals of the Global North, without recognition of cultures and conditions in the Global South. In effect, WPS is seen as a tool of neocolonialism, with more-or-less standardized NAPs pushed by the North to test the veracity of acceptance. NAPs have also been negatively construed in some countries as a standard by which others will measure or judge them regarding gender equality, and have opted to refrain from development or to instead pursue WPS principles though other routes, including feminist foreign policies. In Latin America, for example, Mexico, Chile, and Colombia have embraced the banner of feminist foreign policies. And not having a NAP does not necessarily mean that gender is ignored in policymaking. As will be discussed in Chapter 9, WPS principles played a key role in the peace talks and agreement in Colombia. In Chapter 12, NAPs are discussed in conjunction with exemplary regional security organizations. In at least some cases globally, NAPs are largely testimonials of good intentions toward garnering international status and legitimacy, and each has its own backstory.

Of the 33 countries in Latin America and the Caribbean, for example, nine have NAPs: Argentina, Brazil, Chile, El Salvador, Guatemala, Mexico, Paraguay, Peru, and Uruguay. Brazil passed its first WPS NAP in 2017 to cover the period 2017–2019, and renewed it in 2019 to extend to 2023. Initially, however, internal political instability hobbled implementation of the NAP, first through neglect and then outright rejection by right-wing strongman President Javier Bolsonaro. According to a 2020 analysis by Brazilian researchers, the WPS framework was not the focus of strong and sustained political will, but survived largely due to the leadership and interest of mid-level public servants at the Ministry of Foreign Affairs, the Ministry of Defense, and other bodies. Regarding the ministries and higher authorities, though, they suggested "Brazil has a NAP *in spite of* strong political will *against* the agenda."[15]

There are four aims stated in the Brazilian NAP. First, increasing the effective participation of women in security-related activities, including in leadership positions, and promoting the effective participation of local women in activities related to conflict and post-conflict that affect them. Second, expanding and enhancing efforts to address gender based-violence and the protection of women and girls' human rights. Third, strengthening the gender perspective in development and implementation of peacebuilding and humanitarian activities undertaken or supported by Brazil. Fourth, extending knowledge about WPS to public agencies, civil society organizations, woman's movements, and the general public.

As in the United States, general awareness of the WPS framework in Brazil appears thin. Further, it is not surprising that considerable attention is paid in the Brazilian NAP to gender-based violence as Brazil has both high rates of homicide generally (60% of homicides are victims are woman) and femicide specifically, with some estimates suggesting that as many as 12 women are murdered per day in Brazil. Though Brazil has made significant strides in passing national legislation to combat these issues, enforcement remains lax.

NAPs are not without foreign policy implications as well. Japan's NAP, for example, is relatively specific, and has a budget attached. While there are aspects related to all four WPS pillars, Japan has been particularly focused on humanitarian assistance, including being a contributing donor to the Women's Peace and Humanitarian Fund, a global partnership working to empower women in conflict zones and humanitarian crises. As a regional Asian power looking to assert and expand its influence, other regional countries can and have interpreted Japan's humanitarian efforts as soft power initiatives.

Regarding developed countries, it is not enough to promote women's rights and gender empowerment in other countries. Parallel efforts must occur at home as well. WPS is not a "do as we say, not as we do" framework. For example, given the persistent pervasiveness of sexual assault within the US military, the July 2022 WPS report includes reference to the DOD's support for an Independent Review Commission on Sexual Assault in the Military that resulted in reforms to the military process for handling sexual and gender-based violence as an indicator of internal commitment to WPS principles. All countries with a NAP must consider both its internal and external components.

Kazakhstan and Morocco are the most recent countries to adopt NAPs. According to UN Women, among the countries in Central Asia, Kazakhstan is a leader on gender equality progress, having jumped 15 positions to sixty-fifth in the Global Gender Index 2022, a report designed to measure gender equality among 146 nations. The ninth-largest country in the world, it is land-locked, with territory approximately the size of Western Europe, and has one of the lowest population densities with a population of just over 19 million people. By global standards, it is an upper-middle-income country. Its five-page NAP, covering 2022–2025, focuses on increasing the number of women participating in defense-related activities, especially those related to conflict prevention and resolution; implementing a gendered perspective in security and defense; and preventing gender-based violence through the media.

The 2021/22 Women, Peace and Security Index published by the Georgetown Institute for Women, Peace and Security (GIWPS) showed Morocco's indicators of gender equality are below international standards, making Morocco ripe for an across-the-board, concerted gender-equality effort, as its NAP suggests that the government supports. When Morocco's NAP was released in March 2022, Morocco's minister of foreign affairs stressed that the NAP was part of a Royal Project for the promotion of gender equality as a basis for a just, democratic, and egalitarian society. He went on to say that it was not

an exercise in formalism, but on the contrary a concrete manifestation of the will of Morocco's commitment to gender equality as well as its conviction that the Women, Peace and Security agenda is an essential component of maintaining international peace and security.[16]

Time and action rather than rhetorical support will tell. Consistently, creating a NAP has been shown easier than implementing a NAP. NAPs are an important step toward gender equality and so security, but not a finish line.

Subsequent to NAPs being developed and adopted, governments and organizations have created policies and programs to address WPS implementation. US efforts regarding the empowering of women to be positive agents of security are largely conducted through the four organizations named in the 2019 WPS Strategy, all of which have developed internal implementation plans. Interactions on WPS with other countries are especially effective when the United States is seen as leading by example. For instance, the US State Department takes a leading role in preventing and minimizing conflicts. Its efforts are aimed at breaking cycles of violence and mitigating conflicts. It learned early the importance of including locals, especially women, in its programming.

In Honduras, for example, the DOS initiated a campaign in 2012 called "Stop the Violence," featuring graphic messaging – dead men on the street. Through focus groups with women and men, the DOS found its approach was too graphic. Specifically, the women said they imagined their loved ones in those pictures, and men rejected it as well, feeling that the individuals in the pictures must have done something to deserve death. After the DOS worked with local women, a revised campaign was launched, this time stressing "no more insecurity," with posters advocating that message placed on streets and public transportation. Subsequently, a demonstration was held where women carried photos of their deceased loved ones and banners demanding government action to stop the violence.

Programs through US military geographical commands similarly include efforts to stabilize society and empower women. Africa Command (AFRICOM), for example, which is responsible for 53 African countries, focused on implementation of WPS principals through military legal advisers, magistrates, and professionals in 2022, toward establishing best practices. State Partnership Programs, where state National Guard units partner with a country, are a part of

DOD efforts as well. In 2022, AFRICOM, the Botswana Defense Force, and the North Carolina National Guard co-hosted the inaugural meeting in Botswana of the Women's African Military Professional Legal Network, bringing together 60 female African military legal professionals from 16 African countries. All of the US geographic commands have active WPS external programs.

USAID focuses on partnering with countries affected by conflict to build foundations for lasting peace and stability. Doing so supports US national security goals by breaking cycles of instability brought on by conflict and violence costly to the United States in terms of both resources and potential spillover. USAID, the DOS, and the DOD work together on the complex challenges associated with WPS implementation toward achieving the right balance of development, diplomacy, and defense – the three Ds of US foreign policy.

DHS led a Unified Coordination Group to resettle vulnerable Afghans through Operation Allies Welcome. More than 79,000 Afghans were assisted with work authorizations, immigration benefits, and other support, including many women and other at-risk individuals, though regrettably almost as many were left behind. DHS has also committed to increasing the number of women as new hires in law enforcement positions by 30% no later than 2023, a measurable goal.

It is important to note that the US government has formally recognized the importance of implementation accountability. In fact, a set of integrated WPS metrics was developed to measure progress on achieving the US WPS Strategy's ambitious goals by 2023. Monitoring, Evaluation, and Learning (MEL) efforts are used toward effective stewardship of taxpayer resources through demonstrating measurable results, reassessing, and adjusting underperforming programming. But, as with all government and many organizational MEL efforts, the difficulty is in achieving truly useful progress rather than activity that primarily satisfies box-checking while the status quo, realpolitik, and realism continue to dominate decision-making.

A key tenet of realism, a traditional IR theory with strong backing during periods of geopolitical tension, is that a country should not risk its own blood and treasure with military intervention abroad if a long-term change beneficial to the intervenor's security will not prevail after its troops leave. And, to borrow from the medical field, "first, do no harm." A populace should not be left in more turmoil or in worse shape than it was prior to intervention. More prudence would keep that adage from being thrown into the wind as it has been in too many cases. Women's lives in Afghanistan are clearly not better there in 2023 than they were in 2002. US officials encouraged women in Afghanistan to come out of their houses, to declare and take their rights, and they did. They identified themselves and now they are Taliban targets. US security goals were not fully achieved, and clearly, internal harm to women has been grievous. Mainstreaming WPS considerations in policymaking and implementation must become part of standard operating procedures.

Data and operationalizing terminology

When concepts like feminism, gender, peace, democracy, and security are involved, definitions can be hard to articulate and soft in specificity. Data is often seen as a way to verify or add granularity to definitions. The importance of data in convincing individuals of the relationship and the importance of gender to security was considered in the 2016 New America Foundation survey. While knowledge was found to be low, 75% of those sampled said supportive data would lead (security-oriented) workplaces to focus more on inclusivity. The challenges to usefully operationalizing terms gathering useful and accurate data are, however, substantial.

In their 2014 book *Sex and World Peace*, researchers Valerie Hudson, Bonnie Ballif-Spanvill, Mary Caprioli, and Chad Emmett discuss the challenges involved with trying to empirically establish causality in the linkages they posit between the security of women and the security of states. They address the philosophical and data impediments to making the kinds of linkages that stand up to scholarly scrutiny, and thereby allow gender-related propositions about international relations to nudge their way into mainstream academia and security communities.

On that point, researchers Dara Kay Cohen and Amelia Hoover Green stated in 2016, for example, that while the UN continues to cite statistics saying 75% of Liberian women were raped during that country's prolonged civil wars, those numbers are not accurate. The numbers, they argue, were drawn from a nonrepresentative sample and continue to be used, though known to be wrong, to draw and keep attention on what is clearly a horrific problem. However, they are concerned about the unintended problems created by using inaccurate data.

Even a small proportion of a population reporting rape in a national sample can represent an epidemic. But if we come to believe that sexual violence is epidemic only if it affects three out of four women and girls, will anyone care when, in the next conflict, "only" 9 percent of women and girls report rape as they were in neighboring Sierra Leone?[17]

Similarly, there is an often-used statistic that asserts that women spend 90% of their income back into their families compared to 35% returned to the family by men. The source of those numbers, however, is unknown and consequently it has been referred to as a "ghost statistic." Reportedly in Ukraine, different nongovernmental organizations (NGOs) require a different level of confirmation regarding gender-violence reporting compared to the United Nations, which can also skew data. Developing and using accurate statistics is clearly an important task for the future.

Decision makers often face data challenges with an immediate impact on policy. Michelle Bachelet, twice-elected president of Chile, explained data issues from her perspective as a policymaker and gender activist.

Only recently have we begun to quantify what is lost when women are excluded from these processes [post-conflict processes]. In general, data have not been widely collected and analyzed on the effects of women's social and political empowerment globally, although what data we do have shows that empowering women is urgently important. But the data gap is especially broad in conflict contexts. Data are missing on such crucial aspects of women's lives as property ownership rates, levels of participation in local government, economic engagement, types of market access and maternal mortality. Conflict-triggered population flight and displacement makes gathering data still more complicated; some of the women most affected by conflict simply disappear from official view. [18]

Because there is little gender-specific data, surprisingly little is known, for example, about what proportion of post-conflict spending is directed toward gender equality and women's empowerment. First, we would have to know what proportion of demobilized combatants and people associated with fighting forces were women. Useful data in that regard is often difficult for several reasons.

In Colombia, for example, women who played support roles like cooking or guarding weapons caches for rebel groups such as the Revolutionary Armed Forces of Colombia (FARC) in the country's decades-long civil war, were frequently not considered combatants by the post-conflict government, thereby skewing data (and denying those women reparations). Further, women were reluctant to admit to having been combatants as the country quickly reverted to a traditionalist view of women's roles after the peace treaty was signed in 2016 and they feared being socially shunned. Similar post-peace reversions to traditional roles for women and backsliding on the equal rights women have experienced during conflict are common, including in countries including Nepal, Sri Lanka, Guatemala, the Democratic Republic of the Congo, Sierra Leone, Liberia, and Eritrea.

Without data, it is also impossible to know what proportion of reparations are, or should be, directed at women as redress for crimes they have suffered and how many individuals, men and women, need to be hired after the conflict ceases to deliver public services. Only recently has there been data collected on how many women are involved in peace negotiations and post-conflict planning, and in what capacity.

Part of the difficulty with gathering gender-related statistics concerns how terms are operationalized and understanding the impact of operationalization. The terms "gender blindness" and "gender neutral" are illustrative. The New American survey addressed that issue, pointing out that some individuals saw "gender blindness" as a virtue; that no gender would be shown preference. Ambassador Donald Steinberg has offered his experience regarding what he thought and intended the term "gender neutral" to mean, and what it came to mean when he was involved with the Lusaka Protocol negotiations. Asked in 1994 about the role of women in negotiating and implementing the protocol, Steinberg said he proudly proclaimed the document *gender neutral*. That designation was also intended to positively indicate that no gender was favored. In practice, however, both gender neutral and gender blind mean that gender will not be considered. Consequently, Ambassador Steinberg explained that negotiations reverted to the status quo, which meant male dominated. Women were not included in either the peace negotiation or the implementation process. Gender neutrality/blindness resulted in ignoring the issues of half the population.

There are other instances of good intentions going wrong, including in a developed country and involving professional women, where "gender blindness" again ended up favoring men. Given the underrepresentation of women in the senior ranks of skilled occupations, American institutions have begun adopting family-friendly policies to allow women time to have families and careers. In an effort at fairness, in many instances the same parental benefits granted to new mothers are also granted to new fathers. But in a 2016 study using a unique data set on the universe of assistant professor hires at the top-50 economics departments from 1985 to 2004, the authors "show that the adoption of gender-neutral tenure clock stopping policies substantially reduced female tenure rates while substantially increasing male tenure rates."[19] Women received the parental benefits and used them to recover from pregnancy and childbirth, and then they were mainly responsible for child care during their time away from the job, while men disproportionately used the time to conduct research and publish. So, while gender neutral on paper, the policies were not gender neutral in effect. The findings are thought applicable to other high-intensity career fields as well, having the effect of hindering gender equality. That doesn't mean that family leave isn't a good idea, just that gendered outcomes need to be considered as well as overall intent.

While there is some gender-specific data available for researchers and policymakers, it is often incomplete. The United Nations has the largest and broadest data collection. The Woman's Indicators and Statistics Database (WISTAT) includes data from 206 countries or areas of the world. The WOMANSTATS Project based at Texas A&M University specifically focuses on women and security-related statistics, relating women to security issues: Women's Physical Security; Women's Economic Security; Women's Legal Security; Women's Security in the Community; Women's Security in the Family; Security for Maternity; Women's Security through Voice; Security through Societal Investment in Women; Women's Security in the State.

Of related interest is the data being gathered by organizations like Promundo, an organization founded in Brazil in 1997 to promote gender justice by engaging men and boys in partnership with women and girls. It produces the International Men and Gender-Equality Survey through household surveys and field research, yielding important conclusions for addressing root causes of violence.

> Men who witness violence against their mothers growing up are 2.5 times more likely to repeat it later on. Men who experience childhood violence and witness violence against their mothers are four times more likely to report using violence against women. Men who have a sense of entitlement to sex, who hold inequitable values, who think they can get away with it and who have hostile attitudes toward women, are all more likely to use violence against women. [20]

Only when men and women work together can gender-related challenges be effectively addressed.

Another challenge regarding gender-related data gathering is a reluctance by women, their families, or governments to share data on culturally accepted but legally and internationally frowned-upon practices. Honor killings, acid throwing, and rapes often go unreported due to feelings of personal and family shame, or because the victim perceives that the judicial system will not be responsive. Maternal deaths in rural regions go unreported because there is no one to report them to. The high global rated of Indigenous women who are killed and go missing, but whose cases go uninvestigated or are underinvestigated evidences that some women are "seen" more than others. The work of individual researchers, program managers, or anyone in a position to gather data can bring light to subjects where policy has been made based on little or no reporting, underreporting, or based on assumptions that turn out to be incorrect.

Conclusions

What will it take to convince skeptics that gender matters in security affairs, when the evidence is already clear?

> A growing body of research definitively establishes a link between gender equality and global prosperity and security. Closing the gender gap in workforce participation could add as much as $28 trillion to the global gross domestic product (GDP). Ensuring women's meaningful participation in peace processes would make agreements more likely to last and be implemented. Greater numbers of women in parliament decrease the likelihood of human rights abuses and conflict relapse. Equalizing access to agricultural resources for women could reduce global hunger for up to 150 million people. The bottom line: nations seeking to advance national security, maximize the utility of foreign aid, and bolster stable and democratic partners should prioritize women's advancement. [21]

Regardless of the good intentions of many individuals, the reality is that women's rights are often resisted or become bargaining chips in the world of realpolitik, where short-term political practicality takes precedence over long-term consequences. The Coalition Provisional Authority in Iraq, led by Paul Bremer, showed no interest in working with Iraqi women. Iraqi writer Zainab Salbi stated, "[The Americans'] patriarchy and chauvinism was harder on Iraqi culture than Iraqis themselves." [22] In Afghanistan, warlords who had committed atrocities against women were accepted at negotiating tables and offered full immunity for their crimes in return for a promise of something considered more politically important than women's rights. Until gender equality is recognized as *need* rather than *desired but negotiable* where long-term security is the goal, women will continue to be excluded or marginalized in decision-making and gendered perspectives ignored.

The WPS framework provides an empirically supported way forward, but the path forward is fraught with challenges including lack of knowledge and understanding of what it is, the need for more gender-specific data, misinformation, organizational and societal resistance to change, and resources. It has been more than 20 years since UNSCR1325 was passed and it is just now that most countries are entering a nascent stage of implementation. Individuals can't implement what they don't know about, so knowledge and understanding is the first step.

Notes

1 www.usip.org/gender_peacebuilding/about_UNSCR_1325#What_are_the_four_pillars_of_Resolutio n_1325_
2 "Women, Peace and Security: Shifting From Rhetoric to Practice," *NATO Review*, August 3, 2017. www.nato.int/docu/review/2017/Also-in-2017/women-peace-security-violence-conflict-sexual-resolut ion-angelina-jolie/EN/index.htm
3 For an in-depth review of the legal implications and enforcement actions of security council resolutions, see the International Court of Justice opinion on Legal Consequences for States of the Continued Presence of South Africa in Namibia (South West Africa) notwithstanding Security Council Resolution 276 (1970), 1971 I.C.J. 16 (Advisory Opinion of June 21) known as the "Namibia Opinion."
4 Christine Chinkin and M. Reese. Commentary on Security Council Resolution 2467. Center for Women, Peace and Security and Women's International League for Peace and Freedom, 2019. www.researchg ate.net/publication/337676410_The_Women_Peace_and_Security_Agenda_The_Unfinished_Story_ of_Feminist_Revolution_versus_Compromise_in_Global_Politics
5 Valerie Hudson et al., *The First Political Order: How Sex Shapes Governance and National Security Worldwide*, Columbia University Press, 2020, p. 3.
6 Aaron Pressman, "Biased Artificial Intelligence Aps Could Cause Problems," *Fortune*, September 14, 2018. https://fortune.com/2018/09/14/fight-algorithmic-bias-joy-buolamwini/
7 Susan R. Fisk, "'Who's on Top' Gender Differences in Risk Taking Produce Unequal Outcomes for High-Ability Men and Women," *Social Psychology Quarterly*, 8, no. 3 (2018); Stacey Daughters et al., "Gender Specific Effect of Psychological Stress and Cortisol Activity on Adolescent Risk Taking," *Journal of Abnormal Child Psychology*, July 2013;
8 Irene Van Staveren, "Lehman Sisters Hypothesis," *Cambridge Journal of Economics*, March 21, 2014, pp. 995–1014.
9 Donald Steinberg, "Looking through the Gender Lens," *Women on the Frontlines of Peace and Security*, National Defense University, 2015, pp. 14–16.
10 Carol Cohn, "Gender and National Security: Thinking Complexly and Creatively about Security," Ploughshares Fund, April 3, 2019. https://ploughshares.org/issues-analysis/article/gender-and-natio nal-security
11 Valerie Hudson, "Of Coalmines," Open Democracy, December 2014 www.opendemocracy.net/en/ 5050/of-canaries-and-coal-mines/; Brenda Oppermann, "Hawks, Doves and Canaries: Women in Conflicts," *Small Wars Journal*, August 2014. https://smallwarsjournal.com/jrnl/art/hawks-doves-and-canaries-women-and-conflict; Melissa Deehring, "Lessons Learned from Afghanistan: The First Political Order," *Washington Quarterly*, 44, no. 4, pp. 7–28.
12 G. Alpak et al., "Post Traumatic Stress Disorder among Syrian Refugees in Turkey: A Cross-Sectional Study," *International Journal of Psychiatry in Clinical Practice*," March 2015, pp. 45–50.
13 New America, *A Guide to Talking Women, Peace, and Security inside the US Security Establishment*, February 21, 2017. www.newamerica.org/better-life-lab/policy-papers/guide-talking-women-peace-and-security-inside-us-security-establishment/

14 Heidi Hudson, "The Power of Mixed Messages," *Africa Spectrum,* 52, no. 3, 2020, pp. 3–29.

15 Renata Avelar Giannini and Pérola Abreu Pereira, "Building Africa Brazil's National Action Plan: Lessons Learned and Opportunities," London School of Economics, March 3, 2020, italic in orginal. https://blogs.lse.ac.uk/wps/2020/03/03/building-brazils-national-action-plan-lessons-learned-and-opportunities/

16 "MFA Nasser Bourita Chairs Launching Ceremony of the First National Action Plan of the Kingdom of Morocco on Women, Peace and Security." Morocco Ministry of Foreign Affairs, March 23, 2022. www.diplomatie.ma/en/mfa-nasser-bourita-chairs-launching-ceremony-moroccos-first-national-act ion-plan-women-peace-security

17 Dara Kay Cohen and Amelia Hoover Green, "Were 75 percent of Liberian women and Girls Raped? No. So Why Is the UN Repeating That Misleading 'Statistic'?" *Washington Post*, October 26, 2016.

18 Michelle Bachelet, "Women as Agents of Peace and Stability: Measuring the Results," *Women on the Frontlines of Peace and Security*, National Defense University Press, 2014, p. 99.

19 Heather Antecol, Kelly Bedard, and Jenna Sterns, "Equal But Inequitable: Who Benefits from Gender-Neutral Tenure-Clock Stopping Policies," IZA DP 9904, April 2016. http://ftp.iza.org/dp9904.pdf

20 Gary Barker, "Engaging Men to End Violence against Women," Council on Foreign Relations blog, June 17, 2016. http://blogs.cfr.org/women-around-the-world/2016/06/17/engaging-men-to-end-viole nce-against-women/

21 Jamille Bigio and Rachel Vogelstein, *Understanding Gender Equality in Foreign Policy: What the United States Can Do*," Council on Foreign Relations, Discussion Paper, June 2020. www.cfr.org/rep ort/understanding-gender-equality-foreign-policy

22 Valerie M. Hudson and Patricia Leidl, *The Hillary Doctrine*, Columbia University Press, 2015, p. 43.

Further reading

Adami, Rebecca, and Dan Plesch. *Women and the UN: A New History of the Women's International Human Rights Movement*, Routledge, 2023.

Beard, Lucas, Jonathan Dunn et al. *Shattering the Glass Screen: Gender Inequality in Media and Entertainment*, McKinsey, 2020. www.mckinsey.com/industries/technology-media-and-telecommuni cations/our-insights/shattering-the-glass-screen

Chang, Patty, Mayesha Alam, Roselyn Warren, Rukmani Bhati, and Rebecca Turkington. *Women Leading Peace*, Georgetown Institute for Women, Peace, and Security, 2015.

Davies, Sara E., and Jacqui True (eds.). *The Oxford Handbook of Women, Peace and Security*, Oxford University Press, 2018.

de Jonge Oudraat, Chantal, and Michael Brown (eds.). *The Gender and Security Agenda: Strategies for the 21st Century*, Routledge, 2020.

Enloe, Cynthia. *Bananas, Beaches and Bases*, 2nd ed., University of California Press, 2014

Hudson, Valerie M. et al. *Sex and World Peace*, Columbia University Press, 2012.

Hudson, Valerie M., and Patricia Leidl. *The Hillary Doctrine*, Columbia University Press, 2015.

Hudson, Valerie M., Donna Lee Bowen, and Perpetua Lynn Nielsen, *The First Political Order*, Columbia University Press, 2020.

LePrince, Caroline, and Cassandra Steer. *Women, Peace and Security: Feminist Perspectives on International Security*, McGill-Queens University Press, 2021.

Olsson, Louise, and Theodora-Ismene Gizelis (eds.). *Gender, Peace and Security: Implementing UN Security Council Resolution 1325*, Routledge, 2015.

O'Neil, Cathy. *Weapons of Math Destruction,* Crown Publishing, reprint 2017.

Shepherd, Laura J., and Caitlin Hamilton, eds. *Gender Matters in Global Politics: A Feminist Introduction to International Relations*, 3rd edition, Routledge, 2023.

Siegel, Mona. *Peace on Our Terms: The Global Battle for Women's Rights After World War I*, Columbia University Press, 2020.

Women on the Frontlines of Peace and Security, National Defense University Press, 2014. http://ndupress. ndu.edu/Portals/68/Documents/Books/women-on-the-frontlines.pdf

2   The role of feminist theory

Redressing inequality

The Women, Peace, and Security framework is intended to bring more women into security-related discussions and decision-making. Part of doing that is to unpack how and why they have been left out. Human rights are women's rights, and women's rights are human rights. While that seems a simple enough statement, the reality is, as many individuals and groups have acknowledged, no country treats its women the same as it treats its men. The United Nations has championed all types of human rights since its post–World War II founding. The International Covenant on Civil and Political Rights and the International Covenant on Economic, Social and Cultural Rights, both adopted by the General Assembly in 1966 and entered into force in 1976, are considered the two oldest, most universal, and most widely adopted statements on human rights. But without specifically stating that the rights in those documents applied to women, it was later realized that they were not necessarily assumed to do so by many signatories. In twentieth-century documents championing universal human rights, women were not considered inherently included in the protections.

Traditionally, laws have been made by men, thereby favoring men, resulting in gender inequality. That reality forms the basis of feminist theory. Like all theories, though, there are variations within that general characterization. Some of the common variations within feminist theory are labeled liberal/mainstream feminism, radical feminism, and socialist/Marxist feminism. All of these variations seek to understand and redress gender inequality, with the differences among them generally stemming from what is considered the root cause of the inequality. In overly simplified terms, radical feminism focuses on patriarchal gender relations, liberal feminism on legal systems, and socialist feminism on class conflict, with considerable overlap among all three. All also focus on key concepts including sex, gender, discrimination, equality, agency, and intersectionality.

The Canadian Institutes of Health Research (CIHR) provides a useful definition of the differences between sex and gender.

> Sex is usually categorized as female or male but there is variation in the biological attributes that comprise sex and how those attributes are expressed.

> Gender refers to the socially constructed roles, behaviors, expressions and identities of girls, women, boys, men, and gender diverse people.[1]

Sex is based on physiology, whereas gender is a social construct with expectations attached, expectations that can change and which vary according to factors such as culture and religion, but in all cases those who vary from those expectations are often subject to punishment. Neither

DOI: 10.4324/9781003413417-3

is a simple concept. Though sex has been thought of as binary, for example, that is no longer the case even within the legal and medical fields.

Dutee Chand was one of India's fastest female runners in 2014. Her speed and success, however, prompted competitors and their coaches to report her "suspicious physique" to India's governing sports federation. Subsequently, she was subjected to numerous invasive and humiliating medical tests – including measuring and palpating the clitoris, vagina, and labia, and scoring pubic hair on a five-grade scale – to determine whether Chand was a woman or a man. Subjecting women athletes to "sex verification" protocols and chromosome tests is not new. Woman Olympians were required by the International Olympic Committee to have "sex certificates" between 1968 and 1998. But geneticists and endocrinologists disagree about whether chromosomes alone determine sex since relying on "normal" ranges does not tell a full or fully accurate story. "Relying on science to arbitrate the male-female divide is fruitless [...] because science could not draw a line that nature itself refused to draw."[2]

While there are "normal" levels of estrogen and testosterone for women and men, as with any bell curve, there are individuals with outlying but not impossible levels from the norm. Initially, Chand was disqualified from racing because her testosterone levels were above the "female" range set by the sports federation. In 2015, however, a three-judge appellate panel ruled in Chand's favor, stating that while her higher testosterone levels may have weighed in her favor, nobody could tell by how much. They further stated that while high testosterone levels may have given Chand an advantage, other competitors may have received advantages in other ways, including better training and diet. Chand's case exemplifies the complications of even seemingly simple definitions. As the CIHR definition states, gender is a social construct, and so it is equally or potentially even more complex and dynamic than sex to define and overcome.

There are two basic types of barriers to gender equality, structural and cultural. Structural barriers are those that can be redressed through laws and policies. The change in US policy that allowed women to serve in ground combat forces was a structural change. Cultural barriers are those imposed based on gender-based stereotypical expectations: men are warriors, women are homemakers; men are strong, women are weak; men protect women, women need protecting. Cultural barriers to gender equality are often maintained after structural barriers are overcome, or where there were no official structural barriers to begin with, just societal expectations.

In 2015, Captains Kristin Griest and Shaye Haver became the first two women to successfully complete the US Army Ranger School, known as one of the most emotionally and physically challenging military schools in the world. Traditionally, less than half of those who attempt the combat leadership and small-units tactics course succeed. In the 2015 class, 380 men began and 94 graduated. Nine women began and two graduated. That means that those two women did better than 286 men. While not all women are as physically strong as men, some clearly are. Tradition tells us that men are stronger than women, but that is a cultural stereotype. While men and women are different, all individuals are different, including within sexes.

The response to Griest and Haver breaking that stereotype initially included death threats. But more women have graduated from Ranger School since 2015 and their success has largely been accepted. Gender expectations can change. It is important to remember too that gender diversity opens perspectives and breaks stereotypes for men as well as women. The reality of the global labor market, for example, is that traditionally male-dominated physical labor jobs have decreased (largely due to automation, globalization, and creative destruction), while the demand for care-related work typically held by women has increased. But sometimes men are reluctant to enter female-dominated areas of work, some known as "pink jobs," due to self-imposed or peer challenges to their masculine identity. That reluctance works to their economic detriment.

Equality is another key concept of feminist theory. Though often used interchangeably, there are important differences between equality and equity. Equality focuses on the provision of equal opportunity, while equity focuses on leveling the playing field for all individuals. For example, a 2013 study by Norwegian defense researcher Elin Gustavsen compared the attitudes of men in the Norwegian and US air forces toward women in the military, illustrating the differences between equality and equity views. While all the men generally supported women in the military and supported mixed-gender units, Norwegian men supported equal *treatment* of men and women while their American counterparts focused more narrowly on creating equal *opportunity* for women. Equity attempts to level the playing field for all, while equality simply says everyone should have access to the field. The difference between equality and equity becomes particularly important in the context of agency.

Agency is a significant but often overlooked concept. Personal agency, simply stated, is the ability to take meaningful action in your own interest. It often correlates with feelings of happiness and life satisfaction because agency gives individuals control of their own lives. Agency is choice. But views regarding how one gets and maintains agency differ even among women. In the United States, for example, liberal women generally support policies and laws advancing women's rights overall and thereby seek to grant agency to women as a group. Conservative women, however, tend to support traditionally held conservative tenets of gender blindness, limited government, individualism, and traditionalism – thereby making agency an individual issue and placing emphasis on personal tenacity and self-reliance. They believe that people get ahead if they work hard. Conservative women often associate feminism with "victimization" and reject any such association, focusing instead on positive personal achievement. Rather than #MeToo, "moving on" is the mantra of conservative women, as a superior vision of female empowerment. These differing views of agency can keep women from cooperating with each other.

Having agency and feeling comfortable in using one's agency can also be more difficult for women than men. The so-called "ladder of interference" regarding exercising agency stems from the (often unconscious) thinking process that individuals go through when moving from recognition of a fact to a decision to act on that fact. It demonstrates how two people can observe the same raw data and arrive at very different conclusions. Specifically, every individual's personal frame of reference influences the conclusions that person draws from facts and whether they subsequently will or will not take action. For example, women may experience overt harassment in their workplace, but based on their own negative experiences or observing negative experiences of others who have reported harassment, they may decide not to report it. When that happens, women have agency based on employment law principles, but are not exercising it because of the interference of personal negative experience.

Differing views on agency also reflects that women are not a monolithic group. Women are not a Borg with one brain, nor do they all have the same life experiences, opportunities, or challenges. American law professor Kimberlé Crenshaw coined the term "intersectional feminism" in 1989. Originally related to a court case involving Black women auto workers, it has evolved to refer to women experiencing prejudice in varying configurations and degrees of intensity depending on identity subcategories such as race, sexual orientation, disability, financial circumstances, and ethnicity. Intersectionality considers how different types of discrimination and opportunity interact.

Intersectionality issues occur because identities have more than one component, with more than one view within components. Women of color have often, for example, felt excluded from the traditional feminist movement. American feminist theorist Gloria Jean Watkins, better known by her pen name "bell hooks," began talking about interlocking forms of oppression in the 1980s, specifically race, gender, and class.

Transgender women have had a complicated relationship with feminism, often feeling excluded from the movement. But in 2021, Terry O'Neill, former president of the American National Organization for Women (NOW), stated that the struggle against transphobia is a feminist issue, with NOW affirming that "trans women are women, trans girls are girls."[3] That affirmation was especially important given the unchecked transphobic rhetoric between 2016 and 2020 during the Trump administration, which especially affected Black and Latinx women. The transgender community suffered more than 44 killings in the United States in 2020, making it the deadliest year on record for that community.

American author Mikki Kendall's book *Hood Feminism* (2020) argues that the focus of mainstream feminism should be on ensuring the basic survival of the many – food security, a living wage, access to education and medical care – rather than increasing privilege for the few, as she contends it has been. Similarly, third world feminism, much like hood feminism, argues that the issues and intersectional challenges of women in the developing world differentiate it from "first world feminism."

Indigenous women in Latin America live a strikingly different reality than white and mestiza (mixed race) women. The intersection of ethnicity and gender in many cases serves to doubly marginalize Indigenous women. According to a 2015 World Bank study, titled "Indigenous Latin America in the Twenty-First Century," Indigenous women in Ecuador face very high levels of gender-based violence, aggravated by discrimination in the labor market and access to healthcare. In Brazil, homicide rates are almost twice as high among Indigenous women as other Brazilian women. In Peru, Spanish is the official language, but Indigenous women often speak regional languages such as Quechua and Aymara, which, though also official languages, are often less familiar to professionals and consequently can often make language a barrier to education, healthcare, and employment. More than half of the people in Peru who lack access to healthcare speak Quechua. Indigenous women in Latin America face discrimination both as women and as Indigenous people.

Given these considerations, it is legitimate to ask "what is feminism?" and "who is a feminist?" The *Merriam-Webster* dictionary defines feminism as "the theory of the political, economic, and social equality of the sexes," and "organized activity on behalf of women's rights and interests."[4] It is not surprising that people have had to seek a dictionary definition regarding what feminism means, as there has been considerable distortion and disagreement about its intentions.

Nigerian novelist Chimamanda Ngozi Adichie's 2014 essay "We Should All Be Feminists," adapted from her earlier TED Talk of the same name, is among the finest efforts to define feminism. It is neither fiery nor abrasive. It simply argues that being a feminist means understanding and acknowledging that sexism exists. But she also warns that there is "the danger of a single story" that creates homogenized, fruitless, and potentially counterproductive portrayals of people, places, and their possibilities. It talks about the link between economic dependency and power, and the conundrum women face of potentially being considered aggressive if they speak up for themselves, or being mistreated if they do not. But whether said softly as Adichie does, or bluntly stated as others such as US Senator Elizabeth Warren has done – "If you're not at the table, you're probably on the menu" – the point is the same.

The first wave of feminism was a global movement that took place in the late nineteenth and the early twentieth century, focused largely on suffrage. But even within that movement, there were women who did not want the vote and campaigned against women's suffrage being granted, feeling equality would hurt them individually and their families, or feeling it simply wasn't needed. The Cult of True Womanhood or the Cult of Domesticity describes what historians consider the prevailing value system of middle- and upper-class women in the nineteenth century.

Most women at that time were not well educated; education often required their fathers' permission; and women were fully dependent on their husbands to financially support them.

Feminists include anyone who believes in equal rights for men and women, including political, personal, and economic rights, and social equality. Feminism was founded under the view that societies favor men, and efforts to change that include the fight for the right to vote, own property, hold public office, protect women and girls from violence, receive an education, earn equal pay, receive maternity leave, and maintain equal rights within marriage. It is a social justice platform with – referencing the WPS framework – increasingly revealed implications for community, national, and global security. It does not, however, mean support (especially by women) for anything a woman does. It does not include, as author Jessica Valenti stated in a 2018 *New York Times* opinion piece, "blind support for any woman who has risen to power" (May 19, 2018).

Not all women are feminists, nor are all feminists women. United Nations Women's Goodwill Ambassador Emma Watson reiterated and clarified in a 2014 speech that feminism is not synonymous with man-hating. Watson gave that speech when launching a program called HeForShe, emphasizing the need for men to be allies and advocates for gender equality. Then-UN Secretary General Ban Ki-Moon was the first person to officially sign on to HeForShe. The media blitz that followed caused the UN Women website to crash. Celebrities including Hugh Jackman, Jared Leto, Harry Styles, Russell Crow, and Eddie Redmayne have been among those who have aligned themselves with HeForShe.

Watson was later criticized, by other women, for appearing in a semi-topless *Vanity Fair* photo. Critics questioned how she could claim to be a feminist and do so. Watson fired back that the criticism

> reveals to me how many misconceptions and what a misunderstanding there is about what feminism is. Feminism is not a stick with which to beat other women with. It's about freedom, it's about liberation, it's about equality. Feminism is about giving women choice.[5]

Ironically perhaps, some individuals recoil at the word "feminist," though say they are not against gender equality.

Feminism, in terms of gender empowerment, is also not synonymous with nonviolence or a renunciation of use of the military in support of national interests. In fact, Hillary Clinton – a lifetime champion of women's rights – was labeled a "hawk" for her foreign policy views as secretary of state. "Feminist hawk" was a term that emerged after 9/11, wedding hawkish tendencies with a feminist frame, such as believing that gender equality is a national interest for which nations should be willing to commit troops and treasure. Pioneering British Prime Minister Margaret Thatcher was also known as a hawk for her foreign policy views, but was not known for supporting feminist causes, and was aggressive and masculine in her leadership style. Indeed Thatcher has been referenced as evidence that "a successful woman doesn't always mean a step forward for women," and that while she smashed the glass ceiling as Britain's first woman prime minister, she "pulled the ladder up right after her."[6]

What feminism means and who represents feminism has become a source of polarization in and of itself. A 2020 Pew poll showed that while 61% of American women (including almost 50% of conservatives polled) say the term "feminist" describes them well, 45% also said it is polarizing and that they would not describe feminism as inclusive. Though 68% of all women surveyed, Republican or Democrat, positively associate feminism with empowerment, using the words "feminism" and "feminist" can set off a firestorm. In Latin America, far-right movements and leaders have associated feminism with an "ideology" that promotes moral disorder and threatens children, marriage, and the natural order. In South Korea, which has one of the worst women's rights records in the developed world, President Yoon Suk Yeol ran an anti-feminist campaign, appealing to young male voters who see gender equality as a form of reverse discrimination – their mantra is "Me First" – that jeopardizes their jobs. In Poland, feminism has been coupled with a radical "homosexual agenda" that would, again, undermine the natural order, the "natural order" meaning a traditional spindle/spear society. Words matter even beyond right-wing agendas. The word "woman" can encumber the intent of a program as a security program rather than a social justice program. The Australian Defense Forces, for example, refers to its Women, Peace, and Security initiatives as Gender, Peace and Security to demonstrate its support for inclusive – men, women, boys, and girls – conflict prevention, conflict resolution, peace processes, and post-conflict state-building.

With the continued debate, misinformation (deliberate and unintended), and outright resistance to gender equality that remains in 2023, it is perhaps then not surprising that women's rights were not recognized or accepted as human rights in the 1970s. It was for that reason that the UN Convention on the Elimination of All Forms of Discrimination Against Women (CEDAW) was adopted in 1979. CEDAW has been described as an international bill of rights for women. It defines discrimination against women as:

> any distinction, exclusion or restriction made on the basis of sex which has the effect or purpose of impairing or nullifying the recognition, enjoyment or exercise by women, irrespective of their marital status, on a basis of equality of men and women, of human rights and fundamental freedoms in the political, economic, social, cultural, civil or any other field.[7]

CEDAW is the only human rights treaty that affirms the reproductive rights of women and targets culture and tradition as influential forces shaping gender roles and family relations. Parties to the treaty are required to commit to a series of proactive steps toward women's empowerment, including the establishment of laws to end discrimination, the punishment of those who do not abide by laws, and the reporting every four years of steps taken and steps still needing to be taken. While the number of countries to sign CEDAW, 187 of 194 countries, surpasses both prior human rights covenants, six countries – Iran, Palau, Somalia, Sudan, Tonga, and the United States – have not ratified the convention.

Many states, however, signed the convention with "reservations," excluding them from certain obligations, especially those found in Articles 9–15 dealing with "family" or "personal status" rights. Those reservations permit states to become parties in name only, while not requiring actual changes in the country's laws or cultural practices considered potentially intrusive into families, where power struggles begin.

US President Jimmy Carter signed CEDAW in 1980, but it has been stalled in the Senate Foreign Relations Committee ever since. The failure of the United States to ratify CEDAW largely reflects debates within American domestic politics. Conservative groups argue that CEDAW does not reflect American values "enough" but rather largely reflects the views of radical feminists. Supporters argue that CEDAW transforms American values regarding women into international norms.

Momentum for gender equality initially gained global energy with the Fourth World Conference on Women, held in Beijing, China, in September 1995. Then-First Lady Hillary Clinton addressed that group, bringing the diverse audience together and citing similar challenges that were being faced across cultures and continents, including profound violations of human rights. She did this in the capital of an authoritarian regime not known for passively accepting dissident views. Clinton's speech has been called "a watershed" for the United States and the world, taking gender-equality issues out of the shadows and inserting women into the foreign policy world dominated by men. The so-called Beijing Declaration that resulted, stating principles of women's empowerment from that conference, pushed women's issues forward and galvanized the attention of organizations within civil society and eventually the United Nations.

Power hierarchies

A team of researchers including Valerie Hudson and Mary Capriole drew from evolutionary biology and psychology to consider the roots of power hierarchies in a 2008 *International Security* article. They noted that there are three basic differences that individuals recognize when coming into contact with a stranger: age, gender, and race. Everyone, however, eventually moves into another age group, thereby somewhat diluting age-related differences. Perhaps surprisingly as well, they state that race differences can sometimes be "erased" and, citing psychologist Alice Eagley, that "gender stereotypes trump race stereotypes in every social science test." That, the authors conclude, makes gender differences "the primary formative fixed difference experienced in human society and sexual reproduction is the strongest evolutionary driver of human social arrangements." In that scenario, "human social structures are profoundly – even predominantly – shaped by selection for reproductive fitness."[8] In evolutionary biology, competition among males focuses on access to the best females for breeding purposes.

In the 1990s, evolutionary biologist and feminist Barbara Smuts began suggesting that both feminist theory and evolutionary biology were concerned with issues of power. Smuts argued that the evolution of conflict between sexes was based on differences in levels of required physiological commitment for reproduction, and subsequently, differences in definitions of success. The amount of time commitment required by females for reproduction is substantially longer than that by males. Female commitment involves internal gestation, childbirth, and lactation at the very least. Male commitment is largely finished with egg fertilization. Consequently, females seek to partner with males who will help them with food and protection during their prolonged period of vulnerability.

> For females more than males […] reproductive success is limited by the time and effort required to garner and transfer energy to offspring and to protect and care for them. Males therefore are usually more eager than females to mate at any time with any partner who may be fertile, whereas females are usually more careful than males to choose mates who seem likely to provide good genes, protection, parental care, or resources in addition to gametes.[9]

In evolutionary biology terms, male mating success is based on quantity, whereas female mating success is based on quality, thus creating inherent conflict between the sexes. From this perspective as well, when women can no longer bear children, they lose their value and are quickly relegated to the back of the cave, whereas men can continue to reproduce much later in life.

Smuts also suggested that males have limited patience and that if females spurn their courtship advances, violence becomes their next approach.

> Male interest in mate quantity, combined with female interest in mate quality, creates a widespread conflict of interest between the sexes. The conflict is mitigated when males court females by offering them the benefits females want from males, such as food, protection, or help in rearing young. These benefits are often costly regarding male time and energy, however, and males can sometimes overcome female resistance to mating at lower cost to themselves by using force or the threat of force--in other words, through sexual coercion.[10]

Hence, violence becomes a pragmatic option against women who resist males in power struggles.

Australian researcher Cordelia Fine challenged the premises behind evolutionary biology in her book *Testosterone Rex* (2017), statistically suggesting that the probability of a woman becoming pregnant from a single, randomly timed act of intercourse is about 3%. She further argued that historically and in traditional societies, at any given point in time as many as 80% to 90% of women of reproductive age might be pregnant or not ovulating because they were breastfeeding. Therefore, she says the theoretical possibility of a male being able to produce dozens of offspring if he mated with dozens of females is of little consequence if, in reality, there are few females available to fertilize. From that she concluded monogamy –requiring competition for a female only once – might have looked like a reasonable option to men rather than constant competition for various females. In that respect, Fine is in agreement with others that for every instance of conflict creation in evolutionary biology, there is also evidence of conflict mitigation techniques being developed.

Smuts does not lay all the blame for gender inequality at the feet of men. She states as well: "In pursuing their material and reproductive interests, women often engage in behaviors that promote male resource control and male control over female sexuality,"[11] as when women marry rich men and those men can then demand certain behaviors from the women. Thus women, as well as men, contribute to the perpetuation of patriarchy.

French feminist Simone de Beauvoir, writing after World War II, authored *The Second Sex* (1949) and there referred to women as "the other" to men. She argued that women lacked the concrete means to organize themselves into any type of opposition to men's dominance because their lives were more tied to men – tied by homes, work, economic interests, and social conditions – than to other women. Women were dependent on men. She went on to say that though men may also depend on women in various ways, men didn't grasp these ways as dependence, and women didn't seem to be able to leverage men's dependence on them for their collective liberation. She stated that women who opposed suffrage and socialism believed that this "liberation" would reduce the special protections (American conservative activist and anti-feminist Phyllis Schlafly referred to them as "privileges" in the 1970s) and routes of influence available to women, would destroy the family, and would increase the number of socialist-leaning voters. Women were, as de Beauvoir stated, tied more closely to men than to other women.

The idea that women who are dependent on men influences their outlook about and support of other women has been explored further as "linked fate theory." Linked fate addresses perceptions of how much an individual believes their fate is linked to that of a group, and consequently, how group-linkage affects, for example, their politics and voting behavior. Linked fate theory has long been used to explain voting patterns of racial minority groups, where individuals feel that they will benefit more personally if their group does better, and so group support takes priority over individual preferences in voting. Among women, perceptions of a gender-linked fate has been found contingent upon two factors, race and marital status. Heterosexual marriage has been shown to make White women feel less connected to other women, with the disconnect to other women increasing along with the duration of the marriage. For example, long-married (and so, older) conservative married women have seen their fate more linked to men – if their spouse did better, they would do better – than to other women and therefore felt little or no reluctance to vote against issues that would benefit women as a group, or for misogynistic candidates. While linked fate certainly does not account for the views and voting patterns of all conservative women, dependence on a male provider can be a significant factor in women's attitudes and consequently voting behavior.

Further, in their 2008 article, Hudson et al. took heart that even considering biological differences between the sexes, male dominance is not inevitable. They suggest first that male dominance can be avoided by strong female alliances, though making those alliances can be difficult due to both male and female peer pressure to not upset norms. Additionally, cultural selection – nurture – can modify tendencies imposed by nature through engineering of social structures and moral sanctions. There they cite the imposition of monogamy into some cultures, leading to the depersonalization of power through democracy and capitalism, an early suggestion of linkage between democracy and gender equality. Third, they suggest that improved female status in some societies leads to emotional and physiological changes in females that can be passed to their female offspring, making them less likely to succumb to coercive male behavior, therefore changing "nature."

The caveman days of females needing protection from woolly mammoths are gone. Theoretically, state or societal rules protect individuals. However, when state or societal protections fail, gangs/terrorist networks or families become fallback security systems. Hence family-level power structures become important, with patriarchies dominant.

Power: taken, given, and fought over

Many feminist writers consider women in history as passive, duped, and powerless. Consequently, in some cases, women have voluntarily given up power, which often rested in childbirth. According to political scientist Harris Mirkin, in Western society women gave up the last vestige of their power when they rejected midwives in favor of male gynecologists. Perhaps women are taking some of that power back given that as of 2022, 85% of gynecologists in the United States were women. Beyond childbirth-related issues, it was women, as agents of men, who actively participated in and enforced the rules of the traditional (gratefully now obsolete) practices of Hindu Suttee, where a widow threw herself on her husband's funeral pyre, and of Chinese foot binding. Women also have supported the not obsolete practice of female genital mutilation. So, while women have been victims of male subjugation and aggression, they have also sometimes been complicit victims. Consequently, women who would try to ban together to fight against their circumstances would be shunned by both men and other women not wanting to be seen as co-conspirators, demonstrating women's difficulties in forming alliances. There are also examples of women who issue commands to commit sexual violence in wartime. Women are not above violence. Cultural anthropologist Margaret Mead believed that women fight less often than men, but fight more fiercely because women are not taught the rules of war; instead, they are taught compliance.

In poor economies, especially in rural areas, women are often treated as little more than chattel. The importance given to the male side of the family and to sons who can inherit and carry on the family name, and are believed better able to financially support the parents in their older years, results in daughters inherently having less value than men, and females' primary responsibility becomes childbearing. Before marriage, girls are a source of family income to be sold, or a financial burden to be relinquished as quickly as possible. In some countries, women cannot own land, have a job to allow them financial independence, open a bank account, and have little access to the legal system, thereby making them fully dependent on men for survival. Marriage becomes imperative and provides women few options for escape even if their husbands brutalize them. That dependence only heightens when children come, and most often children come quickly. It is important to note that it is not only in developing countries and rural areas that the link between women and children is critical.

Becoming pregnant is the most dangerous thing a woman can do in many countries. Fine points out in *Testosterone Rex* that even in the United States, being pregnant is about 20 times more likely to result in death than is a sky dive. Women of color in the United States are three times as likely to die from pregnancy-related complications as White women. Sociologist Ann Crittenden, in her book *The Price of Motherhood* (2001), explains how/why having a child – motherhood – is the single largest risk factor for old-age poverty in the United States. Motherhood is unpaid labor with few or no structural benefits. Mothers are marginalized if they have careers and are unable to be free at all hours, every day. Social safety nets often do not fully provide for divorced or single mothers to keep them out of poverty. And mothers spend their incomes primarily on family benefits.

In the Philippines, researchers found that when women control family savings, expenditures shift toward the purchase of durable goods such as washing machines or kitchen appliances that benefit the family. After Haiti's devastating earthquake in 2010, Haitian authorities distributed food vouchers to women, stating that by doing so, food would more likely be distributed equitably within households. Sociologist Catherine Kenney found that in the United States, in low- to moderate-income families, children are less likely to experience food insecurity when the family income is controlled by their mother rather than their father. Yet men – and complicit women, with their voices often the loudest to garner favor with power brokers – continue to attempt to control childbearing expectations and rules, most often in authoritarian-leaning countries.

Reproductive rights are key to women having the agency to make decisions for their own and their families' welfare. Since 2000, 31 countries have expanded access to abortion, including such religious countries as Mexico, Argentina, and Northern Ireland. The term "Green Wave" has become synonymous with the successful movement for legislation supporting women's right to safe and accessible abortions in Argentina. Only four countries have rolled back access to abortion: El Salvador, Nicaragua, Poland, and the United States. According to the World Population Review, El Salvador is considered a hybrid regime, Nicaragua an authoritarian regime, and both Poland and the United States have recently slipped from being a full democracy to a flawed democracy. Researchers have found that access to abortion is often linked to a rise in democracy, and that the inverse is the case as well. As nationalism and right-wing populism – and authoritarianism – rises, access to abortion is tightened, hence the view that reproductive rights are not about babies but rather about power. The status of women is determined by the status of democracy. As democracy weakens, so too does support for women's reproductive rights.[12]

In 2016, the United States dropped from a "full democracy" to a "flawed democracy" and remains so ranked in 2023. On the global level, during debate over the passage of UNSCR 2493 (2019) during the Trump administration, the United States resisted the term "full implementation of the WPS agenda" based on the view that the reproductive rights portion contradicted US foreign policy on women's sexual and reproductive health. While Biden administration policies seek to redress rollbacks in areas critical to democracy like voting rights, the environment, and reproductive rights, Trump supporters in state legislators and on the courts continue to push the previous administration's agenda.

At the national level, in *Dobbs v Jackson Women's Health Organization* (2022), the US Supreme Court reversed *Roe v. Wade*, holding that the Constitution does not confer a right to an abortion, and returned the authority to regulate abortion back to the people and their elected representatives. When left to the people of Kansas shortly thereafter, a state that had strongly supported Donald Trump for the presidency, the people convincingly voted not to amend the state constitution to ban abortion rights, indicating that restricting abortion rights does not represent the will of the people, at least in Kansas. Subsequently, bans on abortion in the United States have been largely made by state legislators, notoriously elected by relatively small percentages of the population rather than voters at large.

In April 2023, federal district court judge Matthew Kacsmaryk, a Trump appointee, ruled in Texas to suspend the US Food and Drug Administration's approval of mifepristone, one of two drugs commonly used together to induce an abortion. Such a ban would virtually prohibit the sale of the pills across the country, thereby denying use and impacting hundreds of thousands of patients who use the medications, often prescribed via telemedicine, sent by mail and dispensed at retail pharmacies, for both abortions and treating miscarriages. It represents an attempt to force women into unwanted births.

El Salvador declared in 1998 that personhood begins at conception. All abortions are banned, with no exceptions. Subsequently, over 140 women have been arrested and imprisoned as being in violation of El Salvador's abortion law, some of whom had experienced a miscarriage rather than having had an abortion, charged with aggravated homicide and sometimes receiving decades-long prison terms. Not surprisingly, the abortion ban has disproportionately affected poor and Indigenous women.

Nicaragua's total ban on abortion was adopted in 2006. It is estimated that some 1,300 girls between the ages of 10 and 14 become pregnant annually through rape in Nicaragua, resulting in forced pregnancies. Though data is difficult to come by, human rights activists report that dozens of women have died from pregnancy complications, sometimes due to doctors refusing to treat pregnant women even if they are hemorrhaging for fear of being charged as accomplices to abortions. Not surprisingly, women have also been driven to alternative methods of terminating their pregnancies, including the usage of herbal medicines, and to often-unsafe underground abortion clinics.

Anti-abortion activists in Poland, backed by the Catholic Church, began chipping away at abortion rights almost immediately after the fall of communism. In 2021, Poland officially abolished abortion except in cases of the mother's life being in danger and when the pregnancy is the result of a criminal act, like rape. One aspect of Poland's abortion law that is particularly insidious is that pregnancies are now recorded in a national patient information database. Women's rights advocates fear that the state can now question women in Poland about their pregnancy at any time.

Poland provides another interesting case study of a country with somewhat paradoxical government positions on gender equality generally, as represented by reproductive rights, and support for WPS principles, as represented by having a NAP. University of Bath researchers Jennifer Thomson and Sophie Whiting suggest in a 2022 article in the *European Journal of International Security* that several factors allowed a Women, Peace, and Security NAP to be developed within a very anti-gender equality Polish political context. They argue that the NAP was created by only select actors, with little involvement of civil society, that its aims are both conservative and vague, and that the NAP was largely symbolic, responding to international pressure. In effect, they say NAP development was a "bandwagoning" effort that will likely have little or no effect on domestic policy.

According to the Guttmacher Institute, in 2022, 93% of pregnancies in low-income countries were unintended; 67% in middle-income countries, and 34% in high-income countries, with significant differences between low- and high-income groups within each group. Abortion is most often linked to unintended pregnancy. If liberals and conservatives in any society agree that fewer abortions is a desirable goal, and that seems a clear consensus, then the strategy with the unequivocally highest proven potential for success to achieve the goal is to increase the affordability and availability of contraception. The US Centers for Disease Control and Prevention includes contraception as one of the 10 great public health achievements of the twentieth century. The benefits of contraception include reduced maternal and infant mortality, health benefits of pregnancy spacing for maternal and child health, female engagement in the work force, and self-sufficiency for women. Control of their reproductive health is a prerequisite for women's agency.

Assuring all women have easily accessible, affordable contraception is the answer if reducing the number of abortions is the desired goal. Even American traditionalist Phyllis Schlafly supported contraception. "Contraception is not controversial," she said in 2012. "The issue is not access. It's who's going to pay for it," relating back to differing views of agency and self-reliance versus government support. But in the United States and some other countries, not just abortion but also contraception has become a political and judicial target, against the views of a majority of the populace.

In developing countries, statistics demonstrate an even more desperate situation. In March 2022, the United Nations Populations Fund (UNFPA) released its State of the World Population Report. UNFPA executive director Natalia Kanem emphasized the importance of contraception in crises and conflicts that was evidenced in the report:

> If you had 15 minutes to leave your house, what would you take? Would you grab your passport? Food? Would you remember your contraception? In the days, weeks and months after a crisis starts, sexual and reproductive health and protection services save lives, shield women and girls from harm and prevent unintended pregnancies. They are as vital as food, water and shelter.[13]

In Afghanistan alone, war, disruptions to the health system, and rollbacks in women's rights are expected to lead to some 4.8 million unintended pregnancies by 2025, which will undoubtedly factor into internal stability.

Gloria Steinem once said, "If men could get pregnant, abortion would be a sacrament." Similarly, the statement "If men could get pregnant, birth control would be free and taste like bacon" is so iconic, it has no attribution. Of note, though, after the 2022 reversal of *Roe v. Wade* there was an increase of over 850% for the search term "where can I get a vasectomy," mostly from Texas and Florida. That staggering figure indicates it is not just women who are concerned about unwanted pregnancies. Nevertheless, men cannot get pregnant and patriarchal attitudes persist. Therefore, the structure of patriarchal systems and the consequences for women warrant further examination.

Feminist Foreign Policy

Besides the Women, Peace, and Security framework, Feminist Foreign Policy (FFP), a second framework that also addresses issues of gender inequality, has also drawn attention and support since first introduced in 2014. Both drawn from feminist theory, there are similarities and differences between them that deserve consideration. Overall, the goals of both the WPS framework and FFP – gender equality and peace – are the same. The differences between the two are largely due to differing approaches, and those differences sometimes creates tensions between the two[14] but provide opportunities in countries where, for reasons already discussed in Chapter 1, NAPs are sidestepped.

Both WPS and FFP seek to redefine the concepts of peace and security. Norwegian peace activist Johan Galtung first differentiated *negative peace* and *positive peace* in the 1960s. Negative peace is defined as the absence of violence but without a society's tendencies toward harmony and stability, whereas positive peace is more lasting and built on sustainable investments in economic development and institutions, and characterized by societal attitudes that foster peace. WPS exemplifies positive peace through inclusiveness and consideration of gendered perspectives of policies and programs that lead to increased stability of all political orders. Yet feminist critiques of the WPS framework often focus on the *protection* pillar. The argument is that the WPS framework not only solidifies the militarized state but, in some cases, provides justification for conflict. The US-led war on terror, for example, was at least in part framed as a fight for the rights of women. Further, University of Sydney professor Laura J. Shepherd has argued that multiple logics behind the "prevention" pillar – a logic of peace, a logic of militarism, and a logic of security – creates a paradox that "collapses back into a logic of security"[15] contrary to the ultimate goal of peace. That is, in order to have peace, security must be obtained and retained through a heavy military presence and potentially military action, thus justifying such.

FFP seeks to change the very definition of "security" to go beyond the absence of armed conflict to include economic and political security, freedom from fear of a global pandemic and climate change, and the feeling of safety within one's own community and home. The security issues discussed in FPP are explicitly broadened to include access to drinkable water, the ability to walk home safely at night, the number of weapons in a country outside of the military, and many others. FFP advocates argue that WPS is too focused on the individual rather than the system. The FFP framework seeks to change the institutions and processes that support gender inequality. It seeks to diversify more than just the voices in the room; it seeks to expand the information collected, analysis conducted, and solutions considered to go beyond the traditional decision-making process, thereby making the solutions considered more diverse.

Sweden's foreign minister, Margot Wallström, was the first to announce adoption of an FFP in 2014, thereby setting an early model for other countries. Similar to the premise of WPS, FFP was posited on the conviction that sustainable peace, security, and development cannot be achieved if women are excluded. Rather than the WPS 4 pillars, Sweden's FFP was based on 3R's: rights, representation, and resources. The intent of Sweden's FFP was to support women's and girls' full enjoyment of human rights, which includes combating all forms of violence and discrimination that restrict freedom of action. Regarding representation, the intent was to have the Swedish Foreign Service promote women's participation and influence in decision-making processes at all levels and in all areas, and seek dialogue with women representatives at all levels, including in civil society. With respect to resources, the intent was to have the Swedish Foreign Service work to ensure that government resources were allocated to promote gender equality and equal opportunities for all.[16]

In the first three years of FFP's implementation, Sweden worked to raise the visibility of and combat destructive masculine norms, and to strengthen the country's capacities to prosecute GBV perpetrators, assist crime victims, and reintegrate soldiers. Sweden also contributed to a growing body of knowledge about the link between the uncontrolled spread of weapons and sexual violence against women. Implementation, however, proved not without challenges. Sweden struggled in 2015, for example, regarding the balancing of human rights promoted by the FFP with lucrative Swedish arms sales to countries like Saudi Arabia,[17] with Wallström eventually tearing up a long-term, very profitable arms trade agreement with Saudi Arabia.

Since 2014, several countries have announced different versions of an FFP. Norway developed both an Action Plan for Women's Rights and Gender Equality in Foreign and Development Policy 2016–2020 and a National Action Plan on Women, Peace and Security. Canada's feminist International Assistance Policy, announced in 2017, targets gender equality and the empowerment of women and girls at its core: "This is a matter of basic justice and also basic economics. We know that empowering women, overseas and here at home, makes families and countries more prosperous."[18] The French government's FFP, adopted in 2019, says that gender equality should be considered in all issues, from poverty reduction to sustainable development, peace and security, defense and promotion of fundamental rights, and climate and economic issues.[19]

Other countries have followed suit: Mexico in 2020, Luxembourg in 2021, Spain in 2021, and Germany in 2023.

Discussions about incorporating a feminist approach to foreign policy are also taking place in the European Union, Chile, Denmark, Malaysia, Norway, New Zealand, South Africa, the United Kingdom, and the United States, some with more potential for adoption and implementation than others. Further, governments are many-armed creatures, sometimes with activities of one arm having no relation to another. Interest in or adoption of an FFP does not inherently mean a gender-equal society, or even full government support of women. Though Mexico, for example, adopted an FFP in 2020, it has one of the highest global rates of violence against women.

Applying both frameworks to a specific example illustrates differences between the frameworks. Within the WPS framework, the US government would have included a push for women to be involved in the negotiations with the Taliban in 2019–2020. Many Afghan, global, and US activists did make the case before and during the negotiation process, during which the Trump administration ignored implementing its own (bipartisan, Trump-signed) WPS Act.[20] An FFP would have gone further. The scope of the negotiation issues would have been expanded from ending the war to ensuring strong Afghan institutions that serve its citizens and turning the country back over to its people. The balance of power and those engaged in the negotiation process would have been modified to include both the American and the Afghan people rather than the US military and the Taliban.

The differences in approach for WPS and FFP are not insignificant, with WPS more incremental and FFP more encompassing. Both, however, strive for gender equality, women's empowerment, and a safer world, and would benefit from more cooperation among advocates. There is also an important postscript to this discussion of FFP. In October 2022, the new Swedish foreign minister, Tobias Billström, announced that Sweden was abandoning its groundbreaking FFP. While stating the country's support for gender equality, he said that the label "obscures" that Swedish foreign policy must be based on Swedish values and interests, implying that FFP was not. Pushback against raising the profile of women's roles in security affairs can occur even in countries known as pioneers in recognizing the importance of overcoming gender-based prejudice and that gender equality plays an active role in achieving broader foreign policy objectives.

Conclusions

Feminist theory adds another dimension to the underpinnings of international relations. It does not negate considerations put forth by the more standard IR theories of realism, liberal internationalism, or even constructivism, but it does suggest that a serious consideration has been missing. How that consideration gets inserted into government policies and programs, whether through an FFP or Women, Peace, and Security, ought not to matter as much as that it gets inserted somehow. Power remains at the heart of gender equality struggles and that will not change in the near future. Advocates of both frameworks must work toward assuring that both internal and external efforts toward gender equality become more than box checks or dispensable after an election. That will likely be especially difficult in that countries which once led WPS efforts, like the United States, are now struggling to remain full democracies and be able to support other democracies globally.

Notes

1 Canadian Institutes of Health Research. https://cihr-irsc.gc.ca/e/48642.html. Accessed February 7, 2022.

2 Ruth Padawer, "Too Fast to Be Female," *New York Times Magazine*, July 3, 2016, p. 35. www.theguard ian.com/film/2016/may/23/angelina-jolie-new-role-visiting-professor-lse-william-hague

3 https://now.org/media-center/press-release/now-celebrates-transgender-day-of-visibility/

4 www.merriam-webster.com/dictionary/feminism

5 Luchina Fisher, "Emma Watson Fires Back at Critics of her Topless *Vanity Fair* Photo." *ABC News*, March 6, 2017. http://abcnews.go.com/Entertainment/emma-watson-fires-back-critics-topless-vanity-fair/story?id=45941009

6 Hadley Freeman, "Margaret Thatcher Was No Feminist," *The Guardian*, April 9, 2013. www.theguard ian.com/commentisfree/2013/apr/09/margaret-thatcher-no-feminist

7 www.un.org/womenwatch/daw/cedaw/

8 Valerie Hudson, Mary Caprioli, Bonnie Ballif-Spanville, Rose McDermott, and Chad Emmett, "The Heart of the Matter," *International Security*, 33, no. 3 (Winter 2008), pp. 9–13.

9 Barbara Smuts, "The Evolutionary Origins of Patriarchy," *Human Nature*, 6, no. 1, 1996, p. 5.

10 Smuts, 1996, pp. 5–6.

11 Smuts, 1996, pp. 18–19.

12 Atina Krajewska, "Connecting Reproductive Rights, Democracy, and the Rule of Law," *German Law Journal*, September 15, 2021. www.cambridge.org/core/journals/german-law-journal/article/connect ing-reproductive-rights-democracy-and-the-rule-of-law-lessons-from-poland-in-times-of-covid19/ CE048E79D093FFEE33326F7C4E889BB7; Multiple essays are available at: "Abortion Rights are Essential to Democracy," Brennan Center for Justice, www.brennancenter.org/series/abortion-rights-are-essential-democracy; Hanna Kozlowska, "Where Democracy Falters, So Do Reproductive Rights," *Foreign Policy*, March 16, 2022. https://foreignpolicy.com/2022/03/16/where-democracy-falters-so-do-reproductive-rights/;

13 "Nearly Half of All Pregnancies Are Unintended," United Nations Populations Fund, March 30, 2022. www.unfpa.org/press/nearly-half-all-pregnancies-are-unintended-global-crisis-says-new-unfpa-report

14 Much of this section is drawn from Joan Johnson-Freese and Susan Markham, Reconciling Two Key Frameworks: Feminist Foreign Policy and Women, Peace, and Security, Women in International Security Policy Papers, May 23, 2022. https://wiisglobal.org/publication/reconciling-two-key-fra meworks-feminist-foreign-policy-and-women-peace-security/. Accessed February 17, 2023.

15 Laura J. Shepherd, "The Paradox of Prevention in the Women, Peace and Security Agenda," *European Journal of International Security*, September 30, 2020. www.cambridge.org/core/journals/european-journal-ofinternational-security/article/paradox-of-prevention-in-the-women-peace-and-securityage nda/5D47238B224CFD8BFEE1CEDD4A1E76CF

16 Handbook for Sweden's Feminist Foreign Policy, www.government.se/492c36/contentassets/fc115607a4ad4bca913cd8d11c2339dc/handbook---swed ensfeminist-foreign-policy---english.pdf

17 "Major Arms Exporter Sweden to Put Human Rights before Weapon Sales," Reuters, June 26, 2015, www.reuters.com/article/sweden-arms/major-arms-exporter-sweden-to-put-human-rights-beforewea pon-sales-idUSL8N0ZC12020150626

18 Government of Canada, Canada's Feminist International Assistance Policy, www.international. gc.ca/world-monde/issues_development-enjeux_developpement/priorities-priorites/policy-politique. aspx?lang=eng

19 France, Ministry for Europe and Foreign Affairs, Feminist Diplomacy, www.diplomatie.gouv.fr/en/fre nch-foreignpolicy/feminist-diplomacy/

20 Melissa Deehring, "Lessons Learned from Afghanistan: The First Political Order," *Washington Qu*arterly, 44, no. 4 (2022), pp. 7–28.

Further reading

Adichi, Chimamanda Ngozi. *We Should All Be Feminist*s, Anchor Books, 2015.

Disch, Lisa, and Mary Hawkesworth (eds.). *Oxford Handbook of Feminist Theory*, Oxford University Press, 2018.

Foster, Stephenie, and Susan Markham. *Feminist Foreign Policy in Theory and Practice*, Routledge, 2023.

hooks, bell. *Feminist Theory: From Margin to Center*, 3rd edition, Routledge, 2014.

Kendall, Mikki. *Hood Feminism: Notes from the Women That a Movement Forgot*, Penguin Books, 2020.

Leidig, Eviane. *The Women of the Far Right: Social Media Influencers and Online Radicalization*, Columbia University Press, 2023.

Mackinnon, Catherine. *Toward a Feminist Theory of the State*, Harvard University Press, 1989.

Pitts, Andrea (ed.). *Theories of the Flesh: Latinx and Latin American Feminisms, Transformation and Resistance,* Oxford University Press, 2020.

Sjoberg, Laura. *Women as Wartime Rapists: Beyond Stereotyping and Sensationalism*, NYU Press, 2016.

3   Patriarchies

Sex and world politics

As stated in the previous chapter, security is provided to individuals either through states or when that is missing, through gangs/terrorist networks or family networks, most often patriarchal networks. British primatologist Richard Wrangham and his coauthor, Dale Peterson, succinctly summed up their perspective on patriarchies in their book *Demonic Males* (1996):

> Patriarchy is worldwide and history-wide, and its origins are detectable in the social lives of chimpanzees. It serves the reproductive purposes of men who maintain the system. Patriarchy comes from biology in the sense that it emerges from men's temperaments, out of their evolutionary derived efforts to control women and at the same time have solidarity with fellow men in competition with outsiders […] Patriarchy has its ultimate origins in male violence.[1]

Patriarchies are those societies where men hold dominant power. More specifically, traditional patrilineal societies are those where land, titles, rights, names, and so on are inherited through the male side of the family.

The patrilineal line is also known as the "spear" side of the family, as opposed to the female, or "spindle" side, and in patriarchies the two must never mix. Humanities professor Peggy McCracken references the 1997 film *G. I. Jane* as exemplifying the American military cultural reluctance to mix spear and spindle in a scene where female protagonist Lt. Jordan O'Neil moves into the formerly all-male barracks. "The men with whom she will share quarters express a mixture of outrage and horror when they see that Lt. O'Neil is putting what one recruit calls 'her stuff' into her locker: What about the tampons?" he cries to the other men. "Don't you care about the tampons?"[2] McCracken posits that the recruit sees feminine menstrual blood and heroic blood, traditionally defined as masculine, as incompatible.

When change is introduced into any organization, including families as the first political order, there is to-be-expected friction in the forms of confusion, anxiety, false starts, and frustration regarding change efforts. Friction is different from overt and covert resistance. Introducing and promoting gender equality into social, cultural, economic, and political structures that have been male dominated since forever, as the WPS framework seeks to do, is not a small change. It is monumental. Consequently, it is not surprising that gender equality is often considered threatening by those benefiting from those existing male-dominant structures, and that WPS has encountered both friction and resistance.

Malala Yousafzai was a 14-year-old girls' education activist in Pakistan when Taliban gunman boarded her school bus in 2012, asked for her by name and then point-blank shot her in the head. Sixteen-year-old Swedish environmental activist Greta Thunberg, who openly talks

DOI: 10.4324/9781003413417-4

about having been diagnosed with Asperger's syndrome, was mocked as having "anger management" issues by US president Donald Trump in 2016. Twenty-two-year-old Mahsa Amini was killed in Iran in 2022 for not properly wearing a hijab. How threatened must these individuals – representing political groups – and governments be to attack young women? From the family level to the global level there has been not only friction but many forms of resistance, including violence, some rationalized by nature.

Political scientist Francis Fukuyama's 1998 *Foreign Affairs* article "Women and the Evolution of World Politics" concluded that there was a limited role for women in international relations. His reasoning began by referencing studies on evolutionary biology, attaching special relevance to the commonalities between chimpanzees and humans. Chimps are the closest evolutionary relatives to humans at both a genetic level and regarding behavioral similarities. Chimps are like humans in that they are intensely social creatures whose lives are consumed by attaining and maintaining dominance.

Fukuyama conveys a story about a peaceful group of some 30 chimps in Tanzania, referenced in Wrangham and Peterson's *Demonic Males* book, to make his case.

In the 1970's, this group broke up into what could only be described as two rival gangs in the northern and southern part of the range [...] Parties of four or five males from the northern group would go out, not simply defending their range, but often penetrating into the rival group's territory to pick off individuals caught alone or unprepared. The murders were often grisly, and they were celebrated by the attackers with hooting and feverish excitement. All the males and several of the females in the southern group were eventually killed, and the remaining females forced to join the northern group. The northern Gombe chimps had done, in effect, what Rome did to Carthage in 146 B.C.: extinguished its rival without a trace.[3]

Wrangham and Peterson had written that of some 4,000 mammals and ten million or more other animal species, only humans and chimpanzees live in patrilineal, male-bonded communities.

From this study of chimps, Fukuyama posits differences between gender behaviors. Females bond according to emotion; males bond, or make alliances, for pragmatic reasons. Females have relationships; males carry out realpolitik. The key questions Fukuyama then asks and answers are: what do these gender differences mean for international relations and power structures, and how might including more women in decision-making change security-related decisions?

Fukuyama suggests that the human desire to dominate generally, and among males specifically has not changed through evolution. What has changed is that being a warrior and killing people on the battlefield are no longer the only options available for gaining the status requisite for power, through domination or prestige. There are now literally thousands of ways to achieve social status – wealth, talent, entrepreneurship – many of which not only do not lead to violence, but rather, in many cases involve socially productive activity. It is important to note as well that there are differences between dominance and prestige, which can also be reflected by social status, with dominance based on coercion, threat, and fear-based respect, while prestige is based on admiration and so deferential influence, with agreement between parties given rather than taken.

However, demographics and technology both offer conditions that perpetuate the violent side of human nature. For example, some populations are more reluctant to accept military casualties than others. Accepting casualties is easier in populations with a youth bulge and where gender imbalances exist, resulting in an excess of testosterone-pumping, hotheaded young men being untethered to families and communities by marriage. Regarding technology, Fukuyama points out that there are problems created by technology that outpace policy to assure it is used safely and constructively. Scale is affected as well. Whereas the Gombe chimps could only kill individually, guns and drones facilitate multiple killings and at a distance, and nuclear weapons can vaporize tens of millions in seconds.

Thus, Fukuyama anticipated more women being involved in politics in the developed world and questioned the wisdom of too much "feminization" of politics generally and international relations specifically. Women, he suggested, were less likely than men to see force as a legitimate tool for resolving conflicts. So, while bringing more women into international relations and security affairs would, based on biology, potentially tamp down the violent instincts of men, it would not tamp down the violent instincts of *all* men, and in a competitive global system the best regimes are forced to adopt the practices of the worst to survive. In summary, tough, aggressive men are required to deal with tough, aggressive men. Counterarguments included consideration of many men hating war as much as women (especially those who have experienced it), rejecting the idea that women are inherently nonaggressive, questioning the premises behind the use of the Gombe chimp example, questioning the entire biological premise of domination, and largely negating the complex interactions of states in favor of focusing on violence.

Since 1998, much has changed, and much has remained the same. Technology continues to outpace the human ability to consider its consequences, but at an even faster pace. Malicious cyber activities were not even on most threat assessments in 2007, but by 2015 they were ranked number one. On the other hand, not as much "femininization" of politics as Fukuyama anticipated, or feared, has occurred. According to UN Women, as of September 2022, 30 women served as heads of state and/or government in 28 countries and/or governments, and at the current rate of advancement, gender equality will not be reached at the highest levels of power for another 132 years. Further, only 21% of government ministers were women, most commonly handling portfolios in: family/children/youth/disabled; followed by social affairs, environmental/natural resources/energy; employment/labor/vocational training; and women's affairs/gender equality. Women are not running the world.

It has, however, been recognized that women are the thread that holds together the fabric of communities, often fragile communities, together. In conflicts from Northern Ireland to Liberia, it has been the women – women on different sides of the conflict and/or from different ethnicities or religions – who have worked together to keep children in school, been responsible for the food security of their families, and championed peace. This focus on family was the subject of Fukuyama's later book, *The Origins of Political Order* (2011), where he states that because humans are social creatures, it is natural for humans to favor blood relationships for survival. Reliance on families for security can, however, leave women in vulnerable positions, and inter- and intra-family rivalries are common.

Women in patriarchal systems

The value of women in patriarchal, especially patrilineal, systems is determined by the value of women's labor and the availability of women for marriage. If women's labor is valued – if they can contribute to the family's well-being through physical labor, household responsibilities, reproduction, capital generation, and so forth – the local culture may allow men to take more than one wife, called polygyny (polygamy is having more than one spouse). But if there is a scarcity of women, men are often expected to pay a "bride price" for a wife – a gender bias that works against men financially but establishes a presumption that women are property. In parts of rural India where there is both a shortage of women and a strong desire to keep rural land holdings intact, women can be secured from poor families or lower castes into polyandrous marriages. The woman becomes a "wife" to not one husband, but also sometimes his brothers and even his father, in effect becoming little more than a sex slave.

Securing a bride through payment establishes the premise that she can be treated as property. In Uganda, paying a bride price remains common practice. Until recently as well, if a woman sought a divorce, she had to repay the bride price – as though property were being forfeited – making leaving an often violent and abusive marriage impossible for many women. In 2015, the Ugandan Supreme Court ruled the practice of repayment unconstitutional, and dehumanizing. While the court ruling was a step forward for women in Uganda, the custom of paying a bride price perpetuates women being considered the property of their husbands.

Political theorist and anthropologist Jane Schneider has studied honor-shame cultures where patriarchies are prevalent, in particular as sources of conflict. In the Mediterranean region, she found conflict stems from intrusions to boundaries, usurpations of water rights, discourteous pasturing, animal theft, crop destruction, adultery, and murder. Each violation is considered a challenge to the honor of the property owner. "Thus honor can be thought of as the ideology of a property holding group which struggles to define, enlarge and protect its patrimony in a competitive area."[4] Extending that idea, she states that honor can attach to any human group from a family to a nation.

Feminist philosopher Bonnie Mann's book *Sovereign Masculinity: Gender Lessons from the War on Terror* (2013) advances the post–World War II work of de Beauvoir, arguing that gender has ontological weight, meaning going to the very core of a being. Therefore, the worst insult, the deepest humiliation that can be given a man is to call him a woman or have his peers see him as a woman, the inference being weakness. Unfortunately, it is still common today to hear or see men belittling other men with references to them being a woman. Golf legend Tiger Woods handed his opponent a tampon after outdriving him on the golf course in 2023.

Mann goes on to say that "not only individuals, but also nations, prefer to see themselves as manly,"[5] and relates gender identification to US actions post-9/11. Humiliated by the terrorist attack, the United States assumed a hyperbolic masculine identity – symbolized by, for example, 2003 imagery of President George W. Bush in flight gear on the deck of the USS Abraham Lincoln in front of a banner pronouncing "Mission Accomplished" – to reclaim its manhood and justify revenge not only in Afghanistan but also Iraq. Protecting its masculine identity became part of US national interests.

National interests refer to what a country is willing to spend its blood and treasure on. The 2022 US National Security Strategy states US national interests as: protecting the security of the American people; expanding economic prosperity and opportunity; and realizing and defending the democratic values at the heart of the American way of life. In some cultures, honor dominates considerations of what is worth fighting for, and strategies are developed to get, maintain, and increase honor.

The reciprocal of honor is shame. For men, shame is equated to inadequacy and weakness. Honor becomes especially important to women in patriarchies when women are a contested resource and women's comportment defines the honor of social groups. "Like all ideologies, honor and shame complement institutional arrangement for the distribution of power and the creation of order in society."[6] In fragmented societies there are weak government institutions and fissures between population groups and between the population and the government. Consequently, the government cannot be relied upon to protect civil and individual liberties, and so the head of a family must constantly make decisions to maintain or advance the family status, including economic interests and family protection. Family leaders are uncertain of the loyalty of those around them, sometimes including family members, and therefore must continually be willing to demonstrate their strength, without being offensive to other power brokers.

When women carry the family honor literally as their bodies, it must be vigilantly protected and ruthlessly cleansed when tarnished. Consequently, even women who are raped are nevertheless sometimes considered to have "soiled" the family honor.

In some countries and cultures, women are kidnapped and raped so that they are considered soiled goods and consequently a lower bride price can be paid to their families after the fact. The promise of providing potentially otherwise financially unobtainable brides to fighters in Nigeria's militant Islamic group Boko Haram played into the kidnapping of young girls from their school and forcing them into marriage. The horror is not only with the act, but with what happens to the girls if and when they are released. Their families often shun them due to "shame" brought on the family through no fault of the girls.

Conversely, if women are not considered valuable as workers and it is a buyer's bride market, the family of the bride pays a dowry to the groom's family. The dowry can consist of cash payments but traditionally can also include furniture, appliances, and all things needed to set up a household, plus personal items such as jewelry. This puts a considerable financial burden on families with daughters and has been linked to dowry-related physical and emotional abuse of daughters. When daughters are seen either as a commodity to be sold or a burden to be rid of, families can be anxious to see daughters married off.

Consequently, adolescent and early marriage remains a common practice in many patrilineal societies and developing countries, which often overlap. In fact, one in nine girls marry before the age of 15 in the developing world. Early marriage means less education for girls, as children soon follow marriage. Complications from pregnancy and childbirth are the leading cause of death for girls between 15 and 19 in many countries. Child brides are also more likely to experience domestic violence. If present trends continue, 150 million girls will marry before their eighteenth birthday over the next decade, equating to 15 million girls each year. The countries with the highest overall child marriage rates are in Western and sub-Saharan Africa, but when considering population size, the largest number of child brides reside in South Asia.[7]

Research suggests households facing a difficult financial situation will marry off the least productive members of the family, meaning a girl, to secure a "bride price" from her future husband or his family.[8] An increase in early marriages when families need money, including times of instability, exemplifies another instance of daughters being largely considered a commodity. Expanding access to credit markets could tamp down parental pushes toward early marriage, but obtaining credit can be challenging, especially for low-income groups and unprepared, often illiterate women who are thrust into the role of head of household during or after conflicts.

Money is not the only motivation behind early age marriages. Since a family's honor rests with its women, families are sometimes anxious to marry off daughters as marriage transfers responsibility for their honor to the husband's family. Consequently, in honor/shame societies girls are often married at or just before they reach puberty. The marriage is arranged by her father or nearest male relative. The bride likely does not even meet the groom before the ceremony and knows little or nothing about sex. Typically, the groom is a decade or more older than the bride, making her wedding night little more than child rape. These marriages are said to be with the bride's consent, but the bride's father, without even her knowledge, can give her consent.

Demographics, pressure to marry, and security

China exemplifies a country facing a security problem regarding men left without brides, and there are other countries similarly situated, including India. In China, the bride shortage is a result of prior government policies aimed at controlling population growth, with complex unintended consequences that the Chinese government now views as directly affecting its domestic security. A closer look at the Chinese situation is illustrative of the complexity of issues related to patrilineality and gender imbalances.

The Chinese government maintained a one-child policy from 1979 to 2015. During that period, families seeking to perpetuate the family lineage would often resort to sex-selective abortions, made easy by widely available ultrasound technology, to assure their one child was a male. Consequently, some 20 million more men than women have been born since 1979, creating a sex ratio – a comparison of the male/female population – that reached a high in 2015 of 1,047 males per 1,000 females, leaving many Chinese men unable to find wives and subsequently being left detached from society. So, the Chinese government now wants women to marry young. But just the opposite is happening.

Simultaneous to the one child policy, China also instituted a policy to better educate its population, women included. Many of the younger generation of women who benefited from that policy became anxious to continue their education into graduate school and get jobs in their fields. Consequently, many have opted to hold off on marriage, leaving them in a cultural bind.

"Leftover Women" (*sheng nu*) is a derogatory term used to refer to women stigmatized – including by their parents – because they are single. In 2015, the prestigious international skin care brand SK-II launched a global campaign to inspire and empower women to shape their own destiny, called #changedestiny. As part of that campaign, a Swedish advertising agency was commissioned to create a four-minute video, "Marriage Market Takeover" (available on YouTube), targeting a specific segment of Chinese women, those called "leftovers" by government definition because they had not married by age 27. That video quickly went viral.

Physical attractiveness is considered key for women seeking to attract a husband. In the SK-II video, one mother said, as her daughter sat next to her fighting back tears, "We always thought our daughter had a great personality. But she's average looking, not too pretty. That's why she's leftover." Not surprisingly, plastic surgery to enhance women's attractiveness among those seeking marriage is booming in China. But other marriageable Chinese women are consciously holding out for a love match or are focused on careers for financial independence. Even among those single by choice, though, there is no feminist revolution, but instead a slow, emotionally charged crawl away from tradition, societal, and not inconsequential governmental demands on them.

In 2021, almost 56% of Chinese males were single, versus 39% of females, leaving many men unable to find brides. Too many "bare branches," as unmarried men are called, can create societal problems regarding economic development, an aging population, labor shortages, and elder care. Further and more generally, not just in China, frustrated men unable to find brides are considered to greatly increase the risk of social instability and insecurity, thus demonstrating the importance of balanced gender demographics to overall security considerations.

> According to sociologists, young adult men with no stake in society – of the lowest socio-economic classes and with little chance of forming families of their own – are much more prone to attempt to improve their situation through violent and criminal behavior in a strategy of coalitional aggression with other bare branches.[9]

Domestic stability is a consistent top priority of Chinese leadership. Also, a direct relationship is often found between Chinese domestic stability or instability, and the aggressiveness of Chinese foreign policy, toward diverting domestic angst into nationalism against foreign powers. Monitoring this type of gender-related data can provide small but important "edges" in strategic competition.

The Chinese government began banning doctors from revealing the sex of an unborn child to parents in the 1980s, but the practice has widely continued. The government imposed a crackdown on the practice of sex determination more recently, with doctors threatened with losing their licenses and with jail terms for performing ultrasounds to determine a baby's sex, but with only limited success. And so, it becomes even more imperative to the government that all available females marry and have children.

The Chinese Ministry of Education officially began defining unmarried women over the age of 27 as *sheng nu* in 2007. It then went even further, stating that failure to find a husband was due to overly high expectations among women for marriage partners. Women, according to the Chinese government, were being too picky. Subsequently, in 2011 the All-China Women's Federation, a state agency established in 1949 to protect women's rights and interests, posted a controversial article titled "Leftover Women Do Not Deserve Our Sympathy," revealing highly misogynistic attitudes including assessments of "worth":

> Pretty girls do not need a lot of education to marry into a rich and powerful family. But girls with an average or ugly appearance will find it difficult [...] These girls hope to further their education in order to increase their competitiveness. The tragedy is, they don't realize that as women age, they are worth less and less. So by the time they get their MA or PhD, they are already old – like yellowed pearls.[10]

That post has since been removed and the term "leftover women" replaced with the equally disparaging term "old unmarried women" on the agency website. But common usage of the term *sheng nu* remains, as does the implication and societal stigma.

The term "the *sheng nu* economy" recognizes that educated single women are an economic force. Chinese women are discovering their agency. But utilizing that agency is tempered by feelings of traditional obligation and expectations – their ladder of interference. A feminist revolution in China is unlikely, but change is happening, and more positively than in many other countries, where coercion to marry goes far beyond emotional reasons.

Control as power or protection?

Overlapping restrictions based on culture, religion, and law inhibit women's lives in countries like Saudi Arabia, with its long-time prohibition on women driving often cited as a key example. Saudi Arabia was the last country in the world to ban women from driving until the ban was lifted in 2018, with considerable impact on women's lives. Government restrictions on driving had effectively prevented Saudi women from full participation in public life. Saudi Arabia had a customary ban on women driving until 1990, when the ban became official policy. Saudi Arabia's top Islamic cleric defended the ban on female drivers as intended for women's safety, which was benevolent sexism.

A June 2018 picture of a glamorous Saudi princess behind the wheel of a car that appeared on the cover of *Vogue Arabia* drew attention to the implementation issues. Women's rights activists pointed out that while the photo was intended to celebrate the pioneering women of Saudi Arabia, mostly from powerful families, other women who had fought for the right to drive had been jailed and deemed traitors. Driving activist Loujain al-Hathloul was jailed until February 2021 on counterterrorism charges leveled against her just before the driving ban was lifted.

The driving ban was rescinded as part of the Kingdom's "Vision 2030" plan, intended to create economic strength through economic diversity and less dependence on oil, to reform society, and to build a more sustainable future.[11] Raising women's employment from 22% to

30% by 2030 was an important part of the plan. Previous to the ban being lifted, women had to pay male drivers to get around or be driven by a male family member, severely limiting their employment potential. The website for Saudi Arabia's first driving school for women drew 165,000 applications within three days of the ban being lifted. Yet two years later, only 2% of Saudi women had been issued a driving license (totaling 148,081 licenses).

A 2021 research collaboration between the Alnahda Society, Duke University, and Uber looked into the reasons behind the low percentage of licenses having been issued. The findings fell into two primary categories: financial and safety. Eighty-three percent of the Saudi women surveyed in the study indicated that the cost of car ownership was a major obstacle for them, and 62% indicated that the costs associated with getting a driver's license were prohibitive, creating substantial barriers for low-income Saudi women. Mandatory driver's training through a licensed training center costs six times more for women than men. About a quarter of the women surveyed also cited safety as inhibiting – road accidents being a leading cause of death in Saudi Arabia – and potential harassment if involved in an accident.

The situation in Saudi Arabia continues to evolve. By 2022, there were more than seven driving schools for women, women-only car showrooms, and a ride-hailing app exclusively for women, with women drivers. For the first time in 2021, government figures showed 30% female labor force participation, and it has been estimated that increasing women's workforce participation could add up to $90 billion to the Saudi economy by 2030. The impact of lifting the ban for those women who wanted and were able to obtain a driving license has often been significant. A woman in Jeddah said in a 2021 interview, "I feel like I am in charge of my life and I am grateful every day for this freedom. It is hard for me to imagine how we lived for all these years without this basic right."[12] Being able to drive gave this woman and others agency.

More broadly, though, men have traditionally been the legal guardians of Saudi women throughout their lives, making women perpetual minors in the eyes of the law. Women have had to have permission from their fathers, husbands, or nearest male relative to travel, get a passport, and marry. They could be required to have male consent to attend school or get a job, or even leave the house and under what conditions they could go to school (what to study and where), be employed (type of position, and hours) or leave the house (accompanied or not, and when). A July 2016 report by Human Rights Watch stated, "In Saudi Arabia, a woman's life is controlled by a man from birth until death."[13]

In May 2017, also part of Vision 2030, the Saudi government announced a royal decree loosening (sometimes unofficial and arbitrary but nevertheless invoked) rules restricting women's actions without the permission of a male guardian. The decree allows women greater freedom in areas like access to healthcare, jobs, and higher education, and since 2019 women have had the right to get their own passports, travel abroad, and live independently. Human rights activists, while positive about the changes, remain cautious. A 2020 *New York Times* article summarizes the situation in the still highly patriarchal country, one where, for example, there is still no law criminalizing marital rape.

> But whether reality lives up to the law depends on the dice roll of birth. Day by day, it still falls to women in many households to negotiate their freedoms with the fathers, husbands, brothers and sons who serve as their legal guardians.[14]

Australian journalist Geraldine Brooks' book *Nine Parts of Desire* (1995) explored choices made by women in Islamic countries, beginning with that of a Western educated Islamic woman named Sahar who suddenly gave up her job as a journalist in Cairo to embrace wearing a burqa and an overall conservative lifestyle. What, Brooks wondered, would compel her to do that?

Sahar's answer was complex: partly religious – "Islam is the answer" became her mantra – and partly personal. Sahar said her new identity gave her a sense of physical security, that veiled women don't get raped. She also cited a sense of sisterhood with her new network of women that gave her access to certain government departments and organizations she had not had access to prior. And there was a rejection of the West:

> The West's soaring crime rate, one-parent families and neglected elderly proved to Sahar the bankruptcy of our secular ways. At the root of it, to her, was Western feminism's insistence on an equality of sexes that she felt ignored women's essential nature.[15]

Sahar, Brooks said, seemed comfortable with her new self.

In her book *Excellent Daughters: The Secret Lives of Young Women Who Are Transforming the Arab World* (2016), journalist Katherine Zoepf interviewed young Saudi women who professed to not just accept but also like the guardianship system, feeling that their guardians looked out for them. They felt the system is intended to protect them. They admitted there were cases where guardianship was abused, but did not feel the system was broken on a wholesale level. Again, women are not a monolithic group. Some women embrace a conservative life and even the guardianship system. Feminism supports the rights of women to choose a traditional lifestyle as an exercise of their agency if it is freely chosen.

Make no mistake, wearing a head scarf as a sign of respect to her religion and/or culture doesn't mean an Arab woman isn't a feminist. Women proudly serve in Arab militaries in roles from nurses to fighter pilots and special forces, sometimes against the inclinations of their male colleagues, just as Western women in the military do. In the Middle East, though, religion plays into cultural stereotyping as well. As a Jordanian colonel explained to me, her religion expects her to be kind, and she is whenever possible. But she is also a leader who knows what it takes to get a mission done, and so when necessary, tells her troops to ignore her feminine cheek dimples, which are prominent when she smiles, and follow her orders.

Control indicators

Even in countries without comprehensive guardianship laws, women can be controlled in a variety of ways including, as already considered, through restricting reproductive rights, as well as educational opportunities, access to food, and access to money as each inhibits women's agency. Even at the most basic, subsistence level, a woman's place in patriarchal societies often puts her at a disadvantage.

Food security is comprised of two primary requirements: the availability of food and the ability of households to acquire food through income. The role of gender comes into play regarding both. Researchers have found that even in regions where women play key roles in agricultural production, societal norms still dictate their household status in ways that impair their food and nutritional security. Women eat last, often meaning eating less, and have less dietary variety as they eat whatever is left when the men and children finish. Consequently, it is often food producers who go hungry.

Without access to money, a woman – any individual – becomes trapped in her circumstances. Economic independence is good for women individually and good for their communities, nations, and security. Yet indicators for women's economic independence and inclusion in their country's economy show that a considerable amount of work remains to be done.

According to the 2022 *Little Data Book on Financial Inclusion* produced by the World Bank, the global tech revolution has prompted a sharp rise in digital financial services, including in developing countries. The report states that even small merchants in rural areas receive and make payments with mobile phones, and that millions more women have a financial account, thereby narrowing the financial gender gap from nine to six percentage points in developing countries and from seven to four globally. Yet many women are still less likely to have even a simple form of identification necessary for a wide range of finance-related activities, to possess a mobile phone, or to use digital payments, which is especially problematic for those who live far from a bank branch, all of which hinder their inclusion in their local and national economies.

Looking at key indicators from 2022 data, globally, 74% of individuals 15 and older had an account at a financial institution in 2021, as did 74% of women. Sixty-four percent of all individuals made or received digital payments in the past year, though only 61% of women. Fifty-nine percent of all individuals and 55% of women found it not very difficult to access emergency money in 30 days, though the total figure dropped to 45% in the poorest 40% of households. Access to emergency money is especially important, having been found related to early-age marriages for girls in places where bride prices are paid and when emergency money was needed in a family. Breaking down these global numbers by region presents a clearer picture of where gender-related gaps are most prevalent.

The Middle East and North Africa region (combined) and the sub-Saharan Africa region had the lowest numbers regarding individuals with an account at a financial institution, with women's numbers in those regions below 50%. The Middle East and North Africa, South Asia, and sub-Saharan Africa all showed less than 50% of women having made or received digital payments in the last year, with South Asia the lowest at 27%. In Latin America and the Caribbean, South Asia, and sub-Saharan Africa, less than 40% of women said that they had not found it difficult to access emergency money in 30 days.

These percentages break down further by income groups within regions and, not surprisingly, individuals at lower income levels are the least likely to have an account at a financial institution, have made or received digital payments, or have found it not very difficult to access emergency money in 30 days. Though in some cultures bartering offers women access to goods and sometimes even subsequently power, generally without access to their own money, women have few options in life. Not surprisingly also, there is a strong correlation between an individual's level of education and their subsequent ability to become active members of their local and national economies. While the gender gap in education has narrowed, especially in primary education, gaps remain. Bridging those gaps would increase women's capabilities, thereby making it more likely they will join the labor force and utilize financial services.

The United Nations Educational, Scientific and Cultural Organization (UNESCO) estimates that globally, 129 million girls are out of school, 32 million are of primary school age, 30 million are of lower-secondary school age, and 67 million are of upper-secondary school age. Gender parity in primary education has been achieved in only 49% of countries, with that number dropping to 42% for lower secondary schools and 24% in upper secondary education. In conflict zones and extremist patriarchies, the effects are most pronounced. UNESCO estimates that girls are almost two and a half times more likely to be out of school in conflict zones like Syria and Yemen. In 2022, the Taliban began to enforce an education ban barring most women in Afghanistan from education beyond the sixth grade. The barriers to girls' education are several and often interrelated. Poverty, child-marriage, early-age pregnancies, gender-based violence, families favoring investing in education for boys, lack of safety, hygiene and sanitation needs of girls, and overt and tacit control of women's access to resources and mobility create complex obstacles to educational parity that creates empowerment.

There are several gender gap/gender equality/gender inequality indexes useful for comparative purposes. Each uses slightly different indicators and algorithms in its calculations. As a tool for comparative benchmarking, the United Nations, through its Human Development Reports, produces an annual Gender Inequality Index. It looks at issues related to reproductive health, political empowerment, and labor participation to produce an inequality index. Switzerland, Norway, Iceland, Hong Kong, and Australia were the top five ranked countries for equality in 2022. The United States ranked 21 (up from 44 previously), Russia 52, and last place went to South Sudan. The rise in the US ranking is at least partially attributable to the increased number of women being elected to Congress, as the United States has previously not fared well in that regard.

The World Economic Forum issues a similar annual Global Gender Gap Index, with countries scored based on indices of economic participation and opportunity, educational attainment, health and survival, and political empowerment. Its 2022 rankings place Iceland, Finland, Norway, New Zealand, and Sweden at the top five spots for equality, with the United States at 27, China at 102, Japan at 116, Saudi Arabia at 127, and last place going to Afghanistan, not surprising given the gender apartheid that has occurred with the return of the Taliban to power. The prevalence of inequality even among developed countries indicates the necessity of considering what other forces are at work that stifle empowerment beyond patrilineality. All the indexes have noted effects on women from the Covid-19 pandemic, with the 2022 Global Gender Gap Index concluding that gender parity is not recovering; it will increase the previously predicted number of years to close the gender gap globally from 100 to 132.

The Georgetown Institute for Women, Peace and Security also produces an annual index, that focuses on women's inclusion as measured by indicators of inclusion, justice, and security. Norway, Finland, Iceland, Denmark, and Luxembourg top its rankings, with the US at 21, China at 89, Russia at 53, and Iraq, Pakistan, Syria, Yemen, and Afghanistan at the bottom. Its 2022 edition also demonstrated discouraging trends in gender-equality advancement, with the global advance of women's status slowing and disparities widening across countries.

There are other, more focused indexes as well, such as the Women's Workplace Equality Index, developed by the Council on Foreign Relations. Formal legal obstacles to women in the workplace, such as gaining access to institutions, protecting women from violence, providing incentives to work, and eliminating barriers to jobs, are measured globally to create its list of countries doing well, and not so well. Australia, Canada, New Zealand, Spain, and Mexico topped their latest list as doing well. Also, the European Institute for Gender Equality produces an annual index of EU countries. It notes that in 2022, for the first time in its reporting, there was a decrease in several domains of equality measurement due to the impacts of Covid-19.

Conclusions

Political sociologist Johan Galtung observed that the amateur who wants to dominate uses guns, the professional uses social structure. The status of women in many countries today remains subordinate to men. Traditional male dominance prevails, perpetuated by forces intent on maintaining the status quo. In fact, systemic patriarchies appear to be making a comeback in countries once thought bastions of liberalism. While linkages between women's empowerment and development, and development and security are clear, the linkage between all of them has yet to be fully recognized and accepted. If they were, decision makers might act them upon more aggressively as a matter of self- (or national) interest, as was the case in Saudi Arabia. Allowing more women to drive enabled more women to be employed, part of the Saudi Vision 2030 plan. Women, Peace, and Security programs seek to make those linkages, supported by empirical gender studies research done within and between disciplines.

Further, the need to employ gendered perspectives in decision-making could not be made clearer than by the status of women in Iraq and Afghanistan subsequent to US military interventions into those countries, as indicated by multiple indexes. The US government's withdrawal from Afghanistan in August 2021 was an utter failure by most accounts. While 124,000 people were airlifted out of Afghanistan before the last troops flew out on August 30, 90% of the Special Immigrant Visa holders were left behind with their families. The number of Afghans who remain in danger because of their association with the 20-year American presence in their country must be counted in the hundreds of thousands. Afghanistan is now a humanitarian crisis. Food security is acute as the Afghan economy has no cash to pay salaries or buy food. With considerable amounts of Western aid suspended because the Taliban government includes designated terrorists, millions of Afghans have been left to face acute malnutrition and starvation. We can and must do better.

Notes

1 Wrangham and Peterson, *Demonic Males: Apes and the Origins of Human Violence*, (New York: Mariner), 1996, pp. 24–25, cited in Hudson et al., 2008, p. 14.
2 Peggy McCracken, *The Curse of Eve: The Wound of the Hero: Blood, Gender and Medieval Literature*, University of Pennsylvania Press, 2003, pp. 2–23.
3 Fukuyama, 1998, pp. 24–25.
4 Jane Schneider, "Of Vigilance and Virgins: Honor, Shame and Access to Resources in Mediterranean Societies," *Ethnology*, 10, no. 1 (January 1971), p. 2.
5 Bonnie Mann, *Sovereign Masculinity*, Oxford University Press, 2014, p. 3.
6 Schneider, p. 2.
7 International Center for Research on Women, www.icrw.org/child-marriage-facts-and-figures/
8 Lucia Corno and Alessandra Voena, "Selling Daughters: Age at Marriage, Income Shocks and Bride Price Tradition," Working Paper, January 2015. www.economicdynamics.org/meetpapers/2015/paper_1089.pdf
9 Valerie Hudson and Andrea M. Den Boer, "Bare Branches and Danger in Asia," *Washington Post*, July 4, 2004. www.washingtonpost.com/wp-dyn/articles/A24761-2004Jul2.html
10 Leta Hong Fincher, "China's Leftover Women," *New York Times*, October 12, 2012. www.nytimes.com/2012/10/12/opinion/global/chinas-leftover-women.html
11 Lubna Rizvi and Zahid Hussain, "Empowering Women through Legal Reforms – Evidence from Saudi Arabian Context," *International Journal of Law and Management,* June 2021.
12 Miriam Nihal, "Driving Ambition: Saudi women reflect on three years at the wheel," *The National*, June 24, 2021. www.thenationalnews.com/gulf/saudi-arabia/driving-ambition-saudi-women-reflect-on-three-years-at-the-wheel-1.1247629
13 Human Rights Watch, *Boxed In: Women and Saudi Arabia's Male Guardianship System*, July 16, 2016. www.hrw.org/report/2016/07/16/boxed/women-and-saudi-arabias-male-guardianship-system
14 Vivian Yee, "Saudi Law Granted Women New Freedoms. Their Families Don't Always Agree," *New York Times*, March 14, 2020. www.nytimes.com/2020/03/14/world/middleeast/saudi-women-rights.html
15 Geraldine Brook, *Nine Parts of Desire*, Doubleday, 1995, pp. 10–11.

Further reading

Atwood, Margaret. *The Handmaid's Tale*, Houghton, Mifflin, Harcourt, 1985.
Brooks, Geraldine. *Nine Parts of Desire*, Doubleday, 1995.
Fincher, Leta Hong. *Leftover Women: The Resurgence of Gender of Gender Inequality in Asia*, Asian Arguments, 2015.

Fine, Cordelia. *Delusions of Gender: How Our Minds, Society and Neurosexism Create Difference*, W.W. Norton, 2010.

Fine, Cordelia. *Testasterone Rex*, W.W. Norton, 2017.

Fukuyama, Francis. *The Origins of Political Order*, Farrar, Strauss and Giroux. (reprint) 2012.

Koepf, Katherine. *Excellent Daughters: The Secret Lives of Young Women Who Are Reforming the Arab World*, Penguin Press, 2016.

McCracken, Peggy. *The Curse of Eve: The Wound of the Hero: Blood, Gender and Medieval Literature*, University of Pennsylvania Press, 2003.

Wrangham, Richard, and Dale Peterson, *Demonic Males: Apes and the Origins of Human Violence*, Mariner Books, 1996.

4 Prejudice and enculturation

It still happens…

In April 2021, two European Union leaders visited Turkish president Recep Tayyip Erdoğan, European Commission president Ursula von der Leyen, and European Union Council president Charles Michel. However, only two chairs were set up at the front of the room, one for Erdoğan and one for Michel. Von der Leyen was left standing until she was seated on a side sofa, fully undermining her place at the meeting.

Gender inequality issues are not exclusive to patrilinealities, traditional societies, or developing countries. But while gender inequality in developed countries can be more subtle than in developing countries and is often more culturally based than structurally based, its effects are no less threatening to individuals, communities, and nations. It has been pointed out that the Women, Peace, and Security framework has both internal and external expectations attached to it. The internal expectations relate to addressing internal gender equality issues. To again draw from the medical field – physician heal thy self. That adage applies to all countries on the development spectrum.

Gender-based prejudice

The terms bias, prejudice, and discrimination are often used interchangeably. But while similar, there are differences. Bias is simply a preference for something, and can be positive or negative. A person might be favorably biased toward a certain type of food, for example. Prejudice, however, references a strong, often negative bias. Discrimination references actions taken based on prejudice. Females can face prejudice and discrimination even in utero.

Women no longer make up half of the global population, as they would if the sex ratio were left to nature alone. UN statistics estimate the overall 2022 global sex ratio as about 102. That means there are 102 males for each 100 females or 98 females for each 100 males, or some 48 million more men than women in the global population. While there are significant differences in sex ratios among countries, overt practices in some countries put women at a disadvantage even before birth and throughout their lives.

Sex-selective abortion and female infanticide are well-documented practices in countries including China, as discussed prior in Chapter 3, and India. Female infanticide also has been reported in North Korea, South Asia, the Middle East, and parts of Africa. As already described, in patrilineal, poor, or developing societies, a girl child is viewed as culturally and economically less advantageous to a family than a boy child.

In areas where such a prevalent anti-girl attitude prevails, women sometimes resort to female infanticide and feticide, deliberately aborting a female fetus, to protect their daughters from

DOI: 10.4324/9781003413417-5

what mothers anticipate as a life of objectification and subjugation in male-dominant societies. Conflicts exacerbate already difficult conditions for women. Said one rural Afghani woman in 2011: "The only thing we can hope is that our lives will be short and that we do not give birth to daughters. I would rather kill my daughter at birth than have her live a life like mine."[1] Less overt and extreme prejudice, but prejudice nonetheless, is found in many venues, though its existence often goes unspoken.

Prejudice often relates to in-group, out-group struggles for dominance, as illustrated by the Gombe chimps in Chapter 3. The male chimps, the in-group, fought among themselves for dominance, but the female chimps were passed among them as the out-group. Though fights – in the case of the chimps, to the death – for dominance occur, once dominance is settled, members within the dominant group are treated in ways and with respect not deemed necessary in dealing with out-groups. Psychologist Gordon Allport's 1954 book *On the Nature of Prejudice* is considered a classic on prejudice and discrimination among groups. There he states that as early as age five, individuals begin to understand they are members of groups, and by age ten can have fierce loyalties to their groups.[2] Individuals begin to differentiate between those in their group and those outside their group. Women are the perpetual, global out-group.

Prejudice and discrimination can be structurally sanctioned through rules, regulations, and legislation, offering a group advantages or imposing disadvantages. Banning women from certain roles in the military and suffrage restrictions are examples of structural bias.

Bias can also be cultural and imposed through implicit expectations of how women should "behave."

US Senator Elizabeth Warren was interrupted and ordered to stop reading a letter written by Coretta Scott King at the 2017 Senate confirmation hearing of Senator Jeff Sessions for attorney general, based on an arcane parliamentary rule that forbids impugning colleagues. King's 1986 letter opposed the nomination of Sessions to an earlier federal judgeship based on what King referred to as "intimidation of elderly black voters." Raising concerns about confirming an attorney general with a history of voter intimidation was taken as "impugning" Session's good name. Senate Majority Leader Mitch McConnell said, "Sen. Warren was giving a lengthy speech. She had appeared to violate the rule. She was warned. She was given an explanation. Nevertheless, she persisted."[3] Male senators Tom Udall, Sherrod Brown, and Bernie Sanders were later allowed to read from the same letter without rebuke. Prejudice, in this case against Senator Warren, perpetuates a view of women as subordinate, even in so-called developed, liberal democracies. Consequently, prejudice impedes women's voices from being heard, from women being viewed as leaders, and from women being seen as appropriate for inclusion in security matters.

Fifty years after the publication of Allport's work, a group of scholars looked back at it to reflect on and update its premises. There, social psychologist Laurie Rudman pointed out that (perhaps as a function of when he was writing), while Allport saw bias against groups based on race, religion, and occupation, he largely ignored gender. Rudman likens Allport to "the proverbial fish – blind to the water he swims in."[4] In other words, Allport failed to recognize a key feature of his environment.

Women as well as men can be blind fish. US Ambassador Swanee Hunt recalled hosting two rounds of formal negotiations between warring parties in the Balkans in 1994. She had an "aha" moment when she looked into the auditorium where the talks were being held and realized it was all men. She, an avid feminist, had failed to require that women be included. Both men and women have been enculturated to associating "men" with security issues.

Nonrecognition of prejudice perpetuates sexism, if only through benign neglect. While there are many different definitions of sexism, here it refers to actions that foster stereotypes of social roles and, as such, foster further prejudice and discrimination. Sexism then becomes considered an acceptable form of prejudice, often through sexist microaggressions including offhand comments, interruptions, talking over women, and other professional slights, and assumptions. Research has shown that sexist behaviors are most common in environments where gender equality policies are not enforced, incidents are not taken seriously, and there is no punishment for perpetrators. As the adage says, "The culture of any organization is shaped by the worst behaviour the leader is willing to tolerate." Women become penalty-free targets, making organizational culture key to whether an environment is a sexist or inclusive.

Offhand comments can degrade women. Indian prime minister's Narendra Modi's 2015 praise of Bangladeshi prime minister Sheikh Hasani's zero tolerance for terrorism "despite being a woman" is an example of an unintended "blind fish," sexist comment. Assuming that New Zealand prime minister Jacinda Ardern and Finnish prime minister Sanna Marin were meeting in November 2022 because they were of a similar demographic, as did a reporter, rather than as heads of state who had governmental issues to discuss, demeans their status as leaders. CNN anchor Don Lemon apologized in 2023 after commenting on-air that former South Carolina governor and potential Republican presidential candidate Nikki Haley, age 51 at the time, was "not in her prime." Though (perhaps) no foul was intended in any of these examples, they nevertheless negatively affect how women are viewed as professionals and leaders.

Researchers have studied since the 1970s the phenomenon of men interrupting women. Some of the interruptions are attributed to men simply talking more than women in meetings, though men often "hear" conversations differently, which is called "listener bias." Australian researcher Dale Spender found, for example, that when women speak 30% of the time in meetings, men perceive it – hear it – as women talking 90% of the time. Returning to the idea of offhand comments distorting images and perpetuating myths, according to Japanese prime minister Yoshiro Mori, "When you increase the number of female executive members, if their speaking time isn't restricted to a certain extent, they have difficulty finishing, which is annoying."[5] Even in the hallowed halls of institutions like the US Supreme Court, it has been found that female Supreme Court justices are interrupted three times as often as their male colleagues. They are interrupted not only by their male colleagues but by male attorneys, something highly unlikely to happen to a male justice.

There have even been new words coined for some microaggressions, including hepeated, mansplaining, manels, and manterrupting. "Hepeated" refers to a woman suggesting an idea and having it ignored, only to have the same idea eagerly embraced when a man says the same thing. Mansplaining refers to a man explaining something to a woman in what is considered a condescending or patronizing manner. It includes having a man with potentially little or no knowledge explain a woman's field to her, the man apparently assuming that she could not possibly be an expert in anything. A website called "Academic Men Explain Things to Me" collected experiences of women being mansplained in academia. "Manels" reference the until recently common practice of professional panels in male-dominated fields such as security, excluding women. The same premise holds true for professional reading lists that exclude women authors, and use of women-authored readings missing in academic curricula. Manterrupting, interrupting, and/or speaking over women, is a common way men dominate conversations and belittle women's contributions.

The assumption that women either do not like or cannot "do" certain fields, such as science, technology, engineering, and math (STEM), has been repeatedly disproven. The Massachusetts Institute of Technology conducted a study in 2016 on women in engineering.[6] It found that, counter to assumptions, women like to "tinker," too, yet their work is virtually invisible. The 2016 movie *Hidden Figures* chronicles the work of three African American women mathematicians who worked on the Apollo program, all but forgotten in history until a moviemaker brought their work to light. The public reaction was largely one of surprise, and "who knew?" It turns out that women in India have also made significant contributions to that country's space achievements, not previously acknowledged until the 2016 movie prompted broader considerations about women perhaps having a role in science.

Microaffirmations can also come into play regarding expressions of bias. Bias can be expressed as a positive feeling toward individuals and groups. Giving frequent expressions of praise to a single person or groups from a superior, and spending more time with, smiling at, or asking the opinions of only certain individuals or groups can signal positive bias as well. Among all individuals, but especially women, there can also be both "halo" and "horn" cognitive effects often associated with such single traits as physical attractiveness. Good-looking individuals can receive advantages – like others forgiving their mistakes or opening opportunities to them – not offered to others. For women, physical attractiveness can also work against them as they rise higher in rank/authority, by others dismissing them as only-a-pretty-face rather than leaders. The "horn" effect refers to the cognitive process whereby negative attitudes are attributed to someone based on their appearance or a single aspect of their character. Unfortunately, for example, overweight individuals in the populace are often stereotyped as lazy or irresponsible. Overweight male leaders, however, are often considered "stately." Being overweight can be almost inexcusable for women leaders.

While women have their foot in the door in nontraditional fields, bias persists. Nontraditional fields are those where one gender makes up less than 25% of the workforce, thereby affecting organizational culture, including at the sub-unit level. Women military officers in, for example, the nursing profession likely do not encounter the same gender-related retention and promotion issues as their female pilot counterparts. The first women promoted to flag rank (a military officer holding the rank of general or admiral) in both the US Army and the Navy commanded the Nurse Corps, nursing being an "accepted" profession for women.

Repeated studies evidence that gender identification on job applications matters. When applicants are randomly assigned a male or female name for a science-related position, the résumés of those with male names were considered more highly qualified and hirable by faculty reviewers. Similarly, it has also been found that both men and women were more likely to hire a man for a job that required math. Studies demonstrating STEM-related prejudice against women have been supplemented with anecdotal evidence. A female US military cyber officer pointed out in a 2020 *Military Times* article that women in that career field are largely tracked into jobs like network administration and operations by their male-dominant superiors, rather than cyberwarfare, and argued against using photos, names, and race in application packages to alleviate that perhaps implicit bias.[7]

Changing people's actions can sometimes be easier than changing their attitudes. For many years, hotels left signs in guest rooms asking guests to turn off the lights when they left the room, and those signs were often ignored. So instead of asking guests to turn off the lights, hotels installed card readers that required guests to insert their room key (card) for the lights to turn on, thereby automatically turning the lights off when the guests removed the key when leaving the room. Similarly, when it was recognized that orchestras were predominantly male and that it was unlikely that men were simply more musically talented, auditions began to be held behind a curtain (including so that judges were not able to see shoes), and the number of women hired went up considerably. The prejudice had been removed and musicians were judged solely on their musical talent. Increasingly, companies and organizations are considering ways to remove prejudice by actions rather than attitudes, with attitudinal change hopefully coming after the fact.

Women in patrilineal societies experience more overt types of discrimination. The consequences of cultural prejudice in patrilineal societies are considered cloying in Western culture. But Western culture has not escaped bias either. While the results are (most often) not as physically threatening and legally constraining, nevertheless they can be insidiously degrading and restrictive.

Objectification and enculturation

In eighteenth-century German philosopher Immanuel Kant's *Lecture on Ethics*, he spoke about sexual objectification, the idea that individuals can be treated as objects. Philosopher and ethics professor Martha Nussbaum extended that consideration in her 1995 identification of seven features that come into play with objectification:[8]

- *instrumentality*: the treatment of a person as a tool for the objectifier's purposes;
- *denial of autonomy*: the treatment of a person as lacking in autonomy and self-determination;
- *inertness*: the treatment of a person as lacking in agency, and perhaps also in activity;
- *fungibility*: the treatment of a person as interchangeable with other objects;
- *violability*: the treatment of a person as lacking in boundary integrity;
- *ownership*: the treatment of a person as something that is owned by another (can be bought or sold);
- *denial of subjectivity*: the treatment of a person as something whose experiences and feelings (if any) need not be taken into account.[9]

Feminist writers have represented the objectification of women by men as a central problem in women's lives.

Through objectification, women see their value as based on appearance and sexual performance. Sigmund Freud's Madonna-Whore complex, whereby men divide women into two types, Madonna (virginal) and Whore (debased prostitute), is an aspect of objectification. The dysfunctional aspect for men comes in desiring a highly sexualized woman but being unable to respect her and wanting to marry a woman they respect, but cannot seem to desire. Though Freud posited his views in the early twentieth century, the premise still survives. Rapper/performer Usher says in his 2004 hit single "Yeah": "We want a lady in the street and a freak in the bed," modified by Ludacris in 2008 in *Nasty Girl* as "Lady in the streets, but a freak in the bed." "Would you rather have a lady in the streets or a freak in the sheets?" was ESPN's radio show *Off the Bench* question in a 2020 "Would You Rather?" segment.

The dysfunction for women comes in trying to satisfy those contradictory desires and subsequently being judged differently than men. After admitting to an affair with President Bill Clinton as a 22-year-old White House intern, Monica Lewinsky was shamed, humiliated, and stigmatized. She has talked about being unable to get a job or escape the Internet shaming, including by women, for years. She became reclusive and left the United States at different points after the affair was exposed. Yet Clinton left office with a Gallup poll approval rating higher at the time than any president since Harry Truman. Not until 2018 and the #Metoo movement, and due to his seeming obliviousness to his repugnant behavior toward women, did Democratic candidates started rethinking, and rejecting, Clinton's once formidable help on the campaign trail.

Prominent men in the United States, including Donald Trump, Steven Bannon, Rudy Guiliani, Roger Ailes, Bill O'Reilly, and Newt Gingrich have all been involved in high-profile adultery or domestic abuse scandals that did not touch their careers. There is an expectation among some men that a celebrity status entitles them to sexual relations with women of their choice. Trump stated as much in the 2005 *Access Hollywood* tape released during the 2016 presidential campaign. "You know, I'm automatically attracted to beautiful – I just start kissing them. It's like a magnet. Just kiss. I don't even wait. And when you're a star, they let you do it. You can do anything."[10] Though he later wobbled about acknowledging this when the remarks became a campaign issue, just before the election Trump admitted – almost proudly and defiantly – the words as his. Later, in 2023, during the civil rape and defamation trial filed by E. Jean Carroll, Trump unleashed a tirade of remarks, including defending his *Access Hollywood* comments, suggesting that because he was rich and famous, he should be insulated from accountability.[11] "Well, historically, that's true with stars," he said. "If you look over the last million years, I guess that's been largely true," he continued. "Not always but largely true. Unfortunately or fortunately."[12] There is nothing fortunate about objectifying women. Yet forgiveness and rehabilitation seem reserved for men, while scorn saved for women.

In *Toward a Feminist Theory of the State* (1989), Catherine MacKinnon wrote that women live in objectification as fish live in water, meaning that it surrounds them. Adolescent girls exposed to sexualized media material that objectifies women plays heavily into self-objectification issues. Because historically women have had to rely on men for their physical, social, and economic well-being, "being liked" was a sometimes a life/death imperative. In her book *Reviving Ophelia: Saving the Selves of Adolescent Girls* (1994), therapist Mary Pipher discussed the societal pressures on young women to be *liked*, including early sexualization for which they may not be ready and that too often results in transforming confident young girls into self-conscious adolescents. Women are often viewed as either likable or competent, and girls learn that at an early age. Being *liked* often translates into trying to satisfy the Madonna-Whore expectations of men, thereby objectifying women.

The psychological and economic effects of objectification include striving for a sometimes impossible body image, linked to bulimia, anorexia nervosa, and high-risk dieting as well as depression, anxiety, and other mental health issues. A plethora of organizations worldwide have been created to help girls and young women develop self-esteem to counter the social pressures they face. The Girl Scout organization was created in 1912 and continues today with various names in 146 countries, toward helping girls build courage, confidence, and character. More recently, former *Vogue* Brazil fashion editor Yasmine McDougall Sterea created the Free Free "movement" in Brazil in 2018 to empower girls and young women through educational programs and directed activities including fashion-related events that encourage girls' personal sense of expression, healing, and liberation. Tapping into the idea that women's perfection is a myth that keeps women in a gilded cage exposed to all sorts of abuse, Free Free has spread to five countries in less than five years. Commercial industries not only profit from this objectification through women far outspending men on personal care products, but also exploit it by charging women more for basically the same products as sold to men at a lower price, called the "pink tax."

The media "sells" the idea that women's value lies in youth, beauty, and sexuality, whereas boys are shown that their value comes from dominance, power, and aggression. That warped value system affects women in power struggles. The political effects of objectification include women being underrepresented in leadership roles. Not being in leadership roles inherently inhibits equality or even considerations of gender-related issues. The reality is that when legal barriers are removed, women still face significant challenges with being accepted into nontraditional roles, including those involving leadership.

While evolutionary biology suggests that gender roles are based on nature, nurture is involved as well through enculturation – learned behavior. A cache of outstanding books have examined various aspects of the enculturation of damaging sexism attitudes. Caroline Criado-Perez examines the adverse effects on women caused by data bias in big data collection in *Invisible Women* (2019). In *Who Cooked the Last Supper?* (first published in 1988), Rosalind Miles pointed out that men have largely written history, and largely written women out. Elizabeth Lesser takes that idea further in *Cassandra Speaks* (2020), asking what might have been different if women had been the tellers of stories that shape societal views. But women have not been the storytellers until recently, and are still having to push their way in.

Virginia Woolf commented on the literature of her time in her 1929 essay *A Room of One's Own.*

> All these relationships between women, I thought, rapidly recalling the splendid gallery of fictitious women, are too simple. [...] And I tried to remember any case in the course of my reading where two women are represented as friends. [...] They are now and then mothers and daughters. But almost without exception they are shown in their relation to men. It was strange to think that all the great women of fiction were, until Jane Austen's day, not only seen by the other sex, but seen only in relation to the other sex. And how small a part of a woman's life is that.

The premise that women play only supporting roles to men in literature was later extended to modern movies, and shown valid, by a test developed by Scandinavian feminists.

Called the Bechdel test, it considers women's roles in motion pictures through three test components: (1) that at least two named women are featured in the movie being tested, (2) that these women talk to each other, and (3) that they discuss something other than a man. The number of movies which pass that test is shockingly low. The test can also be applied to television shows, video games, and comics. The Geena David Institute on Gender in the Media monitors statistics such as the number of named female characters, protagonists, co-protagonists, writers, and directors in films, all low compared to men. When history is written by men and the world is seen and portrayed largely through male eyes, as de Beauvoir said in the 1940s, women become merely "the other."

Inclusive diversity

The benefits of diversity, including innovation, expanded problem-solving techniques and capabilities, and varied strategic perspectives are well documented. Research has also shown, however, that visible signs of diversity, such as race, gender, and age, can initially have negative effects on teamwork because it cues an increased likelihood for differences of opinion within the team. With time, however, even that cueing can enhance the team's ability to handle conflict, because members expect it and therefore handle it better when it surfaces. So what initially "feels good" for the group may not be what is best for the group in the long term, and what "feels bad" can increase group effectiveness. Consequently, current organizational research focuses on "how" rather than "if" diversity should be an organizational goal. A key point regarding effective diversification of the workforce is that diversity is useless without inclusivity. Harvard University simply defines an inclusive culture as one "that accepts, values and views as strength the difference we all bring to the table."[13] In other words, inclusive diversity is more than statistics and more than toleration. Inclusive diversity means that all individuals feel an accepted part of a group, can voice opinions without fearing retribution, and that their input is valued rather than dismissed.

Data and demographics are again important. Environments do not necessarily or even ordinarily move directly from being healthy to one of overt sexual harassment. Sexism is the missing link in a continuum between having a healthy environment and a toxic environment, sexism consisting of the microaggressions that occur regularly without rebuke, often by or with full awareness of leadership. It includes being ignored, patronized, or the target of passive-aggressive behavior. Ignoring that missing link is, however, done at the peril of the organization as research demonstrates there is a link between sexism, sexual harassment, and sexual assault. It is all part and parcel of attitudes. Without addressing sexism within organizations and institutions, problems on the gender-inclusive continuum are being addressed only at a surface level and will not be abated. Again, data becomes critical, and is often missing or manipulated.

Issues in gathering and drawing conclusions from attitudinal data within gender-dominated organizations can be a problem. In an organization of 400 individuals, for example, only 25 might be women. If a survey question is asked regarding whether the organization condones sexism, and all 25 women answered "yes," how the statistics are interpreted is critical. If the percentage of women who see sexism as a problem is considered, the answer is 100%. If, however, the percentage of the overall population that views sexism as a problem is considered, the answer is 6.25% and that figure might not be considered statistically significant and therefore worthy of attention. The latter approach is certainly the safer approach if organizations don't want to reveal internal issues, don't want the data known within higher levels of the organization, or potentially made available for public release.

While a prevailing majority opinion in a population can be reversed by as little as 10% of the population, that requires the 10% to be committed agents who "consistently proselytize the opposing opinion and are immune to influence."[14] But in one-gender dominated fields, until the demographic mix reaches a tipping point considered as 30%,[15] that number identified by what is known as critical mass theory, the minority is acutely prone to influence, including bullying, and their views are easily discarded. A female member of the Swedish parliament pointed out that the same group of women who were once in a small minority in the legislature talked, acted, and voted differently when their proportion significantly increased.[16]

However, "body counting" alone as an indicator of diversity fails to consider the context of social relations, subjectivities, experiences, and processes by which inclusivity occurs. Focusing on numbers fails to consider that an established, sometimes hostile culture remains in place after women or minorities are hired, largely invisible, subjective, and often unchallenged due to its embedded nature. The presence of minorities, even in the upper layers of institutions, though encouraging, cannot be taken as a definitive indicator that organizational cultures and structures are significantly changing, as changes to organizational culture are among the hardest changes to make. Leader support for cultural change – male or female – is a necessary, but not sufficient condition for change. Accountability of middle managers for implementing diversity initiatives is equally or more important, as they are the gatekeepers for retention and advancement. While women have increasingly entered nontraditional career fields, their entry often is not welcomed, and sometimes is actively resisted.

Michelle Howard was named the US Navy's first woman four-star admiral in 2014. She was also the first African American woman to command a US naval ship, as well as being the first African American woman to achieve the rank of admiral in the navy, all through an exemplary operational record as a surface warfare officer. While her promotion was a significant event for the navy, the military, and for women, Howard herself admitted in 2012, "There were individuals who didn't want me there or wanted to undermine what I was trying to do."[17]

A *Navy Times* article chronicled the prejudice, resistance, and resentment Howard encountered "from her Induction Day in 1978," and that continued even as a flag officer.[18] A navy investigation report cited one of her peers, Rear Adm. Chuck Gaouette, as suggesting to others that Howard "may not have had to cross as many hurdles in the same fashion to get where she was at," and her race and gender may have "sped up" her selection for vice admiral. Gaouette, who was fired from command of the John C. Stennis Carrier Strike Group mid-deployment in 2012, admitted his comments were "petty" and said he'd apologize to Howard.[19]

Unquestionably, women are sometimes placed in organizational positions as "props" to demonstrate organizational commitment to diversity, which only perpetuates the kind of attitude expressed by Gaouette and considerable backlash,[20] and puts women into competition with each other for those one-only slots. Consequently, the resentment experienced by Howard is not uncommon and often goes unchecked. It is especially important to note how resistance such as that experienced by Howard, could undermine her ability to be an effective leader.

American video game designer Brianna Wu became the target of bullying on Twitter in 2014, including both rape and death threats, about #GamerGate, a hashtag by "the freewheeling catastrophe/social movement/misdirected lynch mob"[21] trying to drive women out of the male-dominated video game design industry. Tactics used by GamerGaters included online harassment and doxxing – the publishing of personal or private information about a person with malicious intent. Wu was forced to move from her home and relocate to another state, where she cofounded an independent video game development studio.

While video gaming specifically is not directly related to security, the more general cyber field is, and women are being shut out of there as well. The global cybersecurity workforce was short some 3.5 million workers in 2021, which means that the workforce was significantly shy of demand. Organizations have unfilled cybersecurity positions that can create security vulnerabilities. While women comprise 39% of the overall workforce and 38% of the STEM workforce, they only make up 25% of the cyber workforce.

Women in the cyber field report discrimination in pay, according to (ISC)², a nonprofit that focuses on cybersecurity training and certification. Their 2022 research found that 32% of men working in cybersecurity earn an average of $50,000–$100,000 annually, while only 18% of women in cybersecurity occupy that same income bracket. Further, 25% of men earn $100,000–$500,000 annually, versus 20% of women.

Additionally, (ISC)² found that the majority of women who work in the field report discrimination. Nearly all of the women in the survey (ISC)² conducted, reported having experienced unconscious bias, and 19% said they had been subjected to overt discrimination. The women also cited unexplained delays in career advancement (53%) and exaggerated responses to errors (29%) as barriers to women in the field. Prejudice and discrimination hurt national security if women are being kept from or run out of vacant positions in areas critical to national defense.[22]

The #MeToo movement evidenced the breadth and depth of the sexual harassment problem. Started within in the entertainment industry in 2017, women from other fields, including national security, subsequently stepped forward exposing sexual harassment issues. A total of 223 women signed an open letter titled #metoonatsec, stating, "abuses are born of imbalances of power and environments permitting such practices while silencing and shaming their survivors."[23] Some women declined to sign the letter, fearing backlash in the work environment, including men avoiding working with women.

#MeToo in fact generated both good news and bad news. The good news is that a 2022 Pew Research study reported that women now feel safer at work and #MeToo has positively changed how organizations manage instances of sexual harassment and assault. The bad news is that research reported in *Forbes* in 2022 also showed a clear link between #MeToo and backlash against women, including male managers being reluctant to hire, work with, or mentor women. That has made the workplace sometimes even more difficult for women than before #MeToo.

In Sweden, traditionally known as the feminist capital of the world, a successful defamation law suit against writer and actress Cissi Wallin after she named her rapist online, has created a substantial chilling effect on other Swedish women stepping forward and naming their abusers. Subsequently, avoiding and abating backlash has become an area of study in itself.

Competence, confidence, and mentorship

Three highly related factors have been found key to all employee hiring, retention, and promotion: competence, confidence, and mentorship. However, they work entirely differently for men than women, as issues related to Social Dominance Orientation (SDO) come into play for women.[24] SDO is a personality trait measuring an individual's support for a standing social hierarchy and the extent to which they feel justified in viewing their in-group as superior to out-groups. In male-dominated professions, organizations, and cultures, SDO represents the status quo. So, while not all women are more, or even equally qualified for all or particular positions than all men, SDO-based assumptions made about women's competency, what competencies are career relevant, and whether women's competency is perceived to pose a threat to the status quo, can work against women trying to climb nontraditional career ladders.

Sociologists have examined how meritocratic ideals and performance awards play out in organizations, including those that see themselves as committed to diversity, and found what they call "the paradox of meritocracy." Even when an organization's core values emphasized meritocratic values, managers confer higher monetary awards to male employees than to equally performing female employees. Individuals who say they support diversity assume themselves objective and unbiased, but do not necessarily monitor and scrutinize their own behavior. Rather, they just assume that they are acting appropriately and their assessments accurate. But organizations need to take a hard, honest look at themselves, with accountability for actions matching rhetoric at all management levels often key to long-term change.

Though Harvard Business School (HBS) saw itself as gender supportive before 2010, the facts spoke differently: women who arrived with the same test scores and grades as their male counterparts fell behind academically, and a third of female HBS junior faculty left from 2006 to 2007.

> Many Wall Street-hardened women confided that Harvard was worse than any trading floor, with first-year students divided into sections that took all their classes together and often developed the overheated dynamics of reality shows. Some male students, many with finance backgrounds, commandeered classroom discussions and hazed female students and younger faculty members, and openly ruminated on whom they would "kill, sleep with or marry" (in cruder terms). Alcohol-soaked events could be worse.[25]

Drew Gilpin Faust, Harvard's first female president, decided something had to be done.

That led HBS to do a curricular, instructional, and environmental "gender makeover" in 2010.

Faust appointed a new HBS dean to change the curriculum, rules, and social rituals to foster the success of women as well as men. Those changes required overt, sometimes intrusive actions such as placing stenographers in classrooms to guard against biased grading, monitoring against female students being interrupted, and not allowing males to dominate discussion. Private coaching was provided for students and untenured female professors. In the end, "women at the school finally felt like 'hey, people like me are an equal part of this institution,'"[26] said Rosabeth

Moss Kanter, a longtime professor. Inclusive diversity did not come easy, and not without a certain amount of angst from both the women and especially the men about the intrusiveness of the measures taken to change the environment.

Studies have consistently shown a general tendency to evaluate men and women differently on performance reviews. Reviewers, regardless of gender, tend to give female employees more negative feedback than they give to male employees. Negative feedback, using very masculine language, given to women often includes personality criticism of some sort, such as being "abrasive," "judgmental," or "strident," not often found in men's reviews. Women are judged by different standards than their male counterparts, and in personalized ways that can mar confidence.

These findings have held true in a variety of organizations. Research conducted based on data gathered through the website RateMyProfessor has found that students evaluate women professors differently than men. Men professors are more often considered brilliant and funny, while women are either nice, or rude and bossy. A study of a large-scale US military leader performance evaluation data set similarly found that women were subjectively assigned significantly more negative attributes than men, such as being scattered, opportunistic, excitable, and temperamental, even though their performances were the same by objective measures.[27] These evaluation practices – focusing on a woman's appearance or personality and on a man's skills and intelligence – reinforce people thinking more highly of men than women in professional settings, and praising men for the same things they criticize women for.

Although women in nontraditional career fields win awards and commendations for outstanding performance, it has been questioned whether competence is in fact a benefit once in the workforce. London Business School researchers conducted a study of 200 US military commanders responsible for performance evaluations. They found a high correlation between SDO and performance evaluations "when the evaluator was male and high social-dominance oriented and when the female subordinate's objective on-the-job performance was high."[28] They concluded that in hierarchical organizations, past accomplishments can actually be detrimental to women in evaluations from men who want to maintain the traditional gender balance because women's accomplishments can be viewed as threatening. Simply stated, equal consideration of qualified women cannot be assumed. Further, once hired, advancement and retention in nontraditional fields is riddled with challenges. While competency remains an entrance and advancement prerequisite, it is not enough. Confidence comes into play as well.

Women, including those in top leadership positions, often suffer from a type of imposter syndrome, one stemming from lack of confidence. The prevalence and manifestations of imposter syndrome are backed by numerous studies. Researchers have found, for example, that women have more self-doubt about their job performance and careers than men. This self-doubt can lead to women giving up on a task before even starting, fearing failure or demonstrating incompetence. Men, for example, will apply for a job if they match only a very few of position qualifications listed on recruitment ads, while women apply only if they can match nearly all.

There is, however, a link between competence and confidence that is important and deserves consideration as well. Women have long assumed that demonstrating competence will lead to acceptance by their male colleagues. The International Space University hosted a panel of four highly trained, highly competent women astronauts, from the United States, China, South Korea, and Canada during its 2014 Summer Session in Montreal. Asked by an audience member what is their biggest challenge day-to-day in being an astronaut, Canadian astronaut Julie Payette answered without hesitation. "Getting male colleagues to take me seriously and having to prove my competence over and over again."[29] Her astronaut colleagues nodded vigorously in agreement. Confidence can be hard to sustain if your colleagues do not take you seriously. Research cites women having to repeatedly prove themselves as one of five reasons women, particularly women of color, leave STEM fields.[30]

Sexist attitudes enculturated through the media ingrain SDO attitudes. In a September 2014 segment of *The Five* on Fox News, panelist Greg Gutfield commented on the United Arab Emirates' first woman military pilot, Major Mariam al Mansouri, launching bombs against the Islamic State of Iraq and Syria. "Problem is," he quipped, "after she bombed it she couldn't park it." Another panelist, Eric Bolling, then made a play on the common military phrase "boots on the ground" asking, "Would that be considered boobs on the ground, or no?"[31]

The Dunning-Kruger effect is a cognitive bias whereby individuals with low ability, expertise, or experience substantially overestimate their own abilities in particular areas, based on erroneous readings of both their own abilities and those of others. Basically, the less competent someone is, the more they can tend to overestimate their own abilities. Researchers have extended that premise to consider the relationship between female competence and confidence. On a quiz of scientific skills designed to test both competence and confidence, women tend to rate themselves more negatively than men on skills, yet on average performed at about the same level. Studies have shown that too often, confidence is mistaken for competence.

A female US Naval officer explained to me in an email how her tendency to defer when she felt there were others more competent than she on a subject, plays out to her disadvantage in practice.

> When I receive a tasker or request for information regarding a topic on which I do not consider myself an expert, my first reaction is to try to find someone who is better qualified to answer than I am, rather than venturing my own, ill-informed and incomplete opinion. If I do feel that I am the most knowledgeable person on the subject, I don't hesitate to answer confidently, even forcefully if required. But I am much less willing than most of my male colleagues are to act like an expert when I'm not. Leaders should be aware that women may be less likely to volunteer themselves, though they are usually in reality equally competent to the men around them. Leaders should also be trained to view the humility indicated by this deferral as a strength, not a weakness.[32]

Her experience is not unique; women generally err on the side of being conservative regarding their capabilities. Her point about leadership needing to be aware that humility can be a strength demonstrates how "confidence" is too often confused with competence, regardless of the underlying substance.

Between having to overcome doubting themselves, doubt sometimes being reinforced by male colleagues and generated by years of societal enculturation, and feeling the need to be hyper-competent, women are left in a precarious position. Yet according to *Forbes* contributor Bruce Kasanoff, "senior leaders perceive that they perpetually confront the same problem [...] they can't find women who are both confident and competent."[33] Nevertheless, perceived "overconfidence" can be a problem for women as well.

Gender-based stereotypical perceptions remain a key issue for women in nontraditional career fields. Researchers have conducted studies regarding expected gender attributes for decades, such as one where participants were shown fictional biographies of two state senators. The biographies were identical except for the names associated with them; one was John Burr and the other Ann Burr. "When quotations were added that described the state senators as 'ambitious' and possessing 'a strong will to power,' John Burr became more popular. But the changes provoked 'moral outrage' toward Ann Burr, whom both men and women became less willing to support."[34] Ann Burr had stepped beyond the culturally acceptable lanes of women's behavior.

Studies continue to document what many women already know: If women behave in too feminine a manner, they are seen as weak and not as leaders, but if they are too masculine, they can experience backlash from being seen as too aggressive. There have also been suggestions that women need to know how to switch on and off masculine behaviors of aggression, assertiveness, and confidence. For example, while speaking up first can get a woman viewed as bossy, piggybacking on a male comment would likely be more acceptable to male colleagues. Or, rather than directly disagreeing with a male colleague, first stating the merit of his premise before gently suggesting another option, would be less threatening to male colleagues. A recent book by Australian sociologists titled *Engaging Men: Reducing Resistance and Gaining Support* (2021), was written as a kind of practical "how-to" work with men. While admittedly practical, having to cajole the male ego can often put women in a position of having to "mommy" their male colleagues. It can be very helpful for women to have other women to lead them through the minefield of gender relations in the workplace. More generally, mentors can mean the difference between success and failure in the workplace.

Every organization has rules and, generally speaking, those who join organizations tacitly (or explicitly) do so agreeing to follow those rules. But there are always official rules, provided and conveyed through organizational human resources departments, and unwritten rules, which are equally or potentially more important for advancement in the organization. In his first year as an attorney at a big New York law firm, my son was sent an email from a partner – a boss way above my son's immediate boss, who was also copied on the email – asking my son a legal question. My type-A son did the all the required research and sent his lengthy, comprehensive response to the partner, copied to his immediate boss. His immediate boss came to my son's office shortly thereafter and offered him advice, based on an unwritten rule of the organization. "Never send a partner an email longer than three sentences. They don't have time to read it and it will be useless to them." If his immediate boss had not offered that advice, my son would have gone on repeatedly making the same mistake, and likely his performance review would have suffered due to a mistake that he didn't know he was making. Mentors tell you the unwritten rules, give you advice and feedback that you might not want to hear but will help you, and generally help you navigate organizational cultures. But women in nontraditional careers are far less likely to have mentors than men.

W. Brad Johnson and David Smith argue in support of more men mentoring women in *Athena Rising: How and Why Men Should Mentor Women* (2016). Asserting that mentorship is key to attracting, retaining, and promoting the women needed to develop an inclusively diverse workforce needed for the future, they find six reasons – most rooted in gender stereotyping – that contribute to what they dub "reluctant male syndrome." *Persistent gender bias*, such as thinking of women as "nice" rather than "leaders," results in a tendency "to see assertive and action-oriented males as excellent leaders, while viewing similarly oriented women as abrasive, cold-hearted, and bossy."[35] Also related to stereotypes, Johnson and Smith suggest *gender expectations* can inhibit men from mentoring women they have been, for example, socialized to "protect" into leadership positions. Some men, they state, are simply *uncomfortable with nonsexual intimate relationships*. Men can also *fear public or office perception and gossip* if they are thought to spend too much time with a woman. They can also fear (even inadvertently) *saying or doing the wrong thing,* and *worry what their spouse will think*. All of these concerns make it easier for men to simply keep their distance and maintain sterile relationships with women colleagues.

Women can be reluctant to mentor women as well. Organizational structures frequently create competition between women. Men mentoring men, including pulling them up the advancement ladder with them, is accepted. In the navy, that's called having a "Sea Daddy." Women doing the same, however, can be perceived and characterized as showing favoritism. Women leaders must be constantly vigilant about not showing other women favoritism.

Before entering into a mentoring relationship, mentors weigh the expected costs – whether mentoring will be more trouble than it is worth, the possibility of a dysfunctional relationship, whether a protégé will reflect poorly on the mentor – and how much energy it will require. For women mentors, top on the list of expectations is a low-risk profile and a relationship where the rewards outweigh the costs, as even after women have climbed the career ladder, they still face more challenges, and hostility, than their male colleagues.[36] Women at the top of their fields cannot afford mentoring someone who will reflect poorly on them or their organizations.

The reality is that in testosterone-heavy career fields, men often nitpick women's behavior, looking for signs of weakness, signs of immaturity, of being "too-girly," or not being girly enough. When General Mike Flynn, Trump's short-lived national security advisor, was at the Defense Intelligence Agency, women were sent a memo from his office telling them "to monitor their levels of makeup, avoid flats, and err on the side of skirts and dresses" and that "make-up helps women look more attractive."[37] Women were told to avoid the "plain Jane" look.

Women walk a very thin line of behavior and deportment. Women mentors are acutely aware (having heard all jabs about wrong-doers in the halls and in meetings) of the multitude of potential faux spas young women can make – like twirling their hair – and have no choice but to limit themselves to protégées who understand organizational culture and expectations. The cold hard fact is, at work employees are fulfilling a role that an organization needs to accomplish its mission.

Women might be allowed into all career fields, but their rise and tenure are still determined by factors very different from their male counterparts. Rather than "climb the ladder," some women opt out to raise families or attend to other personal issues. Accommodation of women's overlapping career and biological clocks, and later care of aging parents, is a structural issue rarely addressed by organizations. Whereas women in the past often simply expected to have to choose between a career and a family life, women today more often expect to have both.

Women often base their decision on whether to stay or leave a career path on what has been called the "fight-or-flight" moment, about ten years into their career. Dubbed the Athena Factor, researchers have found that multiple reasons play into highly qualified, talented women opting out at about the ten-year mark, many of them gender-centered. Many women in nontraditional career fields find hostile environments, working in isolation or near-isolation, and mysterious career paths are commonalities found tied to not having an internal support network, along with having to walk the precarious line between aggressiveness and assertiveness that can often derail women's careers.

Toward inclusivity

Sociologist and HBS professor Rosabeth Moss Kanter's seminal book *Men and Women in the Corporation* (1977) was an examination of a large, mock corporation and how behavior and relationships within it were affected by power and powerlessness. In the book, Kanter introduced the idea of "empowerment," stating that organizations are most productive when all their employees are empowered to make and take decisions on their own and authority is devolved rather than centralized. That, however, goes against the very nature of hierarchical power. She further argued that structural issues – the structure of opportunities, power, and the proportions of people from different groups – explained the behavior of these groups within the corporation:

It was not the behavior of women, for example, that determined their relative lack of success within corporate life, but the structure of the organizations for which they were working. If there were to be any progress on issues such as the glass ceiling, it would come about because organizations changed, not people.[38]

For many years, there was a belief that women who have achieved success then fail to help and sometimes even thwart the progress of other females, see them as competitors. It even had a name, first coined in the 1970s: Queen Bee Syndrome. But a Columbia Business School study debunked the Queen Bee myth.[39] Instead, the authors faulted hidden organizational quotas as the culprit for low numbers of women in high positions. Other researchers have similarly found that workplace conditions set women up to compete with each other in ways men do not experience. When women perceive that only so many of them will be allowed into the senior ranks, often through tokenism, they begin vying for those spots. "When there appear to be few opportunities for women, research shows, women begin to view their gender as an impediment; they avoid joining forces, and sometimes turn on one another."[40] The organizational structure and culture position women against each other, creating a situation known as triangulation, where women are not only competing with men but with each other, which unfortunately extends to both personal and professional environments.

It is also interesting to note that there is no derogatory male equivalent of the Queen Bee Syndrome; cattiness has been only assumed for women. Catty women, or Queen Bees, do exist, but they are not the norm. Women are not any nastier to women than men are to one another. Women are just expected to be nicer, thereby creating bias toward ambitious women.

Referencing Allport's work regarding in-groups and out-groups, bias is explained there as

a human trait resulting from our tendency and need to classify individuals into categories as we strive to quickly process information and make sense of the world. Bias can be explicit, where individuals are aware of their prejudices or attitudes, and implicit, which is more sub-conscious feeling, perceptions, attitudes and stereotypes.[41]

Everyone has implicit biases and the very process of recognizing and discussing negative biases can help "manage" them. Harvard University's Project Implicit provides a testing vehicle for self-identifying hidden biases. Google also developed a program, called Jailbreak the Patriarchy, that allows users to "genderswap" pronouns in everything read, with the intent of demonstrating differences in the way women and men are referenced.

The reality is that increasingly, women must learn to forgo striving to be liked, and instead strive to be respected. Further, striving to be liked turns out not to be good training for dealing with and accepting the often-personalized criticism of women seeking advancement in non-traditional careers. The required first step toward inclusivity is awareness, not being a blind fish or complicit in sexism. Breaking the Ophelia Syndrome requires concerted effort on the part of women, and inclusive diversity requires male allies.

Masculinity and male allies

None of the changes regarding gender equality required to achieve a more stable and peaceful world are possible without men as allies in that quest, and men are currently going through some serious reconsiderations of what it means to be a man.

Globally, men are confronted with two broken bargains that have turned their economic and social status upside down – and consequently many are alarmed, worried, and indeed, angry.

The first broken bargain involves the evolutionary nature of capitalism from Fordism to globalization. During Fordism, a man could be hired into and retain a manufacturing job forever, a job that could support a family, but was limited in potential advancement. That was the bargain. Automation and manufacturers' realization that there's always cheaper labor to be found broke that bargain. Furthermore "creative destruction" – the abolishment of some fields but the opening of others – was accelerated by the influx of information technology that accompanied the wave of globalization which swept the globe at the turn of the millennium. Goodbye, mining and manufacturing sectors, hello, information technology and knowledge-based economies. That reality has left many men virtually unemployable.

Second, both ambition and economic need during the second wave of feminism in the 1960s and 1970s, drove more women into the workforce to compete for what were then considered "men's jobs." Women earning their own money also reduced women's economic dependence on men. Women now make up 41% of all primary breadwinners in the United States. As such, the nuclear family model prevalent in many Western countries with working-class men as providers has become the exception rather than the rule. Nonetheless, the "real man" version of masculinity – which idealizes toughness, strength, social respect, heterosexism, sexual potency, and stoicism – is centered on the belief that men are the head of the household, the breadwinner, and the provider (alongside being the protector of women, children, and the family). We cannot, however, put this genie back in the bottle and return to the 1960s. Rather, new social, economic, and policy approaches are needed alongside values, attitudes, and beliefs that support equality of life and livelihood.

For example, feelings of loss of control among primarily white, often poor, American men have given rise to the great replacement theory – a racist, sexist, anti-immigration theory that blames their negative circumstances on others and pushes authoritarian responses to address their woes. Men who believe this theory feel angry at women, believing they are among those "stealing their jobs" and robbing them of their masculinity, and control. Given the traditional dominance of men, including in writing and interpreting laws, they were previously allowed to suppress women's agency. Now, the shifting sands of who is gaining and losing personal agency and perceptions of whose "fault" that is, have affected both men and, occasionally, women, and not just in the United States. UK home secretary Suella Braverman has been referred to as the commander in chief of Britain's culture wars for her populist and often inflammatory anti-migrant views, often bleeding over into rants regarding transgender rights and climate activists.[42] Recent South Korean anti-feminist backlash stems from the men professing the same "I'm the victim" reasoning. In all cases, these interpretations of fault go hand in hand with rising misogyny.

American educator and activist Tony Porter is known for his advocacy to stop violence against women. He has argued the societal dictates to "act like a man" can lead to disrespect, mistreatment, and abuse of women, and each other: in other words, mistreatment of out-groups and fights to dominate among Alpha male in-groups. He argues that men need to break free of the "man box" that society has placed them in.

In *Of Boys and Men: Why the Modern Male Is Struggling, Why It Matters and What to Do about It* (2022), Richard Reeves suggests that boys are being left behind due to structural issues rather than societal issues. He points out, for example, that boys are 50% more likely than girls to fail at all three key school subjects: math, science, and reading. More generally, men are underperforming in education, which then leads to subsequent problems with employment and wage earning. Concerning that problem, he suggests delaying boys' entry into school by a year to allow their brain chemistry to catch up to that of girls because boys brains develop more slowly; delayed school entry is a strategy that has long been used by parents of boys who anticipate that their sons will eventually be competing for limited spots in top colleges. Reeves also suggests more male teachers would be beneficial to boys' learning, but that requires more men to accept teaching as a manly profession, teaching having traditionally been left largely to women, especially at the primary levels.

Reeves also correctly notes that it is not useful, and is in fact counterproductive, to simply direct social hostility toward men with labels of "toxic masculinity." He argues that the term has become an overly broad reference to perfectly normal male behavior, that few boys/men are actually involved in the type of behavior that might warrant such a label, and that men don't respond well to being called "toxic." Actually, nobody – men, women, boys, or girls – likes being labeled "toxic." The term "toxic feminism" has, for example, been associated with "Karens," the vigilante-style, most often middle-aged White women with a sense of entitlement who try to dictate conduct and police others. Karen is the outraged woman who always wants to speak with the manager. Unfortunately, there are examples of any woman speaking up for herself being labeled a Karen, but Karens can also be a complicated study of the connection between racism and sexism.[43]

What Reeves fails to consider is that certain cultures perpetuate versions of masculinity that do include violence. For example, a disproportionate 20% of the defendants in the Capitol riot cases served in the military – a profession described as one where members kill people and break things when told to – while only about 7% of American adults are veterans. That 20% includes a veteran and member of the Oath Keepers convicted of seditious conspiracy (the plan or effort to overthrow the government), and recent indictments of members of the Proud Boys for sedition made up primarily of military veterans. In fact, research has identified a correlation between certain versions of masculinity and violent extremism, mass violence, and mobilized violence. Further, adherence to the "real man" narrative of masculinity has correlated with mass violence, as noted by the Secret Service's 2022 website headline "Secret Service's Latest Research Highlights Mass Violence Motived by Misogyny."[44] Indeed, misogyny has been called "the glue" that binds together right-wing extremists.

All this to say that just as women have self-corrections to make among themselves, so too do men, but they can also work together while doing so. HeforShe through the UN, Promundo in Brazil, and Mobilizing Men as Partners for Women Peace, and Security through the non-profit Our Secure Future are all working to create relationships with men, thereby broadening the supportive stakeholders.

Through both patrilineal structures and objectification, social constructs of gender have conferred a higher social value on men than women, and privilege the masculine over the feminine. Male violence against women and girls stems from that privilege. Consequently, working with men and boys to encourage expressions of what has been called "positive masculinity," while empowering women and girls, offers a way forward, away from the gender-focused violence that prevails. A training guide for developing positive masculinity used in Nairobi, Kenya, explains the concept:

> Violence is all about power; men as the main perpetrators of violence exert "power over" women or other men that they perceive to be weaker than them. Positive masculinity is about tapping the "power within" and exercising "power with" others, be they women or fellow men.[45]

In *Good Guys: How Men Can Be Better Allies in the Workplace* (2020), W. Brad Johnson and David Smith explain the difference between performative and actual allyship. Performative allyship is, as it sounds, voicing support for gender equality with no actual follow-up. It is especially insidious as it signals to others that there is nothing actually expected from them either. It is often done to either avoid scrutiny for past actions or to check a box. Also counterproductive is allyship with a tone of "rescueship" – let's help the ladies – as it infers weakness among women. Actual allyship involves gender equality support, follow-through, and commitment to embedding change in organizations so that progress isn't reliant on particular individuals being in particular positions.

There are a multitude of ways that men can act as actual allies from the micro to the macro level and everything in between. Being an ally at the micro level includes simple things like, if a woman/Susan is cut off in a meeting, suggesting to colleagues that he (any male ally) would like to go back to Susan's comment and hear more of what she had to say, thereby acknowledging the value of her input. On a more macro scale, the American Bar Association (ABA) has issued multiple reports focused on long-term experiences of women in the nation's largest law firms, concluding that in many cases their relative lack of advancement was a structural issue. In 2021, that finding was challenged – by a woman – suggesting instead that women had too many "distractions," which meant they couldn't or wouldn't invest the time needed to advance. Ten women ABA past presidents responded with an "open letter" addressing the need for policies and cultures at law needed to allow women to thrive. But where were the men past presidents? As allies, they might have publicly stood by their women colleagues.

Conclusions

Discussions about bias, prejudice, and discrimination are difficult as they are often infused with perceptions – or direct accusations – of blame. Focusing on blame or perceptions of blame, however, serves no one's interests. Instead, focus must be kept on addressing problems that inhibit gender equality for men, women, boys, and girls, for global security.

Whether trying to maintain a positive peace or work toward positive peace, empirical evidence confirms that countries with gender equality are more economically prosperous, less corrupt, more democratic, and less likely to consider force as standard operating procedure for conflict settlement. But as long as women are portrayed and treated as subordinate, their roles as decision makers will be limited. Full implementation of the WPS framework optimizes nations' potential to reach positive peace.

It is in the interest of every nation to hire, retain, and advance the best and the brightest. It is the responsibility of the relevant organizations to provide the best and the brightest the opportunity to reach their full potential and an environment conducive to doing so. It is the responsibility of women in these careers to prepare themselves for the challenges they will face. Everyone will benefit from taking their responsibilities seriously.

Notes

1 Conveyed in Valerie Hudson and Patricia Leidle, *The Hillary Doctrine*, Columbia University Press, 2013, p. 250, from an interview by Leidle in 2011.

2 Gordon Allport, *On the Nature of Prejudice,* Addison-Wesley, 25th anniversary edition, 1979, p. 29.

3 Amy B. Wang, "Nevertheless, She Persisted Becomes New Battle Cry after McConnell Silences Elizabeth Warren," *Washington Post*, February 8, 2017. www.washingtonpost.com/news/the-fix/wp/2017/02/08/nevertheless-she-persisted-becomes-new-battle-cry-after-mcconnell-silences-elizabeth-warren/?utm_term=.d1bebf45428a

4 Laurie Rudman, in John Dovidio, Peter Glick, and Laurie Rudman, eds. *On the Nature of Prejudice: Fifty Years after Allport*, Wiley-Blackwell, 2005, p. 107.

5 "Who Won't Shut Up at Meetings? Men Say Women. It's Not." *Washington Post*, February 18, 2021. www.washingtonpost.com/outlook/2021/02/18/men-interrupt-women-tokyo-olympics/

6 Carroll Seron, Susan Silbey, Erin Cech, and Brian Rubineau, "Persistence Is Cultural: Professional Socialization and the Reproduction of Sex Segregation," *Work and Occupation*, December 13, 2016. pp. 178–214.

7 Lillian Warner, "This Is What the Air Force Can Do to Recruit and Train Women Cyber Warriors," *Military Times*, December 3, 2020.

8 "Objectification," *Philosophy and Public Affairs*, Fall 1995, pp. 249–289. www.mit.edu/~shaslang/mprg/nussbaumO.pdf

9 "Feminist Perspectives on Objectification," *Stanford Encyclopedia of Philosophy*, https://plato.stanford.edu/entries/feminism-objectification/http://www.dol.gov/wb/factsheets/nontra2009.htm.

10 *Access Hollywood* transcript, *New York Times*, October 8, 2016. www.nytimes.com/2016/10/08/us/donald-trump-tape-transcript.html?mcubz=3

11 Ja'Han Jones, "Trump Unleases Unhinged Tirade Attacking E. Jean Carroll, MSNBC, May 4, 2023. www.msnbc.com/the-reidout/reidout-blog/trump-e-jean-carroll-rape-trial-response-rcna82923

12 Jarad Gans, "Trump Defends *Access Hollywood* Comments," *The Hill*, https://thehill.com/regulation/court-battles/3990841-trump-defends-access-hollywood-comments-historically-thats-true-with-stars/

13 http://hr.fas.harvard.edu/inclusive-culture; See also T. Hudson Jordan, "Moving from Diversity to Inclusion," *Diversity Journal*, www.diversityjournal.com/1471-moving-from-diversity-to-inclusion/

14 J. Xie, S. Sreenivasen, G. Koniss, W. Zhang, C. Lim, and B.K. Symanski, "Social Consensus through the Influence of Committed Minorities," *Physical Review E*, July 22, 2011.

15 Joy McCann, "Electoral Quotas for Women: An International Overview," Parliament of Australia, November 14, 2013. www.aph.gov.au/About_Parliament/Parliamentary_Departments/Parliamentary_Library/pubs/rp/rp1314/ElectoralQuotas

16 Swanee Hunt, "Let Women Rule," *Foreign Affairs*, May/June 2007; Sarah Gordon, "The 30% Club, How Women Have Taken on the Old Boys Network," *Financial Times*, December 4, 2015. www.ft.com/content/43177e48-8eaf-11e5-8be4-3506bf20cc2b

17 "Vice Admiral Michelle Howard First African-American Woman to Reach the Rank of Three Star," October 12, 2012. WJLA-TV Washington, www.wjla.com/articles/2012/10/vice-admiral-michelle-howard-first-african-american-woman-to-reach-rank-of-three-star-officer-80588.html

18 "Howard's Path to Navy History," *Navy Times*, January 4, 2014.

19 David Lerman, "Black Woman Named to a Top US Navy Job Says Wimps Fail," Bloomberg News, December 20, 2013. www.bloomberg.com/news/articles/2013-12-20/black-woman-named-to-a-top-u-s-navy-job-says-wimps-fail

20 CDR Salamander: Diversity Thursday, July 27, 2017. http://cdrsalamander.blogspot.com/2017/07/diversity-thursday_27.html

21 Caitlin Dewey, "The Only Guide to GamerGate You Will Ever Need to Read, *Washington Post*, October 10, 2014. www.washingtonpost.com/news/the-intersect/wp/2014/10/14/the-only-guide-to-gamergate-you-will-ever-need-to-read/?utm_term=.8731d63ad655

22 David Panhans et al. "Empowering Women to Work in Cybersecurity," BCG, September 7, 2022.

23 Maya Rhodan, "Sexual Harassment: National Security Women Sign Open Letter," *Time*, December 1, 2017. http://time.com/5039104/we-too-are-survivors-223-women-in-national-security-sign-open-letter-on-sexual-harassment/

24 See Carol Cohn, "How Can She Claim Equal Rights When She Doesn't Have to Do as Many Push-ups as I Do?" *Men and Masculinity*, 3, no. 2, pp. 131–151.

25 Jodi Kanter, "Harvard Business School Case Study: Gender Equality," *New York Times,* September 7, 2013. www.nytimes.com/2013/09/08/education/harvard-case-study-gender-equity.html?pagewanted=all&_r=0

26 Kanter, 2013.

27 David G. Smith, Judith E. Rosenstein, and Margaret C. Nikolov, "The Different Words We Use to Describe Male and Female Leaders," *Harvard Business Review*, May 25, 2018.

28 M. Ena Inesi and Daniel M. Cable, "When Accomplishments Come Back to Haunt You: The Negative Effects of Competence Signals on Women's Performance Evaluations," *Personnel Psychology*, 67, no. 3 (2014).
29 The author was in attendance at that presentation on July 10, 2014. See also: Daniel Oberhaus, "Sexism in Space," *Motherboard*, April 2, 2015. http://motherboard.vice.com/read/sexism-in-space Hastings
30 Joan C. Williams, Katherine W. Phillips, and Erika V. Hall, *Double Jeopardy*, UC Hastings College of Law, 2015. www.uchastings.edu/news/articles/2015/01/double-jeopardy-report.pdf
31 www.huffingtonpost.com/2014/09/24/fox-the-five-sexist-jokes_n_5879358.html. Accessed May 6, 2023.
32 Email correspondence between Joan Johnson-Freese and Lt. Cmdr. Elisabeth Erickson, March 17, 2017.
33 Bruce Kasanoff, "Women: If You're Competent, It's Time to Be Confident," *Forbes*, March 23, 2015. www.forbes.com/sites/brucekasanoff/2015/03/23/women-if-youre-competent-its-time-to-be-confident/
34 Victoria Brescoll and Tyler Okimoto, "The Price of Power: Power Seeking and Backlash against Female Politicians, *Personality and Social Psychology Bulletin*, June 2, 2010.
35 p. 56.
36 K. Lyness, & D. E. Thompson, "Climbing the Corporate Ladder: Do Female and Male Executives Follow the Same Route?" *Journal of Applied Psychology*, 85, no. 1 (2000), p. 101.
37 Katie Zavadski, "Gen. Mike Flynn's Office Told Women to Wear Makeup, Heels, and Skirts," *Daily Beast*, November 18, 2016. www.thedailybeast.com/articles/2016/11/18/gen-mike-flynn-s-office-told-women-to-wear-makeup-heels-and-skirts.html
38 "Rosebeth Moss Kanter," *The Economist*, October 24, 2008. www.economist.com/node/12492049
39 Cristian L. Dezsö, David Gaddis Ross, and Jose Uribe, "Is There an Implicit Quota on Women in Top Management? A Large-Sample Statistical Analysis," *Strategic Management Journal*, November 15, 2015.
40 Olga Khazan, "The Queen Bee in the Corner Office," *The Atlantic*, September 2017, p. 53.
41 *Understanding Bias: A Resource Guide, Community Relations Services Toolkit for Policing*, US Department of Justice. www.justice.gov/crs/file/836431/download
42 Rob Pincheta, "A Trump Tribute Act: Meet Suella Braverman, the Commander in Chief of Britain's Culture Wars, CNN, May 7, 2023. www.cnn.com/2023/05/07/uk/suella-braverman-profile-migration-gbr-intl/index.html
43 Joan Johnson-Freese, *Women vs. Women: The Case for Cooperation*, Routledge, 2022, pp. 72–73.
44 www.secretservice.gov/newsroom/releases/2022/03/secret-services-latest-research-highlights-mass-violence-motived-misogyny. Accessed May 6, 2023.
45 Nelly Njoki et al., *Positive Masculinities Training Guide*, Community Education and Empowerment Center, 2012. http://ceec.or.ke/wp-content/uploads/2017/02/Training-Guide-Positive-Masculinities.pdf

Further reading

Allport, Gordon. *On the Nature of Prejudice*, Addison-Wesley, 25th anniversary edition, 1979.
Criado, Caroline Criado. *Invisible Women*, Harry N. Abrams, 2021.
Diehl, Amy, and Leanne Dzubinski. *Glass Walls*, Rowman and Littlefield, 2023.
Dovido, John, Peter Glick, and Laurie Rudman (eds.). *One the Nature of Prejudice: Fifty Years After Allport*, Wiley-Blackwell, 2005.
Flood, Michael. *Engaging Men and Boys in Violence Prevention*, Palgrave Macmillan, 2019.
Flood, M., O'Donnell, J., Brewin, B., and Myors, B. *Engaging Men: Reducing Resistance and Building Support.* Melbourne: Eastern Health, Eastern Domestic Violence Service (EDVOS), and Queensland University of Technology (QUT), 2021.
Johnson, W. Brad, and David Smith. *Athena Rising: Why Men Should Mentor Women*, Harvard Business Review Press, 2016.
Johnson, W. Brad, and David Smith, *Good Guys: How Men Can Be Better Allies for Women in the Workplace,* Harvard Business Review Press, 2020.

Johnson-Freese, Joan. *Women vs. Women: The Case for Cooperation*, Routledge, 2022.
Kanter, Rosabeth Moss. *Men and Women of the Corporation*, Basic Books, 2nd edition, 1993.
Lesser, Elizabeth. *Cassandra Speaks*, Harper Wave, 2020.
Pipher, Mary. *Reviving Ophelia*, Riverhead Trade, 2005.
Porter, Tony. *Breaking Out of the Man Box*, Skyhorse, 2021.
Stewart, Dianne. *Black Women, Black Love*, Seal Press, 2020.
Traister, Rebecca. *All the Single Ladies*, S&S, 2016.

5   Gender-based violence

The specific inclusion of a "protection" pillar in the Women, Peace, and Security framework evidences the pervasiveness of violence against women. But gender-based violence (GBV) is not limited to women. Over 7,000 Bosnian Muslim men and boys were targeted and killed by Bosnia Serb forces over a two-week period in the July 1995 Srebrenica massacre, carried out because their gender made them potential fighters against the Serb forces. More recently, two boys made allegations in 2023 that ISIS women in a Syrian detention camp were trying to force them and other teenage boys to impregnate dozens of camp women to create more ISIS fighters. Sixteen percent of US male military service members reported sexual assault in 2021. Like all of the Women, Peace, and Security pillars, the protection pillar is relevant to men, women, boys, and girls.

GBV is, however, most widespread among women. Without personal safety, their participation in security discussions and decision-making is severely limited. The threat to the status quo that the inclusion of women presents to those who enjoy the benefits, is evidenced by violence specifically aimed at Women Human Rights Defenders (WHRD).

In Afghanistan, there was a 25 per cent increase in the deliberate killings of women in public roles, including WHRDs, perceived to be rebelling from prevailing gender norms in 2017. As the UN Mission there was renewed, the Security Council voted to remove provisions referencing women's rights and participation. In 2018, the Inter-American Commission on Human Rights reported increased violence towards WHRDs during the armed conflict in Colombia, noting they face "differentiated risks and disproportionate effects based on their gender [...] the rights they defend, their sexual orientation and gender identity". Killings of WHRDs there increased nearly 50 per cent in 2019 compared to the previous year and rose dramatically since the signing of the Peace Accords in 2016.[1]

GBV limits the agency of women and those who identify as women from the micro to the macro level.

There are multiple forms of GBV, including child and forced marriages, female genital mutilation, human trafficking, acid throwing, virginity testing, stoning, forced pregnancy, infanticide, deep fake pornography, incest, and sexual violence. Doxxing and deep fake pornography are among the more recent and increasingly used GBV methods.

Intimate partner violence (IPV) and non-intimate partner violence are the most pervasive and recognized form of sexual violence and together represent a global epidemic. According to the World Bank, an estimated 30% of women worldwide have experienced intimate partner or non-partner sexual violence. IPV is more prevalent in the United States than breast cancer. IPV too

DOI: 10.4324/9781003413417-6

often turns fatal. The UN estimates that in 2020, 47,000 women and girls were killed by their intimate partners or family members. That averages to one killing every 11 minutes. Increases in killings in some regions of the world have been considered Covid-19 stress related.

Estimates of violence against transgender individuals are even higher than against the general population. The US Department of Justice estimates that one in two transgender individuals are sexually abused or assaulted at some point in their lives. Other reports estimate even higher numbers of up to 66%, often coupled with physical assault or abuse. Globally, there were 375 reported deaths of gender-diverse individuals in 2021, most of them in Central and South America (70%), and the most deaths in a single country occurring in Brazil, 33% of the total number. Many of the victims were sex workers or migrants. For the first time as well, cases from Greece, Kazakhstan, and Malawi were reported.[2]

Beyond (and often combined with) sexual violence, women and girls are subjected to other various forms of GBV. Women and girls comprise an estimated 70% of global human trafficking victims. Virginity testing (also known as the "two finger" test) is still performed by doctors, police officers, and community leaders in some 20 countries for reasons including establishing a woman's marriage eligibility or even at the request of potential employers. It is a gynecological inspection of female genitalia carried out under the false belief that such the inspection can determine if a female has had vaginal intercourse.

Forced pregnancy is defined as a female becoming pregnant without having sought or desired it, and abortion is denied, hindered, delayed, or made difficult. Forced pregnancy denies women agency, and in 1998, the International Criminal Court expressly listed it as a crime against humanity and a war crime. The US Supreme Court ruling in *Dobbs v. Jackson Women's Health Organization* (2022) has raised references back to the days when slave owners could control enslaved people's reproduction. Even more indicative of the war against women in the United States is the Heartbeat Protection Act signed by Florida governor Ron DeSantis in April 2023 requiring rape, incest, or human trafficking victims to provide proof of those acts through a police or medical report in order to gain an exception to Florida's abortion ban.

Anti-abortion laws, in effect forced pregnancy laws, have also raised considerable discussion over the national security implications, as it will not be just women who are reluctant to serve in the military for fear of being sent to a state banning abortion under restrictive or all circumstances, but also men with wives and daughters. Women have died from being denied abortions. Further, the UN Office of the High Commissioner for Human Rights has referred to *Dobbs* as a "monumental setback for the rule of law and for gender equality" and denounced the Court for "completely disregarding the United States' binding legal obligations under international law."[3] The United States is now positioned almost in isolation to the rest of the world regarding reproductive rights.

Doxxing is part of GBV in that it often leads to other criminal offenses like harassment, stalking, or sexual violence. The address of a councilwoman in Norman, Oklahoma, was published by the police department after she advocated cutting the police budget. A woman living in the other half of her duplex was raped only days later by an assailant who allegedly made a political threat. Idaho State Representative Priscilla Giddings doxed a teenage female student intern on Facebook and in her newsletter to supporters after the intern reported being raped by Giddings' male colleague. Doxxing is often and increasingly used in connection with women speaking out against sexual abuse and against women politicians.

Women are taking steps to protect themselves, frequently with the help of advocate organizations or through institutional initiatives. Grannies – women, 60, 80, and even up to 100 years old– are learning martial arts in the Korogocho slum area of Nairobi, Kenya. The classes began after the Gender Recovery Center of Nairobi's Women's Hospital reported that a significant number of their sexual assault patients are over 60. Older women often live alone and are seen as easy targets by young men with no jobs, no wives, no prospects, and who spend much of their days drinking, thereby leading to dangerous and careless behavior at night, seeking to assert their power and dominance through violence. The Grannies are taught to protect themselves through a group called Streams for Hope and Peace. The key to deterrence is teaching the women to target vulnerable parts of their attacker's body, to have accuracy, and to yell NO loudly to attract the attention of others.

Women in Egypt created HarassMap in 2010 because street attacks on women were becoming "normal." Using texting and online reports of sexual harassment and assault, HarrassMap workers, often working with other organizations, mobilize volunteers to rescue women being harassed and assaulted by crowds. The extent of the harassment and assault problem in Egypt is evidenced by the practices of the rescuers. Teams of male rescuers wearing special identifying vests and carrying flares and extra clothing to help victims, sometimes must form a human chain around the woman to get her to safety. Some rescuers may carry sticks to deter offenders. The organization works on the principle that if more people start taking action when sexual harassment happens in their presence, the epidemic of harassment and assault can be stopped.

There is something horribly wrong with these situations and many others like them. They reflect the efforts of individuals to live their everyday lives in what is considered "peaceful" areas, under "normal" circumstances. But there is nothing either peaceful or normal about them. The problems experienced by many women are comparable in many ways to the lives of women in conflict zones: unpredictable and dangerous.

When violence becomes "normalized"

Women are not inherently nonviolent. Historically, the Irish Republican Army, the Baader-Meinhof group in Germany, the Italian Red Guard, the Popular Front for the Liberation of Palestine, the Tamil Tigers in Sri Lanka, and more recently Boko Haram in Nigeria have successfully used women as suicide bombers. Women have also been known to resort to violence against other women to protect their position in society. Women have become radicalized for "causes." The first ever all-female ISIS cell was discovered in London in 2018. Motivations for these women becoming killers include being indoctrinated, threatened, and having been brutalized. For centuries, and often going unrecognized, women have also acted as effective combatants. However, systemic and societal violence against an out-group is largely directed "at" rather than "by" women.

Nobel Peace Laureate Mairead Maguire summarized the problem of violence against women:

I think there is a socialization that goes on where violence becomes acceptable. You have to change that and say, "No, that's not acceptable, rape is not acceptable and neither is any form of violence against women. We must not be ambiguous about violence. The greatest war is fought inside our own hearts, a war of anger and resentment and greed. So we start within ourselves and then with our families and our communities."[4]

As long as violence is tolerated, it will shake the foundations of civil societies, which then threatens stability and therefore security. Unfortunately, too, violence is often not just tolerated but also considered "normal."

In 2016, a unanimous US jury convicted 19-year-old Stanford University freshman and potential Olympic swimmer Brock Turner of three counts of sexually assaulting an unconscious woman. The assault occurred behind a dumpster near a fraternity house where both Turner and the 23-year-old victim had been drinking at a party. At trial, Turner said the victim had consented, and blamed the party culture and college risk-taking behavior for his actions. The prosecutors asked for six years in state prison in accordance with the two-year minimum guidelines, but Judge Aaron Persky sentenced Turner to six months in county jail and three years of probation, with Persky stating that a prison sentence would have "a severe impact" and "adverse collateral consequences" on Turner. While public outrage ensued, the leniency of the sentence, it turns out, is not uncommon for male athletes in similar situations.[5]

Turner blaming the college "party culture" implies that alcohol was to blame for his abhorrent behavior. But research regarding the effects of alcohol on sexual assaults at college campuses has found otherwise. Law and ethics professor Martha Nussbaum's book *Citadels of Pride: Sexual Abuse, Accountability and Reconciliation* (2021) examines how sexual harassment and assault stem from pride of ownership and control. While alcohol can exacerbate proclivities in behavior, men who commit sexual assault when drinking alcohol are similar to men who commit sexual assault when sober in most aspects of their personality and attitudes, specifically, hypermasculinity and belief in rigid gender norms have been found most influential.

The Turner case occurred two years after a White House report titled *Rape and Sexual Assault: A Renewed Call to Action* specifically cited campus sexual assault as a problem. While the link between gender inequality, campus rape, violence against women generally, and international relations may seem tenuous, the linkage is in fact direct. When violence becomes acceptable – or even excusable – in a family or a society, it can span the spectrum of societal, intrastate, and international relations. Using data from 1960 to 2001, Mary Caprioli concluded from her research that states characterized by gender inequality are more likely to be involved in intrastate conflict. She noted later, in 2005, that though the literature on intrastate violence largely omitted considerations of gender inequality, "both structural violence and cultural violence are keys to understanding societal levels of violence because they create the fundamental justification for violence."[6] Violence breeds violence as it becomes normalized. Normalization is a process.

Pervasive and systematic exploitation of a group creates an inherently violent environment such as referred to by Caprioli. The environment is characterized by unequal distribution of labor benefits; by exploiter control over the consciousness of the exploited, resulting in their acquiescence; by keeping the exploited separated from one another; and by marginalization of the exploited.[7] Consequently, open, public violence is rarely needed to maintain the structure. However, "it is based on open or implicit violence in the private sphere of the home. Norms of cultural violence diffuse within religion, ideology, language, and art, among other aspects of culture."[8] Norms can be changed, often slowly, as small deviations becoming accepted over time.

Sociologist Diane Vaughn's book *The Challenger Launch Decision* (1996) examined the decision-making behind launching the space shuttle *Challenger*. On a frigid Florida day almost certain to push the rubber O-ring seals between rocket booster segments beyond their limits, decisions were made that resulted in tragedy. In that book, she coined the phrase "normalization of deviance" to describe a cultural drift where circumstances formerly classified as "not OK" are slowly reclassified as "OK." Once a slight deviation from the acceptable norm for launch conditions was made, the deviation became the new norm, susceptible to slipping ever further from the original standard.

Normalization refers to social or cultural processes by which ideas and even actions come to be seen as "normal," taken-for-granted, or "natural" in the home and everyday life. With normalization, behavior modeling can become based on inappropriate norms. Australian researchers have studied the influence of pornography on sexual behavior in relationships. They found first that pornography has become more violent over recent years, often including the abusive treatment of women. Additionally, since pornography is often a male's first experience with sex, behavior in pornography is sometimes assumed to show what is "normal." Researcher Maree Crabbe states, "Pornography is now our most prominent sex educator" and modeling sexual relations on pornography has led to "costly experiences" for men and their partners.[9]

Through both patriarchal attitudes and objectification, violence against women has become not just normalized but also regularized as a social norm that is widely adopted by society. Further, social regularities are not just what people do, but what society holds they *should* do, resulting in members of society feeling obliged to conform to the norm social regularities create, or risk sanction from other members of society. Sadly, violence against women and its prerequisite attitude of gender superiority is a social norm, with three interrelated factors said to play key roles in "training" individuals to become more violent toward women: modeling, immediate reinforcement, and male-bonded groups.

Modeling is first and most prominently done in homes, since relationships in homes are considered as the first political order, through children parroting parental actions. Children learn acceptable behavior within their families and from role models. "John Stuart Mill argued that the tyrant at home becomes the tyrant in the state and the tyrant at war with other nations."[10]

Actress Merle Streep expressed concern in a 2017 award speech about President Trump's mocking of a disabled reporter, serving as a negative model to others. The same year, the *New York Times* surveyed 615 men about how they conduct themselves at work. Men in blue-collar jobs, those who were white or Republican, and those who described a feeling of resent-ment or being unappreciated at work were more likely to acknowledge harassing behavior. Of those, 68% strongly or somewhat approved of the job Trump was doing as president. Individuals in leadership positions are important in conveying what is acceptable behavior.

Immediate reinforcement refers to the fulfillment of emotional or physical needs, such as exerting power, physical gratification, even material gain. The pull toward giving in to imme-diate reinforcement temptations is especially heightened when the chances of punishment are considered low, as is often the case with acts of violence or subjugation against women. Immediate reinforcement can also refer to gratification through acceptance and approval of peers. Male bonding then links various types of gratification.

Male bonding refers to the previously referenced findings within evolutionary biology that men bond more closely with men, than women do with women. Several considerations flow from that finding. First, competition within groups will lead to in-group aggression, and even more certainly to out-group aggression. Women comprise the largest out-group, with strata among them through intersectionality. Also, while men learn primarily from the behavior and peer requirements of other men, as previously pointed out, even when women associate with other women, their allegiance can be linked primarily to the male heads of their households and male beliefs. Women learn from experience and from other women that men's beliefs are para-mount. They have traditionally done so because, according to Petersen and Wrangham, they have sought protection for themselves and their children.

Because war has been considered an inherently "male" activity, the intensification of male-bonded groups – male in-groups fighting male out-groups – is heightened. There are comrades and there is the enemy, and an often life or death battle between them. Individuals learn from their comrades, and are subject to peer pressure from their comrades. Modeling occurs within hypermasculinized environments during conflicts, including overt efforts to strip away all aspects of feminization. One way to do that is to demonstrate control over females, through sexual violence. Thousands of Korean comfort women were pressed into sexual slavery to sat-isfy the sexual demands of Japanese troops during World War II, while also serving a political purpose of "shaming" the Korean men who had been unable to defend the women.

Only rarely have individuals been held responsible for the rape or sexual slavery of women during conflicts. An international tribunal estimated that Japanese soldiers raped some 20,000 Chinese women in Nanjing in 1937, during the second Sino-Japanese war. While Imperial Japanese Army leaders were not prosecuted for establishing the institution of military sexual slaves (the Korean comfort women), trial proceedings did reference the "Rape of Nanjing." Two Japanese officials were convicted of failing to prevent rape.[11]

During World War II, there were numerous accounts of Russian soldiers raping German women, and of German soldiers raping Russian women. Along with death in concentration camps, incidents of rape and sadism against Jewish women were perpetrated during World War II. Nazi doctors simulated numerous types of battle wounds for study at the Ravensbrück concentration camp, often specifically choosing attractive women to mutilate. Yet rape was not listed as a "crime against humanity" in the Nuremburg Trials (1945).

The Foča Rape case, decided in 2002 by the International Criminal Tribunal in favor of the former Yugoslavia, marked the first time that anyone was convicted of rape as a crime against humanity, the most serious category of international crime after genocide. There, three Serbian defendants were each found guilty of acts of rape, torture, and enslavement of non-Serbian women between 1992 and 1993 during the Bosnian conflict, and sentenced to a total of 60 years in prison. Unfortunately, however, that conviction has not stopped or even largely deterred the crime. Impunity remains the norm.

The International Criminal Court (ICC) sentenced former Congolese vice president Jean-Pierre Bemba to 18 years in prison in 2016. In an unprecedented ruling, Bemba was held responsible for the actions perpetrated by his subordinates involved in a 2002–2003 campaign of rape and murder in the neighboring Central African Republic. His case was the first to focus on rape as a weapon of war by the ICC. He was convicted on two counts of crimes against humanity and three counts of war crimes. Though it was hoped that the Bemba conviction would signal an end to impunity, on appeal in 2018 the ICC acquitted Bemba of his crimes based on a legal technicality.[12]

During Guatemala's 36-year internal military conflict that ended in 1996, Indigenous Mayan women were targeted for sexual violence. In February 2016, a Guatemalan court sentenced two former military members to 360 years in jail for murder, rape, and sexual enslavement of women. It was the first successful prosecution for sexual violence committed during the violent 1980s. Testimony was heard during the trial about rape being used as a tool of war, intended to pollute and thus dilute the Mayan population. Jubilant Indigenous women celebrated the court ruling, though most with their faces covered in fear of retribution for speaking out and fighting for their legal rights.

For too long and too often, rape has been

mischaracterized and dismissed by military and political leaders – those in a position to stop it – as a private crime, a sexual act, the ignoble conduct of one occasional soldier, or, worse still, it has been accepted precisely because it is so commonplace.[13]

The omission of rape as a crime against humanity at Nuremberg gave way to subsequent military excuses, such as rape being characterized as "regrettable excess" in Peru in the 1980s.

The concept of a social contagion, raised in Chapter 1, referring to the spread of behaviors and attitudes through group conformity, is directly related to the normalization of violence. Violence can become expected social behavior. The expression "rule of thumb" comes from the group expectation that it is acceptable to beat a woman as long as the stick used is no thicker than a thumb. Considerations of how to counter social contagions stem largely from social psychology research regarding rewards and punishment. A reward is useful to increase the probability or rate of a behavior when the event is contingent on the behavior. Rewards reinforce behavior. As researchers such as B. F. Skinner have shown, though, punishment is a consequence that decreases the probability of a behavior. Therefore, when a negative social contagion such as GBV is being considered, rewards are not enough to stop it; punishment must be involved as well. Bad behaviors have to be called out and individuals held accountable.

The breadth and depth of violence

As sad as statistics regarding incidents of abuse are, the statistics about low prosecution rates, light sentencing, and acceptance by women that violence is their lot in life are even more so. When violence against women (and children) is accepted, the step toward accepting violence as the primary method of solving disputes – including state security – becomes easier. Violence has become normalized, accepted by society and individuals, including women.

A 2005 Amnesty International report on domestic violence in Russia began by chronicling Anna, a Russian domestic abuse victim. When Anna filed divorce papers, the violence increased. More than once, her husband tried to set her on fire, and attacked her with a pike and a knife. Police largely dismissed her cries for help. Eventually, Anna's husband was charged with attempted murder. After considering the years of abuse, the judge finally sentenced Anna's husband to one year in jail. None of Anna's story is all that unusual, regardless of where it geographically occurs. The striking part of Anna's story is the family and societal attitudes involved:

> Anna's husband continues to receive a lot of sympathy from others. His sister reportedly told her, "He has such a difficult life, he does not have work and he is an alcoholic, but you – you are an active woman, you have work and continue your studies. You need to take better care of him, so that everything will be as it used to."
>
> Anna says that other victims of violence in the family told her: "That is our fate. If he is aggressive, you should just go shopping until he calms down." She said: "Women, including female judges, do not show solidarity. They consider I should solve my problems myself. Four times in 2004 the police and judges of the peace refused to open a criminal case."[14]

Being abused was considered Anna's "fate."

Some Russian writers attribute Russian attitudes toward domestic violence to the so-called *Domostroi*, a manual written by an unknown Russian author in the sixteenth century on how to discipline family members and servants. It affirmed the right of husbands to beat their wives. Western societies provided similar guidance through axioms like "spare the rod and spoil the child" and "wives and bells must be struck regularly."

American educator and trauma specialist Marilyn Murray lived and worked in Russia for ten years. She recalled conversations she had with Russian men and women when she was a guest on a Russian radio talk show:

> "But to be Russian is to be violent. You can't be a Russian man and not have the freedom to be violent."
>
> "Aggression is normal here in Russia. Being aggressive is who we are."
>
> "We understand that Russia is a violent place, and we just have to learn how to adapt to it. And that means we have to learn how to protect ourselves and be violent too."[15]

High rates of alcoholism exacerbate domestic violence rates in Russia as well, aggravating already existing cultural propensities toward gender stereotypes that link to violence.

There is little indication that the domestic violence situation in Russia will positively change in the near future; indeed, it continues to worsen as strongman President Vladimir Putin's tenure goes on. Ultra-conservative Russian senator Yelena Mizulina successfully lobbied for Russia's 2012 "gay propaganda" law and spearheaded efforts to decriminalize domestic violence in 2016. "Battery carried out toward family members should be an administrative offence," said Mizulina, "You don't want people to be imprisoned for two years and labeled a criminal for the rest of their lives for a slap."[16] As Russia becomes increasingly authoritarian, it appears to be returning to its conservative roots, sometimes with the help of women politicians. It is interesting to note, though, that a group of Russian feminists called the Feminist Anti-War Resistance was instrumental in helping Russian men leave the country to avoid conscription during the first days of the unprovoked Russian invasion of Ukraine.

Russia is by no means alone among countries in its domestic abuse problems, though comparisons are often difficult to make. Studies have pointed out difficulties with comparing rape statistics among just European countries because of differing definitions and operationalization of legal terms, resulting in some countries having more reported rapes than others and other countries having lower levels of detected rapes than others. Sweden's laws and statistical recording practices, for example, tend to drive reported rape statistics up, and the rate of detected rape cases down, "detected" being one of the terms with multiple operationalizations among countries. In some countries, "detected" refers to whether or not a suspect could be identified, in others it refers to whether or not the case was disposed of through the courts or withdrawn by complainants.

Attitudes within Europe regarding sexual assault and rape have evidenced considerable and increasing misogynism. According to a 2016 European Union survey of almost 30,000 individuals, 27% of European respondents said that rape might be justified in some circumstances – up to 55% in some countries. These circumstances included being drunk, women walking alone at night, and women not clearly saying no or fighting back. In 2017, an Italian judge dismissed a sexual assault case because the rape victim "didn't scream" during the attack. The woman said only, "Stop it" and "Enough" without crying out or calling for help. A 2022 study considered reasons behind the rise of sexism among European Union countries and found that young men, not members of older generations, were most likely to perceive advances in women's rights as a threat to men's opportunities. This was found especially true for young men who resided in regions with recent increases in unemployment, resulting in increased competition for jobs, and those who considered public institutions in their areas as biased against them.[17]

In the United States, if a woman is raped, becomes pregnant as a result of the violent act, and subsequently decides to keep her baby, state law determines the visitation and parental rights of the rapist. Rape victims are sometimes forced to co-parent with their attacker:

> In making the decision to keep their babies, however, these victim mothers face the possibility of psychologically painful and damaging prolonged contact with their rapists. In most states, rapist fathers enjoy the same parental rights as any other biological parent. The existence of these parental rights means that the rapist father may seek physical custody, legal custody, or visitation with the child. If granted any of these rights, he is subsequently able to assert a significant level of control over the victim mother's life through his control over the child's life and upbringing.[18]

In a very real sense, the woman's assault becomes chronic.

Research has examined why young women do not report instances of sexual harassment and abuse. The term "heteronormative" refers to a worldview promoting heterosexuality as the normal, or preferred sexual orientation, and sees sexual orientation as binary.

Young people are socialized into a patriarchal culture that normalizes and often encourages male power and aggression, particularly within the context of heterosexual relationships. As men's heterosexual violence is viewed as customary, so too is women's endurance of it [...] These discourses shape embodied experiences normalizing the presumption that men's sexual aggression is simply "boys being boys" [...] Girls are thus expected to endure aggression by men because that is *part* of man.[19]

Unhealthy attitudes are established early by both sexes.

Violence against women is an issue from a human rights perspective. But it is also an issue from a national security perspective. Gender equality, power politics, and state security can no longer be considered separate spheres. Examples of culturally accepted violence against women illustrate the pervasiveness and effects of GBV.

Female genital mutilation

Female genital mutilation, or cutting (FGM/C), is practiced as part of patrilineal societal norms and the deep entrenchment of gender inequality. In practicing societies, men and women support FGM, and anyone who dares go against the norm could face condemnation, harassment, and ostracism. It is an extreme form of discrimination against women. But it is difficult for individuals or even families to abandon the practice as all could face negative consequences. Consequently, most often it is the women in the family who push the continuance of the practice, and carry it out. Wider community support is necessary to change the community norm.

The number of women who have been subjected to FGM/C is unknown. According to the World Health Organization, the practice refers to all procedures involving partial or total removal of the female external genitalia or other injury to the female genital organs for non-medical reasons. It is estimated that at least 200 million girls and women have been cut in some 30 African and Middle East countries. However, women frequently are reluctant to admit to involvement, making underreporting a serious issue. FGM/C is also practiced in certain Asian ethnic groups and communities in South America. It is even practiced in diaspora groups in Australia, Europe, the United States, Canada, and the United Kingdom. According the British government, an estimated 137,000 girls in the United Kingdom have undergone FGM/C and some 60,000 girls under 15 are at risk there.

Terminology matters. Some individuals working with individuals who support FGM/C encountered resentment at the "mutilation" terminology used by outsiders; as supporters see it as "value loaded" to convey disgust. Consequently, "cutting" is sometimes the preferred terminology. FGM is used on all United Nations documents referencing the practice, as it is considered a violation of human rights. The term "female circumcision" has also been used, though it has drawn criticism from the health community because male circumcision and female cutting are not comparable. Female cutting is not a health-related practice, as circumcision is. Men in Eastern and Southern Africa are encouraged to be circumcised to reduce the risk of human immunodeficiency virus (HIV) transmission, while FGM/C can increase the risk of HIV transmission in women. The term "female genital surgery" is also sometimes used, although these procedures are often far from anything a medical practitioner would consider surgical. According to the United Nations Population Fund,

FGM is carried out with special knives, scissors, scalpels, pieces of glass or razor blades. Anesthetic and antiseptics are generally not used unless medical practitioners carry out the procedure. In communities where infibulation is practiced, girls' legs are often bound together to immobilize them for 10–14 days, allowing for the formation of scar tissue.[20]

In some instances, women appear to embrace the custom as a rite of passage. Anthropology professor Bettina Shell-Duncan has studied FGM/C in a number of countries, including among the nomadic Rendille ethnic group in eastern Kenya. Among the Rendille, circumcision is part of wedding ceremonies, which are drawn out over several years. The first part of the ceremony, where the bride is transferred to the groom, includes FGM. When a Rendille woman marries, she goes to live with the husband's family, as is the case in most patrilineal cultures. It is therefore important that she become part of the female network of her husband's kin, all of whom are circumcised. Consequently, FGM becomes part of demarcating insider and outsider status. Being part of the group of elder women who have power in their society requires women to "prove themselves" to one another through circumcision.

There are no health benefits to any levels of the FGM/C processes, only potential harm. There are immediate risks of hemorrhaging, shock, tetanus, wound infection, and septicemia. Long-term risks include menstrual and bladder disorders, complications with childbirth, cyst formation, and an increased risk of HIV transmission. Though for many years it was believed that an education campaign to spread knowledge of the health risks among women would curtail the practice, that has been proven wrong. Women often recognized the health risks involved, but felt the societal benefits outweighed the risks. Therefore, a better understanding of the nature of support behind FGM/C, and how to address and curtail the practice is needed. The timing of "cutting" often correlates to motivations, generally categorized as: religious; psychosexual; sociological and cultural; hygienic or aesthetic; and socioeconomic, with overlap between the categories.

FGM/C is sometimes intended to control a woman's sexuality. Though neither Islam nor Christianity requires or sanctions FGM/C, both closely value virginity and modesty. In certain Muslim groups, strict cleanliness is expected before praying to Allah, with circumcision considered part of cleanliness. In some cultures, uncircumcised women are considered impure, and assumed promiscuous. Female sexual desire is depicted as negative and so circumcision saves her from temptation. In the Rendille culture, however, both men and women are sexually active before marriage, so circumcision is more sociological and cultural. However, Rendille women were repulsed by the idea of an uncircumcised woman delivering a baby. Crossing most if not all of the motivational categories for FGM/C are families concerned that if their daughters are not circumcised, they will not be considered marriageable material, a key socioeconomic goal.

There is evidence of a generational change in attitude among some young women, with an increasing number favoring abolishment of the practice, though with significant variance among cultures and countries. While some governments have passed legislation prohibiting the practice, these laws must be accompanied by culturally sensitive education and public awareness, to have a lasting positive impact. Communities that have employed a collective decision-making process have been most successful in abandoning the practice, as it removes the onus of abandoning cultural norms from individuals. Targeting individual mothers has little affect, as they are vulnerable to community pressures.

The role of the medical community in abating FGM/C practices is precarious. In West Africa, some women began going to healthcare providers to have their or their daughters' procedure performed, to make it safer, but certain places banned it from being done in healthcare facilities. Nurses would sometimes take annual leave to return to their villages and perform procedures. Doctors who performed procedures were caught between trying to prevent short-term complications and perhaps sanctioning a harmful practice.

Physicians attending to diaspora communities have been drawn into the ethical quandary as well. Beginning in 1996, for example, doctors at a Seattle hospital agreed to offer its female

Somali patient population a ritual genital "nick," calling it "female genitalia alteration." They reasoned that unless they agreed to this option, girls would be taken back to Somalia for a far more extensive procedure in less hygienic surroundings. Other physicians objected to that approach, based on medical, ethical, and procedural considerations.

Eliminating FGM/C is not something that can be done distinct from the empowerment of women, as FGM/C is one of many tools that deliberately keep women subservient. In research conducted in Egypt, a correlation was found between education and women's attitudes toward FGM/C. The more educated a woman, the less she favored FGM/C. Similarly, research regarding men's attitudes about abandonment of FGM/C practices has also found a correlation between education and attitudes toward abandoning FGM/C. FGM/C is not the only culturally accepted practice of violence against women.

Acid attacks

When acid is thrown on a person's face, the eyelids and lips may burn off completely. The nose may melt, closing the nostrils, and the ears shrivel up. Skin and bone on the skull, forehead, cheeks and chin may dissolve. When the acid splashes or drips over the neck, chest, back, arms or legs, it burns every inch of the skin it touches.

When the wounds from an acid burn heal, they form thick scars that pull the skin tight and cause disfigurement. In 90 percent of cases, the eyesight of the victim is adversely affected, causing blindness. And then there is the psychological trauma. With a high survival rate among victims, acid attacks are rarely carried out with murder in mind. They are intended to disfigure and mutilate – to condemn the victim to a lifetime of suffering.[21]

An acid attack involves throwing, spraying, or pouring a corrosive substance on a person, usually their face, and is intended to maim, disfigure, blind, torture, or kill that person. It is very personal, unlike a bomb or even a gunshot. Women are most often the victims of acid attacks (also called acid throwing or vitriolage) perpetrated by men. Most often, the weapon of choice is sulfuric acid, used in car batteries and so easily obtainable from cars and garages. Traditionally, disputes over issues like dowries and bride prices trigger this form of violence as retribution against women, with the intent behind the atrocity being to destroy the merchandise. But "the merchandise" is a human being, and a woman's beauty often determines her "value" on the marriage market. Attacks can also be brought on as retribution – and warnings to others – when women dare to spurn suitors, seek divorce, anger powerful community leaders, or transgress from their socially prescribed roles by undertaking independent decision-making. Perpetrators of acid violence are particularly sadistic and malicious as their intent extends beyond lifelong physical damage, to deliberate imposition of the ostracism, severe psychological issues, and economic dependency survivors regularly suffer.

Acid attacks are most prevalent in South Asian countries. Beyond the traditional reasons just cited, acid attacks in countries like Bangladesh have more recently been linked to the forces of globalization. Garment industries that have moved there tend to hire women rather than men because they can pay women less. That can disrupt patriarchal family structures by making men financially dependent on women, thereby triggering issues of shame and subsequently violence.

Women sometimes also perpetrate acid throwing against other women. In societies where women are socially and economically insecure without a male provider, a woman may attack another woman she considers a competitor for her husband or partner, to break up the relationship. By disfiguring the victim, the perpetrator intends to secure her own position. Even when driven by more personal motives, such as jealousy or vengeance, the perpetrator's knowledge that punishment is unlikely, perpetuates the practice.

The reporting situation regarding acid attacks must be viewed from a wider socioeconomic context. Most victims are poor, often illiterate, and live in areas where access to basic human needs like clean water is sporadic, let alone advanced medical care or any type of justice system. An example from Pakistan is illustrative:

> More than half of all acid crimes arise in South Punjab, an agricultural area commonly referred to as the "cotton belt," historically marred by low socioeconomic indicators and where acid is readily available in local markets and often used to clean cotton. The psychology of feudalism, institutionalization of patriarchy, and religious distortion arising from growing fundamentalism produces wide disparities among populations and general indifference to issues concerning vulnerable groups. Gender-based violence and crimes against weaker populations have gained little political interest among powerful elites.[22]

Without controlling access to acid, acid attacks being made a crime by the state, and punishment being enforced – the three consistently enabling factors behind acid attacks – acid crimes will continue and likely rise.

Regarding data, before 2013, acid attacks in India were classified under the category of a "grievous harm." That made it impossible to determine the number of acid attacks reported, let alone how many attacks had actually occurred. However, in 2012 Indian public attention to acid crimes, and other gender-targeted crimes, rose after the fatal gang rape of a young Indian woman on a bus. Subsequently, in 2013 acid attacks became a specific crime for reporting purposes. Nevertheless, statistics on acid attacks widely vary.

If victims have access to medical care, upward of 15–20 surgeries can be required for just functional rather than cosmetic repair. While some countries have legislated compensation for victims, victims say it is an insufficient amount to cover the extensive medical care needed. Many survivors are forced to live out their lives in shelters, shunned by their families and ostracized by society.

Hanifa Nakiryowa had not even heard of acid throwing until it happened to her when she tried to leave her abusive husband in Uganda. No one was ever held accountable for her vicious, disfiguring attack. She lost an eye and underwent many surgeries, eventually coming to the United States with her children, where she pursued graduate education and became an advocate for other survivors. She founded the Kampala-based Center for Rehabilitation of Survivors of Acid and Burns Violence and has become a symbol of hope and inspiration for others, her beauty shining through her disfigurement, inspiring the depiction on the cover of this book. It is hoped that survivor stories like Hanifa's will raise awareness regarding the issue, and force governments to address the enabling factors behind acid attacks. Filmmakers Sharmeen Obaid-Chinoy and Daniel Junge chronicled two Pakistani survivors' struggle for justice and healing in their 2012 Oscar-winning film *Saving Face*, which pushed the Pakistani government to make changes in laws against acid throwing perpetrators.

Honor killing

In August 2015, a 22-second video of 25-year-old Pakistani Qandeel Baloch posted on Facebook went viral. Wearing large sunglasses and standing in front of a middle-aged man, she flirted with the camera, "How I'm looking? Tell me how I'm looking." Then she answered herself, "Extraordinary." The video made her famous as a social media star – referred to as Pakistan's

Kim Kardashian – and it was the first of many provocative videos to follow. She supported her extended family from her social media- and modeling-generated earnings. In August 2016, Qandeel's brother, Waseem Zaeem, killed her. He then turned himself into the police, proudly admitting to having drugged and strangled her. "Girls are born only to stay at home and to bring honor to the family by following family traditions, but Qandeel had never done that," Waseem said in a press conference that followed his confession.[23] Qandeel's mother later said Waseem had killed her after being taunted by his friends.

A "cultural defense" is often offered by honor killing perpetrators.

In many countries, honor killings are cultural practices that members of the society do not readily question; they become part of the "rules of the game," in other words, a social norm [...] Moreover "norms constrain an individual's behavior, but not through the centralized enforcement of a state. If they constrain, they do so because of the enforcement of the community." In some instances an honor killing might be motivated simply because a woman believes, or is perceived to believe, in values that are in conflict with the norms of her culture.

Once the family decides, rightly or wrongly, that an assault on the family's honor has occurred, shame and humiliation cry out for revenge. This revenge can only transpire through the death of the female family member who has violated the prevailing moral norms. "Her male relatives cannot walk in the village with heads high. To reclaim their manhood in the eyes of other men, they cleanse their honor by stabbing or sometimes stoning her [to death]." However horrendous cultural outsiders may view this to be, adherents to the practice of honor killings believe this form of violence is a "family problem" or a "domestic situation."[24]

Through the eyes of her brother, Qadeel Baloch had violated societal norms, and societal norms as he saw them then expected – indeed demanded – that he take steps to reinstate his family honor through revenge. He was restoring societal order by reminding women of "their place."

Obaid-Chinoy addressed the issue of honor killings in her 2015 Oscar-winning film *A Girl in the River: The Price of Forgiveness.* The film chronicles the story of Saba, a 19-year-old Pakistani woman shot, dumped in a river, and left for dead by her father and uncle for eloping with a man her family considered of an inferior class. Saba survived the shooting, but her trials were not over. The law in Pakistan allows "honor" murderers and attackers to go free if forgiven by the victim's family, or in her case, Saba herself. The pressure she faced from her family to "forgive" her attackers was enormous, and eventually she did so. Saba's "justice" came through the making of the film, which her in-laws supported. Finding a survivor allowed Obaid-Chinoy to make her film, but there are not many such survivors. Sadly as well, many honor killing victims are brutally tortured before they are killed.

An estimated 5,000 honor killings are committed each year, primarily in India, Pakistan, Afghanistan, and Arab countries. However, that number is considered a gross underestimation by many organizations and researchers due to non-reporting by victims or because honor crimes are considered domestic rather than criminal issues where they are committed. Honor killings have also spread to diaspora communities. While awareness of the issue is growing, so too is the conservativism that culturally endorses or at the very least, legally overlooks or minimizes honor-related crime.

Legislation and enforcement are the structural requirements of change that are needed to stop honor killings. The even more difficult requirements are cultural/societal. That women are sometimes perpetrators or accomplices in honor-related crimes evidences the complicated nature of the issue. The most often cited motivation was that the victim was considered by the female perpetrator as having become "too Westernized."

It will take men and women working together to end honor-crimes. In her acceptance speech for her *A Girl in the River* Oscar, Obaid-Chinoy thanked all those who had helped her make the film, including "the men who champion women," and pointed out the power of men and women working together toward changing both structural and societal/cultural impediments to gender equality. "This is what happens when determined women get together," Obaid-Chinoy said. "This week the Pakistani Prime Minister has said that he will change the law on honor killing after watching this film. That is the power of film."[25] Enculturation can be positive as well as negative.

Sex trafficking

Sex trafficking is a sub-category of human trafficking. Human trafficking of men and women includes involuntary servitude, peonage, debt bondage or slavery, including child soldiers, expunging ancestral debts and domestic servitude. Further, a victim does not have to be physically transported from one location to another for a trafficking crime to occur. Individuals are lured, tricked, trapped and otherwise coerced into sex trafficking in many ways, with traffickers targeting them for value and vulnerability, and then traded like a barrel of oil. The Islamic State of Iraq and Syria (ISIS) published a sex slave price list, with boys and girls under 9 drawing the highest price.[26] Members of the LGBTQ+ communities can be particularly vulnerable to falling prey to sex traffickers as they represent a disproportionate share of the runaways and homeless youth population.

There is a significant difference between sex trafficking and other forms of GBV. The motivation behind sex trafficking is money, making the economics of sex trafficking important to understand.

> These sex slaves are forced to service hundreds, often thousands of men before they are discarded, forming the backbone of one of the most profitable illicit enterprises in the world. Drug trafficking creates greater dollar revenues but trafficked women are far more profitable. Unlike a drug, a human female does not have to be grown, cultivated, distilled or packaged. Unlike a drug, a human female can be used by a customer again and again.[27]

Women and children are high return-on-investment commodities. They are provided as a "pull" factor for tourism in places like Southeast Asia. They are brought in to be available to workers in extractive industries like mining in Colombia, Peru and Senegal just as food and housing are brought in. They are brought to areas near military camps around the world.

The violence involved with sex trafficking goes beyond the horrific sexual exploitation of being raped multiple times daily. Victims are controlled with drugs, some are whipped, burned with cigarettes, suffer broken bones, and starved. Psychological threats to their families are employed as well. The brutalities they suffer are perverse and brutal.

Researchers have found that violence, self-harm and suicide are common among sex trafficking victims. According to Ligia Kiss, a lecturer at the London School of Hygiene and Tropical Medicine: "Staff of post-trafficking services often don't feel equipped to deal with mental health problems, especially with situations involving suicidal intent and alcoholism."[28] Sex trafficking victims are also susceptible to physical ailments including HIV/AIDS, vaginal/anal tearing, and rectal trauma, as well as tuberculosis, hepatitis, malaria and pneumonia due to unsanitary and dangerous living conditions.[29]

Even defining sex trafficking and child sex trafficking is difficult. Definitions must be carefully crafted toward closing as many of the legal loopholes as possible that trafficking perpetrators might attempt to employ, often focusing on force, fraud, coercion, or any combination of such means as critical elements of trafficking. Otherwise, perpetrators claim that individuals are voluntary sex workers. Sex trafficking is an umbrella term that may include commercial sex work such as involuntary prostitution, pornography, exotic dancing, stripping, live sex shows, mail-order brides, military prostitution, and sexual tourism. By the US DOS definitions, for example, if coercion of any type is involved, sexual acts are considered exploitive. Because of the extremely lucrative nature of the sex trafficking business, perpetrators often have considerable resources available to fight legal charges against them. Sex trafficking is estimated to generate upward of $150 billion annually.

SHE'S CRAZY

Women's underreporting of GBV is a serious problem, often over fears of "victim blaming" all too familiar to women. One particularly insidious method of victim blaming is dismissing women as simply unbalanced – crazy. Troublesome women, usually wives, were shipped off to insane asylums in the 1800's if they refused to be bow to their husbands' authority. These uppity women were subsequently subjugated through imprisonment in mental hospitals, where they were forcibly sedated with medications and "treated" by electroshock therapy. Between 1907 and 1963 over 64,000 (mostly minority) individuals in the United States were forcibly sterilized for reasons including (alleged) mental disabilities. Similarly, female genital mutilation was also committed in the United States until the 1960s to control women's "hysteria" and sexuality. Many of those women had merely dared use their voices to stand up for themselves or challenge the status quo. Calling women crazy – the hysterical woman trope – has long been a tactic to silence women, including subsequent to their allegations of gender-based violence.

Former Republican Senator Martha McSally graduated from the Air Force Academy and served in the US Air Force from 1988 until 2010, retiring at the rank of colonel. She was the first American woman to fly in combat and the first to command a fighter squadron. Fighter pilots sit at the top of the food chain in the Air Force.

Her willingness to take on a fight was evidenced in her successful law suit against the DOD in 2001 (*McSally v. Rumsfeld*), challenging the military policy requiring American (and British) servicewomen stationed in Saudi Arabia to wear a body-covering abaya cloak when leaving their base. McSally took on the system. Women are increasingly willing to do so once they have achieved a position with some power. Earlier in her life and career, however, McSally acquiesced to the system and kept quiet about being raped, as many women do.

In March 2019 while a Senator, McSally admitted at a Congressional subcommittee hearing on sexual assault in the military that during her Air Force career she had been raped by a male superior officer but did not report it. Like many women in the military, McSally said she didn't report it because she felt powerless. "I blamed myself. I was ashamed and confused. I thought I was strong but felt powerless,"[30] she said. Like many others as well, McSally learned "to mask all vulnerability in order to survive an aggressively masculine military culture in which women were barely seen as equals, let alone capable of leading."[31] Yet the month before her testimony, McSally had declined to support a bill brought forth on behalf of other military rape victims, to shift decisions about sexual-assault prosecutions from military commanders to military lawyers experienced in sexual-assault investigations. While McSally agreed that in many instances commanders had not fulfilled their responsibilities in pursuing sexual assault investigations and cases, as a former commander herself she still supported matters being left to them, though offered no plan for holding them accountable. McSally's unwillingness to support the efforts of her gender cohort was perhaps in part because she identified more with her military cohort. It is not uncommon for women who are made to feel powerless to identify with their abusers when the abusers offer a cloak of safety.

Just a few months later in July 2019, McSally declared US Army Col. Kathryn Spletstoser's allegations of sexual assault against Air Force Gen. John Hyten to be "false," in a Senate hearing on Hyten's promotion to the second highest position in the military. Spletstoser sat just a few feet away from her. McSally's statement was unequivocal. "Sexual assault happens in the military. It just didn't happen in this case," she added. "I pray the accuser gets the help she needs and finds the peace she is searching for. But it cannot be by destroying Gen. Hyten with false allegations…I didn't take coming to this conclusion lightly. I knew the message it could send to sexual assault survivors who haven't seen all the information on the case that I have," she said. "I will continue to fight to ensure the best possible outcomes and to fight for real victims."[32] Spletstoser would ultimately condemn the hearing as "political spectacle."[33]

Spletstoser had served on Hyten's staff and had glowing fitness reviews in her military file, including from Gen. Hyten himself. In 2017 he had rated her as in the top 1% of all colonels he had seen in his 36 years of service and that "Kathy will be the kind of general officer the Army needs, ready today for brigadier general, unlimited potential to lead."[34] Less than a year later, an Army investigation called Spletstoser, "an unstable and irrational person who was headstrong and thought she knew best."[35]

McSally would later also say she was sexually abused in high school by a sports coach, though she didn't tell anyone about it for a decade. McSally said, "At the time, I was so afraid. I now understand—like many girls and boys who are abused by people in authority over them—there's a lot of fear and manipulation and shame." The man identified as her coach denied the allegations and responded. "I believe she's nuts," he said. "That girl is the most scheming woman I ever met."[36]

Two women who had risen to the highest ranks in the military were both written off as unstable. The "he said, she said" accusations of sexual abuse such as in the testimonies McSally, Spletstoser – and of Anita Hill and Dr. Christine Blasey Ford, both of whom also have been referenced by critics and accusers as "unstable" – are often doubted when there is no physical or conclusive evidence. The waters are muddied with "he said, she said" questions, echoing the old asylum tactics. Gaslighting, manipulation where someone tries to get an individual to doubt their own perception of reality, is used as a means of casting doubt over victim's eyewitness accounts. That leaves the woman's character and words vulnerable to attack and their voices diminished by labeling them as crazy. Women being labeled as crazy – even diagnosed as such by the medical profession – happens all too often.

Women, for example, are diagnosed with borderline personality disorder (BPD) three times as often as men in both the general population and in the US military, many of those women also sexual assault victims. Understanding the gravity of the diagnosis is important in shining light on the problem of minimizing the validity of or dismissing victims' reports altogether. Clinicians are beginning to consider whether gender bias plays into the overrepresentation of women in these diagnoses because of the pejorative stigma attached to it.

Women diagnosed with BPD are often characterized as manipulative, needy, seductive, fearful of being rejected and willing to go to great ends to avoid rejection. The 1987 film *Fatal Attraction* is considered a classic portrayal of that characterization and is an example of encul- turation of a stereotype. More recently, that is how actor Johnny Depp's paid expert witness portrayed Depp's ex-wife Amber Heard in his 2022 court testimony, "diagnosing" Heard with BPD after two meetings with her.

However, research suggests that it is men diagnosed with BPD who tend to present with an explosive temperament, risk-taking and substance abuse. In fact, research suggests that men present more externalizing symptoms while women present with more internalizing symptoms[37] and that many other BDP presentations overlap with PTSD presentations. Such symptoms include feelings of detachment, being "on edge," self-harm, impulsivity, anger, difficulty regulating emotions, difficulty managing relationships and feelings of guilt and shame. It is important to note the profound difference in both stigma and prognosis associated with BPD versus PTSD. The former can be both career-ending and psychologically punitive and debilitating, while the later offers appropriate sympathy and treatment to those suffering from trauma brought on by something outside of the individuals' control.

According to clinicians, BPD is pervasive and longitudinal, meaning symptoms begin to present by adolescence and in most areas of the person's functioning, whereas PTSD is grounded in a traumatic event. Personality disorders are considered manageable, but likely incurable and largely untreatable beyond psychotherapy and sedating psychotropic medications for management. Once a woman is given a BPD diagnosis their reported experiences are often interpreted as semi-psychotic perceptions. In other words, they are deemed "crazy."

To meet the qualifications for a BPD diagnosis, the person's reported symptoms, perceptions, and behavioral presentations must be longitudinal and pervasive. In assessing such psychological and behavioral history, there is considerable room for interpretative subjectivity. Some standard questions a clinician would ask might include, "Can you ever remember a time or times when they had difficulty managing their anxiety, felt disappointed, helpless, hopeless, or had considered hurting themselves?" It is then not much of a stretch to imagine that most women talking to a medical professional who they felt had their best interests in mind would likely answer yes to at least one of these, especially young women and women from less privileged backgrounds. Research on South African women diagnosed with BPD found that most of them came from violent backgrounds, which would certainly generate feelings of anxiety and hopelessness. Women's answers to assessment questions can suggest as much about the collective experience of women as psychopathology.

The National Alliance on Mental Health suggests that men may be equally affected by BPD, but they are far more often assigned diagnoses of PTSD or Major Depression. It is reasonable to assume that the reverse may also be true, that women assigned diagnoses of BPD may in fact be suffering from PTSD or Major Depression. In light of the diagnostic disparity, it is important to consider why assessors might make attributional errors when interpreting symptoms presented by men, as opposed to women. Given the extreme, potentially negative implications of a BPD diagnosis, assessors might require a higher standard of presentation for men when considering a BPD diagnosis. Since society has traditionally viewed men as protectors and providers, it is easier to sympathize with them as depressed or traumatized than it is helpless, hysterical and manipulative. But the stereotype that it's "all in her head," or "she has an overactive imagination" that has traditionally been used to silence women's voices must stop.

Equally insidious is the rise of credibility given by US courts to claims of parental alienation, where one parent accuses the other of alienating the children, against women in divorce-related contested child custody cases.[38] Based on junk science, men make the accusation against women almost six times more than women level it against men. A 2020 study found that "when mothers alleged abuse and fathers responded by claiming alienation, the mothers stood a startling high chance of losing custody."[39] Further, alienation claims create opportunities to send "alienated" children to camps whose sole goal is to make money, to help them reconnect with the parent they've rejected, sometimes their abusers, with camp owners often consequently happy to propagate alienation claims. While courts have a vested interest in keeping both parents involved in their children's lives when that involvement is healthy for the children, the outwardly gender-biased assumptions made against mothers by courts requires immediate reexamination.

Conclusions

Women are not the only victims of violence. Men are victims of domestic abuse, sexual assault – in untold numbers as many times it is not reported – violent crime and conflict related violence. There is no intent to minimize or disregard their victimization and suffering. The focus of this chapter, however, is on how violence is being used to perpetuate a male-dominated power structure.

Addressing systemic violence used to subjugate women will take a multipronged approach, working with men and boys and women and girls. No country is immune. It is important to remember as well that vulnerability is a function of context. Is a female college student walking in public in a tank top and shorts on a hot day putting herself at risk? Not if she is in Cambridge, Massachusetts. Is a man carrying a gay pride flag in danger? He is if he is in Uganda. Is a girl of 9 allowed to be married to a stranger decades older than she is? It depends on where she lives. Social norms dictate vulnerability, and that is where ameliorating efforts must be focused, otherwise social norms can metastasize to other political orders.

When violence becomes a normalized part of civil society, it is not a far leap for violence to be a standard response to problem-solving more broadly. With that normalization of violence, the domestic security of a country can become easily threatened, opening a Pandora's Box of bad domestic and foreign consequences.

The "protection" pillar of the Women, Peace, and Security framework is not intended to legitimize military violence, as some critics have contended. Rather, it is intended to address a very pervasive reality faced by many men, women, boys, and girls. Conflict-related sexual violence is at one end of the GBV spectrum, violence within the home and family at the other. Neither can be ignored, nor can any of the plethora of intimidation and subjugation tactics in-between.

Notes

1 Amy Dwyer, *Women Human Rights Defenders: Left Behind in the Women, Peace & Security Agenda*, London School of Economics, Policy Brief, February 1920. www.lse.ac.uk/women-peace-security/ass ets/documents/2020/PBS01Dwyer.pdf

2 Jamie Wareham, "375 Transgender People Murdered in 2021 – 'Deadliest Year' since Records Began," *Forbes*, November 11, 2021. www.forbes.com/sites/jamiewareham/2021/11/11/375-transgender-peo ple-murdered-in-2021-deadliest-year-since-records-began/?sh=310a7ee1321c

3 Heather Zimmerman and Justin Cole, "Retrenchment of the Federal Right to Abortion: How Dobbs Threatens National Security," *Just Security*, July 26 2022. www.justsecurity.org/82520/retrenchment-of-the-federal-right-to-abortion-how-dobbs-threatens-national-security/

4 Marianne Schall, "Peace Laureates Take on War on Women," *Huffington Post*, June 14, 2011. www.huf fingtonpost.com/marianne-schnall/peace-laureates-take-on-t_b_876348.html

5 Janette Gagnon and Emanuella Grinberg, "Ad about Brock Turner's Sentence? It's Not Uncommon," *CNN*, September 4, 2016.

6 Mary Caprioli, "Primed for Violence: The Role of Gender Inequality in Predicting Internal Conflict," *International Studies Quarterly* 49 (2005), p. 163.

7 Johan Galtung, "Cultural Violence," *Journal of Peace Research*, August 1990, pp. 291–305.

8 Hudson et al., *International Security*, September 2008, p. 21.

9 Denise Ryan, "Teachers Urged to Address Porn Factor," *Sydney Morning Herald*, February 13, 2012. www.smh.com.au/national/education/teachers-urged-to-address-porn-factor-20120210-1sjtl.html

10 Valeria Hudson and Patricia Leidl, *The Hillary Doctrine*, Columbia University Press, 2015, p. 91

11 Yuma Totani, "The Case against the Accused," Chapter 11 in *Beyond Victor's Justice? The Tokyo War Crimes Trial Revisited*, edited by Yuki Tanaka et al., Nijhoff, 2010.

12 Mereana Hond, "ICC Bemba Case: Appeal Court Overturns Conviction," *Al Jazeera*, June 9, 2018. www.aljazeera.com/news/2018/06/icc-bemba-case-appeal-court-overturns-conviction-180609110400 636.html

13 Dorothy Q. Thomas and Regan Ralph, "Rape in War: Challenging the Tradition of Impunity," *SAIS Review*, 1994. www.hrw.org/legacy/women/docs/rapeinwar.htm

14 Amnesty International, *Russian Federation: Nowhere to Turn: Violence Against Women in the Family*, December 15, 2005, p. 6. www.amnesty.org/en/documents/eur46/056/2005/en/

15 Marilyn Murray, "When Violence Is So Typical It Becomes Normal," *Moscow Times*, December 16, 2012. https://themoscowtimes.com/articles/when-violence-is-so-typical-it-becomes-normal-20232

16 Daria Litvanova, "Russian MP Seeks to Decriminalize Domestic Violence," *The Guardian*, August 18, 2016. www.theguardian.com/world/2016/aug/18/russian-mp-seeks-to-decriminalise-domestic-violence

17 Gefjon Off, Nicholas Charron, and Amy Alexander, "Who Perceives Women's Rights as Threatening to Men and Boys? Explaining Modern Sexism Among Young Men in Europe," *Frontiers of Political Science*, August 15, 2022. www.frontiersin.org/articles/10.3389/fpos.2022.909811/full

18 Rachel Kessler, "Due Process and Legislation Intended to Restrict the Rights of Rapist Fathers," *Northwestern Journal of Law and Social Policy*, Spring 2015, p. 201.

19 Heather Hvlaka, "Normalizing Sexual Violence: Young Women Account for Harassment and Abuse," *Gender and Society*, February 28, 2014, pp. 339–340, italics in original. http://journals.sagepub.com/doi/abs/10.1177/0891243214526468

20 www.unfpa.org/resources/female-genital-mutilation-fgm-frequently-asked-questions#instruments

21 Harsimran Gill and Karen Dias, "Indian Acid Attack Victims Share Their Stories," *Al Jazeera English*, March 10, 2016. www.aljazeera.com/indepth/features/2016/03/indian-acid-attack-victims-share-stories-160309074926141.html

22 Ameena Ilahi, "Acid Crimes: A Growing Crisis in Pakistan," Asia Foundation, October 1, 2014. http://asiafoundation.org/2014/10/01/acid-crimes-a-growing-crisis-in-pakistan/

23 Saira Khan, "The Outrageous 'Honor Killing' of a Pakistani Social-Media Star," *New Yorker*, July 19, 2016. www.newyorker.com/news/news-desk/the-outrageous-honor-killing-of-a-pakistani-social-media-star

24 John Alan Cohan, "Honor Killings and the Cultural Defense," *California Western International Law Journal*, Spring 2010, pp.191–194 (footnotes omitted).

25 Maxwell Strachan, "Sharmeen Obaid-Chinoy Delivered the Most Powerful Speech of the Oscars," *Huffington Post*, March 9, 2016. www.huffingtonpost.com/entry/sharmeen-obaid-chinoy-oscars-speech-honor-killings_us_56d3c5f9e4b0bf0dab329872

26 Sangwon Yon, "Islamic State Circulates Sex Slave Price List," Bloomberg, August 3, 2015. www.bloomberg.com/news/articles/2015-08-03/sex-slaves-sold-by-islamic-state-the-younger-the-better

27 *Sex Trafficking: Inside the Business of Modern Slavery*, Columbia University Press, 2006, p. x.

28 Astrid Zwenert, "Violence, Self-Harm and Suicide Common among Trafficked Children," Reuters, September 8, 2015. www.reuters.com/article/us-health-trafficking-children-idUSKCN0R81WP2 0150908

29 Neha A. Deshpande and Nawal M. Nour, "Sex Trafficking of Women and Girls," *Review of Obstetrics and Gynecology*, 1 (2013). www.ncbi.nlm.nih.gov/pmc/articles/PMC3651545/

30 Karina Bland, "Will Martha McSally Help Change the System She Doesn't Trust?" *The Republic*, March 6, 2019. www.azcentral.com/story/news/local/karinabland/2019/03/06/martha-mcsally-help-change-system-she-doesnt-trust/3086971002/. Accessed January 11, 2021.

31 Helene Cooper, Dave Phillips, and Richard A. Oppel, Jr., "I, Too, Was a Survivor": Senator McSally Ends Years of Silence," *New York Times*, March 26, 2019. www.nytimes.com/2019/03/26/us/senator-martha-mcsally-rape-assault.html. Accessed January 11, 2021.

32 Zachery Cohen, "Martha McSally, a Sexual Assault Survivor, Calls Allegations against Gen. John Hyten 'false,'" CNN, July 30, 2019. www.cnn.com/2019/07/30/politics/hyten-confirmation-hearing-mcsally/index.html. Accessed January 11, 2021.

33 Cohen, 2019.

34 "General Hyten Did Something Incredibly Wrong to Me," PBS News Hour, July 31, 2019. www.pbs.org/newshour/show/gen-john-hyten-did-something-incredibly-wrong-to-me-says-col-kathryn-spletstoser

35 "General's Sexual Assault Accuser Was Deemed a 'Toxic, Self-Centered Abuser,' New Docs Reveal," *Defense News*, August 16, 2019. www.defenseone.com/policy/2019/08/generals-sexual-assault-accuser-was-deemed-toxic-self-centered-abuser-new-docs-reveal/159252/

36 Kristina Peterson, "Arizona Rep. Martha McSally Alleges Sexual Abuse by High School Coach," *Wall Street Journal*, April 23, 2018. www.wsj.com/articles/arizona-rep-martha-mcsally-alleges-sexual-abuse-by-high-school-coach-1524518307

37 Qian Xinyu, "Sex Differences in Borderline Personality Disorder," *PLoS One*. December 30, 2022. www.ncbi.nlm.nih.gov/pmc/articles/PMC9803119/

38 Amy Polacko, "Remembering Catherine Kassenoff and Continuing the Fight for Fair US Child Custody Outcomes," *Ms.*, June 25, 2023.

39 Olivia Gentile, "Her son said his stepdad was sexually abusive. A judge gave the stepdad custody anyway. Then she found the photographs," *Insider*, May 18, 2023; Janet R. Johnston and Matthew R. Sullivan, "Parental Alienation: In Search of Common Ground for a More Differentiated Theory," *Family Court Review*, April 2020, pp. 270–292.

Further reading

Bales, Kevin. *Disposable People*, University of California Press, 2012.

Berdayes, Vincente, and John Murphy (eds.). *Neoliberalism, Economic Radicalism and the Normalization of Violence*, Springer, 2015.

Huhtanen, Heather. *Gender Bias in Sexual Assault Response and Investigating: Part 2, Victim Blaming & Selection*. Report by End Violence Against Women International, updated 2022. https://evawintl.org/wp-content/uploads/TB-Gender-Bias-1-4-Combined-1.pdf

Kara, Siddharth. *Sex Trafficking: Inside the Business of Modern Slavery*, Columbia University Press, 2010.

Leatherman, Janie. *Sexual Violence and Armed Conflict*, Polity, 2011.

Lightfoot-Klein, Hanny. *Secret Wounds*, Authorhouse, 2003.

Moon, Katherine. *Sex among Allies: Military Prostitution in US-Korea Relations*, Columbia University Press, 1997.

Pilot, Sara, and Lora Prabhu (eds.). *The Fear That Stalks: Gender-Based Violence in Public Spaces*, University of Chicago Press, 2014.

Pope, Nicole. *Honor Killings in the Twenty-First Century*, Palgrave Macmillan, 2012.

Rittner, Carol, and John Roth (eds.). *Rape: Weapon of War and Genocide*, Paragon House, 2012.

6 Women and development

Development and human security

Pakistani economist, game theorist, and international development specialist Mahbub ul Haq is credited with having a profound impact on global development. His book *Reflections on Human Development* (1995) advanced that development was not simply a measure of economics but also of people's well-being. Subsequently, consideration of human development and positive peace must include not just income growth, but expanding people's ability to live lives they value. They must have opportunity, capability, and agency to prosper. For long-term human development, environmental sustainability must also be factored into plans, and gender equality achieved. Human development and human security are closely linked as both are focused on people. The difference between them is that while human security focuses on identifying and addressing threats and risks, human development involves understanding the threats, toward finding and implementing preventive measures.[1]

The United Nations Development Program (UNDP) has also highlighted two key aspects of human security, "freedom from want" and "freedom from fear."[2] More specifically, seven essential dimensions of human security are considered part of human development: economics, health, personal, political, food, environment and community. These dimensions, and others when appropriate, are part of a flexible approach that can be tailored to different circumstances, contexts, and topics.

> No matter which topic is addressed, a guiding principle of the human security approach is that it requires understanding the particular threats experienced by particular groups of people, as well as the participation of those people in the analysis process. Threats to human security can exist at all levels of development.[3]

Understanding different perspectives regarding threats, and having those perspectives represented in analysis toward addressing the threats, is the essence of the WPS framework. A human security development approach can and should work hand in hand with the WPS framework.

Global development goals

The economic empowerment of women is taking place within the context of global development goals set over the past three decades. The 1990s also saw a series of global conferences held toward setting international development goals and targets on specific subjects. The agendas at these conferences focused on priorities like education (Jomtien 1990), children (New York

DOI: 10.4324/9781003413417-7

1990), the environment (Rio 1992), population (Cairo 1994), social development (Copenhagen 1995), and the status of women (Beijing 1995). Because aid budgets were declining, the Organization for Economic Cooperation and Development began advancing the idea of international development goals in the mid-1990s. Those efforts were eventually shifted to the UN, and at the September 2000 UN Millennium Summit, global leaders produced a historic Millennium Declaration text that condensed a wide-ranging, ad hoc global agenda down to a relatively succinct framework of global priorities, deemed the Millennium Development Goals (MDGs). The MDGs comprise eight time-bound, measurable human development goals.[4]

- To eradicate extreme poverty and hunger
- To achieve universal primary education
- To promote gender equality and empower women
- To reduce child mortality
- To improve material maternal health
- To combat HIV/AIDS, malaria, and other diseases
- To ensure environmental sustainability
- To develop a global partnership for development

The MDGs expired in 2015, replaced by Sustainable Development Goals (SDGs). The effectiveness of the MDGs has been both touted and questioned. According to UN Secretary-General Ban Ki-Moon:

> the MDGs have made a profound difference in people's lives. Global poverty has been halved five years ahead of the 2015 timeframe. Ninety per cent of children in developing regions now enjoy primary education, and disparities between boys and girls in enrollment have narrowed. Remarkable gains have also been made in the fight against malaria and tuberculosis, along with improvements in all health indicators. The likelihood of a child dying before age five has been nearly cut in half over the last two decades. That means that about 17,000 children are saved every day. We also met the target of halving the proportion of people who lack access to improved sources of water.[5]

Others have asserted that the MDGs improved data collection, facilitated cross-sector collaboration in development work, and spurred donor support.[6] According to economist Jeffrey Sachs, perhaps most importantly,

> by packaging these priorities into an easily understandable set of eight goals, and by establishing an easily understandable set of eight goals, and by establishing measurable and timebound objectives, the MDGs help to promote global awareness, political accountability, improved metrics, social feedback, and public pressures.[7]

Communication and incremental, measurable targets are not inconsequential objectives.

But not all critique has been positive. The general nature of the MDGs and the focus on metrics have also generated criticism along the lines of the entire program being a box-checking exercise.

> Derided by their most ardent detractors as "Major Distracting Gimmicks," critics of the MDGs have pointed to the secretive circumstances of their birth, their technocratic and reductionist nature, their failure to address root causes of poverty, their failure to factor

in legal obligations pertaining to social rights, their gender-blindness, their failure to address poverty in rich countries, their weak accountability mechanisms, their limited uptake by social movements in the Global South, the potentially distorting character of target-driven policymaking, and the propensity of the MDGs to "crowd out" attention to important issues that didn't make it into the global list, for example, social security or social protection.[8]

The inherent complexity of global issues makes simplification difficult, and there certainly are instances where statistics have been generated and used inappropriately. The problem is, without goals and metrics of some kind – and whatever goals and metrics are selected for use will never please everyone – the only option is ad hoc measures with no accountability. The SDGs are a second iteration attempt at selecting appropriate goals and metrics, and optimistically, a third version will continue improvement.

The SDGs were built around and integrated into the MDGs, with work beginning during the lead-up to the Rio+20 Summit in 2012 and eventually led by a post-Summit panel including UK prime minister David Cameron, Indonesian president Susilo Bambang Yudhoyono, and Liberian president Ellen Johnson Sirleaf as co-chairs. Officially known as *Transforming Our World: The 2030 Agenda for Sustainable Development*, a set of 17 "Global Goals" with 169 targets between them were developed. The goals reflect the complexity of global challenges toward furthering the efforts of the MDGs, but also expand to include global priorities not addressed prior, such as inequality, infrastructure, and peace and justice. Once again as well, the goals are simply communicated, toward generating public discussion.

Gender equality plays a key role in achieving most of the SDGs. The empowerment of women is a prerequisite to the success of the SDGs overall. The difficulty in reaching those targets differs by country, depending on their individual starting point, and commitment.

Women, development, and security

A landmark McKinsey Global Institute (MGI) report stated in 2015 that advancing women's equality could add $12 trillion to global growth by 2025 – more than the current gross domestic products (GDPs) of Germany, Japan, and the United Kingdom combined. But the study also found several factors which will keep that from happening. First, while women make up almost 50% of the overall global population, only 37% contribute to the global GDP. Second, 195 million more women than men are illiterate. Third, 190 million more men than women have access to an account at a formal financial institution, making credit harder for women to get. Fourth, women spend three times more time on unpaid care work than men. Fifth, 90% of CEOs at S&P 500 companies are promoted or hired from line roles, while less than 20% of women senior vice presidents hold line roles. For the first time since the Fortune 500 list began 68 years ago, more than 10% of Fortune 500 companies were led by women in 2023. It took 68 years to get to 10%. Sixth, less than 50% of employees feel their company is doing all that is needed to achieve gender parity. Thus, finally, the study found that it will take over 100 years at the current rate to achieve 100% gender parity in the workplace,[9] though that number has grown post-Covid-19 to 132 years. In producing the report, MGI mapped 15 gender-equality indicators for 95 countries. No country was highly ranked in gender equality in society but low gender equality in work. Societal empowerment of women correlated with developmental potential.

Economic recovery is widely understood as a key aspect of long-term stability in countries transitioning out of conflict. Since it is women who hold together the social fabric of society and are primarily focused on raising children, determining who has access to post-conflict economic opportunities has implications for sustainable peace, hence the importance of understanding and utilizing gendered perspectives in recovery programs.

Women face multiple barriers to economic opportunity and empowerment, including legal constraints, difficulties in setting up businesses, and limited access to finance and capital. In legal terms, land is an important asset for households in developing countries and laws often perpetuate male control. Female farmers lack equal rights to own land in more than 90 countries.[10] Women represent less than 20% of landowners globally, with those numbers decreasing to 5% in North Africa and West Asia, and 15% in sub-Saharan Africa. Yet almost 70% of employed women in South Asia and 60% in sub-Saharan Africa work in agriculture.

In Uganda, for example, where more women work agricultural jobs than men, women own only 7% of the land they work. It is the norm there that women work land owned by male relatives. That situation weakens women's economic security because they are left out of decisions regarding investment or selling land, especially during times of conflict. During conflicts, women frequently become widows and thus the primary provider in their households, but may be legally prohibited from inheriting the land on which they work.

The potential benefits for women regarding not being tied to land have, however, also been studied. Young women in India, for example, are increasingly able to leave rural areas for better jobs and education in urban areas than some male counterparts. Perhaps not surprisingly, though, women who take the opportunity to leave have also sometimes suffered backlash. Men are resentful of women's increased independence, of women outperforming them economically, seeing women as competitors, and with a 2022 sex ratio of 108 men per 100 women in India, many men are left without brides, again highlighting the interconnected and complex nature of gender-related issues.

Structural barriers to women working still exist in many countries. The Council on Foreign Relations Women's Workplace Equality Index points out that women are required to have their husband's permission to work in 18 countries. Fifty-nine countries provide no legal protections whatsoever to women against workplace sexual harassment. Seventy-five countries restrict women's inheritance rights, meaning they can be left destitute, especially if they are considered "troublesome."

The kinds of jobs that women can hold, often those traditionally held by men and/or high-paying, are restricted in 104 countries. Whether structural or cultural, women are disadvantaged in their economic dependence and consequently can fear using their voices to support personal and political empowerment.

Because of lack of access to capital and often constraints of physical movement, women are often forced to turn to low-paying jobs such as sewing or laundry. Microcredit, small loans with terms intended to lift individuals from poverty, has been a key mechanism in assisting women in building businesses, in and out of their homes. Unlike traditional finance mechanisms, microcredit does not require the use of land or other resources as collateral. At the micro level, without economic independence, women's life choices are few or none. At the macro level, women add to the economic well-being of society in many ways, including helping to keep violent extremism that can fester in the petri dishes created by poverty at bay and societal stability maintained.

The linkage between women, development, and security is not just an issue in developing countries. Japanese prime minister Shinzo Abe launched a "womenomics" strategy in 2013 to mitigate Japan's demographic crises and subsequent labor shortages. He proposed a three-pronged approach to revitalizing Japan's economy: monetary policy, fiscal policy, and structural reform, including measures to reduce barriers to women's participation in the labor force, the latter representing the "womenomics" portion of his strategy.

That Japan undertook the program at all evidences the importance attached to the gender equality "image" in foreign policy even among developed countries. Though considered a highly developed country, Japan has faced considerable international pressure and criticism from human and women's rights activists and organizations for its repudiation of wrong-doing regarding the Korean comfort women issue. A statement made by then-Osaka mayor Toru Hashimoto in 2013 that comfort women had been necessary to maintain discipline in the military, sparked outrage in South Korea and elsewhere. Womenomics was intended to allow Japan to bolster its international image to other countries, financial and international institutions, investors, and human rights organizations by taking action that will benefit the country in two areas, economic growth and gender equality. But cultural barriers are hard to abate.

In 2018, scandal rocked Japan's premier medical school, Tokyo Medical University, when it was revealed that administrators had been surreptitiously lowering women's entrance test scores. Their gender-based manipulation of scores was rationalized based on the assumption that women would get married, have children, and leave the medical profession, so they did not want to waste a coveted medical school position on a woman. Upon further investigation, it was found that ten of the country's most prestigious schools were similarly lowering women's test scores. University procedures changed and in 2022, more women than men qualified for entrance to the Tokyo Medical School and six of the other schools that had been manipulating scores. Nevertheless, many women still feel the need to leave Japan to pursue a career on a (more) level playing field as cultural barriers in Japan and elsewhere remain the biggest obstacle to equality.

National efforts to economically empower women are part of global development efforts, and often done out of national self-interest and that's OK. Saudi Arabia allowed women to drive not because the government suddenly believed in empowerment, but because working women add to economic growth. Abe's Womenomics program was similarly born out of economic and foreign policy national interest, not because of a realization that empowerment was the right thing to do. Convincing more countries of the benefits of women's empowerment is in fact a big part of the task at hand for WPS supporters.

Ideally, global and national efforts are coordinated and addressed with consistent commitment. In reality, rhetoric has proved easier than follow-through, and commitment wanes when juxtaposed with more traditional security considerations. Dr. Flavia Bustreo, former WHO assistant director-general for family, women and children's health, stated in 2015 that "in too many countries, 'women's empowerment' remains a pipedream – little more than a rhetorical flourish added to a politician's speech."[11] Unfortunately, due to the rise of authoritarianism, the Russian attack on Ukraine, the US-China Cold War, rogue states flexing their muscles, the increasingly felt effects of climate change, and the COVID-19 pandemic, the world has been left in what has been called a state of "polycrises" or "permacrises." That state consumes leaders' attention and resources and has not helped women's empowerment. "Gender parity has slipped down the list of priorities and women's progress set back a whole generation,"[12] according to Alex Liu, chairman and managing partner of Kearney Consulting Group.

A spectrum of issues must be addressed related to gender and development. Women who work the fields in Uganda face very different issues than young women trying to get into top schools in Japan, and professional women unable to break the corporate glass ceiling in the United States. Intersectionality comes into play in many different ways.

Three dimensions of gender equality

Gender equality and development are often construed through three interconnected dimensions: the accumulation of endowments, opportunities, and agency. *Endowments* specific-ally refers to education, health, and tangible assets available to a girl or woman. *Opportunities* refers to the ability to use endowments to generate income. *Agency* is the ability to apply those endowments as actions affecting personal and household well-being.

Good health is considered a prerequisite that affects other potential endowments, with the majority of issues relevant to women most frequently cited by WHO also most prevalent and dire in low- and middle-income countries. (1) Cancer. Screening, prevention, and treatment for two of the most common cancers affecting women, breast cancer and cervical cancer, is virtually nonexistent in many countries. Cancer is followed by (2) Reproductive Health, (3) Maternal Health, (4) HIV, and (5) Sexually Transmitted Infections. Especially in developing countries, sexual and reproductive health issues comprise one-third of the health issues for women between the ages of 15 and 44 years, with unsafe sex a key factor. HIV leaves women vulnerable to tuberculosis, a leading cause of death in women between 20 and 59. Untreated syphilis is responsible for some 200,000 reported stillbirths annually, and 90,000 newborn deaths.

Getting contraception to the hundreds of millions of women to whom it is not locally available is key to women's health. Between 2014 and 2016, money from the UN Population Fund is estimated to have prevented 35 million unwanted pregnancies, 11 million unsafe abortions, 93,000 maternal deaths, 272,000 genital mutilations of girls, 8.3 million sexually transmitted infections via one billion condoms, and 188,000 HIV infections.[13] In April 2017, the Trump administration announced the United States would no longer support the program.[14]

Internationally, when the Trump administration reinstated and broadened the Mexico City Policy, denying aid for NGOs providing abortion counseling or referrals, advocating abortion decriminalization, or expanding abortion services, the Netherlands announced it intended to set up its own plan to fill in the funding. The rationale, according to Lilianne Ploumen, the Dutch minister for foreign trade and development cooperation, was that to do otherwise would lead to "dangerous backroom procedures and higher maternal mortality." She went on to say,

> This decision has far-reaching consequences above all for the women it affects, who should be able to decide for themselves if they want a child, but also for their husbands and children and for society as a whole. Banning abortion does not reduce the number of abortions.[15]

That simple fact was lost on the Trump administration and continues to be either lost on many US decision-makers or, more likely, reducing the number of abortions performed is actually a secondary goal to a primary goal of controlling women.

Additional predominant women's health issues, following from those listed prior, are more related to circumstances than physiology, ranked as follows: (5) Gender-based violence affects one in three women under 50, with health workers in developing countries rarely prepared to address the multitude of physical and mental issues that result. (6) Mental health issues. The scars of physical violence against and around them weigh heavily on women. Women have also been found more prone to anxiety, depression, and somatic complaints – complaints that cannot be explained medically. Depression is the most common mental health problem for women, and suicide a leading cause of death for women under 60. (7) Non-communicable diseases. These are deaths related to causes like traffic accidents; tobacco, alcohol, and substance abuse; and obesity. Rates of female obesity have risen significantly in recent years. Finally, (9) Being young and (10) Getting old present health issues for women as well. Young women face an inordinate number of the sexual and reproductive health issues covered, while older women are often left without resources, consequently hindering their ability to take care of their health.

The age dimension associated with women's endowment is important, as women have differing needs – in all areas, not just health – at different points in their lives. Investing in young girls is critical for breaking the poverty cycle, focused on areas like nutrition and education. Women in the working-age population are likely mothers, needing child care and birth control. Elderly women, especially widows, are sometimes the most vulnerable members of society. They need protection in areas like inheritance laws and widows' pensions. Widows are abandoned because they are another mouth to feed, and might try to stake a claim to family property, property men assume as theirs.

Opportunity refers to the ability to use endowments to generate income, thereby providing financial security and independence if desired. According to the *2022 Global Gender Gap Report*, gender parity for workforce opportunities had been slowly declining since 2009, and then took a precipitous decline in 2020 due to the amount of care work falling to women during the pandemic. Consequently, gender parity in the workforce stood at 62.9% in 2022, the lowest level registered since the index was first published in 2006.

Consequently, many women are forced to work in the informal economy where both wages and job security are low. Within the informal economy there are self-employment jobs and wage jobs. Self-employment jobs include those where the employer is engaged in an informal enterprise, such as baking bread to sell at a market, and pays another person to do the actual selling at the market. They also include members of an informal producers' co-op, own-account workers (self-employed without any employees), and contributing family members to formal and informal enterprises. Especially as contributors to family enterprises, women's contributions are expected and often pay no individual wages.

Wage workers in the informal economy include employees of informal enterprises, casual or day laborers, paid domestic workers, contract workers, unregistered or undeclared workers, and industrial outworkers (also called homeworkers). While individuals are paid for their contributions, the work is neither steady nor does it come with health benefits or retirement contributions. Women are consistently overrepresented in the informal and part-time work force.

There are examples of women working in the informal economy taking steps to better their economic positions. The Self Employed Women's Association (SEWA) is a multi-sector trade union founded in India in 1972, where 94% of the women work in the informal economy. SEWA's membership of almost two million women now extends beyond India. Its members work primarily in four categories of jobs: (1) hawkers, vendors and small business women who sell vegetables, fruit, fish, eggs, and other food items, household goods and clothes; (2) home-based workers like weavers, potters, ready-made garment workers, women who process agricultural products, and artisans; (3) manual laborers and service providers in areas like agriculture, construction workers, handcart pullers, domestic, and laundry workers; (4) individuals who invest their labor and capital to carry out their businesses, including in agriculture, cattle rearing, salt workers, gum collectors, cooking and vending, and so on.

SEWA's goal is to organize women workers for full employment, defined within the context of security:

> Full employment means employment whereby workers obtain work security, income security, food security and social security (at least health care, child care and shelter). SEWA organizes women to ensure that every family obtains full employment. By self-reliance we mean that women should be autonomous and self-reliant, individually and collectively, both economically and regarding their decision-making ability.[16]

SEWA seeks to achieve full employment through organization at the local level, asset and capital creation by offering bank accounts and credit, and capacity building through leadership and business training.

The SEWA Cooperative Bank, the first bank for poor self-employed women, was founded in 1974. The initial purpose was to offer credit to women always in debt, and in doing so free them "from the clutches of money-lenders and traders, to enhance their businesses, build up assets in their own name, for their children's education, for the several emergencies including illness that they face and many other purposes."[17] SEWA also assists in organization, local leadership development, collective bargaining, and policy advocacy. While work conditions in the informal economy in India can still be unimaginably hard, especially in rural areas, organizations like SEWA can offer workers some hope of a better future, at the least through networking.

Finally, *agency* references the ability of individuals and groups to make effective choices about themselves and then to transform those choices into desired actions and outcomes. Women's agency influences their ability to build human capital, to take up economic opportunities, and to participate effectively in private and public life. Agency is often considered binary; one either has it or one does not. In that regard, agency is sometimes conceptualized much along the same lines as autonomy and empowerment.

As long as violence against women remains prevalent, with civil and criminal laws failing to criminalize certain acts against women, as long as women are denied reproductive rights, and as long as women's roles in community and political decision-making roles are limited, girls' and women's agency will be limited. Young women and girls are significant stakeholders in peace and security efforts, and too often their roles are marginalized.[18]

Aid and investment

Zambian-born economist Dambisa Moyo created a public stir with the publication of her book *Dead Aid: Why Aid Is Not Working and How There Is a Better Way* (2009). In it she argued that the billions of structural aid (as opposed to emergency aid) dollars sent by wealthy countries to address poverty and spur African development has not just failed, but has trapped many countries into being welfare states rife with corruption. She refers to the structural aid as not just ineffective but also malignant. She goes on to advocate for it being halted to force the continent to develop their own, sustainable economic plans. Whether what some economists and many donors saw as Moyo's Draconian approach was too harsh or not, structural aid has certainly not been without problems.

In *The Hillary Doctrine* (2015), the authors point out that there are often issues at the national level of donors, specifically citing the evolved role of USAID in the post-Cold War period. USAID is not the development agency it was originally designed as during the Cold War, when aid was a persuasion tool used by both the East and West blocs to lure developing countries into their sphere of influence. When the Cold War ended, the US government cut the number of USAID employees, while the USAID budget continued to grow. Consequently, USAID became essentially a contract management agency, doling out contracts to for-profit mega-contractors. The consequence of that is a widening gap between USAID and supposed beneficiaries.

> USAID used to believe in doing work from the ground up by sending highly experienced professionals to the field to work with people there to figure out solutions. Now […] USAID brings in contractors without experience or cultural sensitivity in one-size-fits-all programming […] It's overly ambitious and shortsighted; there's pressure to have the proper indicators on your log, and it becomes overwhelming.[19]

Part of the problem as well has been the attitudes and propensities of some of those administering the contracts.

Many of the contractors, the *Hillary Doctrine* authors point out, are conservative, retired military, who do not establish relationships with the communities they are working in. "It's not an equal relationship; they think of themselves as gods: Very hierarchical, very patriarchal, very pyramidal."[20] Viewing problems through a gender lens often simply does not occur to them, making widespread education, awareness, application, and accountability for implementing WPS principles a clear imperative for all security practitioners.

Further, there have been charges leveled against USAID contracting agencies regarding corruption related to US global war on terror efforts.[21] When spending large amounts of contract money is a prerequisite for getting further large amounts of contract money, the potential for corruption is significant. This reality was evidenced in Iraq and Afghanistan with companies like food service provider Supreme Foodservice, security provider Triple Canopy, and mega-contractor KBR, which provided pretty much anything the military requested.[22] In 2014, for example, Supreme Foodservice, a Swiss corporation, pleaded guilty to major fraud charges in connection with a contract to supply food and water to troops in Afghanistan, and agreed to pay $434 million in criminal penalties and settlement fees.[23] Corruption issues associated with USAID provide ammunition for those who would like to disassociate the United States from addressing human security issues.

The Biden administration appointed human rights specialist and former US ambassador to the United Nations Samantha Power to change the USAID business model. Realistically, however, there is a substantial amount of organizational inertia that must be dealt with, as well as resistance in favor of maintaining the status quo from currently benefiting contractors. In fiscal year 2017, 60% of agency funding went to just 25 contracting organizations, and a 2019 report that surveyed three years of USAID spending found that 43% of the agency's awards achieved, on average, only half of the intended results. In 2021, USAID dispersed $28.3 billion, with an accurate measure of effectiveness still elusive. Experts say that fixing the business model would take a "procurement renaissance"[24] to shed inefficient and ineffective large contractors and make room for medium and small enterprises and organizations. Large contractors with strong vested interests, however, can be politically powerful.

In March 2023, USAID announced a new policy framework, titled "Driving Progress Beyond Programs." The policy includes three overarching priorities: confront what USAID defines as the greatest challenges of our time; embrace new partnerships; and invest in USAID's enduring effectiveness. The need for new partnerships acknowledges that too much money was going to too few contractors, and the critical role locals play in the development of efforts sustainable in the future because very situation is unique. The greatest challenges are to be addressed are: conflict, displacement, and food insecurity; the climate crisis; repression and corruption; fragile primary healthcare systems, and barriers to inclusive growth and equitable opportunity. The intent is that a procurement renaissance actually be achieved.

Beyond aid, many developing economies also depend on remittances sent from abroad to provide for their populations. The World Bank estimated that Africans working and living abroad sent some $80 billion back to Africa in 2020, again evidencing external economic dependency. The sometimes high cost of sending remittances due to bank transfer charges also comes into play regarding how much of the money sent actually provides growth potential to individuals and hence development. How to harness remittances from individual payments to more impactful African investment has been a topic of recent economic discussions and debates.

The problems of aid and remittances are not unique to Africa and they are not the only problems that can hinder development. Even programs heralded as successes have created negative unintended consequences, evidencing the need for both the full inclusion of the local populations affected by aid programs who can often anticipate and address issues, and the need for evaluation, assessment, and potential restructuring of aid and investment programs over time. The history and evolution of microcredit/microfinancing provides an example of what can happen to a good development idea.

In 1976, Mohammed Yunus, then head of the Rural Economics Program at the University of Chittagong in Bangladesh, had a chance encounter with a 21-year-old woman named Sufia Begum in the Bangladeshi village of Jobra. Desperate to support herself, Sufia had borrowed about 25 cents from moneylenders charging exorbitant interest rates approaching 10% daily. She used the money to make bamboo stools that, as a condition of the loan, she sold back to the moneylenders at a price well below market value for a profit of about 2 cents. Her position was basically one of bonded labor. Yunus found others in the village in similar circumstances.[25] So he loaned $27 from his pocket to 42 people in the village so that they could purchase raw materials needed for their trades.

The borrowers repaid their loans promptly, and inspired Yunus to move forward with a simple but revolutionary concept: Provide poor people credit on suitable terms and teach them sound financial principles so that they could achieve financial self-sufficiency. That was the beginning of what has come to be known as microfinancing, or microcredit. Yunus went on to establish the Grameen Bank Project to spread the idea of microcredit, and became a Nobel Peace Prize laureate in 2006 for his efforts in transforming the lives of poor people around the world.

Yunus attracted significant funding from the development community to operationalize his plans for the Grameen Bank. Other banks using the Grameen model began appearing in other developing countries as well. Women are often the beneficiaries of microcredit. Initially, some 97% of microcredit from Grameen Bank went to women. Yunus observed that women put the money they made into bettering family conditions. Further, while repayment rates at commercial banks where middle-class men are the primary credit recipients, are typically around 70%, poor women borrowers at Grameen have had much higher repayment rates, reaching as high as 97% in some years, with no collateral backing their loans. Yunus also initiated a social element as part of the loan process, specifically requiring borrowers to attend weekly meetings to learn about economics and gain support for their repayment from others in their small group. Yunus was also known to be willing to make special flexible plans for those in trouble, in effect bending the rules a bit when borrowers were delinquent. Loans were personalized.

While the idea of microcredit flourished, the concept and Yunus have also not escaped criticism. One analyst retrospectively compared microcredit as a way to alleviate poverty to East European central planning in the 1980s and characterized it as an interesting idea that went wrong, formulated by "possibly" well-meaning individuals.[26] Yunus personally came under fire after deciding to create his own political party in Bangladesh in 2007 to potentially run for prime minister. While his run for office was short-lived, his political opposition accused him of "bloodsucking" the poor.[27]

Beyond attacks on Yunus personally, the commercial microcredit industry overall has been targeted for exploiting the poor, as their goal was not development aid but profit. In a 2011 *New York Times* op-ed, Yunus explained that two very different models of microcredit had developed. One type was designed to help the poor, the other to maximize financial returns to program managers and Wall Street investors who became involved when the microcredit banks went public. He said trouble began in 2005 when lenders began "looking for ways to make a profit on the loans by shifting from their status as nonprofit organizations to commercial enterprises."[28] Compartamos and SKS Microfinance were among the first microcredit institutions to commercialize. Compartamos, a Mexican commercial microcredit institution, had charged its borrowers an annual interest rate of almost 90%, nearly three times the 15% average charged by Mexican commercial banks. In India, there were reports of suicides when borrowers could not repay high-interest loans to SKS Microfinance, as only in death would the debts be forgiven. Honor/Shame societies are particularly susceptible to internalizing strong coercion tactics.

Whether or not microcredit generally alleviates poverty or empowers women has been the focus of many studies. Researchers at MIT began randomized studies of microcredit success in 2009. They found no significant changes in health, education, or women's empowerment in the areas of Hyderabad, India, they examined where microcredit loans were available. They followed up two years later and still found no significant impact.[29] Regarding empowerment, in many cases it has been found that while most microcredit loans are given to women – approximately 75% as of 2022 – women only maintain control of small loans. Larger loans are often requested for and under the control of husbands, though the women remain responsible for repayment. Nevertheless, microcredit organizations continue to evolve and are now part of international development, though not the only part. Entrepreneurship through microfranchising has also been added to the mix.

Africa has perhaps a higher rate of female entrepreneurship than anywhere else in the world. "Women are considered the drivers of growth in Africa through cross-border trade throughout sub-Saharan Africa: selling used clothes and tin kitchenware, as hairstylists and owners of fashion salons and running small food stores."[30] Entrepreneurial businesses like Solar Sister, Living Goods, and VisionSpring originated based on the "business-in-a-bag," direct sales microfranchising model, perhaps best known in the West through Avon cosmetics. Solar Sister entrepreneurs sell renewable energy products, Living Goods healthcare products and services, and VisionSpring eyeglasses. Beyond the bag used to carry products, business-in-a-bag operations share other similarities. They provide their entrepreneurs with training; offer financing or consignment models for the initial inventory provided; use systematized promotion and marketing strategies, including branded uniforms; have strict protocols that include penalties for rule breaking; and help entrepreneurs develop a reputation within their communities as well-informed service providers. They give the women a community and a support system.

More than 8,500 Solar Sister entrepreneurs operate in sub-Saharan Africa, specifically Nigeria, Tanzania, and Kenya, bringing clean, sustainable, last-mile energy technologies to more than 3.7 million people in those countries. Solar Sister Entrepreneurs (SSEs) proudly wear orange T-shirts and sell solar-powered lamps and clean stoves within their communities. Solar Sister is a nonprofit organization run by local women who, simply put, create personal and community impact.

SSEs are required to make an initial capital investment to show personal commitment, but under organizational terms and amounts realistic for individuals. They are then provided training, support, and perhaps most importantly, a community to help them grow their businesses to whatever level they choose. Business Development Associates assist SSEs with everything from establishing bank accounts if the women want them (and not all do), to acquiring bicycles so that they can travel farther to sell their products.

It is important to understand where most of the SSE live and work. They may be an hour by car from the nearest power grid, in areas accessible only by dirt roads. The SSEs often walk miles, through all types of weather, to reach potential customers. Potential market saturation makes it incumbent upon the organization itself to continue to expand its product portfolio.

Solar Sister products are all high quality as it is important that SSEs earn the trust of their customers and communities. Lamps are durable, easy to use, and sell at a price of $15 to $50. That is a big initial investment compared to the $2 paid regularly for kerosene to fuel lamps (that produce toxic fumes), but with these solar lamps being reusable, the investment pays for itself in a few months. The lamps can also be used to recharge cell phones, are convenient for the lamp owner, and are a potential revenue source if they charge others to use that capability. The benefits are wide ranging, including provision of four-plus hours of solar light that allows students in the home more study time. The easy-to-use and energy-efficient clean stoves are sold to replace the traditional, smoky, three-stone cook stoves used in many parts of Africa and often associated with burn injuries.

Solar Sister is a learning organization that fully captures and incorporates key lessons learned in its operations, specifically the importance of local knowledge, management, and ownership, and the need for both initial training and continued mentorship of the local women involved. The women receive a commission on each sale. The Solar Sister website states the organizational goals.

> Solar Sister eradicates energy poverty by empowering women with economic opportunity. We combine the breakthrough potential of clean energy technology with a deliberately woman-centered direct sales network to bring light, hope and opportunity to even the most remote communities in rural Africa.

The organization has had and declined the opportunity to partner with other groups, selling items for personal care, for example. One of the important aspects of Solar Sister is that the women become known as technology specialists, a rare and respected position for women within their communities.

The Solar Sisters website also points out what has already been shown time and time again, that women invest the bulk of their income into their family's well-being. Independent research has shown the Solar Sister model to improve not only a woman's personal income, but also her (and often her family's) health, education, and status. Nevertheless, SSEs are working in a very male-dominated environment and so different women have different experiences. Some husbands support their wives working, even providing capital for their initial investment, whereas others are more reluctant or even initially forbid them from doing so. Many SSEs are single women and mothers, or from marginalized communities, with the income they produce allowing them to support themselves and their families.

The impact on communities of having off-grid power available goes beyond what might be expected from nonprofit organization operations. It is estimated that families not having to constantly buy kerosene has cumulatively generated $340 million in additional income to local economies where Solar Sister operates. Development stabilizes communities. Further, in Tanzania, it is estimated that Solar Sister products generate 25% of off-grid lighting. One lamp, one household at a time, Solar Sister has become the equivalent of a utility company.

Similarly, Living Goods uses the business-in-a-bag model to distribute healthcare products. Headquartered in Kenya, Living Goods operates primarily in Kenya, Uganda, and Burkina Faso.

> At Living Goods we empower people to improve the health of their families, friends and communities.
>
> Living Goods supports networks of "Avon-like" health entrepreneurs who go door to door to teach families how to improve their health and wealth and sell life-changing products such as simple treatments for malaria and diarrhea, safe delivery kits, fortified foods, clean cook stoves, water filters, and solar lights. By combining the best practices from business and public health, we are dramatically lowering child mortality AND creating livelihoods for thousands of enterprising women.[31]

A randomized controlled trial in Uganda showed that Living Goods-supported community health workers, reduced under-five mortality by 27% and stunted growth by 7%, all for less than $2 per person annually.

Women, typically mothers between 25 and 50, are carefully selected to be Living Goods' Community Health Providers. They wear a uniform with the Living Goods logo to signify quality and trust to clients. Typically one in five women who apply to be community health providers are accepted, based on references, tests, and role-playing as selection tools. Living Goods then provides them with a kit containing the tools required to serve a client's health needs and build a successful business for themselves. The kit includes

flip books that convey health messages via easy-to-understand illustrations with local language translations, a thermometer to check for fevers, and measuring tape to chart growth. Most importantly, the kit includes a smart phone with diagnosis and pregnancy support apps designed by Living Goods. Living Goods provides each agent with an inventory loan to ensure that she is always in stock.[32]

The women become micro-franchise owners.

While many new businesses – anywhere – fail, franchises generally do better than average. Franchises support one in eight jobs in America. They are businesses that have been tested over and over for best practices. Franchises provide an assured supply chain, low-cost inputs (because the franchiser can buy in bulk), supply training for managers and employees, and come with a trusted brand.

For Living Goods, empowering women by creating capital is one goal. Bettering healthcare availability is the other. Researchers with Innovation for Policy Action conducted a three-year independent study and found that "drug prices fell 17 percent at clinics and drug shops near where Living Goods operates, and that the prevalence of fake drugs fell by 50 percent, suggesting positive competitive pressure."[33]

These micro-franchises learn as they go. VisionSpring, for example, found that while the entrepreneur-centered model worked where a product was being sold, it did not work as well with eyeglasses. So it modified its approach.

VisionSpring's early work involved training local people, or vision entrepreneurs, to conduct outreach and sell quality, low cost eyeglasses in their communities. Despite the clear need for basic eye care in these communities, the vision entrepreneur model soon proved unsustainable in isolation, with limited potential for scale. VisionSpring recognized that in order to maximize access to this underappreciated tool for socio-economic development, we needed to create businesses that would eventually scale with a blend of commercial, impact, and philanthropic investment. Accordingly, VisionSpring refined our interventions to incorporate the successful elements of the vision entrepreneur-based model into a hub and spoke approach where VisionSpring optical shops operate as hubs and vision entrepreneurs act like spokes conducting outreach in the communities surrounding the optical shops.[34]

VisionSpring uses a high-volume, low-margin approach to be able to provide eyeglasses in a nontraditional manner, with a small profit being made by distributors. In that way, both the distributor and the recipients economically benefit from the sale. The VisionSpring website tells the story of Dipti, a potter from Bangladesh. Before getting eyeglasses, she was only able to make two clay pots each day, earning $1.50 for each. With corrected vision, she was able to make ten pots each day, substantially bettering her family's livelihood.

When trying to involve women in innovation, special attention must be paid to an often-encountered technology gender divide.

Technology and empowering women

Information and communication technology (ICT) is an important development tool in many countries. ICT can provide weather reports and warnings of impending natural disasters such as tidal waves, provide tele-education and tele-healthcare in rural areas, allow individuals in cities to send money back to rural villages, allow women to feel more secure regarding their physical safety, and be a critical asset in developing social and political rights and business opportunities. During a 2015 talk, Anupama Suresh, a representative of an Indian NGO that works to empower women through ICT, gave examples of how information centers established by her organization equipped with a computer with an Internet connection or a mobile phone that could be shared by a group, had changed women's lives.

in the village of Kattemalavadi, in Karnataka State, a group of women who visited the newly established information centre learned the details of how much rice "below poverty line" households were entitled too and for what price under the government run Public Distribution System. Thus realizing that the local Fair Price shop owner had been inflating prices, they were able to come to him with these facts and he in turn had no choice but to start selling rice quotas at their lawful prices. All households in the village are thus reaping the benefits of cheaper grains, to which they are legally entitled. In another case, a group of women who had lost their spouses found out that they were entitled to certain benefits under the government's Scheme for Widow Pensions, and were helped to submit a claim to receive the needed support. In yet another, Sundaramma, a local banana farmer, was able to obtain a subsidy to support her economic livelihood.[35]

Yet women have both less involvement with development of and less access to ICT than men.

In terms of development, as of 2022 the overall percentage of women graduates in STEM has been growing, largely due to specific programs to recruit and retain women in those majors, but the gender split still shows women at about 26%. That figure also translates to women in the STEM workforce, with women making up 24% of individuals in those fields.[36] The example of omitting women of color in AI development, discussed in Chapter 1, points out the dangerous unintended consequences of a non-diverse workforce. It is important to note as well that STEM has been widened to STEAM and STREAM in recent years. STEAM adds an "A" for arts, as arts are considered to spark imagination and creativity in ways that naturally align with STEM learning. STREAM adds one more component, the "R" referencing literacy (reading and wRiting) as an essential part of a well-rounded curriculum for development, as writing has long been recognized as a skill critical to organized thinking.

In terms of access, the International Telecommunications Union (ITU) provides an annual snapshot of where the world stands regarding gender parity and, for example, Internet usage:

Globally, in 2020, 62 per cent of all men were using the Internet, compared with 57 per cent of all women.

Gender parity is deemed achieved when the gender parity score, defined as the female percentage divided by the male percentage, stands between 0.98 and 1.02.

In all regions, the gender Internet divide has been narrowing in recent years. Thus, the global gender parity score has improved from 0.89 in 2018 to 0.92 in 2020.

Much of the acceleration in Internet access is attributed to the Covid-19 pandemic and the consequent need to work from home and the desire for social contact during isolation.

Findings also show that globally, women value mobile phones and recognize them as a tool that enhances their lives, making them feel both more autonomous and connected, able to access new opportunities, and saving them time and money. In an ITU survey of mobile phone ownership in 60 countries within the 2018–2020 time frame, 30 countries achieved gender parity, and in ten more countries, more women than men own a mobile phone. Nevertheless, in 21 countries, women still lag behind men in mobile phone ownership, in some cases by a large margin.

As pointed out earlier, access to mobile phones and use of digital banking is an important part of both development and empowerment. The company Mobile Money, for example, began providing banking services via mobile phone in 2005 to the estimated two billion people[37] in developing countries who otherwise would have no access to banking services. The Covid-19 pandemic was an accelerator of no-contact electronic banking such that the value of transactions handled by Mobile Money has surpassed the trillion-dollar mark, or almost $2 million worth of transactions per minute.

Barriers to women using ICT fall into multiple categories: cultural, technical, affordability, coverage, and literacy. Culturally, in conservative societies ICT use can be associated with promiscuity, as a way for women to secretly and inappropriately interact with men. Further, women may feel uncomfortable or be unable to interact with a male agent to buy a mobile phone, putting the technology out of her reach.

Technically, women may feel intimidated by the idea of using technology simply because of inexperience, which makes user-friendly product design imperative. Because a significant number of women have less access to and control of resources than men, affordability can also be a problem. In some geographical regions as well, prices remain beyond that affordable by much of the population for both ICT equipment and access. Access also assumes that mobile coverage is available, which can still be a problem in rural areas. However, if women have access to a phone, there is a high probability of cell service available to use it.

Finally, text messaging and reading information provided on the Internet also assumes literacy, where women are again at a disadvantage because of their lower levels of education. There are ways to address all of these issues. Oftentimes, all that is needed is resources and ingenuity.

In Qatar, for example, Vodafone developed their Al Johara initiative in 2009 as a network of female sales agents sporting red signature suitcases to sell mobile phones to other women in the privacy of their homes. The women were all recruited from very connected, traditional communities so they would be seen as positive role models within their cultures. Recruitment, however, was not without challenges given that few women in Qatar work, and written permission from their male guardian was required before even an interview could be conducted. Once the "Joharas" began their businesses, the personal challenges they faced were also significant.

Despite their participation having been sanctioned by their male relatives and despite the adherence to Qatari societal norms, the Joharas still met extreme resistance from certain sections of the community. With the support of Vodafone, their families and each other, they persevered and achieved some excellent results.[38]

Similarly, in 2012, Iraq Asiacell, a Qtel Group Company, enrolled 1.2 million new female subscribers (a 40% increase) in one year by launching targeted services to meet conservative women's needs. The "Almas" line was developed to provide unique features considered appropriate for Iraqi women, including lower rates for extended calls during the day to talk with friends and family from their homes; free number blocking; and discounted health, cooking, and beauty content. Indonesia instituted a similar program managed by Indosat, another Qtel Group Company, and gained close to two million women subscribers in the first year through products targeted at stay-at-home moms. They too offered a reduced rate for calling friends and family during the day, as well as a family finder service to ensure moms could know their kids were safe.[39] So, while mobile phones are associated with women being promiscuous, they also allow women to keep in touch with their families, and allow them to use phone apps like HarrassMap to call for assistance in places where sexual violence is common.

Having the technical capability to communicate and doing it effectively is also an important consideration toward empowering woman. In areas where literacy rates among women are low, voicemail is often the preferred method of communication. Launched in 2010 as a collaborative effort between USAID, Johnson & Johnson, and the United Nations Foundation, the Mobile Alliance for Maternal Action (MAMA) program was a $10 million project to provide basic healthcare advice to pregnant women in rural areas of Africa and South Asia. The messages could be sent in either texts or as voicemails, because for women unable to read, voicemail was the better option. The messages cover what may seem simple things to those in developed countries, like good eating habits through pregnancy and the first year of a baby's life. The results were impressive.

Today, the MAMA message model is used by more than 160 organizations in more than 54 countries around the world. Studies have pointed to the effectiveness of the program, including research by the Health Alliance Foundation of Timor-Leste, which found that women who received MAMA messages were:

- Twice as likely to use a skilled birth attendant and have their baby in a health clinic
- Five times as likely to have a postpartum care visit within two days of delivery
- Five times as likely to have their newborn's health checked within two days of birth[40]

A South African study also found a significant increase in the average number of antenatal care visits attended and improved outcomes for pregnant women and newborns among women who had received MAMA messages. The same type of communication system had been used earlier to spread information about HIV/AIDS.

Conclusions

Women act as key agents of social stability. Development cannot occur when half the population – the half most likely to reinvest in the family – is left out. The nexus between development and security is clear. The nexus between development and gender empowerment is clear. Yet the nexus between women, development, and security too often remains unrecognized or ignored in the dispersal of development aid, the gathering of gender-specific development metrics, development program planning, and program implementation.

UN Sustainable Development Goals, the Human Security approach to development, and the Women, Peace, and Security framework are all intricately intertwined means to achieve primarily the same end: a world where gender parity increases the potential for a sustainable, stable future where more individual lives can prosper in positive peace. Their approaches differ somewhat, but that should not make them competitive. One of the bureaucratic/organizational challenges for the future will be to assure that they do not become so.

Notes

1 Duralia Oana, "Human Security and Human Development – Behavioristic Approach," *Studies in Business and Economics,* 2016, p. 28. ftp://ftp.repec.org/opt/ReDIF/RePEc/blg/journl/11203duralia.pdf

2 Oscar A. Gomez and Des Gasper, Human Security: A Thematic Guide Note for Regional and National Human Development Report Teams, p. 2.

3 Gomez and Gasper, p. 2.

4 Mac Darrow, "The Millennium Development Goals: Milestones or Millstones? Human Rights Priorities for the Post-2015 Development Agenda, *Yale Human Rights and Development Journal*, 15, no. 1 (2012), p. 57.

5 *The Millenium Development Goals Report*, 2014, p. 3. www.un.org/millenniumgoals/2014%20 MDG%20report/MDG%202014%20English%20web.pdf

6 Darrow, p. 58.

7 Jeffrey Sachs, "From Millenium Development Goals to Sustainable Development Goals," *Lancet*, June 9, 2012, p. 2206. http://peoplebuildingbettercities.org/wp-content/uploads/2013/04/MDGs-to-SDGs-Lancet.pdf

8 Darrow, pp. 59–60.

9 Jonathan Woetzel, Any Madgavkar, Kweilin Ellingrud, Eric Labaye, Sandrine Devillard, Eric Kutcher, James Manyika, Richard Dobbs, and Mekala Krishnan, *The Power of Parity*, September 2015. www.mckinsey.com/featured-insights/gender-equality

10 Monique Villa, "Women Own Less Than 20% of the World's Land. It's Time to Give Them Equal Property Rights," World Economic Forum, January 11, 2017. www.weforum.org/agenda/2017/01/women-own-less-than-20-of-the-worlds-land-its-time-to-give-them-equal-property-rights/

11 www.who.int/life-course/news/commentaries/2015-intl-womens-day/en/

12 Kim Piaget, "5 leaders on Why We Must Focus on Gender Parity in Times of Crisis," World Economic Forum, March 6, 2023. www.weforum.org/agenda/2023/03/international-women-s-day-5-leaders-on-why-we-must-focus-on-gender-parity-in-times-of-crisis/

13 UN Population Fund, cited by Nicholas Kristof, "They Call this Pro-Life?" *New York Times*, April 23, 2017, p. 11.

14 Feliz Sullivan, "US Ends Funding for UN Population Fund," *Time*, April 3, 2017. http://time.com/4724 227/unfpa-funding-trump-mexico-city-policy-abortion/

15 James Masters, "Abortion Funding: Netherlands Acts after Trump Reinstates 'Gag Rule'," CNN Politics, January 26, 2017. www.cnn.com/2017/01/25/politics/netherlands-trump-global-gag-rule/

16 www.sewa.org/About_Us.asp

17 www.sewa.org/Services_Bank.asp

18 Leslie Pruitt, "The Women, Peace and Security Agenda: Australia and the Agency of Girls," *Australian Journal of Political Science*, 49, no. 3 (2014), pp. 486–498.

19 Valerie M. Hudson and Patricia Leidl, quoting Ann Jones in *The Hillary Doctrine*, Columbia University Press, 2015, p. 200.

20 Hudson and Leidl, 2015. pp. 201–203.

21 Jeffrey Young, "Probe of Suspended USAID Contractor Deepens," *VOANews*, February 9, 2015. www.voanews.com/a/probe-of-suspended-usaid-contractor-deepens/2634844.html

22 Adam Weinstein, "The All-Time 10 Worst Military Contracting Boondoggles," *Mother Jones*, September 2, 2011. www.motherjones.com/politics/2011/09/contractor-waste-iraq-kbr/

23 US Justice Department Press Release, December 8, 2014. www.justice.gov/opa/pr/defense-contractor-pleads-guilty-major-fraud-provision-supplies-us-troops-afghanistan

24 Walter Kerr and Maya Guzdar, "USAID Needs to Rethink How It Spends Its Money," *Foreign Policy*, May 18, 2021. https://foreignpolicy.com/2021/05/18/usaid-biden-power-contracts-money-procurement/

25 Evaritus Mainseh, Schyler Heuer, Aprajita Kalra, and Quilin Zhang, "Grameen Bank: Taking Capitalism to the Poor," Columbia Business School, *Chazen Web Journal of International Business*, Spring 2004. www0.gsb.columbia.edu/mygsb/faculty/research/pubfiles/848/Grameen_Bank_v04.pdf

26 Milford Bateman, "The Rise and Fall of Muhammed Yunus and the Microcredit Model," International Development Studies, January 2014, p. 3. www.micro-fiancegateway.org/sites/default/files/mfg-en-paper-the-rise-and-fall-of-muhammad-yunus-and-the-microcredit-model-jan-2014.pdf

27 Parminder Bahra, "Micro-finance: Is Grameen Founder Muhammed Yunus a Bloodsucker of the Poor?" *Wall Street Journal*, December 6, 2010. https://blogs.wsj.com/source/2010/12/06/micro-fiance-is-gram een-founder-muhammad-yunus-a-bloodsucker-of-the-poor/

28 "Sacrificing Microcredit for Megaprofits," *New York Times*, January 14, 2011.

29 Abhijit Banerjee, Esther Duflo, Rachel Glennester, and Cynthia Kinnan, "The Miracle of Micro-finance? Evidence from a Randomized Evaluation," March 2014. http://economics.mit.edu/files/5993

30 Nuket Kardam and Fredric Kropp, "Women as Social Entrepreneurs: A Case Study," *Women in the Global Economy*, Global Education Research Report, 2013, p. 21.

31 https://livinggoods.org/what-we-do/

32 https://livinggoods.org/what-we-do/the-living-goods-system/

33 https://livinggoods.org/what-we-do/; Tom Murphy, "'Living Goods' Avon-Style Model Is More Than a Novelty, It Saves Lives," *Humansphere*, December 6, 2016. www.humanosphere.org/social-business/2016/12/living-goods-avon-style-model-novelty-saves-lives/; "An Entrepreneurial Model of Community Health Delivery in Uganda." www.poverty-action.org/study/entrepreneurial-model-community-health-delivery-uganda

34 http://wp.visionspring.org/making-markets-work/

35 Caroline Horekens, "Using Information Technology to Better Women's Lives," UN Women, May 4, 2015. http://asiapacific.unwomen.org/en/news-and-events/stories/2015/05/using-information-technol ogy-to-better-women-s-lives

36 www.stemwomen.com/women-in-stem-percentages-of-women-in-stem-statistics#:~:text=Over all%2C%20the%20percentage%20of%20female,with%20women%20making%20up%2024%25.

37 www.gsma.com/mobilefordevelopment/programmes/mobile-money

38 Vodafone, "Case Study: Vodafone Qatar's Al Johara: Empowerment through Entrepreneurship," 2013. www.gsma.com/mobilefordevelopment/wp-content/uploads/2013/01/mWomen_Case_Study_Vodaf one_Al_Johara_FINAL.pdf

39 Ann Mei Change, "Bridging the Technology Gender Divide," *Women in the Global Economy*, Global Education Research Report, 2013, p. 54.

40 Mobile Alliance for Maternal Action (MAMA), www.thriveagency.uk/work/mobile-alliance-for-maternal-action-mama/#:~:text=The%20Mobile%20Alliance%20for%20Maternal,to%20new%20 and%20expectant%20mothers.

Further reading

Armendariz, Beatriz, and Jonathan Morduch. *The Economics of Microfinance*, MIT Press, 2nd ed., 2010.

Beneria, Lourdes and Gunseli Berik, Maria Floro (eds.). *Gender, Development and Globalization: Economics as if All People Mattered*, Routledge, 2nd ed., 2015.

Bhalla, Surjit. *The New Wealth of Nations*, Simon and Schuster, 2018.

Eyben, Rosalind, and Laura Turquet, (eds.). *Feminists in Development Organizations*, Practical Action, 2014.

Moyo, Dambisa. *Dead Aid: Why Aid Is Not Working and How There Is a Better Way for Africa*, Farrar, Straus and Giroux, 2010.

Nussbaum, Martha. *Women and Human Development: The Capabilities Approach*, Cambridge University Press, 2001.

Sireau, Nick (ed.). *Microfranchising: How Social Entrepreneurs are Building a New Road to Development*, Routledge, 2011.

Tierney, Trish (ed.). *Women in the Economy: Leading Social Change*, Institute of International Education, 2013.

van Staveren, Irene, Diane Elson, Caren Grown, and Nilufer Cagatay (eds.). *The Feminist Economics of Trade*, Routledge, 2007.

Visvanathan, Nalini, Lynn Duggan, Nan Wiegersma, and Laurie Nisonoff (eds.), *The Women, Gender and Development Reader*, Zed, 2nd edition, 2011.

Yunus, Mohammed. *Creating a World Without Poverty: Social Business and the Future of Capitalism*, PublicAffairs, reprint, 2009.

7   Gender, the environment, and climate change

Climate stability

Assumptions regarding a stable climate are built into every aspect of daily life. That needs to be said again. Assumptions regarding a stable climate – the average state of the weather – are built into every aspect of daily life. Farmers plant crops according to anticipated weather conditions. If those conditions radically change or become unpredictable, food security will be affected. Housing is the primary determinant of people's financial security and an anticipated rise in weather-related natural disasters will impact housing. In 2020, two hurricanes hit southwest Louisiana in the United States within a month of each other, largely affecting homes of working-class residents. Some homes survived the high winds of the first hurricane only to be flooded during the second, and some homes in rural areas were simply destroyed outright. Forty percent of the global population live with 100 kilometers (about 62 miles) of the coast and homes built on coastlines are progressively endangered by rising sea levels. Increasingly common heatwaves have been shown to have multiple negative effects on mental health, including heightened reports of depression and anxiety, and suicide attempts. The list of anticipated and multifaceted problems related to climate change is extensive and a stable climate can no longer be assumed.

In fact, just the opposite – climate instability – must be assumed. Sea levels are rising at a rate of 3.77 mm annually. Earth's temperature has risen an average of 0.14 Fahrenheit (0.08 Celsius) per decade since 1880, or about 2 degrees F total. The rate of warming has increased since 1981 to a rate of .31 degrees Fahrenheit (0.18 degrees C) per decade. Semi-arid lands are being converted to deserts. Extreme heat events are on the rise. From June to August 2022, Europe was affected by persistent heatwaves, resulting in over 20,000 heat-related deaths. The highest temperature recorded was 116.6 degrees Fahrenheit (47.0 degrees Celcius) in Pinhão, Portugal, on July 14.

In areas where temperatures are rising and rainfall patterns changing, there will be increases in tropical diseases including malaria, dengue, West Nile virus, and Lyme disease carried by mosquitos and other insects as they are able to expand their habitats. Malaria is considered the deadliest mosquito-borne parasitic disease, killing over a half million people annually and afflicting some one billion people in countries throughout Africa, Asia, and Latin America. Data indicates that malaria-carrying mosquitoes are already adapting to traditionally temperate regions. While both a malaria and a dengue vaccine are available, they are not universally available to everyone. Changing African temperatures and rainfall could increase yellow fever deaths by up to 25% by 2050.

Climate change presents a security risk to individuals, communities, and nations that nations across the globe are taking very seriously. US defense secretary Lloyd Austin has called climate change an "existential threat," a term reserved for threats that can fundamentally disrupt the

DOI: 10.4324/9781003413417-8

American way of life, like nuclear weapons. The US military has released a Climate Adaption Plan (2021), a Climate Risk Analysis (2021), multiple climate strategies, and the 2022 National Defense Strategy, which calls climate change a "destabilizing and potentially catastrophic transboundary challenge." Speaking at the United Nations in 2022, the French delegate said, "the fight against climate change is also a fight for international peace and security." Australian researchers indicate that

climate change will likely undermine Australia's national security by disrupting critical infrastructure, by challenging the capacity of the defence force, by increasing the risk of domestic political instability in Australia's immediate region, by reducing the capabilities of partner countries in the Asia-Pacific region, and by interrupting important supply chains.[1]

The security implications of climate change are reflected in many ways, including civil unrest. American sociologist James Davies introduced the J-curve political/economic hypothesis in the 1960s. It states that when periods of economic growth and improvement in people's lives are followed by a sharp economic decline, social and political unrest can occur. That is, people develop rising expectations when improvements to their life are sustained for prolonged periods, and when a gap develops between their expectations and reality, that gap can reach an unacceptable level that creates unrest. Political scientist Ted Gurr expanded the J-curve premise in the 1970s, suggesting that when there is too much deviation between what individuals have and what they think they should have, there is a risk of violence, even of revolution. When livelihoods are lost, including through climate-related events, a petri dish is created for risky behavior, criminal activity, violence, and extremism.

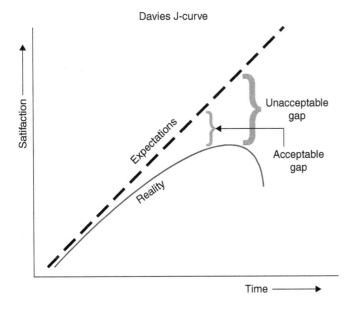

Figure 7.1 J-curve/relative deprivation.

Source: Adapted from MBN News

Climate change has the potential to create chaos in many different ways, largely by aggravating already existing challenges, many of them gendered. Yet only 17 out of 80 states mention climate change in their WPS National Action Plans, and only Finland, Ireland, and the United States specifically recognize the imperative to address climate change, in relation to the WPS "prevention" pillar. Only 5 of 75 UN Member states recognized gender as an important consideration in a 2019 open microphone event on the impacts of climate-related disasters on international peace and security. The nexus between climate, gender, and security is real but still largely unseen.

Chaos hits women first, and hardest, and climate change will result in chaos in many ways and in many areas of the world. Consequently, the WPS imperative to include more women at all levels of decision-making and to assure that gendered mitigation policies and plans are developed and implemented becomes vital. Women know things. Women get things done. If carefully managed, change consequent to climate change offers the potential to open up new spaces for women in economic activity, decision-making, and leadership. When gendered dynamics are ignored, however, new risks and vulnerabilities can be created for men and women by climate change. As USAID administrator Samantha Power said in 2022, "climate change is sexist." The response to climate change shouldn't be.

Climate change as a threat multiplier

The strong nexus between gender, climate, and security results in both challenges and opportunities. In many regions of the world, women's development gains, which contribute to community and national gains and hence political stability, are threatened by severe droughts and rising temperatures, leading to food insecurity and loss of livelihoods. Agriculture provides more jobs for women and girls in low- and lower-middle-income countries than any other employment sector.

Loss of livelihood in association with climate events can be catastrophic for both men and women. When events like droughts occur, pastoralist migration patterns can shift, resulting in families being forced to split apart, increasing household responsibilities for women and exposing men to insecure routes of travel. Girls may be forced to leave school to help their mothers with augmented burdens. Women and girls may be again pushed to pursue riskier strategies of survival, as may men in similar situations. "The loss of livelihood due to environmental change, regardless of whether it is caused mainly by global warming or more by governance, is often the starting point of resource-related conflicts on the micro and mesa levels."[2] Weak or poor governance allows hardships to fester and go unaddressed. In fragile or conflict settings, violence, limited governance, and political instability can leave communities unable to cope with a changing climate, exacerbating already existing internal and external tensions. Competition for resources can then lead to violence. The conflict in Syria is an example of a country where climate change combined with poor governance resulted in a food shortage, which then contributed to uprisings, violence, and forced migration.[3]

In some parts of the Sahal region of Africa, the traditional livelihoods of both farmers and herders have been negatively affected by the rapid decrease in both fertile land and reliable water supplies due to extended drought periods, unpredictable rainfall, poor agricultural policies and practices, and violent conflict in neighboring regions. Low levels of education among both populations limit the potential to develop alternative income sources, particularly for marginalized groups. "Together, these stress factors have spurred competition over resources in the area, undermined trust, created new patterns of migration, and provoked an increase in localized violent conflict between the different livelihood groups."[4] Problems are most acute near border areas where the vulnerability of the populations is heightened by distance from state services and governance.

Regarding migration, it has been estimated that there are 100 million displaced people globally, meaning 1.2% of the global population are living at a location they did not want or intend to be. While some people have migrated due to conflict, many others relocate due to changes in climate. It is estimated that there are some 21.5 million climate migrants each year, with up to 700 million predicted by 2050. Climate migration is gendered: women and girls initially tend to migrate locally, while men and boys venture farther looking for work. That element of climate migration alone presents multiple further considerations. When men leave their homes to seek work, women often become more vulnerable. They are left to provide for the family, with fewer options and opportunities than men, if only because of cultural dictates regarding what is allowed and acceptable for women.

What women are "allowed" regarding migration has historical roots. In Tanzania, for example, male migrants traditionally left their villages seeking work in urban areas or colonial plantations. However, female migration was discouraged through not just practices but also colonial policies. In some cases, for example, women were required to be in possession of a valid marriage certificate, a rarity in colonial days, in order to accompany a male contract laborer to his place of employment.

In Tanzanian towns, single females were rounded up and deported to their home areas since they were considered "undesirable." Another reason behind restricted female migration was emphasis on the need for them to keep their place in society. Women were expected to produce on the farm rather than being "parasitic" and a "liability" in urban areas.[5]

The idea that women need to stay close to home took root, especially in rural and agricultural communities.

It is often women from the poorest communities who depend on natural resources for the livelihoods that have the least capacity to respond well to climate events, especially climate shocks like droughts, landslides, floods, and hurricanes. During extreme events, poor women are 14 times more likely to die than men due to factors including being responsible for staying at home, having little or no voice in family decision-making, and lacking education or access to information. When cyclone Gorky hit Bangladesh in 1991, 90% of the fatalities were women, their deaths attributed to factors including, as is the case with most women in Bangladesh, being unable to swim, wearing restrictive clothing, having responsibilities for children, and knowing that they feared and faced increased risk of sexual and physical abuse outside of their homes.[6] These gendered factors must be considered in future prevention, preparedness, and relief and recovery efforts.

Acknowledging challenges specific to women is not to say that men are not vulnerable to environmental stress, but only that women's vulnerability is heightened due to deeply rooted imbalanced power relations and gender roles. For example, the Upper Indus Basin of India and Pakistan is a region particularly affected by climate change due to fluctuations in the snowmelts that feed the Indus River and unpredictable precipitation. However, only men are allowed to migrate as an adaptation strategy, leaving the women to care for the household and dependent on also unpredictable natural resources and agricultural work.

If people decide they must leave their local areas due to climate-related issues, they face many of the same kinds of challenges that are experienced through conflict-based migration. Pre-existing divides and biases can be exposed and deepened through migration. Discrimination can surface toward immigrants based on a variety of in-group and out-group markers: race, ethnicity, religion, social and economic status, education, ability, and place of origin, origin reflecting a combination of several other markers.

For example, Ukrainian refugees, mostly Christians and women, due to Ukrainian conscription laws, are benefiting from what some analysts have called unprecedented kindnesses from nearby countries. A Temporary Protection Directive from the EU allows Ukrainian refuges to reside, seek employment, and attend school in EU countries for three years, without official asylum approval. Even countries that had exhibited strong anti-immigrant policies previously, have allowed Ukrainian refugees entry without papers. "In 2016, Hungarian leader Viktor Orbán described immigration as a 'poison,' yet he recently exclaimed that Ukrainians are 'welcomed by friends in Hungary.'"[7]

In contrast, in 2015 when the Syrian refugee crisis erupted, sending floods of, mostly Muslim, refugees to Europe, the EU refused to activate the Temporary Protective Directive, incentivized other countries to impede the flow of refugees, and let human rights violations against asylum seekers by border guards go unpunished.

Non-Ukrainian refuges have been physically assaulted by Polish and Belarussian patrolmen; left to freeze in the winter; detained in unhygienic camps in Greece; "trapped in limbo" between Poland and Belarus; assaulted with tear gas and water cannons near the Greece-Turkey border; and bombarded with xenophobic and anti-migrant rhetoric, especially in Poland, Hungary and Slovakia. Former German Chancellor Angela Merkel – widely hailed as a champion of refugee rights, funded Turkey's refugee camps so that President Erdoğan would hinder the passage of refugees into Greece, an EU member. Meanwhile, Poland erected a border fence, started to build a wall, passed legislation to make entry more difficult, and only accepted about 5.7 percent of asylum applications in 2020. As more refugees entered Europe, detention increased, and former European Council President Donald Tusk even called for 18-month detention camps.[8]

Women comprise about half of the Syrian refugee population.

The United Nations High Commissioner for Refugees (UNHCR) case of Ioane Teitiota in January 2020 was the first of its kind in recognizing the right to claim refugee status due to the climate crisis (though his particular application for asylum in New Zealand from Kiribati was denied). Climate refugees, just as conflict refugees, are often desperate and subsequently engage in risky behavior with often unscrupulous individuals including migrant smugglers, in an attempt to escape to safer conditions. This, in turn, makes them vulnerable to exploitation through trafficking in persons (TiP) and other forms of exploitation and abuse such as sexual exploitation, forced labor, forced marriage, and organ removal. Whether through sudden-onset disasters that require immediate evacuation or slow-onset circumstances where migration is an adaptation strategy, there are individuals waiting to take advantage of people's desperation.

Traffickers are likely to recruit in areas afflicted by climate change, in climate migrant camps, and also at migrant destinations like urban slums. Increased desperation perpetrated through either crisis situations or after long bouts of crop failures, water shortages, or other challenges can push affected populations into the hands of criminal actors and even into colluding with them: men selling their wives or other female relatives; parents selling their children; and women being forced into prostitution or transactional sexual relations to obtain food for themselves and her children in order to cope with the losses associated with a changing climate.

The Asia-Pacific region is home to over 4.2 billion people, making it the world's most populous region. There is also a high rate of regional human mobility as internal migration is considered a "mixed flow" of migrants from different backgrounds moving for different reasons, including seeking economic opportunity, climate refugees, conflict refugees, and victims of human trafficking. Much of the regional migration is from rural to urban settings. TiP routes are basically the same, facilitated by organized criminal groups or networks mainly to India, Malaysia, and Thailand.

> Large numbers of victims of trafficking are exploited in brick kilns, fishing boats, manufacturing and the sex sector, in domestic work, as well as on construction sites. In parallel with this trend of human trafficking, the region faces extreme vulnerability to climate change. Asia-Pacific's diverse topography, ranging from landlocked mountainous countries to low lying atolls, increases exposure to a range of natural disasters.[9]

While most refugees like to think they will be returning home, quickly or eventually, the reality is that protracted displacement is increasingly common, forcing displaced communities to live in camps, where residents are also vulnerable to the promises made by traffickers.

Several policy instruments have been developed and adopted to address various issues connected to the significant human mobility that is occurring and will only increase due to climate change. These include: the Kampala Declaration of Refugees, Returnees and Internally Displaced Persons in Africa; the Global Protection Cluster; the Platform for Disaster for Disaster Displacement; the Global Compact on Migration; the Global Compact on Migration; and the Global Compact on Refugees. These instruments are intended to facilitate cooperation among countries and, as stated in the Kampala Declaration, "to address the plight as well as to find durable solutions for refugees." Implementation, however, has been haphazard and lacks full commitment from signatories. Additionally, gender considerations and concerns of especially vulnerable individuals must be integrated into these initiatives to assure that the needs of men, women, boys, and girls be met, rather than exacerbating existing inequalities or creating new ones.

Climate activism

Time magazine's 2019 Person of the Year, Greta Thunberg from Sweden, is perhaps the most well known of a troupe of women climate activists, many not even or just barely out of their teens. Thunberg stunned the world with the words of her 2019 speech at the United Nations.

> You have stolen my dream and my childhood with your empty words. And yet I'm one of the lucky ones. People are suffering. People are dying. Entire ecosystems are collapsing. We are in the beginning of a mass extinction, and all you can talk about is money and fairy tales of eternal economic growth. How dare you!

Hilda Heine, former president of the Marshall Islands, has taken the global stage to talk about the precarious situation in her country, which she calls "the front line" of climate change. Rising sea levels, salt water seeping into fresh water lands, and drought make the country's future precarious. Others include Hindou Oumarou Ibrahim in Chad who is trying to bridge the gap between what's talked about in international forums and the reality on the ground, demonstrating the importance of local knowledge in addressing climate change issues. Research scientist and science writer Kate Marvel uses storytelling on social media to cut through misinformation that has been spewed for years and that kept climate change from being recognized as "real" for too long. Sunita Narain is trying to raise the voices of those in the Global South from India. They are making a difference.

Young climate activists were at World Economic Forum annual meeting at Davos in full force in 2020, including Vanessa Nakate from Uganda, Luisa Neubauer from Germany, Greta Thunberg and Isabelle Axelsson from Sweden, and Loukina Tille from Switzerland. They all appeared together at a joint press conference and a photo was taken. Yet when the Associated Press news service ran its photo, Nakate was cropped out. It was, as she said, as though she wasn't there. Climate change is a global issue, not a first-world issue, and solutions will require inclusive diversity. Since Nakate's experience in 2020, there has been considerable attention paid to what has been described as a culture of silencing marginalized communities, often communities disproportionately affected by the climate crisis. Africa contributes only 4% of the global greenhouse gas emissions but is taking the brunt of a far higher proportion of climate change effects. Every voice is needed and the on-the-ground expertise of local communities familiar with culture, customs and conditions will be critical.

It is increasing recognized too that when environmental and climate change activists speak out, they put themselves at risk. In 2018, 77% of human rights defenders whose murders were recorded (more likely went unrecorded) were defending land, Indigenous peoples', and/or environmental rights. Many more have been silenced through intimidation, arrests, violent attacks, and lawsuits. In 2021, alone, some 200 environmental activists were killed, including 54 in Mexico, the most dangerous country for activists, followed by Colombia with 33 murders and Brazil with 26 murders. In Mexico and Colombia, mining rights were being challenged by activists, while in Brazil clashes focused on land and resources within Brazil's Amazon, where most of the murders took place. According to a report by Global Witness, "With powerful agricultural interests at the heart of Brazil's export-focused economy, it is the setting for a battle over land and resources that has intensified following the election of Brazil's far-right president, Jair Bolsonaro, in 2018."[10] Indigenous rights commonly suffer under populist far-right governments.

While the majority of recorded murders are of men, women activists face specific and unique risks, especially in patriarchal societies. In those societies, women are often barred from owning land, from natural resource governance, and from decision-making generally. So, speaking out is a risk in itself, and the legitimacy of their voices is challenged.[11] Women activists have been subject to smear campaigns, sexual violence, rape, and murder especially in the context of standing up to extractive industries on Indigenous lands. Thunberg has been targeted with a mis/disinformation campaign that suggests she is mentally ill, linked to the Antifa movement, linked to George Soros, and part of a climate-industrial complex, all to discredit her.

The 2016 murder of Indigenous environmental activist Berta Cáceres, known as the "guardian of the rivers" in Honduras, sparked international attention. So too did the April 2021 murder of the Indigenous governor in southwest Colombia, Sandra Liliana Peña Chocué. She had fought for the eradication of coca crops in Caldono before being killed near her home by armed men. Too often, though, attacks against environmentalists, men and women, are ignored. In Mexico, an investigation by federal officials concluded that local authorities were likely involved in 40% of environmental activist killings. Only 2 out of 45 cases have resulted in a suspect being charged.[12] In many instances, attacks take place in rural, isolated areas far from the reach of government. All this considered, individuals who are threatened or attacked frequently choose not to report it.

Planning ahead

Plans for a future where climate instability is a reality must include sustainability and resilience as key components. Consequently, best solutions to challenges will touch on as many of the UN SDGs as possible. For example, empowering women and providing clean, sustainable energy through programs such as delivered by Solar Sisters, discussed in the previous chapter, relates to at least nine SDGs (named here according to their UN numeric): 1) No poverty, 3) Good health and well-being, 4) Quality education, 5) Gender equality, 7) Affordable and clean energy, 8) Decent work and economic growth, 10) Reduced inequalities 11) Sustainable cities and communities, and 13) Climate action. Integrated action on gender dimensions of climate-related security risks is required for resilience and sustainability. The future of food, SDG 2 (End hunger), exemplifies the need for new, holistic and sometimes radical thinking given the complexity of the interrelated challenges climate change presents.

According to Abraham Maslow's hierarchy of needs, food and water are strong motivators of human action, given they are physiologically necessary for survival. Consequently, an argument can be made that all wars are about food and water, whether to gain direct access or to obtain or increase financial resources to buy food and water. The importance of land to grow food and access to water is evidenced by companies in countries with little or no arable like Saudi Arabia leasing some 14,000 acres of land in the Western United States in 2014. A Saudi company, Fondomonte, then began growing thousands of acres of alfalfa crops to ship back to Saudi Arabia to feed their cattle. It only took a few years before the state of Arizona and the Saudi company were at odds over the water being used to irrigate the alfalfa crops, at the expense of Arizona residents who found wells running dry. Water and food are precious commodities now and will be even more so in the future, but food production doesn't come without a tax on the environment.

Approximately 34%, or one-third, of global greenhouse gas emissions come from food production. That percentage will rise to almost 75% in the next decades. Seventy-one percent of food emissions come from agriculture and associated land-use activities, with the remainder coming from retail, transport, consumption, fuel production, waste management, industrial processes, and packaging. People must eat, but eating habits must change. Those changes fall into many categories, including creating less waste and considering what we eat.

In 2023, enough food is produced to feed the entire global population of eight million people. In fact, the world's farmers grow enough food to feed to ten billion people, the expected global population expected by 2050. And yet, almost 800 million people are hungry, 345 million are facing severe hunger, 43 million people in 51 countries are on the brink of famine, and at least 850,000 people are already facing catastrophic levels of hunger. Conflict, economic failure, political instability, and weather conditions contribute to food distribution problems. Among the countries where hunger is most prevalent, over 30 million children are severely hungry, meaning they have or will suffer from recent and life-threatening weight loss due to a lack of nourishment.

Globally, 30–40% of all food is wasted. That costs the global economy hundreds of billions of dollars every year, depletes resources, and food waste produces an estimated 9% of global food system greenhouse gas emissions. In developing countries, more than 40% of the food lost occurs at post-harvest and processing levels and is most often because of lack of infrastructure. Food producers, wholesalers, and retailers often cannot afford the equipment or the energy costs of drying, adequate storage or refrigerated storage, and transportation. Subsequently, it rots before it can be consumed. India, for example loses 30–40% of its produce due to lack of cold storage facilities. Data shows that China and India are responsible for more household food waste than any other country, at some 92 million and 69 million metric tons annually, respectively, primarily due to their large populations.[13]

In more developed countries, the relatively lower cost of food reduces the incentive to prevent waste and so more than 40% of food lost occurs at retail and consumer levels. In the United States, for example, studies suggest that household food waste ranges between 20% and 50%

of what is purchased, with even the least wasteful household wasting about 9% of the food it acquires.[14] Household food waste is lower among EU countries, estimated at about 20%, with variation among countries. Nevertheless, that still means EU countries waste more food than they import, even though the EU adopted its Farm to Fork strategy as part of the European Green Deal approved in 2020, aimed at making the EU climate neutral in 2050. Culture makes a big difference in shopping habits between the United States and Europe.

Americans tend to shop for cost and time effectiveness, favoring once-a-week grocery shopping and buying bulk, wholesale items with long shelf lives, about 30% of which ends up in landfills. Given busy schedules, cravings, and people's willingness to prepare meals changing daily, people don't use everything they buy. Larger households waste less due to more people being available to eat food items that come in larger quantities, like a head of cauliflower or a turkey. Researchers have also found less waste in households with higher levels of food insecurity, those far from main grocery stores, and in households in which members shopped from shopping lists. Americans are prone to impulse shopping and bulk buying.

Europeans, on the other hand, tend to make multiple trips to the store each week. They buy only what they need for that day's meals and favor small markets for the high quality of products they offer. Small markets do not sell bulk goods.

There is also a significant difference in expected portion sizes between Americans and Europeans, with American portions substantially larger. Even in terms of drinks, US consumers expect quantity. For example, Coke cans are normally 12 ounces, or 355 ml, in the United States, while in Europe they are 330 ml (a 7-Eleven Big Gulp in the United States can be 50 ounces, or 1,478 ml). Americans also lead the world in annual meat consumption per capita, followed by Australia, Argentina, Israel, Brazil, New Zealand, Chile, and Canada. Old habits will be hard to change.

About 36% of food grown is fed to animals. The three biggest greenhouse gas emitters in food production are from meat, dairy, and rice: cows and other animals like goats and sheep emit methane as part of their digestive process, and it is common practice to flood rice paddies during growth, which generates methane-emitting bacteria. The FAO estimates that animal protein consumption will increase by 52% between 2007 and 2030. The World Resources Institute also predicts a 60% gap between protein supply and demand by 2050. Increasing the volume and sale of meat and dairy alternatives is necessary for a sustainable protein supply chain. Thinking differently about what is fed to animals, and humans, is part of many future strategies.

For example, the FAO has been conducting research pertaining to edible insects since 2003, concluding that they can diversify diets, improve livelihoods, contribute to food and nutrition security, and have a smaller ecological footprint compared to other sources of protein.

> Edible insects contain high quality protein, vitamins and amino acids for humans. Insects have a high food conversion rate, e.g. crickets need six times less feed than cattle, four times less than sheep, and twice less than pigs and broiler chickens to produce the same amount of protein. Besides, they emit less greenhouse gases and ammonia than conventional livestock. Insects can be grown on organic waste. Therefore, insects are a potential source for conventional production (mini-livestock) of protein, either for direct human consumption, or indirectly in recomposed foods (with extracted protein from insects); and as a protein source into feedstock mixtures.[15]

The idea is to feed animals protein such as mealworms, thus reducing the amount of feed that needs to be raised. Feeding insects to animals is a more readily accepted idea than growing insects for human consumption, but that is being considered too. While initial reactions might be skeptical (or squeamish) regarding edible insects for humans (in a totally unrecognizable form), cricket flour is commonly used as a protein additive in items like baked goods and protein bars.

Insect farming is already said to be growing at unprecedented rates, though food experts are continuing their call for more. Estimates are that between 1 trillion and 1.2 trillion insects are raised on farms each year, mostly through start-up companies. A French company, Ÿnsect, is building a factory in Amiens, France, that is estimated to be able to produce 200,000 metric tons of insect-based products annually, mainly for pet and animal food. Ÿnsect announced plans in 2022 to expand its insect farm projects to Mexico and the United States. As of 2023, there are 71 insect farming start-ups in the United States alone. In 2022, a Dutch firm, Insect Engineers, announced it was opening the first insect farming school. The intent is to help start-up companies take their processes to an industrial scale.

Insect farming could also be a way to empower women. Several insect farming companies are already in existence in East Africa, specifically Kenya, Tanzania, and Uganda, most of them still microenterprises. In support of the potential seen in insect farming, a number of government agencies, community-based organizations, private organizations, and universities have trained over 57,000 beneficiaries of the training. Among individuals recruited to work on insect farms, over 70% are women. Researchers postulate that "based on the immense potential of BSF larvae […] the various products obtained thereof can directly meet eight (1, 2, 3, 6, 7, 8, 9, and 12) out of the seventeen United Nations Sustainable Development Goals and indirectly promote the rest in Africa."[16]

There has also been considerable interest and activity regarding insect farming in the Asia-Pacific region, which will be home to 4.5 billion people by 2030. Arable land and fresh water for irrigation will be in short supply in many areas. In some countries, arable land is actually decreasing due to unsustainable agricultural practices that have depleted soil nutrients and caused erosion. Public and private ventures in Singapore and Thailand have been actively looking for ways to improve the protein supply chain. One venture, for example, has focused on using insects to quickly break down food waste to speed up the composting process. According to the founder of the Southeast Asia-based company called Nutrition Technologies, "My vision has always been to produce a high-quality insect protein powder that can reduce the pressure on wild fisheries, and minimize the impact of industrial fleets on traditional fishing communities."[17]

Other companies are working on projects to introduce insects directly into the diets of consumers. Insect-based products are already available and, in many cases, popular in countries including Thailand, Cambodia, and Laos as street food. Switzerland approved mealworms, crickets, and grasshoppers as food items in 2017, and at least one grocery chain began selling insect-based products in their stores. In 2021, the EU joined Switzerland in encouraging more human consumption of insect-based products, approving mealworms, migratory locusts, crickets, and lesser mealworms for human consumption. It is estimated that 80% of global countries are already consuming insects as part of their diet. Whether in Africa, Asia, or elsewhere, investment is needed to move beyond start-ups in what promises to be a lucrative new field. As of 2023, only 2% of global investment goes to women. Increased funding for women to work on projects like insect farming would serve multiple SDG goals.

Insect farming is not the only change needed and that can be expected in the global food chain reflective of climate change issues, but it is indicative of the scale and type of change that can be anticipated. The dual goals of healthy people and a healthy planet can only be achieved by through circular production methods, where waste does not exist, but is instead feedstock for another cycle.

Recycling

A circular economy is a systems solution framework to address global challenges like climate change, biodiversity loss, waste, and pollution based on three principles: eliminate waste and pollution, circulate products and materials (at their highest value), and regenerate nature. "It is underpinned by a transition to renewable energy and materials. A circular economy decouples economic activity from the consumption of finite resources. It is a resilient system that is good for business, people and the environment."[18] Waste recycling is a critical part of a circular economy needed for sustainability.

Japan has been recycling paper since the ninth century. The ancient Japanese began recycling paper almost as soon as they learned to produce it. In fact, recycled paper is treated as more precious than new paper, with it often used for paintings and poetry.

World War II brought on a massive effort to recycle tin, steel, paper, rubber, and more in the United States. It was bolstered by a national campaign including posters and newsreels that explained what was needed and why. Americans got on board to support the war effort, but the idea that recycling needed to happen faded when the war ended. Recycling didn't begin to become mainstream in the United States until the 1970s, coinciding with the first Earth Day being celebrated in 1970.

Fast-forward to 2023. The United Nations Environment Program simply states "Our planet is choking on plastic." Between 1970 and 1990 both plastic production and plastic waste generation more than tripled from past years. With the turn of the millennium, the plastic waste generated, increased more in a single decade than it had it the previous 40 years. As of 2023, approximately 400 million tons of plastic waste is generated every year. Cigarette butt filters containing tiny plastic fibers are the most common type of plastic waste found in the environment, followed by food wrappers, plastic bottles, plastic bottle caps, plastic grocery bags, and plastic straws and stirrers. It is estimated that some 36% of all plastics produced are used in single-use plastic products for food and beverages, and about 85% of that ends up in landfills or as unregulated waste. Ninety-eight percent of that single-use packaging is made from fossil fuel, with an associated level of greenhouse gas emissions associated with fossil fuel-based plastics estimated at 19% of the global carbon budget by 2040. Less than 10% of the over seven billion tons of plastic waste generated globally to date has been recycled and "the estimated annual loss in the value of plastic packaging waste during sorting and processing alone is US $80–120 billion."[19] For recycling to have a positive long-term effect on sustainability, though, it must be done properly.

The benefits of recycling paper are several if the process is powered by clean energy. According to the US Environmental Protection Agency, recycling reduces greenhouse gas emissions by avoiding methane emission, saves 3.3 cubic yards of landfill space for every ton of paper recycled, reduces water and energy consumption, and extends the fiber supply and adds to carbon sequestration. When trees are harvested for making paper, carbon is released in the form of carbon dioxide. "When the rate of carbon absorption exceeds the rate of release, carbon is said to be 'sequestered.' This carbon sequestration reduces greenhouse gas concentrations by removing carbon dioxide from the atmosphere."[20] Recent research has posited that the benefits of recycling paper can be negated in some instances if the energy used in the recycling process actually adds to the emissions problem more than new production would have,[21] thereby requiring consideration in circular economy efforts and illustrating the complexity of sustainability efforts.

Women are natural partners in recycling efforts. Research has shown that compared to men, women litter less, recycle more, and leave a smaller overall carbon footprint. The reasons for that gendered behavior have been thought related to women's greater sense of altruism and care for their communities. Research involving more than 2,000 Chinese and American participants has discovered another reason as well:

> We showed that there is a psychological link between eco-friendliness and perceptions of femininity. Due to this "green-feminine stereotype," both men and women judged eco-friendly products, behaviors, and consumers as more feminine than their non-green counterparts [...] Men may eschew green products and behaviors to avoid feeling feminine [...] Ironically, although men are often considered to be less sensitive than women, they seem to be particularly sensitive when it comes to perceptions of their gender identity.[22]

Gender stereotyping is not just bad for individuals, their communities, and national security, but for the planet as well.

In a number of countries, women are leading figures in recycling efforts. The UNDP created a program in Jordan, funded by the government of Canada, that employs 60 women at a recycling center. Twenty women stay at the center sorting and crushing sometimes up to four tons of waste every day, while the other 40 work in town encouraging businesses and households to recycle. Another UN program in South Africa called All Women Recycling, is training women to create new products from plastic bottles and creating local and global awareness about the need to recycle. Women in countries from South Africa to Thailand, Belgium to Serbia, Kenya to the Netherlands are involved in recycling, in many cases trying to start their own businesses. Again, however, more investment in women is needed.

Conclusion

As the grip of climate change gets tighter, inclusive diversity as called for in the WPS framework, will only increase in importance toward finding viable solutions to the problems created and exacerbated by the effects. It is well known and accepted that climate change is a threat multiplier, but far more gender-disaggregated data is needed to maximize planning efforts toward minimizing those effects. Data already shows that women will likely be hit hardest by climate instability, but women's knowledge of on-the-ground conditions, of community cultures, and their altruism will make them invaluable partners in abating the effects of climate instability. Bridging the data gap allows for a better situational awareness, and as pointed out prior, before an effective strategy can be developed to achieve a goal, as complete a picture of the ground situation as possible is necessary.

Notes

1 Tobias Ide, "Climate Change and Australia's National Security," *Australian Journal of International Affairs*, January 25, 2023, p. 26.
2 Christiane Fröhlich and Giovanna Gioli, "Gender, Conflict and Global Environment Change," *Peace Review*, 27, no. 2 (2015), p. 137.
3 Marwa. Daoudy, *The Origins of the Syrian Crisis*, Cambridge University Press, 2020.
4 "Gender, Climate and Security: Sustaining Inclusive Peace on the Frontlines of Climate Change," United Nations Report, 2020. p. 18.
5 Esther Dungumaro, "Consequences of Female Migration in Tanzania," *African Review of Economic and Finance*, December 2013, p. 46.
6 "3 Ways in Which Gender Inequality Interlinks with Climate Migration," Environmental Migration Portal, https://environmentalmigration.iom.int/blogs/3-ways-which-gender-equality-interlinks-climate-migration-adaptation-strategy-exploring-links-between-migration-environment-and-sdg-5

7 Addie Esposito, "The Limitations of Humanity: Differential Refugee Treatment in the EU," *Harvard International Review*, September 14, 2022. https://hir.harvard.edu/the-limitations-of-humanity-differential-refugee-treatment-in-the-eu/

8 Esposito, 2022.

9 *The Climate Change-Human Trafficking Nexus,* International Migration Organization, p. 5

10 "More Than 1700 Land Activists Murdered the Last Decade," *Al Jazeera*, September 9, 2022. www.aljazeera.com/news/2022/9/29/over-1700-environmental-activists-killed-in-past-decade-report

11 "Gender, Climate and Security: Sustaining Inclusive Peace on the Frontlines of Climate Change," United Nations Report, 2020, p. 16.

12 *Al Jazeera*, 2022.

13 Ian Tiseo, "Annual Food Waste by Select Country Worldwide," Statista, February 6, 2023. www.statista.com/statistics/933083/food-waste-of-selected-countries/

14 "How Much Food Does the Average US Household Waste?" *Medical News Today*, www.medicalnewstoday.com/articles/study-suggests-u-s-households-waste-nearly-a-third-of-the-food-they-acquire

15 "Insects for Food and Feed," Food and Agriculture Organization, www.fao.org/edible-insects/en/

16 Chrysantus Tanga et al., "Edible Insect Farming as an Emerging and Profitable Enterprise in East Africa," *Current Opinion in Insect Science*, December 2021, p. 67.

17 Joe Gan, "Why Is Insect-Based Protein Sprouting Wings in Asia," August 20, 2019. https://agfundernews.com/update-why-is-insect-based-protein-sprouting-wings-in-asia

18 "What Is a Circular Economy?" Ellen MacArthur Foundation. https://ellenmacarthurfoundation.org/topics/circular-economy-introduction/overview

19 Our Planet is Choking, UNEP, www.unep.org/interactives/beat-plastic-pollution/?gclid=Cj0KCQjw_r6hBhDdARIsAMIDhV9g7TqkaYlaeAk5RM9GOSrQCXSdUy18Gj8g5E9KWpBCEc9uR1pwNzIaApOMEALw_wcB

20 US Environmental Protection Agency. https://archive.epa.gov/wastes/conserve/materials/paper/web/html/index-2.html

21 Stijn van Ewijk et al., "Limited Climate Benefits of Global Recycling of Pulp and Paper," *Nature Sustainability*, October 19, 2020. www.nature.com/articles/s41893-020-00624-z

22 Aaron Borough and James E. B. Wilke, "Men Resist Green Behavior as Unmanly," *Scientific American*, December 26, 2017. www.scientificamerican.com/article/men-resist-green-behavior-as-unmanly/

Further reading

Detraz, Nicole. *Gender and the Environment*, Polity, 2016.

Halloran, Afton (ed.). *Edible Insects in Sustainable Food Systems*, SpringerLink, 2018.

Hawken, Paul. *Drawdown: The Most Comprehensive Plan Ever Proposed to Reverse Global Warming*, Penguin Books, 2017.

Johnson, Ayana Elizabeth, and Katharine Wilkenson (eds.). *All We Can Save: Truth, Courage and Solutions for the Climate Crisis*, One World, 2021.

Koch, Natalie. *Arid Empire: The Entangled Fates of Arizona and Arabia*, Verso, 2023.

Leach, Melissa (ed.). *Gender Equality and Sustainable Development*, Routledge, 2015.

Letcher, Trevor (ed.). *Plastic Waste and Recycling*, Academic Press/Elsevier, 2020.

Letcher, Trevor (ed.). *The Impacts of Climate Change: A Comprehensive Study of the Physical, Biophysical, Social and Political Implications*, Elsevier, 2021.

Marvel, Kate. *All That We Can Save: Truth, Courage and Solutions for a Climate Crisis*, One World, 2020.

8 Women in conflict

Protests

Conflicts are struggles for power and as often begin with protests as with gunshots. In September 2022, Mahsa Amini, a young Kurdish woman visiting Tehran, was detained by the Iranian morality police "to be educated" for a hijab violation. Though the Iranian police have claimed that she subsequently died of a heart attack, her family and the vast majority of Iranians believe Mahsa was beaten – murdered – and subsequently died in custody. Two Iranian women journalists broke the story and they were consequently imprisoned. Street protests erupted after Mahsa's death, and were maintained, the extent of which hasn't seen since the 2009 Green Revolution. Men and women were seeking justice for Mahsa and civil rights for all women and Iranian citizens.

Iranians have lived under theocratic rulers who maintain power through fear since 1978. Men and women, but women especially, have been under constant surveillance and threat. Women are forced to cover their hair, wear loose clothing, and can't dance in public, drive motorcycles, or travel without parental or spousal consent, among other restrictions. Sometimes, restrictions are eased, but then are quickly pulled back without warning, leaving individuals vulnerable regarding what is allowable at any given point in time.

Iranians have been at their wits end and Mahsa Amini's murder seems to have pushed them over the edge.

People fought back against security forces, though protesters were threatened with the death penalty, and in fact executions have been carried out. Women continue to lead the way. They not just took off their headscarves, they burned them in public. And it's not just women. Young men and women danced in the streets to rap music, messaging to the West that "we are like you," as a plea for international support of the kind that has been critical in other places, like South Africa and Northern Ireland. The more Iranians continue to be involved – men, women, boys, and girls – the harder it will be for Iranian security forces to control them. Unity of action in civil movements is imperative for success.

The brutal military government that seized power in Myanmar in 2021 spawned protests, locally known as the Spring Revolution, bringing together disparate groups of individuals in that country. In this largely Buddhist country, protesters have included individuals from different faiths, ethnicities, professions, and ages. The one group that has been missing is the Rohingya Muslims, having been subjected to widespread and arbitrary murders, village burnings, and mass detentions since 2017. The complicating factor for the continuing Spring Revolution is that the Rohingya genocide began under the civilian administration of Aung San Suu Kyi, so there is an understandable reluctance among the Rohingyas – and the international community – to work with those who supported the prior government's genocide.

DOI: 10.4324/9781003413417-9

A significant portion of the population in Myanmar has grown up under the controlled liberalization implemented by the government of Aung San Suu Kyi. They are also realizing the inconsistency of seeking support for their cause now while they stayed silent when the Rohingya were targeted. There has been a reckoning of sorts within Myanmar about the country's mistreatment of the Rohingyas. The hope is that a common enemy will bring all people of Myanmar together to fight against the brutal military regime. Certainly among women in countries like Northern Ireland and Liberia that happened.

An estimated 60% of the protesters in Myanmar have been women, who fear the loss of the rights they have gained since 1988. The tactics they have employed have been "gender centric." *Htaimein* is Burmese for sarongs and women's intimate undergarments, and are perceived as "unclean" in Buddhist beliefs. Coming into contact with *htaimein* is considered bad luck for men and as diminishing one's *hpone*, or masculine superiority. So, across the country women protesters have lined the street with these garments, to deter the military from attacking them as they protest for fear of breaking this traditional taboo. They have also draped sanitary towels drenched in red paint over pictures of military leader Min Aung Llaing to symbolically humiliate him. The nature of the taboos and source of the humiliation also shows, however, the low status of women in Myanmar society.

Beyond national causes, women have taken to the streets in support of reproductive rights. After *Roe v. Wade* was overturned in the United States in 2022, women all over the United States protested, and supporters in countries including Mexico and Argentina demonstrated at US embassies. Similarly, thousands protested against an amendment to Hungary's abortion laws that forces women to listen to the fetus' heartbeat before making a final decision to terminate their pregnancy, the amendment driven by the government of right-wing nationalist-populist Victor Orbán. In El Salvador, women took to the streets after other women reported being sent to prison following a miscarriage, possibly because of the draconian and ambiguous nature of abortion rollbacks there. Women are not afraid to protest, before and after bullets start to fly. They often do so at risk of peril to themselves.

The Women, Peace, and Security framework has been criticized as too focused on the protection pillar and for merely managing militarized solutions to power struggles rather than abating them. But although gender equality is the ultimate goal toward a more positive peace, the reality is that too many women live with fear and violence as a constant in their lives. Addressing that cannot be overlooked.

Living in a war zone

In many areas of the world, when violence erupts into full-scale conflict, it is largely women and children who are affected. "In Africa's contemporary conflicts, more than 90% of all casualties are women and children, who also are more likely to be targets of sexual and gender-based violence."[1] In war-torn areas like Ukraine, Syria, and Somalia, civilians face horrible choices daily, including whether to stay and try to survive, or to try to make it to a refugee camp. Either way, many of those who die during conflicts, as a result of conflict, or are violently affected by the conflict, are women and children. Hence, there is a growing body of literature related to conflict-related violence against women (CRVAW).

The UNHCR states that there were 6.6 million Syrian refugees worldwide in 2022, with 5.5 million of them hosted in countries near Syria. Almost a million Rohingya refugees have left Myanmar, mostly crossing into Bangladesh and then being housed at the Kutupalong camp. As of February 2023, over eight million refugees from Ukraine have swamped Europe, with another five million estimated to be displaced inside Ukraine. Many refugee camps are reporting hardships and cutbacks as a result of refugee aid "flooding" to Ukrainian refugee efforts. The competition for aid can be extensive, and was exacerbated by the Covid-19 pandemic even before Russia invaded Ukraine. Sexual violence as a weapon of war, the challenges faced by women left as primary caregivers as a result of war, and the trials of women refugees are all humanitarian issues, but also violence-related security issues that too often go unrecognized as such. The trials and tribulations inflicted by conflict must often be "handled" by the women themselves.

While specific situations in war zones differ dramatically there are, nevertheless, commonalities between them, many including survival tactics. In places like South Sudan, riddled with internal struggles over decades, women who had lived through one round of violence worked with international volunteers to teach younger women how to survive the next round of conflict, beginning with surviving attacks. With aerial bombardment a constant threat, digging bunkers and foxholes in safe areas and teaching children that they should use them immediately upon hearing the sound of airplanes, whether their mothers were with them or not, was imperative. Trainers also suggested that local authorities move schools, mosques, and churches, to safer locations, whether that be a cave or in the forest. Whistles were provided to community members to alert the populations to approaching airplanes. Above all, it was stressed that airplanes do not give people time to run. Bombing happens very quickly. Therefore, digging foxholes and having places to seek shelter at as many locations as possible before attacks was imperative.

Beyond surviving attacks, the population was taught how to anticipate and respond to daily challenges. They were encouraged to reduce the size of daily meals to prolong rations, to store food, to gather wild foods, and taught how to prepare those foods, and to pre-position food in various places in case family homes were destroyed. With water sources ruined, compromised, or not safe to access, communities were urged to identify multiple water points, and how to boil water or use water purification tablets if they were forced to drink surface water. First aid training was given, including use of traditional herbs and medicines, since there was only one hospital in the area, serving over a million people. In South Sudan and a myriad of other conflict zones, the primary lesson to be learned by international actors is the importance of working with and funding community-led efforts – often spurred by women – as they are living the experience, know the culture and community, and can best channel external efforts to help.

Women are also drawn into conflicts in numerous of ways, including being used as tools to legitimize forces. Central America was awash with civil violence in the 1970s and 1980s, with gender politics sometimes playing an integral role. Harvard sociologist Jocelyn Viterna examined how the protection of women came to identify the Farabundo Marti National Liberation Front (FMLN) in El Salvador as a "righteous" rather than a "radical" leftist organization in the 1980s. The FMLN was waging guerrilla warfare against the Salvadoran Armed Forces, which was known for slaughtering innocent women and children. The FMLN protected the vulnerable – mothers, children, and the elderly – often moving them to safe places and out of the way of government troops, thereby winning the support of much of the rural populace.

The FMLN was then able to use that support to create an identity for themselves as protectors.

Women's entrance into violent political acts, either as victims or perpetrators, changes those acts with emotion. If men commit political violence against women – and especially against women's sexuality – then most audiences perceive that violence as radical. If men's political violence is committed in the name of protecting women – and especially women's sexuality – it becomes righteous. If women commit violent political acts, the violence is seen as radical, especially if they commit those acts in response to, or in collaboration with, a male sexual partner. But if an organization can demonstrate that many women – especially mothers – are willing to commit political violence on their behalf, then that organization becomes especially righteous. Indeed, the narrative goes, no mother would risk her life or the lives of her children for a cause that was not profoundly just. In short, how groups mobilize gender norms may be critical to solidifying their reputation as either the "good guys" or the "bad guys" in any violent political conflict.[2]

Women were also persuaded to join the FMLN as fighters to protect themselves – better to fight than become victims – and the recruitment of women then shamed men into doing the same. Since women are known as inherently "peaceful," if women felt the cause so important as to fight for, then men felt they must as well.

Rape as a strategy and tactic of war

Journalist and feminist activist Gloria Steinem founded a project in 2012 through the Women's Media Center, called Women Under Siege. The project goals are to investigate how rape and other forms of sexualized violence have been used as tools in genocide and conflict in the twentieth and the twenty-first century. The project was inspired by Sonya Hedgepath and Danielle Saidel's work on rape during the Holocaust and that of Danielle McGuire regarding rape during the civil rights movement. Both of those works explore modern motivations for rape as a weapon of war.

When rape or sexual violence is used as a tool to achieve a goal, such as ethnic cleansing or driving a population from a particular area, it serves a strategic purpose rather than an individual purpose, inherently linking it to security. Ethnic cleansing is a purposeful policy designed by a group or a state to remove the civilian population of another ethnic or religious group from certain geographical areas by violent and terror-inspiring means. The 1990s conflict in the former Yugoslavia brought to light the use of rape as a method of ethnic cleansing, or genocide. Forced impregnation was part of the war strategy of both sides in Bosnia; the perpetrators' aim being to create more babies of their ethnicity and through this, destroy the personal, ethnic, religious, and national identities of their victims. Serbian forces in Bosnia utilized "rape camps" where women and girls were raped until they were pregnant, and then held to prevent them from getting abortions. The Women Under Siege Project points out that rape has been a "creatively diverse" method to destroy populations, ripping at the very core of societal make-up.

The 1994 war in Rwanda, with somewhere between 250,000 and 800,00 Rwandans killed in 100 days and upward of half a million women raped, was a deadly in-group/out-group battle, where the Hutu majority engaged in genocidal slaughter of the Tutsi minority. Machetes were the weapons of choice for the largely rural population that had been whipped into a frenzy of killing, the Hutu government having purchased 750,000 machetes from China a year earlier. A report written for Human Rights Watch explored the targeting of women during the massacre. Rape was carried out on a massive scale, individually and as gang rapes, for perverse sexual gratification, using foreign objects and as part of sexual slavery. Sexual mutilation sometimes followed being raped, with machetes or whatever could be found.

The motivations for rape as a weapon of war can include more than one intent. Ethnic dilution or destruction is one motivation for targeting women in genocides. "Perpetrators of genocide must either annul reproduction within the group or appropriate the progeny in order to destroy the group in the long run."[3] However, the rape of Tutsi women was intended not only to "cleanse" the population but also to break the fabric of society. Survivors were taunted that they were allowed to live so that they would "die of sadness,"[4] through the loss of loved ones, the shame of rape humiliation on the survivor and their families, and the broader social degradation that flows within honor/shame societies. The impact of rape is different for every survivor.

In Rwanda, attacking Tutsi women was associated with the specific sexual identity of these women. Under German and Belgian colonial rule, Tutsi women were considered aristocratic; they were considered better looking than Hutu women and were attributed something of a sexual mystique that made them unavailable to the average Hutu man. The Hutu propaganda machine recalled that not-entirely-forgotten Hutu cultural memory, using it to suggest that Tutsi women considered themselves too good for Hutu men, thereby insulting their masculinity. So, not only did the supposed shunning of Hutu men degrade Hutu ethnicity, but it also insulted Hutu masculinity.

The role of women as perpetrators of violence in Rwanda has been documented as higher than during the Holocaust, than the massacre of Mayan Indians in Guatemala in 1982, and even than during the breakup of the former Yugoslavia. While the reasons are not entirely clear, they relate back to the sexualizing of Tutsi women, thus making them competitors to Hutu women for male protectors.

Traditional Rwandan society was, and remains, extremely patriarchal. During the lead-up to the genocide, Hutu women were encouraged to hate and fear Tutsi women. Propagandistic Hutu publications frequently included pornographic cartoons depicting Tutsi women as traitorous seducers. Ironically, during the 1980s and 1990s, women's roles in Rwandan had started to expand, with women becoming doctors, lawyers, and even soldiers. That put Hutu women not only in positions where they would be caught up in the frenzy of killing but in positions to order and lead this violence,[5] to protect their own positions in society.

Rape as a weapon of war also has been used to drive populations from geographical areas. Serbian troops in the former Yugoslavia used rape as a tactic to drive the non-Serbian population into flight. Control of geography was thereby the strategic goal, with rape was part of an integrated military strategy.

Harvard Kennedy School professor Dara Kay Cohen argued in her 2016 book *Rape during Civil War* that armed groups forced to recruit fighters by coercion, use rape, particularly gang rape, as a tactic to create loyalty and trust between fighters. Gang rape is the most widely reported form of rape in conflict, in stark contrast to peace times when gang rape is relatively rare. In effect, armed groups use traditional "training" methods of modeling, immediate reinforcement, and male bonding to bind their recruits to them, as groups reliant on recruitment through abduction are more likely to perpetrate rape than those comprised of voluntary fighters. Rape becomes a violent socialization serving to cut ties with fighters' past lives and an indication of their commitment to their new group, often necessary to save themselves.

More recently, Cohen's research has focused on lessons learned from the past 15 years of CRSV study confirming, for example, that armed groups that recruit fighters through force are more likely to commit rape than groups formed by volunteers. Additionally, among rebel groups, state actors, and pro-government militias – all types of groups perpetrate CRSV – state actors were found the most common perpetrators, though groups associated with leftist ideologies were less likely to be associated with sexual violence. Further, CRSV has not been not limited to any one form of conflict: Not all ethnic wars include mass rape, and rape is also perpetrated in non-ethnic wars. It was also found that CRSV can be opportunistic or strategic – as most commonly referred to in the past – or "practice," with practice defined as not *ordered* from the top down but *tolerated* from the top.[6]

The brazenness of Russian soldiers in leaving sexually brutalized Ukrainian witnesses, for example, suggests that the troops were not ordered to commit rape, but that their commanders were likely aware of their troops' brutal behavior and the soldiers did not fear being held responsible for these crimes against humanity. In the Ukrainian town of Bucha, for example, about 25 women and girls were systematically raped in the basement of a home, with nine of them subsequently reported pregnant. Russian soldiers told the women and girls that they intended to rape them until they wouldn't want sexual contact any man in the future, thereby preventing them from having Ukrainian children. There is considerable concern that women who have been raped will not be able to receive abortions in nearby Poland if they flee there for safety. Poland is one of the few countries that has rolled back its reproductive rights in recent years, and abortion is now legal only if the mother's life or health is in danger.

In some recent conflicts, women have been used as sex slaves, much as the Korean comfort women were during World War II. ISIS claimed its use of captured Yazidi women as sex slaves adheres to centuries-old religious rulings. According to a pamphlet published by the group, rape of an enslaved woman, even a child, was permissible in all circumstances except one – if the girl or woman was pregnant – the exception ostensibly based on an obscure Islamic law. According to Yazidi women, they were required to take oral or injectable contraception so that they could be passed around. While adherence to the rules was more common by senior leaders rather than junior fighters, a UN-run clinic in Iraq that treated over 700 Yazidi rape victims found only 5% became pregnant during their enslavement.[7] At the individual and religious level, the emphasis on birth control was to maintain surety regarding paternity, essential in patrilineal societies.

For ISIS leadership, the importance of keeping sex slaves available directly related to ISIS' ability to maintain its fighting force. Provision of a sex slave was an appealing recruiting tactic to a young man who would otherwise not have been able to find or afford a bride, relating to the prior discussion of demographics and bride prices.

> The trade in Yazidi women and girls has created a persistent infrastructure, with a network of warehouses where the victims are held, viewing rooms where they are inspected and marketed, and a dedicated fleet of buses used to transport them.
>
> A total of 5,270 Yazidis were abducted last year, and at least 3,144 are still being held, according to community leaders. To handle them, the Islamic State has developed a detailed bureaucracy of sex slavery, including sales contracts notarized by the ISIS-run Islamic courts. And the practice has become an established recruiting tool to lure men from deeply conservative Muslim societies, where casual sex is taboo and dating is forbidden.[8]

Besides literally buying and selling women with price tags on them as sex slaves, ISIS specifically targeted women professionals for harsh treatment for presuming to step out of traditional gender roles.

CRVAW and conflict-related sexual violence (CRSV) "can also reflect widespread acceptance of patriarchal norms and of rape myths that justify and normalize rape, the everyday subordination of women, and men's sense of entitlement to women's bodies."[9] The power structures that require gender inequality must be broken down.

UN peacekeepers: protectors or predators?

Women also have been victims of sexual violence at the hands of those sent to protect them. Any time there are situations of unequal power, or "power-over" dynamics, the potential for abuse increases. Such can be the case with peacekeepers.

United Nations peacekeepers operate under three basic principles: consent of the parties in conflict, impartiality, and non-use of force except in self-defense and defense of their mandate. Their mandates, however, can include not only maintaining peace and security, but also the facilitation of a political process, protecting citizens, assisting in the disarmament, demobilization and reintegration of former combatants, supporting and organizing elections, and protecting and promoting human rights and the rule of law. Peacekeeper mandates are carried out according to rules of engagement that can be very narrow, in some cases resulting in atrocities occurring in full view of peacekeepers.[10] Perhaps even more disturbing, peacekeepers themselves having been charged with committing atrocities, most notably sexual abuse and rape.

The United Nations was rocked in 2015 by charges of sexual abuse by its peacekeepers, many involving charges of "sex for food or money" abuses. The number of cases is difficult to pinpoint though, again pointing out the importance of legal definitions and why it is difficult to gather accurate data. When desperate victims exchange sex for food for themselves or their children, for example, or for money to buy food, it is often recorded as "transactional sex" rather than rape. Between 2010 and 2022, there were more than 1,200 allegations of sexual abuse in UN peacekeeping missions, occurring in some 30 missions.

For the first time, in 2016 the United Nations published a report on sexual abuse by peacekeepers, including a "name and shame" list of countries involved. Peacekeepers from 21 nations were on the list, topped by the Democratic Republic of the Congo.[11] The entire UN system of handling peacekeepers, from training to demographics and accountability, was subsequently placed under review. There has also even been a discussion about whether sex workers should be brought to the front lines of peacekeeper operations to prevent sexual exploitation and abuse of those they are supposed to protect. Not surprisingly, the United Nations has argued that such a practice would not align with UNSCR 1325 goals. Issues surrounding peacekeeping are complex and varied.

A budget of $6.3 billion (for comparison, that is less than the annual budget of the City of Chicago, and is insufficient funding to purchase a single aircraft carrier), funds 12 UN peacekeeping operations ongoing as of 2022. These operations are carried out by 87,000 peacekeepers, with their distinctive blue helmets, from 121, often developing countries. As of December 2021, women constitute 7.8% of uniformed milia, police units, and justice and corrections government-provided personnel in UN peacekeeping missions. Among that group, the highest percentage of women is found in justice and corrections roles, hence the need for and emphasis that security cooperation programs often place on working with women lawyers. Female peacekeepers have been largely relegated to support roles in administration, logistics, and nursing.

Though the UN encourages and advocates for more women being deployed in police and military units, the responsibility for identifying and recruiting women lies with member states. The 2028 target for women serving in military units is 15%, 20% in police units, 30% for individual police officers, and 25% for military observers and staff officers. Under what conditions women can be most effective as all-female units versus integrated units is also a consideration for deployment.

The United Nations explained why more female peacekeepers are needed in 2016, calling it an "operational imperative."

Female Peacekeepers act as role models in the local environment, inspiring women and young girls in male-dominated societies to push for their own rights and for participation in peace processes.

The increased recruitment of women is critical for:

- Empowering women in the host community;
- Addressing specific needs of female ex-combatants during the process of demobilizing and reintegration into civilian life;

- Helping make the Peacekeeping force approachable to women in the community;
- Interviewing survivors of gender-based violence;
- Mentoring female cadets and police and military academies;
- Interacting with women in societies where women are prohibited from speaking to men.

The presence of women Peacekeepers can also:

- Help to reduce conflict and confrontation;
- Improve access and support for local women;
- Provide role models for women in the community
- Provide a greater sense of security to local populations, including women and children;
- Broaden the skill set available within a Peacekeeping mission

Simply put, the presence of women allows peacekeepers to conduct operations conducive to establishing and maintaining peace that they would have otherwise been unable to do.

A 2022 study titled the *Global MOWIP Report* (Measuring Opportunities for Women in Peace Operations) considers how gender impacts military operations. Based on data from four countries, one of the evidence-based findings most relevant to peacekeeping relates to the character profiles of peacekeepers: their attitudes, assumptions, and approaches. Specifically, individuals who hold rigid adherence to gender roles – spindle/spear stereotypes – are mostly likely to engage in behaviors including sexual exploitation and abuse, bribery, drunk driving, and using violence against women, and less likely to report these forms of misconduct to superiors. That indicates a need to prioritize character profiles of peacekeepers as well as military skills. This is especially true given the often high correlation between countries that contribute high numbers of peacekeepers and countries' with often low positions on gender equality indexes.

These findings are backed by anecdotal reports from women peacekeepers. They report backlash from their male counterparts when women peacekeepers' effectiveness is heralded, including resentment, hostility, and a sense of disenfranchisement. Women also say that they perceive their actions as always under a microscope, with no room for error, as the work of one individual will reflect on all women. That reality is universal. When Jack fails at a job, his failure is attributed to Jack. When Jill fails at a job, all women are deemed unsuitable for that job. Women are painted with a broad brush, and even when women succeed, it can be noted in ways that impair their confidence. "One uniformed officer likened the experience to being 'contestants on a show,' as women are watched and applauded while performing routine tasks."[12]

Collective conflict management, as peacekeeping is referred to, has come under fire for gender-related and other reasons, with its future uncertain.[13] The UN Department of Peacekeeping Operations has been tasked with incorporating gender perspectives into all peacekeeping operations, including ensuring that field operations include a gender component and gender training for peacekeeping personnel. Workshops, dialogues, and discussion have been held for almost two decades specifically focused on gender perspectives, toward identifying options, challenges, and good practices with regard to achieving a greater gender balance in UN peacekeeping operations, and toward identifying actions necessary to address the current shortfall of female personnel serving as uniformed peacekeepers. Pilot projects have been established to begin cultivating good gender practices into their deployment strategies, including comprehensive pre-deployment training and ways to increase numbers of women in their national forces. The need is recognized and the processes in place. Implementation within organizations, however, is always harder than intent due to structural barriers, resources, and attitudes.

Women as the head of household

According to the UNHCR, the global population of forcibly displaced persons has grown from 33.9 million in 1997 to 65.6 million in 2016 (driven mostly by the conflict in Syria), and to 100 million in 2022, pushed up from 89 million after the Russian invasion of Ukraine. As of June 2022, the majority of the world's refugees come from Syria, Ukraine, and Afghanistan, with most others from South Sudan, Myanmar, the Democratic Republic of the Congo, Sudan, Somalia, the Central African Republic, Eritrea, Nigeria, and Iraq. Refugee numbers from Afghanistan went down for a period when almost 400,000 Afghans returned home from camps in Pakistan in 2016 due to economic hardship, harassment, and fear of arrest and deportation in Pakistan, but then have risen again with the return of the Taliban to power. Over 50% of refugees are women, and one in four of them are the head of their household. The Universal Human Rights Association characterizes these women refugees as "facing a lone fight for survival."[14]

There are different types of forcibly displaced persons: refugees, internally displaced persons, asylum seekers, those considered part of the "stateless population," and "other groups or people of concern." While their circumstances and legal status differ, they face many similar issues as individuals out of their homes. The UNHCR provides definitions:

> A refugee is someone who has been forced to flee his or her country because of persecution, war, or violence. A refugee has a well-founded fear of persecution for reasons of race, religion, nationality, political opinion or membership in a particular social group. War and ethnic, tribal and religious violence are leading causes of refugees fleeing their countries.
>
> An internally displaced person (IDP) is a person who has been forced to flee his or her home for the same reason as a refugee, but remains in his or her own country and has not crossed an international border. Unlike refugees, IDPs are not protected by international law or eligible to receive many types of aid. As the nature of war has changed in the last few decades, with more and more internal conflicts replacing wars among countries, the number of IDPs has increased significantly.
>
> When people flee their own country and seek sanctuary in another country, they apply for asylum – the right to be recognized as a refugee and receive legal protection and material assistance. An asylum seeker must demonstrate that his or her fear of persecution in his or her home country is well-founded.
>
> A stateless person is someone who is not a citizen of any country. Citizenship is the legal bond between a government and an individual, and allows for certain political, economic, social and other rights of the individual, as well as the responsibilities of both government and citizen. A person can become stateless due to a variety of reasons, including sovereign, legal, technical or administrative decisions or oversights.[15]

The UNHCR considers approximately a million other people as needing protection beyond those defined. They include such individuals as rejected asylum seekers, host populations affected by refugees, and former refugees integrated into local populations.

Studies have been conducted on questions related to what happens to women as head-of-household refugees consequent to the US-led war in Iraq and the ongoing conflict in Syria, asking questions like:

> What happens when life as you know it changes overnight? What happens when your role as a mother, wife, sister, or daughter suddenly switches to that of the main provider and head of the household? How do you cope when thrust into an uncertain terrain that leaves you exposed to unfamiliar risks, and struggling just to make it through the day?

Though certainly with variations among them depending on geographical region and culture, the findings of these studies have revealed that women often face many similar issues based on gender discrimination.

The International Committee of the Red Cross and Red Crescent (ICRC) in Iraq conducted a survey titled *Households Headed by Women in Iraq*, in August 2011. One hundred nineteen women were surveyed from five areas directly affected by conflict. Of those surveyed, 92% were widows and the rest wives of detainees, missing individuals, or divorcees. The ICRC additionally interviewed city officials, village heads, religious leaders, and local NGO workers regarding services and benefits available to these women. From often being secluded wives in conservative societies, banned from many activities without their husband's permission, they suddenly found the responsibility of putting food on the table and trying to keep their children in school thrust upon them. The report estimated that over a million women became the head of their household in Iraq alone.

Many patriarchal societies, especially where Islam is the predominant religion, expect that widows and women left alone return to their father's home or that of their in-laws. But in conflict areas, the entire family is often affected and the traditional fabric of society badly strained if not broken. When women left to head their household seek refuge with extended family, they can become a financial burden. Additionally, due to surrounding conflict and security concerns, relocation of the entire family may occur two or three times. Some women find the means to live on their own, near relatives, with family and neighbors donating furniture and household utensils. Ten percent of the women interviewed in the above-mentioned ICRC study, admitted to having resorted to squatting in abandoned buildings.

Psychologically, these women were also dealing the loss of their husbands, children, and extended family. They were grieving. Most often they had lost someone under violent circumstances and they were dealing with trauma. The report quoted Hiba, a 30-year-old woman whose husband was beheaded in front of her near Kirkuk. "If it weren't for my children, I would pray Allah every day to take me away from this awful life."[16] Between grief and feeling overwhelmed, some women would simply never recover.

The "average" profile of the women in the 2011 ICRC survey was that of a woman in any patriarchal society: almost all were married before age 20, 46% had a primary education, 45% were illiterate, of the few who had ever worked professionally, all of them stopped working after marriage. The widows interviewed had an average of six children each. They were unprepared to care for themselves or their families. That leaves the women and their children dependent on others. Not surprisingly, it leaves all of them extremely vulnerable.

Half of the women interviewed had found jobs, most of them in farming, baking bread, cleaning, or in small shops. Those who had managed to start their own business rather than work for someone else earned 27% more than the others. Cultural and security considerations had to be worked into all of the women's plans and parameters. Fatima was widowed in 2007 when her husband was killed by crossfire in Baghdad.

Women in my neighborhood were complaining that they did not feel as ease going to the market to purchase clothes and items for the house. Last year, I started a clothing business, selling outfits for children and women as well as bed linen. My son helps me purchase all items in the central market, and then I resell them in my living room.[17]

Women can be extremely entrepreneurial when the need arises and the means are available.

The Iraqi government founded a Women's Directorate in 2008. Officially, benefits for families ranged from the equivalent of $43 to $150 per month depending on the number of children. That amount often meant the difference between acute poverty and being able to cope. Unfortunately, however, the Iraqi bureaucracies were underfunded, understaffed, and susceptible to the same kind of ineffectiveness issues most bureaucracies suffer from, only worse. Further, registering for benefits required travel and at least minimal literacy. Consequently, only 19% of the women interviewed by the ICRC had received any benefits.

The survey concluded by asking women what they wanted in the future. The overwhelming answer was to be a good mother. Only 10% of the women expressed a desire to remarry, as most worried that their children would receive inferior treatment compared to children of a husband's first marriage. The women wanted to take care of their children and themselves.

The ICRC survey was conducted in 2011, before ISIS began to get a grip inside Iraq in 2013–2014, when the situation for women left alone in Iraq largely became even worse. Women who were alone reported being seen as victims to be hunted. Women were sometimes responsible for themselves and their children, and for their incapacitated husbands as well. The feelings of many seemed to be summarized by one woman: "I wish to see Iraq like it was in the 70s or 80s – life was different," she said. "We used to feel that we are alive. Now […] we are just machines."[18] The case of women in Iraq is not unique. In fact, it is all too common.

If remaining at "home" becomes too much – too threatening, too financially difficult, too painful, too exploitive – women may decide to take their families and seek refuge elsewhere. Making this decision itself is beyond any they have ever had to make in their prior lives as wives in a male-dominated society. The journey, they inherently know, will be perilous. Amnesty International interviewed 40 women who had traveled from Turkey to Greece and then across the Balkans.

All the women described feeling threatened and unsafe during the journey. Many reported that in almost all of the countries they passed through they experienced physical abuse and financial exploitation, being groped or pressured to have sex by smugglers, security staff or other refugees.[19]

For likely the first time in their lives, many women were forced to be in close contact with males outside of their families.

Women traveling alone or with their children, and children alone, said they felt most threatened in transit areas or refugee camps in Hungary, Croatia, and Greece where men, women, and children were all forced to sleep in the same area. Some women left their designated areas, feeling safer on open beach areas where available. Women were also expected to use the same shower and bathroom facilities as men, and so sometimes avoided eating or drinking so as not having to use a potentially unsafe facility. Reports of being beaten, of sexual harassment, and of being offered assistance in return for sex, including by security officers, was common. All of this was endured to reach "safety." Finding it, however, often proved elusive.

A 2014 United Nations survey report on Syrian women[20] for the UNHCR again found that one of every four of the more than 145,000 refugee families in Egypt, Libya, Iraq, and Jordan were headed by women. Their profiles are largely similar to those of Iraqi women forced to become the heads of their households, and their struggles the same: lack of resources, including not having food; security concerns; and being on their own in a society where that is uncommon, and often unacceptable.

UNHCR special envoy Angelina Jolie spoke about the role of women in Syrian society: "Syrian refugee women are the glue holding together a broken society. Their strength is extraordinary, but they are struggling alone. Their voices are an appeal for help and protection which cannot be ignored."[21] Issues already present in so-called peaceful times are exacerbated during conflicts. Child marriages, for example, nearly doubled when the latest Syrian conflict began.

Child marriage existed in Syria before the crisis – 13% of girls under 18 in Syria were married in 2011. But now, three years into the conflict, official statistics show that among Syrian refugee communities in Jordan [...] child marriage has increased alarmingly, and in some cases has doubled. In Jordan, the proportion of registered marriages among the Syrian refugee community where the bride was under 18 rose from 12% in 2011 (roughly the same as the figure in pre-war Syria) to 18% in 2012, and as high as 25% by 2013. The number of Syrian boys registered as married in 2011 and 2012 in Jordan is far lower, suggesting that girls are, as a matter of course, being married off to older males.[22]

More child marriages, with women then not attending school, having babies before their bodies are ready, and making women totally dependent on their spouses regardless of how they are treated, further strains the society Jolie describes.

Susan Martin Forbes' book *Refugee Women* (1992) first looked at this population of women as a group, with subsequent updates noting progress in tackling identified issues. The issues and best practices identified by Forbes have been generally incorporated into the UNHCR's "5 Commitments to Refugee Women." Those commitments related to life in camps are: meaningful participation; individual registration and documentation; food and non-food items management and distribution; economic empowerment; and prevention and response to sexual and gender-based violence.

UNCHR "encourages" meaningful and active participation of women in the management of the camps. The goal is 50% representation by women, and UNHCR has created leadership-training modules to help women get comfortable with what is for them very nontraditional leadership roles.[23] A Syrian woman refugee who has become part of the camp leadership in Lebanon says: "We women know what's happening," having shouldered responsibility for the well-being of dozens who rely on her for basic necessities. "We know what is lacking in our homes."[24] These needs can range from food and shelter, to protection, to education for children, to feminine hygiene products.

Menstrual hygiene management remains a sensitive, sometimes taboo subject in refugee camps. The risks of ignoring it, however, are substantial. Women have been known to get infections from unsanitary pads, ripped from old pieces of material wherever it could be found. At some camps, menstrual hygiene kits are distributed. Realizing the need for those kits is itself a gender-sensitive issue.

Not surprisingly, there are pros and cons to the opportunities given to women in the refugee camps. First and foremost, few if any want to be there, much preferring their lives at home. But being there, opportunities for more egalitarian gender roles are presented. Even those, however, can come with a downside. Some women have received death threats for teaching in camp schools and for presuming to take traditionally male leadership roles, which obviously can have a chilling effect on their participation.

Standard operating procedures at the camps like individual registration and documentation are intended to offer legal protection for women. The goal is to "provide them with relevant documentation to ensure their individual security, freedom of movement, capacity to register (and trace lost) children, access to essential services, support property claims and ensure political rights on return"[25] on a nondiscriminatory basis. Proof of legal status is necessary to be eligible for and receive state-distributed benefits, as well as food and money from family or other sources. Syrian women especially have experienced legal issues related to proof of marriage. Not having proof of marriage can have consequences for newborn children, who cannot be properly registered without evidence their parents are married. Problems proving divorce are also common for Syrian women, especially if their husbands remained in Syria, have traveled to third countries, or have abandoned the family. All of these issues make already vulnerable individuals even more vulnerable.

Without access to and control over services and resources related to management and distribution of food and non-food items, women's vulnerability is compromised even further. According to the UNHCR, "households are considered to be food secure when they have year-round access to the amount and variety of safe foods that their members need to lead active and healthy lives"[26] Food security includes consideration of a household's ability to secure these needs through its own production, purchases, barter, or other means. Food security's three pillars are availability, access, and utilization. Further, addressing the food security needs of refugee women occurs within the context of relief, aid, and development. Without regular access, women's vulnerability to trading sex for food is heightened.

Most women arrive at refugee camps with few skills, severely limiting their ability to meet the livelihood needs of the family. Emphasis on economic empowerment means assuring that women have equal access to vocational and training programs through the camp. In fact, the economic empowerment principle recommends affirmative action targeting of women to ensure an equitable impact of projects on men and women.

Efforts to empower women in camps must be accomplished within UN Guidelines on Prevention and Response to Sexual and Gender-Based Violence for all individuals. A community-based approach and working with men is recommended, though it is sometimes necessary to begin self-protection efforts at the individual level. An aid worker at a camp in Lebanon explained:

> Street harassment and rape within the camps are also issues. Our partners explain that girls are told it is inappropriate for them to voice anything publicly or to scream, even when they are in danger. So they are working to change this. "Screaming is discouraged because they think it is 'haram' [bad]," explains Mahmoud, adding the importance of workshops that teach girls about screaming and self-defense from harassment and violence. "Recently a young girl [who had been told in a workshop to scream if she felt unsafe] screamed when an older man tried to grab her and people came running out to help her."[27]

It is important to remember how sheltered many of the women in refugee camps were until forced to flee their homes. A new life in a new country under very different circumstances than they were accustomed to, leaves many of them initially shell-shocked. They must learn entirely new ways to live, often facing brutal conditions.

Jordan is host to three refugee camps, Za'atari, Azraq, and Mrajeeb Al Fhood. Azraq formerly served as a refugee camp for Iraqis and Kuwaitis in the early 1990s and was reopened in 2014 to house some 30,000 Syrian refugees. It is geographically the biggest camp, built to avoid some of the crowding issues of Za'atri, but located in a very isolated desert area.

Mrajeeb Al Hood is similarly located in a remote area, offering the refugees little outside of the camp.

Jordan's largest refugee camp, Za'atari, is located very close to the Syrian border, surrounded by a small town. Like the other camps, it experiences temperatures in the summer as high as 113 degrees Fahrenheit, and below freezing with strong winds in the winter. It has evolved since its opening in July 2012 from a tent city to, at its peak, the fourth-largest city in Jordan, home to 120,000 Syrian refugees. In 2022, housing some 80,000 people, it is the largest refugee camp in the Middle East and one of the largest in the world.

Over the years, the tents at Za'atari have been replaced with prefabricated shelters, though over 70% of those have walls, floors, and ceilings considered substandard and certainly not accommodating to extreme weather conditions. Over 20,000 births have been recorded at the camp, averaging about 40 babies per week. Demographically, approximately half the camp's population are children and many never have never lived outside of the camp's 2.046-square-mile perimeter. There is a bustling marketplace, where stores ranging from bicycle shops to vegetable stores can be found. There are eight medical facilities that provide free healthcare to anyone who walks through their doors, and more than 30 aid organizations on-site that keep the camp running. A solar power plant began operating in Za'atari in 2017, intended to provide electricity to residents 12 hours per day, though recently power has been cut to 9 hours per day. UNHCR distributes cash assistance each quarter to camp residents, with cash increasingly being replaced by mobile money. Though the community has worked hard to maintain Syrian traditions and culture, overwhelmingly, the majority of Za'atari residents want to return home to Syria one day. Recently as well, due to the Covid-19 pandemic and the crisis in the Ukraine, life in Za'atari has become harder.

Many residents of Za'atari and other refugee camps were initially afraid to take Covid-19 vaccinations, due to misinformation that had been spread, but most eventually were vaccinated. However, containment measures put into place to curb the spread of the virus resulted in the loss of informal and formal work opportunities – 4% of Za'atari residents have permits to work outside of the camp – pushing vulnerable families into poverty, thus often making it difficult to put food on the table. Then when the war in Ukraine began, food security increased even further. Jordan imports some 90% of its food staples, making it susceptible to supply chain issues and price inflation related to the war, as well as a considerable amount of food aid being reallocated to help Ukrainian refugees. The World Food Program estimated in 2022 that 58% of Za'atari camp households were food insecure, compared to 39.5% in 2020.

Payment for food at the camp's grocery store is state of the art to prevent corruption and theft, to remove paper, and for hygiene purposes, but creates difficulties as well. Customers began checking out at the camp's Safeway supermarket by iris scan in 2016, with payment automatically deducted from their monthly allowance. But that payment method also limits their shopping choices and leaves them vulnerable to high prices, which are often higher inside than outside of camp because the camp's supermarkets pay rent. Camp residents prefer cash so they can shop for lower prices. Overall, it is simply apparent that there are too many refugees and not enough resources to care for them in a humanitarian manner. Given the patriarchal nature of Syrian culture, camp life for women largely reflects the same types of subjugation they experienced in Syria, with women alone or acting as head of their household especially vulnerable.

According to the UN Refugee Agency, as of mid-2022 Turkey and Germany were hosting the most refugees in Europe. Turkey opened its borders to Syrian refugees in 2011, accepted under a state of emergency and initially under the assumption that when the war ended in Syria, they would return home, and refugees in Germany are mostly from Iraq, Afghanistan, and Syria.

Consequently, the initial humanitarian response in both countries focused largely on immediate needs. But the majority of refugees in Turkey are no longer in a state of emergency. It has become increasingly apparent many of the 3.5 million Syrians living in Turkey may be there for a long time, or permanently.

The changed status of Syrian refugees meant plans were needed for long-term care, including for disabled persons, LGBTQ+ persons, and women, and for status beyond that as "guests," which denies refugees employment and education. Turkish legislation in 2016 allowed refugees to apply for work permits, though only with the employer's "blessing" and willingness to pay minimum wage. Those requirements are stringent given that refugees are often hired specifically because they will accept low wages, and are last hired, first fired.

With regard to women Syrian refugees in Turkey, mental health studies have found post-traumatic stress disorder prevalent, a function of both the violence they experienced in Syria and as refugees. It is doubtful either funding or trained individuals to provide necessary treatment are available. And then just when it seemed that things couldn't get worse for the refugees, a 7.8 magnitude earthquake hit Turkey in 2023.

About half of the Syrians living in Turkey reside in the southern Turkish provinces that were devasted by the February 6, 2023, earthquake, and many had found work and accommodations. After the earthquake, though, survivors felt under increasing pressure to return to Syria or move to refugee camps as everyone began scrambling for emergency and recovery resources. With more than 50,000 people killed in Turkey and Syria as a result of the earthquake, and more than two million displaced in Turkey alone, Turkish president Recep Tayyip Erdoğan began facing domestic political pressure to put Turks first, leaving Syrians feeling increasingly unwelcome. Erdoğan also has a long history of saying that women are not equal to men, so women's status as refugees in Turkey has been precarious at best even before the earthquake.

It is important as well to understand the impact of refugees on their host countries. Jordan had a stable population of approximately 3.4 million people before the 1990–1991 gulf war, when Iraqis and Kuwaitis began streaming into the country. Conflict brought more Iraqis and Syrians in the next decade, and the Jordanian population had doubled to over 7 million by 2010 and increased further to 12 million in 2022. Not only must the refugees be accommodated, but national infrastructure becomes strained as well, especially in the cities. Some refugee camps are closed over time, others morph into a city. Baqa, in central Jordan, began as an emergency Palestinian refugee camp in 1967, but has now taken on the dimensions of a city and many of the residents are now Jordanian citizens.

The largest refugee camp globally is Kutapalong in Bangladesh, housing some 635,000 Rohingya refugees. Camp conditions are poor and worsening. Many of the women arriving at the Kutapalong camp since the military crackdown – called "ethnic cleansing" by the US government, genocide by the UN – beginning in 2017, were pregnant as a result of the Myanmar military's widespread rape campaign, then gave birth in unsafe and unsanitary condition while still grappling with the trauma of CRSV. It is estimated that some 76% of the Rohingyas who arrived post-2017 have been women and girls, most of whom have suffered some sort of GBV in Myanmar or en route to Bangladesh. A 2022 study by Bangladeshi researcher Ena Tripura, titled "Confined, Controlled, and Violated," documents the continued violence and trauma faced by Rohingya women in the camps.[28] She states they face confinement and control by the humanitarian regime, not-atypical violence by Rohingya men as expression of their own anger and frustration, and by local Bangladeshi men to demonstrate their own power over Rohingya refugees. The UN has referred to the Rohingyas as the most persecuted ethnic minority in the world, with women bearing the brunt of that persecution.

Relief and recovery

Relief and recovery is one of the four pillars of the WPS framework. It is considered to be both the pillar with the most potential for making significant change, and the pillar least studied or used. It is considered to have game-changing potential because it is employed after some crisis or disaster, natural or man-made. Crisis and disaster by definition infer both time as a critical element (relief) and that infrastructures, physical structures, and social structures have been crippled or destroyed (recovery). Relief and recovery efforts, especially if deliberately linked by bridges between short-term and long-term efforts, offer a window of opportunity for building something new, infrastructures and physical structures that will result in social structures that are more equitable and sustainable than in the past. It must also be realized that women's capacity to participate in relief and recovery is predicated on having socioeconomic security and rights, including and also contingent on reproductive rights.[29]

Unfortunately, however, relief and recovery efforts have too often been undertaken under a one-size-fits-all premise – mostly by the Global North – that caring for and rebuilding the old structures is the fastest, easiest, and most appropriate approach. Relief and especially recovery should, however, strongly relate to women's potential economic participation in society and consequently empowerment as it would then offer women a chance to break the cycle of poverty that may have denied them agency. Additionally, reproductive rights must be a part of the change in women's circumstances in conjunction with economic empowerment. Relief and recovery should be, and could be, transformative.

UN Women argue in support of closing the gender gap in humanitarian relief efforts. In terms of health, both conflict and natural disasters often result in displacement, which then affects healthcare. Sixty percent of preventable maternal deaths take place consequent to conflicts and natural disasters. Livelihoods are affected by crisis and natural disasters as well, potentially leading to an increase in poverty and/or sex work. Up to 30% of internally displaced households in Yemen are headed by females, up from 9% before the current crisis. Girls are often the first to be pulled out of schools during crises, and are 2.5 times more likely to be out of school in conflict areas than their counterparts in conflict-free areas. While there are important differences between time-sensitive emergency relief and long-term recovery efforts, both need gendered approaches, evidencing the need for proactively incorporating gender into emergency and recovery planning, and training for implementation even in chaotic environments.

As in other areas, there has been an increase in global awareness for gendered policies in relief operations, and even in proactive planning. Problems remain, however, in implementation. After the earthquake in Haiti in 2010, many humanitarian aid programs and government agencies had policies that referenced women's vulnerabilities and capabilities and called for women to be involved in on-the-ground decision-making processes. But when chaos and destruction hit, the guidelines weren't implemented. There were policies and plans, for example, regarding the placement of women's latrines with locks on the doors, the need for adequate lighting to get to the latrines, the mapping of gender-based violence service providers, the need for mixed-gender patrols in the camps, and the need for safe and equitable food distribution. In too many cases, however, those policies and plans were ignored, resulting in, for example, latrines without locks and located far from women's quarters with no lighting between the locations. Consequently, up to one-third of the latrines constructed by aid workers after the Haiti earthquake went unused because women and girls feared that by using them, they would expose themselves to abuse. Well-intended policy is a good; successful implementation is considerably harder. Haiti has served as a regrettable but important case to learn from.

Some organizations have become more deliberate in relief planning. The United Nations Children's Fund (UNICEF), for example, has developed four principles related to gendered emergency planning, recognizing that every disaster is unique. 1) Be participatory and inclusive. Diversity matters to assure that all views are heard in the planning process. 2) Ground gender integration on evidence and disaggregated data. Assumptions have proved insufficient and even counterproductive in the past. 3) Engage organizations and networks led by women, girls, youths, and persons with disabilities. Considerations of intersectionality are vital to success, as is the on-the-ground knowledge of women's civil society organizations. 4) Be intentional. Proactively seek out marginalized populations to assure that context-specific considerations can be taken into account in planning.

Anticipating gendered reactions from populations in specific locations, such as whether or not disaster warnings will be heeded, is important in relief planning as well. Studies in Canada subsequent to the 1997 Red River flood have shown that women heed disaster warnings more than men. But that is not true everywhere. Bangladesh, for example, has been consistently vulnerable to cyclone-related disasters. While men in Bangladesh often migrate to the cities, the women, children, and elderly are left behind, and women have been shown to delay more in responding to cyclone warnings, or are simply left behind when others evacuate. Further, they often cannot swim, are constrained by their clothing that physically restricts their movements, and are fearful of leaving due to fear of physical GBV beyond their home. Disaster immobility has been mainly characterized as "non-evacuation behavior" and "involuntary immobility," and witnessed not just in places like Bangladesh, but also in the United States during events like Hurricanes Katrina and Rita. A newer categorization is "trapped populations," referring to climate-induced immobility.[30]

In terms of recovery, a 2022 policy brief from the London School of Economics provided specific recommendations toward making recovery transformative, beginning with an explanation of the basis for those recommendations.

> The recommendations are built on analysis of three distinct but interrelated themes: understanding what is considered legitimate knowledge in decision-making on issues of relief and recovery; the need to move towards more context-specific and localized approaches of relief and recovery, including investing in and championing research by affected communities; and the importance of understanding the dynamics of care in crises and how these relate to feminist relief and recovery.[31]

Those responsible for relief and recovery must recognize that those affected, regardless of age, race, ethnicity, sexual orientation, and education, must be involved in decision-making if the decision-making is to have lasting and transformative effects. That will likely entail breaking down structural barriers that have kept marginalized individuals – most often and specifically women and girls – marginalized.

Their recommendations were threefold:

- Ensure that the processes of knowledge production that shape policy developments are inclusive and respond to diverse realities.
- Ensure the full, equal, and meaningful participation of all groups that are routinely excluded from decision-making spaces, responding to historical and contemporary marginalization in both local and global settings.
- Redress inequality and inequity through making material contribution to cultural and structural power shifts within organizations.

Each of these recommendations is intended to champion context-specific responses rather than past practices that too often supported the status quo. As in many other instances, evidence of past-practice, status-quo support is financial. Ninety-nine percent of development and foundation grants do not reach women's rights and feminist organizations, and women's rights organizations receive only 0.13% of all official development assistance. While funding is the only factor in change, it is, realistically, a big one.

Conclusions

It is unlikely anyone in the United States knew about, let alone considered the fabric of Iraqi women's lives before invading Iraq in 2003. Whether understanding it would have made any difference regarding decisions made in the hypermasculine post-9/11 environment is doubtful. Retrospectively, it is now recognized that when the societal fabric becomes broken, it leaves a power vacuum for organizations like the Taliban or ISIS to fill. President Barack Obama once referred to ISIS as an "unintended consequence" of US intervention in the Middle East.

Part of the unintended consequences of conflict in Iraq, and later Syria, is a refugee crisis unprecedented in recent history. The spillover to US, European, and Middle Eastern domestic politics has been significant, potentially including the outcomes of several elections and referendums. While debates are held in potential refugee host countries regarding what to do, young girls are being married off without their consent; women are squatting in buildings with their children, hungry and vulnerable; and a new generation of males is growing up with few positive behavioral models. Unquestionably, though, the spindle/spear dichotomy previously used to differentiate and describe men and women's lives simply no longer applies. Women are in the thick of "spear" activities.

Utilizing the WPS framework as an analytic tool for anticipating instability – to preempt situations that generate refugee crises – has been repeatedly suggested by framework advocates, yet it is rarely systemically used. WPS advocates Valerie Hudson and Brenda Oppermann, for example, have pointed out that the US Department of Defense political instability forecasting models do not track bride price costs or polygynous marriages, though on-the-ground commanders have seen the importance in operations. They cite the case of a US Army division in Afghanistan in 2010 that recognized that steadily increasing bride price costs were a factor in encouraging young, unmarried Afghan men to fight for the Taliban as a way to earn money to pay that expense. Consequently, the division created a program to offer those young men jobs, as an alternative to the Taliban.[32]

Fully mainstreaming the participation, protection, and prevention pillars would accommodate relief and recovery being transformational. The pillars are not stovepipes; they are reliant on each other to address the challenges faced by women in conflict, and to reduce the further potential for conflict and thus for a more positive peace. That means making WPS implementation a necessity, rather than a nice thing to do in exercises but that is set aside in operations.

Notes

1 "Women, War and Peace," UNIFEM.org. Cited by Carter Ham, "Working with African Nations to Support the Role of women as Agents of Peace and Security," *Women on the Frontlines of Peace and Security*, NDU Press, 2014. p. 114

2 Jocelyn Viterna, "Radical or Righteous? Using Gender to Shape Public Perceptions of Political Violence," in *Dynamics of Political Violence*, Chapter 9 (Bosi, Demetriou, and Malthaner, eds.), Ashgate, 2014. pp. 191–192.

3 Helen Fein, "Genocide and Gender: The Uses of Women and Group Destiny," *Journal of Genocide Research*, 1, no. 1 (1999), p. 43. www.tandfonline.com/doi/abs/10.1080/14623529908413934?journalCode=cjgr20

4 Jonathan Torgovnic, "Rwanda: Legacy of Genocide," *The Telegraph*, October 6, 2007. www.telegraph.co.uk/culture/3668387/Rwanda-Legacy-of-genocide.html

5 Donna J. Maier, "Women Leaders in the Rwandan Genocide: When Women Choose to Kill," *Universitas*, vol. 8, 2012–2013. www.uni.edu/universitas/article/women-leaders-rwandan-genocide-when-women-choose-kill

6 Ragnhild Nordås and Dara Kay Cohen, "Conflict-Related Sexual Violence," *Annual Review of Political Science*, 24 (2022), pp. 193–211.

7 Rukmini Callimachi, "To Maintain Supply of Sex Slaves, ISIS Pushes Birth Control," *New York Times*, March 12, 2016. www.nytimes.com/2016/03/13/world/middleeast/to-maintain-supply-of-sex-slaves-isis-pushes-birth-control.html

8 Rukmini Callimachi, "ISIS Enshrines a Theology of Rape," *New York Times*, August 13, 2015. www.nytimes.com/2015/08/14/world/middleeast/isis-enshrines-a-theology-of-rape.html

9 Patrick Cammaert, "Protecting Civilians from Conflict-Related Sexual Violence," *Women on the Frontlines of Peace and Security*, NDU Press, 2014, p.140.

10 Chris McGreal, "What's the Point of Peacekeepers When They Don't Keep the Peace?" *The Guardian*, September 17, 2015. www.theguardian.com/world/2015/sep/17/un-united-nations-Peacekeepers-rwanda-bosnia

11 "U.N. Report Describes Sex Abuse Allegations about Peacekeeping Missions," *New York Times*, March 4, 2016. www.nytimes.com/2016/03/04/world/un-report-describes-sex-abuse-allegations-about-Peacekeeping-missions.html

12 Robert Nagel, Kate Finn, and Julia Maenza, "Gendered Impacts of Operational Effectiveness of UN Peace Operations," GIWPS, 2021.https://giwps.georgetown.edu/resource/gendered-impacts-on-operational-effectiveness-of-un-peace-operations/

13 Roland Paris, "The Past, Present and Uncertain Future of Collective Conflict Management: Peacekeeping and Beyond," *Journal of Intervention and Statebuilding*, March 17, 2023.

14 www.unhcr.org/en-us/news/latest/2014/7/53bb77049/syrian-refugee-women-fight-survival-head-families-alone.html

15 www.unrefugees.org/what-is-a-refugee/

16 ICRC, 2011, p. 3. www.icrc.org/eng/assets/files/2011/iraq-women-survey-2011-08-eng.pdf

17 ICRC, 2011 (ft 47), p. 8.

18 "Life in Iraq: War Forces Women into Non-Traditional Roles," NBC News, September 25, 2016. www.nbcnews.com/news/world/life-iraq-war-forces-women-non-traditional-roles-n497256

19 Tirana Hassan, "Female Refugees Face Physical Assault, Exploitation and Sexual Harassment in Their Journey through Europe," Amnesty International, January 18, 2016. www.amnesty.org/en/latest/news/2016/01/female-refugees-face-physical-assault-exploitation-and-sexual-harassment-on-their-journey-through-europe/

20 *Women Alone: The Fight for Survival by Syrian Refugee Women* www.unhcr.org/womanalonemedia/

21 Chris Reardon, "Syrian Refugee Women Fight for Survival as They Head Families Alone," UNHCR, July 8, 2014. www.unhcr.org/en-us/news/latest/2014/7/53bb77049/syrian-refugee-women-fight-survival-head-families-alone.html

22 Save the Children, *Too Young to Wed: The Growing Problem of Child Marriages among Syrian Refugees in Jordan*, 2014. www.savethechildren.org.uk/sites/default/files/images/Too_Young_to_Wed.pdf

23 Eileen Pittaway, *Leadership Training for Young Refugee Women*, www.refworld.org/pdfid/464ab7ea2.pdf

24 Emma Gatten, "Syria Conflict: With the Men Away Fighting, Women Take Up the Mantle of Community Leaders in Lebanon's Refugee Camps," *The Independent*, May 9, 2015. www.independent.co.uk/news/world/middle-east/syria-conflict-with-the-men-away-fighting-women-take-the-mantle-of-community-leaders-in-lebanons-10238891.html

25 2001. www.refworld.org/docid/479f3b2a2.html

26 *Strategic Plan for Nutrition and Food Security* 2008, p. 114.
27 "Women and the Refugee Crisis: An Update from Lebanon," www.globalfundforwomen.org/news-upd ate-refugee-crisis/#.WHYyqLHMz-Y
28 "Confined, Controlled and Violated: The Rohingya Women in Bangladesh Refugee Camps," *Feminist Encounters*, September 12, 2022. www.lectitopublishing.nl/download/confined-controlled-and-viola ted-the-rohingya-women-in-bangladesh-refugee-camps-12348.pdf
29 Jacqui True and Sarah Hewitt, "What Works in Relief and Recovery," *Oxford Handbook of Women, Peace & Security*, 2019.
30 Sonya Ayeb-Karlsson, "When Disaster Strikes: Gendered (Im)Mobility in Bangladesh," *Climate Risk Management*, 29, 2020. www.sciencedirect.com/science/article/pii/S2212096320300279
31 "An Inclusive and Sustainable Approach to Relief and Recovery," Center for Women Peace & Security, Our Generation for Inclusive Peace at London School of Economics, Policy Brief, 05/2022. www.lse. ac.uk/women-peace-security/assets/documents/An-inclusive-and-sustainable-approach-to-relief-and-recovery-policy-brief-05.pdf
32 Valerie Hudson and Brenda Oppermann, "Anticipating Instability: The Untapped Potential of Women, Peace and Security," Council on Foreign Relations, June 18, 2021. www.cfr.org/blog/anticipating-inst ability-untapped-potential-women-peace-and-security

Further reading

Bassel, Leah. *Refugee Women: Beyond Gender and Culture*, Routledge, 2014.
Chang, Iris. *The Rape of Nanking*, Basic Books, reprint edition, 2012.
Cohen, Dara Kay. *Rape During the Civil War*, Cornell University Press, 2016.
Crawford, Kerry. *Wartime Sexual Violence*, Georgetown University Press, 2017.
DiGeorgio, JoAnn, and Donna Gosbee (eds.). *Gendered Experiences of Violence, Survival and Resistance*, Women's Press, 2016.
Hedgepath, Sonja, and Rochelle Saidel. *Sexual Violence against Jewish Women during the Holocaust*, Brandeis University Press, 2010.
Helm, Sarah. *Ravensbruck*, Anchor Press, reprinted 2016.
Karim, Sabrina, and Kyle Beardsley. *Equal Opportunity Peacekeeping: Women, Peace and Security in Post-Conflict States*, Oxford University Press, 2015.
Martin, Susan Forbes, and Ruud Lubbers. *Refugee Women*, Lexington Books, 2nd edition, 2004.
O'Brien, Melanie. *Criminalising Peacekeepers*, Palgrave Macmillan, 2017.
Pruitt, Lesley. *The Women in Blue Helmets*, University of California Press, 2016.
Swain, Ailsing. *Conflict-Related Violence against Women*, Cambridge University Press, 2017.

9 Women and peacemaking

Why ignore success?

Statistical analysis has shown that when women are included in peace processes there is a 20% increase in the probability of an agreement lasting at least two years, and a 35% increase in the probability of an agreement lasting at least 15 years. Those are perhaps the most oft-cited numbers arguing in support of the Women, Peace, and Security principles of inclusive diversity in peace processes. Yet, between 1992 and 2011, women comprised only 2% of the negotiators of peace agreements, 4% of signatories, and 9% of mediators. As of 2019, those numbers rose to 13% of negotiators, 6% of signatories, and 6% of mediators in major global peace processes. According to Margaret Vogt, former UN mediator-in-residence,

> It's a power game. And in most of these games, women are not there. So, when it comes to discussing peace [at] the table, the participants – the negotiators – see it as an opportunity to renegotiate power, and they want to restrict the domain as much as possible.[1]

Minimizing an evidenced-based means to a more stable, lasting peace has been standard fare. That must change.

Stop the violence

Peace is not just an absence of war. It is an environment allowing for the growth of a civil society and a government that provides personal security for all. While that must initially include gender-equal opportunity, it must evolve into being gender-equal outcomes. When peace begins with a peace process, excluding women from that process only hampers the odds of a lasting peace. Hence, security extends beyond bullets and battlefields.

Formerly distant, internal, human security concerns of a country – crime, corruption, weak governance, drugs, poverty, access to food, clean water, schooling, and health epidemics – are now recognized as potentially leading to larger concerns because they threaten national unity, stability, and internal peace, with consequent implications for regional and global security.[2] Women are fully involved, positively and negatively, in many of the human security issues associated with day-to-day life.

An expanded definition of security inherently changes the purpose of peacemaking. If peacemaking were intended only to end an armed conflict, then only the belligerents would need to be involved. But conflicts have causes that must also be addressed. With internal warfare still prevalent in many countries, the importance and prevalence of human security issues in peacemaking, and considering women's inputs so that a lasting peace can be built, are key considerations.

DOI: 10.4324/9781003413417-10

Women's inclusion in peacemaking processes between countries, including treaty negotiations to avoid conflict, has been shown important toward achieving strategic goals as well, such as with the women-led team of Western negotiators able to achieve the 2015 Iranian nuclear deal.

Women in conflict areas initially want the violence surrounding them to stop. Whether local, intrastate, or interstate, women will first and foremost advocate for peace, defined as ending armed conflict. But they will then also advocate for other issues to be considered in conjunction with stopping the violence.

Women's secondary demands vary by circumstance but generally fall into several categories. Regarding security and protection, women often petition that gender-based violence be considered a violation of any ceasefire or cessation of hostilities and treated as such. Additionally:

> gender-sensitive training at all levels for national and international armed forces, gender-sensitive security sector reform and DDR (disarmament, demobilization and reintegration), special measures for the protection of women refuges and internally displaced persons, and an end to the proliferation of small arms and light weapons. In approximately 75% of their demands, women have highlighted sexual violence as a special concern, which contrasts with the scarcity of explicit mentions of sexual violence in the text of peace agreements.[3]

Often also included are recommendations and examples of implementation measures, such as quotas for women in security services, or emphasizing the need to protect civilians.

Context then determines specific issues women raise. In Afghanistan, for example, anti-personnel land mines in rural areas were a particular concern of women because of their prevalence. Recruitment of child soldiers was an issue in Sierra Leone, which was elevated to the forefront of issues women wanted addressed. Violence and threats not just against women generally, but also those who support women's rights in the Democratic Republic of the Congo (DRC) have been of special concern there.

Empowerment and socioeconomic recovery are components of peace negotiations of interest to women as well. Women's groups focus on such areas as land ownership and inheritance rights, marriage laws, access to credit (which includes grants and interest-free loans), access to education, and investment in skills training and capacity building. The compounded needs of female heads of household often draw special attention and donors can play a critical role in these areas. Prior to the 2005 Oslo Donors Conference for Sudan, Sudanese women requested establishment of a women's fund within the Multi-Donor Trust Fund being established, specifically devoted to funding women's programs. While a fund was set up in the amount of $250 million from ten donors, including the World Bank, there was nothing specifically focused on women. An evaluation of the fund conducted in 2012 found that the fund "succeeded in delivering some positive results on gender despite very limited explicit acknowledgement of gender-related issues in the planning and design."[4] Gender was included as an afterthought rather than a driver of relief and recovery aid distribution.

When only men are at the negotiation table, the agenda most often focuses on issues such as territorial control, the surrender of weapons, and each side granting amnesty to the other for acts and atrocities committed. Lost or forgotten are human security issues or post-conflict civil liberties like the removal of land mines in areas where women regularly walk in the conduct of their daily lives. Princess Diana made awareness of the dangers posed by the millions of land mines left behind post-conflict in Africa, and the clearance of those mines, a personal cause. She is credited with the successful passage of the Ottawa Mine Ban Treaty, signed months after her death. It becomes the responsibility of those interested in the bigger picture – a lasting peace – to assure that post-conflict considerations be included in efforts to end violence, at all levels, from the home to the state.

Organizations like the United Nations have made commitments to include women in the peace process through mandates like UNSCR 1325, but are rarely able to force inclusion of women or women's issues into peace negotiations. Allowing input from more diverse inputs inherently diminishes the power of the belligerents, thereby generating their resistance. As the International Peace Institute points out: "Perhaps most importantly, a deeper resistance to change and a reluctance to share power is also at play – particularly on the part of the conflict parties themselves."[5] The prevalence of these power struggles means that women have often had to be creative to be heard.

Avenues of participation

The spectrum of avenues available for women's participation in peace actions ranges from acting as mediators and directly participating at the peace process negotiating table as delegates, to observer status, consultations, inclusive commissions, problem-solving workshops, public decision-making, and mass action. These avenues are often most effective when used in combination. While ideally women would be directly involved in the peace process, challenges there remain. The same dynamics of domination that play out in other arenas where women are in the minority, can come into play at negotiating tables as well, resulting in either a woman or a few women finding it difficult to have their voices heard or to articulate a different set of views from the dominant narrative being presented by men.

The importance of having mediators who are fully briefed and trained regarding UNSCR 1325 involved in a peace process cannot be overstated. Even then, however, inclusion is not guaranteed. During the 2014–2015 peace process in Mali, there were 11 co-mediators, including the United Nations, the African Union, and the European Union. While the inclusion of community representatives and women was originally a top priority for the UN and the EU, the lead mediator, Algeria, and many other co-mediators were not convinced of the importance of women's participation, due to "cultural reasons and because they thought it would delay the negotiations."[6] When women's participation is an option, it is an option rarely taken.

Mediation can also be part of an informal process. In 2004, for example, Betty Bigombe took the initiative to act as an unofficial mediator between the government of Uganda and the Lord's Resistance Army. In that role, she helped lay the groundwork for the official peace talks in Juba a few years later.

In El Salvador in the 1990s, women were present at nearly all of the post-peace accord negotiation tables where technicalities were worked out. One technical table, the Reinsertion Commission, was comprised of six women and one man. Through the women's participation, women eventually were one-third of the beneficiaries of land redistribution and reintegration packages. That number roughly corresponds to the number of women combatants or collaborators in the FMLN.[7]

Having a woman as part of a delegation does not guarantee either a peaceful dispute settlement or that gendered issues will be raised. Women can be blind fish too. In the 2005 Ache peace talks, while there were no women on the Indonesian government side, a woman was included on the rebel party delegation.

Later on, this one woman recognized that she was not aware of resolution 1325 (2000), nor did she at the time realize what the exclusion of women and gender issues meant for the future of the peace process. She acknowledged that she would have welcomed advice on a range or gender issues, but no support was available to ensure that mediators and parties to negotiations were aware of the implications of their proposals for gender equality and for women's rights.[8]

The need for men and women working security issues to be educated on WPS principles, and organized, with prearranged information sharing on how and why inclusion might be achieved in specific negotiations, is clear from this example and many others.

In an observer status, women become something of an information conduit. They can provide negotiators with information, and convey information from the negotiating table to a wider outside audience, thereby holding the negotiators accountable. That ability to hold negotiating parties publicly accountable is often not welcome, and so a strong and sympathetic mediator is required to assure that the observer groups are not summarily sidelined.

Consultations are the most broadly used form of inclusionary participation in peace processes. Consultative forums act as advisory bodies. They can be either elite based, for technical matters, or represent broad constituencies. They are sometimes part of the official process, or self-initiated. Women in Kenya set up their own consultative body following mediation after election violence in 2008. Women in Uganda similarly organized women's consultative groups at the village and district levels, and insured that their inputs were fed into the 2006 peace process between the Ugandan government and the Lord's Resistance Army, and the national recovery plan that followed.

Inclusive commissions often precede or follow peace processes. In Colombia, for example, an inclusive commission was set up prior to the peace talks between the government and rebels to prepare an agenda of issues. More often, however, commissions are used to oversee the implementation of peace agreements. Truth and reconciliation commissions are post-peace agreement mechanisms intended to aid in the national healing process by implementing transitional justice against those responsible for human rights abuses. These commissions are often part of the peace agreement, and the more strongly the requirement for an inclusive commission is written into the agreement, the more effective the commissions have been in practice. University College of Dublin researcher Aisling Swaine states, "transitional justice mechanisms have provided significant opportunities for accountability for the harms that women have experienced during conflict. They have also become the most significant spaces where women's experiences of violence are being aired and documented in post-conflict settings."[9]

Commissions often advocate for and accept pardons rather than punishment for many conflict participants, or pardons for many while saving punishment for the most egregious or responsible few, as the norm. Doing so has been almost through necessity in the many postcolonial, transitional societies, as otherwise there would be no moving forward. These commissions are also often responsible for allocating reparations to victims.

Ensuring that reparations are fair and adequate requires a comprehensive understanding of the gendered nature of the harms suffered and assuring that operationalizing the nature of reparations does not exclude, marginalize, or penalize women through gender blindness. Though reparations are a recognized right, and court-ordered reparations are often awarded to victims of sexual violence, few if any victims ever receive compensation or even adequate health treatment. States often argue that they do not have the money or should not be responsible for the actions of individuals, other states, or armed groups.

Women do not often fare well in problem-solving workshops. These workshops are often comprised of individuals close to decision makers – and few women fall into this category – to discuss issues without the pressure of having to reach an agreement. They are a venue to unofficially explore alternatives, before or concurrent with official negotiations. There have been instances of using problem-solving workshops to allow women of different ethnicities or perspectives to meet and agree on a plan of action for all women, to present a united front.

Public decision-making usually takes the form of a referendum. It is a way for elite negotiators to get buy-in from the general public, where women represent half the electorate. Women's groups can be important in generating support for the agreement if they have been involved in the peace process in some other way – directly, as an observer, or through consultations.

Mass action campaigns are especially well suited to women, as women are predominantly active in civil society and grassroots movements. Mass action campaigns can generate generally pro- or anti-peace agreement environments. Liberian women, through their Women in Peacebuilding Network (WIPNET), proved particularly effective in their efforts. Different circumstances allow for different avenues of participation of women, who are learning from each other.

Women seek to both end hostilities and build a lasting peace. They push for commencement or finalization of negotiations. They work toward reconciliation. Their effectiveness stems from women generally having different conflict management styles than men.[10]

There are essentially five main types of conflict management styles: "competing (satisfying one's own concern at the expense of another's), accommodating (sacrificing one's own for the sake of another's), avoiding (neglecting both parties' concerns by postponing a conflict issue), collaborating (attempting to find a solution that satisfies both parties' concerns), and compromising (attempting to find a middle ground, which satisfies only partly both parties' concerns." Studies have shown that women are typically more likely to use cooperative conflict management styles such as collaborating, compromising, or avoiding, while men are more likely to use competing or avoiding strategies in situations of conflict.

In the international conflict context, hard bargaining tactics may be socially costly because, often, innocent lives are on the line. As a result, women's typical collaborative approach may be more productive and efficient than men's inclination toward hard bargaining tactics. Furthermore, given women's actual or perceived aims of maintaining long-term, relational harmony and their sensitivity to interpersonal cues, women are more likely to be more successful in delicate conflicts involving future relationships. These gender distinctions need to be recognized and utilized in conflict resolution. Armed conflict is not a gender-neutral event; therefore, the dispute resolution process designed to resolve armed conflict should not be neutral toward gender.[11]

In negotiations, men largely gravitate toward competition and avoidance management styles. Additionally, men with military backgrounds who are involved in settlements are often of an even narrower perspective than men generally.

Military officers, where men dominate, often view the world in a particular way. They are "can do" individuals focused on winning, so they answer questions from a "how" perspective. Military careers and experience often result in what psychologists sometimes call a 'professional deformation,'[12] which refers to a tendency to view the world through one perspective, shaped by their profession, rather than a more balanced perspective. In the case of the military, it is a necessarily conditioned perspective that is structured, hierarchical and operational. All problems are nails and all answers come through hammers. "Operational problems require operational solutions – fix the problem, and done."[13] They are well trained in combat operations and execution, but may not be well versed beyond that, or even have an interest in the peacebuilding issues required for a long-term stability.

But sending gender experts to negotiations comes with its own set of issues, as discussed in a 2022 article titled "I Wouldn't Want to be a Gender Expert: Gender Experts in Peace Mediation." There the authors argue that

> there is tension between the art of mediation and the art of gender expertise that reflects the gendered power dynamics of peace mediation. We conclude that the strategy of appointing gender experts to peace mediation teams will not "dismantle the master's house." However, we acknowledge that without a gender expert very little will be accomplished on this issue [...] their presence may still be (incrementally) transformative.[14]

Gender experts, it seems, rock a very comfortable boat.

Women contribute considerable positive value to peace negotiations and peacebuilding. There is not a single case of women being involved in peace negotiations or peace implementation evidencing a negative effect in terms of reaching an agreement. Yet for the most part, women continue to be ignored in these processes, or are involved temporarily, only to find a rollback on their roles and even women's empowerment generally after the fact. Such was the case in Northern Ireland.

Northern Ireland

Northern Ireland experienced over 30 years of violence from the 1960s to 1998, a period known as "the Troubles." It was an ethno-nationalist conflict that focused on the constitutional status of Northern Ireland. Largely Protestant Unionists/Loyalists wanted Northern Ireland to remain part of Britain, and were supported by Britain. Largely Catholic Nationalists/Republicans wanted Northern Ireland to rejoin the Republic of Ireland as a united, independent Ireland. With Northern Ireland having a small total population of 1.6 million people during the Troubles, everyone was touched by the violence, through deaths, injuries, and incarcerations. So-called Peace Walls were constructed of cement, barbed wire, sometimes whatever could be found, intended to keep warring parties apart by separating populations within cities, even neighborhoods.

Women were largely excluded from political and other decision-making bodies in Northern Ireland during "the Troubles." Yet, typically, it was left to women to hold families and society together during the conflict. They worked through trade unions, community, and volunteer groups in that regard. Dating back to the 1970s, a women's movement of sorts emerged to deal with the burdens of poverty, domestic violence, single parenthood, and additional struggles caused or exacerbated by living in a conflict setting. Betty Williams and Mairead Corrigan were awarded the Nobel Peace Prize in 1977 for their work with Peace People, a women-led peace organization that had mobilized public support for nationalist and loyalist factions to agree to a ceasefire in 1972. Unfortunately, but not surprisingly, the ceasefire did not hold, leading to the British government instituting "direct rule" from London later in 1972, which further inflamed Nationalists, and the fighting continued for approximately another two decades.

In 1981, the Women's Information Group movement was organized to bring women from diverse local groups together once a month, on neutral ground. They never discussed political issues, but instead focused on social, health, and education issues relevant to all of them. Several women's centers began to be set up as well, to provide advice and support for women on issues like domestic violence and rape, exacerbated by the conflict, and not usually discussed elsewhere. One women's health issue of note was severe depression, with women treated with tranquilizers like valium. The valium didn't solve the problem causing the depression, however, and could lead to further damaging women emotionally and physically. Especially in the

Catholic ghettos, women took "mother's little helpers" "to forget, to escape, to dull the edge of pain, fear and frustration, and theirs is a private hell."[15]

Through their efforts over decades, women's groups developed considerable grassroots credibility. Meanwhile the British began to realize in the 1980s that the Northern Ireland "Troubles" could never be solved through military means, but required a political process, and began to push for that. The strategic goal remained the same, stopping the violence, but the means to achieve it was changed from military to political. As the ceasefires began to hold in the 1990s, it appeared that a settlement could be in the offing. Women began to be concerned about how to stay involved, requiring them to find or develop their own structures, processes, and power bases.

In 1996, the Northern Ireland Forum was created to negotiate a peace agreement. The British were responsible for the process, including determination of who would be at the negotiating table. To ensure that loyalist parties associated with paramilitary groups had an opportunity to participate, a vote was scheduled where political parties would compete for ten spots at the negotiating table. Six weeks before that vote, the Northern Ireland Women's Coalition (NIWC) was formed as a broad-based political party and, coming in ninth within the top ten, won one of those spots. Women on both sides of the conflict, tired of hackneyed arguments for why peace was impossible, took on what has been called a do-it-yourself approach to peace.

The NIWC's approach to getting into the needed top-ten vote-getting category was based on five points. First, they broke down campaign tasks to make them manageable and kept their message simple. Their campaign motto was "Wave Good-bye to Dinosaurs," also the title of the 2017 documentary film recounting their struggle, to signal their support for a new approach and a new attitude focused on moving forward. Second, they used a "list system" on the voting ticket, offering a slate of candidates rather than individuals, to make candidates less vulnerable to personal attack, as women running for political office often are. Third, their core principles were simple, drawn directly from the Beijing Declaration: inclusion, human rights, and equality. Fourth, they stressed inclusiveness through leadership from both sides of the conflict, and not requiring that voters give up their prior party membership to lend the NIWC support. And last, they urged moving away from zero-sum politics to what was called "transversal politics," meaning to keep your own identity while being open to the identity of others.

That approach allowed the NIWC to become a place for those, mostly women, who otherwise felt excluded. A study conducted in 1993 found that when women were asked which party in Northern Ireland best represented the interests of women, two-thirds responded "none."[16] Nevertheless, it would be an overstatement to say that the NIWC presented a united Northern Ireland women's front. Some women felt it had a too nationalistic leaning. Other smaller political parties, the Alliance party in particular, also drew considerable numbers of women. The Women's Coalition did, however, offer a new option.

The Women's Coalition approached the negotiations with two goals, equal footing for women post-conflict and an agreement that would accommodate a stable, lasting peace. Their approach was based on their own internal organizational model of inclusivity and expansiveness. By keeping their goals broad, they avoided rigid bargaining positions. That approach worked well in allowing them to build multiple relationships, with other parties, with the international facilitators, and with parties outside Northern Ireland, specifically the United States and the Irish diaspora in the United States.

The importance of international support in general and oftentimes the support of specific individuals can make a critical difference in peace processes. US president Bill Clinton championed the peace process in Northern Ireland, calling terrorists "yesterday's men." Then First Lady Hillary Clinton galvanized community groups and women's groups on both sides.[17] American statesman and senator George Mitchell headed an international body to independently assess the decommissioning of paramilitary arms, a key part of building conditions for a lasting peace. He developed principles that guided the process. A committed foreign champion, or champions, can mean the difference between success and failure in peace talks.

Not everyone at the multiparty talks welcomed the Women's Coalition. Liz O'Donnell was a representative of the Irish government at those talks, and recalls the Women's Coalition being treated disrespectfully by many participants.

> What passed for "politics" in Northern Ireland was the trading of sectarian insults and abuse. It was small wonder women avoided politics as it was seen as a distasteful way of earning a living. The Chairman of the talks always made time for the Coalition to speak, but their colleagues did not treat them with respect, especially Unionist men, who took to calling them "silly women." This is the male culture in Unionism, where women stay home and make cakes.[18]

Unionists shouted "moo moo moo," mimicking a cow when Women's Coalition members attempted to speak.

A key NIWC focus in the negotiations was the establishment of a Civic Forum. The Forum was intended as a way for ordinary people to have a voice in the post-conflict peacebuilding dialogue processes, to assure those processes did not become an "elites only" venue. Except for a short period in the 1990s, though, the Civic Forum never reached fruition as intended, and collapsed in 2002. Lynn Carville, a member of the Civic Forum, recalled that, "The media were horrible towards the Forum and referred to us as 'do-gooders' and 'lapdogs,'"[19] illustrating the power of the media in shaping stories.

Retrospectively, women who were involved have said that they should have spent less time on the Civic Forum and more time supporting a quota system to assure that women continued to have a voice in Northern Ireland politics, and taking note of who was tasked to do what in terms of implementing the peace agreement. As the peace process was concluding, the Women's Coalition insisted on acknowledgment of women's rights in the agreement, and their proposed wording was inserted into the text. But getting words into the agreement proved not to be enough. Having no champion during the implementation phase, legal enforcement proved elusive. Having no prior experience in the junkyard-dog environment of politics, the Women's Coalition was learning as it went, sometimes too late. Consequently, the slog to equality has been slow.

Margaret Ward, then-director of Northern Ireland's Women's Resource and Development Agency, described the situation in 2005: "A lack of gender parity that exists throughout Northern Irish society is a key factor in hindering the development of a new, shared future."[20] She wrote that after the peace process, women in the Northern Ireland remained "excluded and silenced,"[21] and noted Cathy Harkin of Derry Women's Aid referred to Northern Ireland as an "armed patriarchy."[22] She also referenced Shelley Anderson, coordinator of the International Fellowship of Reconciliation's Women Peacemakers Program, who called for an examination of the links between "private" violence and the "public" violence of armed conflict.

> The attitudes and values that give rise to the former lay the ground work for the latter. Both are rooted in mindsets where domination, control and beliefs in certain groups' superiority and others' inferiority are central. A mindset that permits and justifies the use of physical or psychological force by a "superior" against an "inferior" cannot be safely relegated to one corner of life, such as the home, or certain personal relationships. It will become a part of public life.

Anderson's remarks clearly illustrate that the family is considered the first political order because relationship patterns established there, including the role of violence, carry over to other political units.

For real change to occur and hold requires "a demilitarization at a cultural and ideological level,"[23] but that is still a two-steps-forward-one-step-back process in Northern Ireland. A strategy for peace, called *Together Building a United Community*, was released in 2013, which includes a gender equality strategy, but Ward called that reference "merely tokenism [...] Peace building is still seen as an activity that primarily involves men."[24] Yet the women of Northern Ireland remain strong, and the experience of the NIWC remains one studied by women's groups around the world for its positive and negative "lessons learned."

While Northern Ireland today is not an open conflict zone, it is still far from peaceful. Though often referred to as a "post-conflict society," it might more accurately be described as a "managed" peace. Peace Walls remain even in 2023 to separate some communities, the displaying of certain flags and emblems is prohibited because they are considered too provocative, and reciprocal fear of police and security forces remains high. There are high rates of alcoholism, addiction to prescription drugs, and high unemployment because anyone arrested during "the Troubles" has a criminal record, making their employment difficult. As in other places, violence in Northern Ireland has become normalized. All of this increases women's vulnerability, as well as incidents of domestic and sexual violence. Much of society remains staunchly conservative about the role of women, and women's political participation remains comparatively low, hindering the potential for change. They have, however, had a strong voice in some areas.

Abortion became legal in Northern Ireland in October 2019, following a referendum strongly backing liberalization in May 2018. But, as in many other areas and countries, there is a significant gap between rhetoric and action. Medical abortion involving two sets of pills (mifepristone and misoprostol) is legal up to 10–12 weeks (depending on location within Northern Ireland), but accessibility to both the pills and clinics can still be difficult. Abortion activists in Northern Ireland cite the government's Department of Health as the problem for not adequately organizing abortion services as part of national healthcare, leaving healthcare workers still already overstretched due to the Covid-19 pandemic, untrained and largely unfunded regarding pregnancy termination. There are no private clinics in Northern Ireland that provide abortion services. That leaves women in Northern Ireland navigating a maze of bureaucracy, and some women are still sometimes having to fly to the United Kingdom for an abortion.

The idea of women working has become normalized in Northern Ireland. In fact, according to the 2019 *Women in Work* report produced by PricewaterhouseCoopers, Northern Ireland made the most progress in the United Kingdom toward closing its gender pay gap, reducing it by 13%. Further, the report says that Northern Ireland now has the smallest pay gap in the United Kingdom, as well as the lowest female unemployment rate. However, 70% of lower-paying "care" jobs are held by women, lone parents make up the lowest economic rung in Northern Ireland, and 91% of those are women, and having children greatly reduces women's economic opportunities.[25]

A 2021 study on Northern Ireland and WPS "participation" found women – Catholic and Protestant – still face parallel issues due to lack of equality and participation:

> For this reason, in this paper we do not distinguish women's experiences along political or community lines. We are concerned with the experiences of women as women. The findings reveal a high degree of consistency in women's experiences irrespective of party or political affiliation.[26]

While both the United Kingdom and Ireland have NAPs for implementing WPS, Northern Ireland falls into the gap between the two, still struggling to even agree on a definition of gender equality.

Liberia

The West African nation of Liberia is Africa's oldest republic, founded by freed American and Caribbean slaves and home to 16 Indigenous ethnic groups. The Liberian people suffered through civil war from 1989 to 1997. Liberian women got involved in 1994 with the conception of the Liberian Women's Initiative. Women from all walks of life, regardless of ethnic, religious, or socioeconomic background, joined together and tried to influence the sporadic peace negotiations. While they were a strong voice in pushing for a peace settlement, their larger concerns were muted by traditional approaches focusing on a short-term fix to end the conflict rather joining that to a longer-term view toward building peace. The 1997 peace agreement did not hold.

Hostilities commenced again in 1999. Charles Taylor was a government official in Liberia during the first civil war. He fled to the United States after being accused of embezzling an estimated $1 million and depositing the money in American bank accounts. Taylor was captured and imprisoned while awaiting a decision on extradition. He escaped, made his way back to Liberia, and became a rebel leader – a warlord – training under and becoming the protégé of Libyan leader Muammar Gaddafi. He was elected president in 1997 with 75% of the votes. "For many Liberian voters, electing Charles Taylor was the only way to bring peace to the country."[27]

Taylor's presidency was riddled with corruption and human rights abuse charges. In 1999, intrastate fighting began again, this time between Taylor's forces and rebels. Over the next 14 years of civil conflict, there were an estimated 270,000 casualties, with countless more displaced and traumatized individuals, without access to even basic services. Women bore a large portion of the violence, with sexual violence rampant. Liberian women were being savaged.

Both sides became known for their brutal violence against civilians and the use of child soldiers. Children made up between 10% and 40% of the fighting forces, employing "small boy units" to carry out mass killings.[28] Meanwhile, Taylor claimed to be a fervent Christian, and rebel forces attended mosques. The women of Liberia, Christian and Muslim, again had enough.

> During the years of warfare, Liberian women "had to endure the pain of watching their young sons [...] be forcibly recruited into the army. A few days later these young men would come back into the same village, drugged up, and were made to execute their own family members. Women had to bear the pain of seeing their young daughters used as sex slaves at night and as fighters during the day [...] [w]omen had to sit by and watch their husbands, their fathers, be taken away. In most instances these men were killed, and some of them were hacked to pieces.[29]

The women jointly formed the Women in Peacebuilding Network (WIPNET) and began to take action.

As chronicled in the 2008 award-winning movie *Pray the Devil Back to Hell*, women in white T-shirts, to symbolize peace, began showing up in markets to sing and pray for peace. Charles Taylor claimed he could pray the devil out of hell, so the women wanted to pray the devil back to hell. They peacefully protested in an environment where there was little tolerance for dissent. The women leveraged their respected roles as sisters, mothers, and wives to skirt the edge of personal danger. A Catholic Church-owned radio station publicized their peaceful protests, drawing both more participants and the attention of the mainstream media inside Liberia and beyond. The media shaped the Liberian women's story and told it to the world.

Led by Leymah Gbowee, the women's numbers swelled into the thousands and they organized mass demonstrations, including a sex strike. Gbowee talked in a 2015 interview, about who came up with the idea for a sex strike, and how they used it with the media to further their cause:

A Muslim woman, my colleague, well, very good friend of mine, Asatu Bah Kenneth. She's like, "We're going to do a sex strike." And it was like, "Whoa!" for me, because usually the stereotypes we have about Muslim women is that they are quiet, obedient, and that they do not have those kinds of, you know, mind. But she was the one who came up with the idea.

And once we put it out there, it became a huge issue, first not in our – in our community, it wasn't because sex is exotic, even though it is, but people wanted to know who were these women to even dare their husbands or the men, who are supposed to be in power, to say they won't give sex because of the war. The international media wanted to know: How can you refuse sex, when rape is the order of the day in your culture, in your society? So, all of these lingering questions made it a very good strategy for talking about, because every time we went to do press and they wanted to know about this sex strike, we had to go about every other reason why we were doing it before this, so it became a very good media strategy for the work that we were doing at the time.[30]

The women worked to build pressure on Taylor and the rebels to negotiate, and eventually it worked.

Taylor was finally forced into exile in Nigeria and the warring parties agreed to a meeting, in Ghana. WIPNET recruited about 200 Liberian women refugees in Ghana to keep up the pressure on negotiators, joined by Gbowee and others who had made their way to Ghana on buses. The men negotiators, used to living in spartan field camps as fighters, were in no hurry to leave the relative luxury of the Ghanian accommodations and so had little to show daily as far as progress. Subsequently, the women blocked the doors of the negotiation hall to force negotiators to keep at their work until an agreement was reached, threatening to take off their clothes if the men emerged, an act that would have gender-shamed the men. The men stayed, produced, and signed the Golden Tulip Declaration (named after the hotel where they met), summarizing their demands, and presented it to the delegations. Again, women's demands focused on peace rather than women's issues, as they feared raising those issues would derail the process. They were relentless. After 14 years, the war was finally ended in 2003. The women of Liberia had proved decisive in the peace process. Leymah Gbowee received the Nobel Peace Prize in 2008.

Post-conflict Liberia remains riddled with institutional and societal issues that continue to tug at the social fabric. But the peace agreement has held. Liberian women were intent on giving the agreement they had fought and sacrificed for, every chance of success. After 2003, they next focused on electing a woman president.

In November 2005, Ellen Johnson Sirleaf, often called the Iron Lady of Africa, was elected the first female president of an African country. Born and raised in Monrovia, she was, like many African women, married at 17, and had four children by age 21. She followed her husband to the United States in 1961 and there earned a degree in accounting. Her husband became jealous at how well she did in school and began abusing her. The abuse got worse when they went back to Liberia. Finally, she found the courage to leave him, and got a job at the Ministry of Finance. Having an education allowed her to leave the abusive marriage, which is often not an option for women.

While at the ministry, Sirleaf was asked to give a talk at an economic conference in Monrovia. She did, one highly critical of the government. Consequently, she fled the country after the speech and went on to earn a degree in economics from the University of Colorado, Boulder, and later a Master's of Public Administration at the Harvard Kennedy School. By 1980, she had returned to Liberia and was appointed minister of finance. Sirleaf had become, according to biographer Helene Cooper, a cat with a number of lives.[31]

In 1980, there was a military coup in Liberia. A group of soldiers led by Samuel Doe overthrew the government, killing the president in his mansion. Within a week they had executed everyone in his cabinet as well, except Ellen Johnson Sirleaf. Cooper shared her views on why Sirleaf was spared:

> They spared her because she was a woman. Women were to be raped, to be attacked but not to be killed like that in a public way. And the second reason is because of all those speeches she had been making, complaining – in which she criticized the government. She was viewed by even people opposed to the government as having some street cred. So she was spared, and then Samuel Doe made himself president and invited her to join his government.

Sirleaf joined Doe's government but did not last long. She quit and fled Liberia again, holding posts at banks, the United Nations, the World Bank, and the International Monetary Fund over the course of her international career. In a 1985 speech to Liberian expatriates in Philadelphia while working there for Citibank, Ellen Johnson Sirleaf called Samuel Doe an idiot. Soon thereafter she went to Liberia, where she was promptly put in jail for sedition,[32] and kept there for almost a year. According to Cooper, it was there that she realized she wanted to be part of a better future for Liberia.

In 2005, elections were forthcoming after the end of the devastating war that had ripped Liberia apart for more than a decade. The leading contender was George Weah, an athlete who had once been named FIFA player of the year and African player of the century. He carried with him no political baggage, which worked in his favor, but the women of the country were concerned that he also had no experience running a country and they were unwilling to risk the hard-earned peace settlement on a political novice. Men had already run the country into the ground before. His opponent was Ellen Johnson Sirleaf.

Liberian women again mobilized to motivate women to register and vote. Their message in the campaign between the grandmother and the soccer star was simple: "Vote for Woman!" One woman told of seeing

> young men laughing as she campaigned for a female president. The boys had taken women's panties, had smeared the crotches with tomato paste and were waving them at the women – their unsubtle way of saying that a woman could not be president.[33]

It only motivated the women more.

Weah's supporters utilized the politics of fear in his campaign, promising that if he lost the election, the country would go back to war. That was the same argument Doe had used earlier and the women wanted no part of it again. They campaigned hard and resorted to trickery when they felt it necessary, buying men's voter registration cards with beer, and even hiding voting cards from male family members. They brought babies to long voting lines, urging women to use the babies as props to get to the front of the line, or to pretend to be pregnant. Sirleaf won, 59.4% to Weah's 40.6%, in a runoff after Weah won the first round, but failed to get the constitutionally required 50% plus one minimum to win the presidency.

Ellen Johnson Sirleaf's presidency was marked by efforts to rebuild Liberian society. She says she based reform on four pillars: peace and security, economic revitalization, governance and the rule of law, and infrastructure and basic services. As part of her presidential efforts to clean up endemic corruption in Liberia and so attract foreign investment, she fired the entire Ministry of Finance staff and brought in women to serve as finance minister, chief of police, commerce minister, and justice minister, among others. But she has also been criticized for nepotism, giving her sons plum positions in government, and not doing enough for women at the local level where changes often have the most impact on women's daily lives. The number of women in the national legislature dropped during her tenure in office. Additionally, she did not support a 2010 legislative proposal to mandate that women occupy at least 30% of political party leadership, with a trust fund established to finance their electoral campaigns, and so it was never ratified.

Ellen Johnson Sirleaf's tenure as president was most remarkable in Liberia, which enjoyed more than a decade without internal armed conflict. For many Liberian women, that was a huge triumph. Internationally, she is credited with setting the foundations necessary for implementation of UNSCR 1325 in place, and was awarded the 2011 Nobel Peace Prize in recognition of her efforts to bring women into the peacekeeping process. Domestically, in terms of policy achievements, her tenure has been described as "good enough."[34] Johnson Sirleaf stepped down as president in 2017, succeeded by her previous opponent, George Weah, and she was subsequently elected chair of the Economic Community of West African States, the first woman to hold that position.

Colombia

In October 2016, Colombians rejected a peace treaty between the Colombian government and the FARC, through a yes/no referendum vote with a 50.2% to 49.8% margin. After years of on-again, off-again negotiations, the peace treaty was intended to end one of the longest-running insurgencies. Voter turnout was low at only 38%, as a "yes" vote had been strongly expected to easily prevail.

Arguments against the peace treaty varied. Many Colombians who had suffered at the hands of the FARC, felt that FARC members were being given too much impunity. The treaty included provisions of lesser punishment for those who confessed to their crimes, in some cases including exemption from time in jail. There were also economic provisions for monthly government stipends to FARC members toward reintegration, and political provisions allowing for seats in the Colombian Congress in 2018 and 2022. Many voters simply had serious questions about whether the FARC could be trusted to disarm and abide by the treaty. There were other issues against the treaty as well, including some related to women and the LGBTQ+ community.

Colombia's colonial past set the stage for the modern-day conflict that began in 1948. Colonial Colombian society was based on stratification according to "purity of blood." The elites were the *peninsulares*, persons of Spanish blood born in Spain. Below them were the criollos, those of Spanish descent but born in the colonies. Those groups claimed political power and social prestige in Colombia, and owned the vast majority of land. The vestiges of that system have resulted in political and economic inequities within Colombia society still today. In the 1940s, urban, university-based resistance erupted through the liberation theology-inspired National Liberation Army (ELN) and in rural areas primarily interested in land ownership reform through the FARC, as well as small, often splinter groups. By the 1990s, Colombia had signed peace agreements with five of those smaller organizations. Of the 4,885 ex-combatants in those groups, 1,183, or 24.2%, were women, though that number is considered low as women frequently were omitted from demobilization lists, especially if they were not turning in arms. Having women involved in the conflict as fighters changed the dynamics of the fight and the peace negotiations.

Women and girls in Colombia suffered massive displacements, sexual violence, rape, forced labor, forced prostitution, forced abortions, and enslavement as a consequence of the ongoing violence. Indigenous and Afro-Colombian women were particularly subjected to sexual violence as a weapon of warfare. Many women lost their husbands and had to assume new roles as widows and single heads of households. Breaking with traditional women's roles brought psychological trauma. As one woman noted, "We are the mothers of guerillas, of military, of paramilitary; we are the origins of life."[35]

The 1991 constitution and subsequent legislation and judicial rulings all afford Colombian women a broad range of rights, including penalizing violence against women and gender-based violence, guaranteeing women's participation and leadership roles in peacemaking and peacebuilding, providing equal access to state resources for women, and guaranteeing women's relief and recovery from the conflict. But machismo, defined as strong, even aggressive male pride, is pervasive in Latin American countries, including Colombia.

Colombia is a party to both CEDAW and UNSCR 1325, but as of 2023, it does not have a NAP for implementation. Many of the structural barriers to women's empowerment and equality have been removed. Not surprisingly, though, cultural barriers remain strong.

> centuries of structural discrimination, mistreatment, and gender-based violence, have been exacerbated by a history of colonialism, racism, homophobia, and poverty. Elite political culture is marked by practices of exclusion and indifference to women's contributions. Strong cultural expectations that women's place is in the home prevail. Patriarchal attitudes that position women as inferior to men, discriminatory practices of exclusion and mistreatment of women, and entrenched gender stereotypes and roles continue to be strong barriers to equality.[36]

Consequently, women were initially only minimally engaged in Colombian peace talks.

In peace talks with the FARC between 1998 and 2002, Maria Emma Mejia was named a principal negotiator for the Colombian government. Ana Teresa Bernal, former director of a network of Colombian civil society organizations that coordinates and disseminates information on peace efforts, was asked to channel input from civil society into the process. These women used their positions to try to bring more women into the process, including on the FARC side. Mariana Paez eventually joined the FARC negotiating team. Together ,the women organized grassroots meetings to discuss gender equality as a part of the peace process. Concurrently, UNSCR 1325 was passed, adding an international framework to their efforts. Though they were successful in rallying community support behind them, their efforts gained little political traction at higher levels. Additionally, financial support from the United States through Plan Colombia, which poured money into the Colombian government to eradicate drugs and fight the insurgencies, gave impetus to seeking a military rather than a political solution to the conflict.

When talks collapsed in 2002, the women went back to trying to hold society together in the midst of conflict. They had to be careful, though, as Colombian president Alvaro Uribe widely dismissed those who continued to favor peaceful solutions to problems as guerrilla-sympathizers. Nevertheless, women played significant roles in mediating community conflicts and dialoguing with armed groups regarding the release of hostages. They articulated the concerns of vulnerable communities, including LGBTQ+ persons.

In 2010, the political landscape in Colombia changed. President Juan Manuel Santos was elected president, promising to bring Colombia peace. Formal peace talks with the FARC commenced in Havana soon thereafter. Women were again largely excluded from official positions. However, "at the table, around the table, behind the table, and at side tables, women are having their say and shaping the path to peace."[37] In 2013, following a summit of Colombian women that had the backing of UN Women and key development partners, representatives from Colombian women's organizations presented three key demands: that the parties stay at the negotiating table until an agreement was reached, that women be included at the table and at every stage of the process, and that women's needs, interests, and experiences be considered during the talks. That message further received the backing of UN headquarters, which was in the process of reviewing Colombia's compliance with CEDAW treaty obligations.

As the peace process proceeded, more women were added to the official delegations. The Colombian government appointed two women as negotiators. The FARC added women to their delegations, to the extent that by February 2015, the FARC delegation in Havana was more than 40% women, largely reflecting the gender composition of the FARC as a whole. The FARC women launched their own website to present their perspectives. A Gender Sub-Commission was formed, comprised of representatives of both the government and the FARC, with a mandate to ensure that gender perspectives and women's rights were included in all agreements. Civil society, including victims, women, and LGBTQ+ representatives, provided input to the negotiators to an unprecedented degree. But politics is about power, and power was up for grabs with the new agreement.

While the United Nations, the international community, and the media largely applauded the attention to gender issues, there were some segments of Colombian society that did not, especially statements expressing support for LGBTQ+ groups. Concurrent to the peace talks, the Colombian government released a manual to public school teachers regarding how to prevent discrimination and bullying against lesbian and gay students. Former president Uribe, the leader of the opposition to the peace accords, resisted the introduction of that material into the school system.

Through a group called the National Movement of the Family, Uribe's followers linked the peace-accord provisions that protect people of "diverse sexual orientation and identities" with the new education initiatives, led by openly lesbian Minister of Education Gina Parody, to suggest government attempts to promote a "confused gender identity." Pamphlets promoting a "No" vote on the peace referendum read, "Colombia is in danger! Of falling under the control of a communist dictatorship and the imminent passage of a gender ideology."[38] Uribe, who maintained a strong political following, echoed those views. Religious groups became involved as well. The president of the Evangelical Confederation of Colombia stated that the accords gender perspective could "infringe upon some evangelical principles."[39] How much these views affected the defeat of the initial referendum is not clear, but the intent was clear. Ironically, President Santos was awarded the Nobel Peace Prize in December 2016, after the referendum failed.

Santos and Uribe met after the referendum toward the development of a peace deal that both could politically support. A second peace agreement was reached just six weeks after the referendum with changes made acceptable to all parties, including modifications to appease the religious far right. That agreement was not put to a referendum. Support for women and vulnerable populations acceptable to all parties remain threaded throughout the Final Agreement. Too often, however, after the peace process is over, "promises to take women's concerns seriously often remain just that: promises, unfunded and ignored."[40] According to the Colombian non-governmental Gender Working Group *Género en al Pa*, as of 2022, only 20% of the 122 gender measures in the Peace Agreement have been effectively implemented, and while the LGBTQ+ community has significant rights on paper, the rights and protections afforded them are rarely enforced.

Afghanistan

Conflict has been the norm in Afghanistan for decades, involving warlords, the Russians (then Soviets), the Taliban, al-Qaeda, the United States, and always the Afghan people. After the 2001 Taliban ouster from power by the United States, an attempt was made to form a democratic Afghan national government, but the country was fractured and public support slim, especially outside the cities. It took two decades of fighting for the United States to accept, as it had to do in Vietnam and Iraq as well, that democracy can rarely be exported. The United States wanted out and began talks with the Taliban in 2018 in Doha, Qatar. The Trump administration negotiated a deal in February 2020 – without the inclusion of the Afghan government – that freed 5,000 imprisoned Taliban fighters and set a date for final withdrawal of US troops by May 1, 2021. Troop reductions began even as the Taliban continued to attack Afghan government forces and welcome al-Qaeda into their ranks.

Though intra-Afghan peace talks were to begin in Doha in March 2020, talks were delayed until September 2020 and the Taliban impetus to negotiate with the Afghan government was nil. Furthermore, the Afghan government delegation remained fractured, without even a full consensus of what "peace" would mean. Though the Biden administration delayed the May 1 withdrawal date, it was clear that US troops were leaving. The Taliban just had to wait. Their return to full power took only ten days after the withdrawal of US troops in August 2021.

Women's participation in Afghan political affairs is highly constrained by cultural barriers regardless of who is in power. There have been arguments that their political participation is barred by religion, though religious scholars have found that argument not theologically valid. Rather, widespread societal acceptance of GBV, ideological barriers, and cultural norms have actively excluded women from traditionally male-dominated political spaces. The degree of societal acceptance of GBV in Afghanistan cannot be discounted or forgotten, rampant even when US troops were in the country theoretically tamping down that behavior by their presence. A US Army doctor serving in Kandahar in 2005 recalled instances such as a woman brought to the army camp by family members after purportedly falling into a cooking fire with burns over 90% of her body, and another who was unable to straighten her limbs after having clearly been confined in a cage. Women's medical treatment always required the husband's permission.

Additionally, even before the Taliban's return, there were considerable differences between life for women in cities and those in rural areas, where poverty, low levels of literacy, and GBV are most extreme. With the Taliban's return, women's movement outside of their homes is again restricted in both cities and the countryside. Many women who were encouraged to leave their homes and speak up for their rights by Americans are now on Taliban hit lists. There were no contingency plans for them beyond evacuation for the lucky ones. Four women participated in the Afghan government's 21-member team that negotiated, ultimately unsuccessfully, for an inclusive government and protection of women's rights at the intra-Afghan talks in Doha, Qatar, in 2020: Fawzia Koofi, Habiba Sarabi, Sharifa Zurmati Wardak, and Fatima Gailani. All are now in exile.

All of the women on the negotiating team were focused on two goals: ending the decades of conflict that had plagued the country and making sure that all of the post-Taliban advancements and achievements made by Afghan women would be preserved into the future. All had cautioned, repeatedly, that US support in Afghanistan was critical to the peace process, and that a premature

US exit would result in state collapse and a breakdown of the institutions painstakingly built over the years. All felt abandoned by the US withdrawal.

When the Biden administration decided it would move forward with the withdrawal plans developed by the Trump administration, a conference was called in April 2021, to be held in Istanbul, to gather all parties to the conflict to reach a final agreement. Over 100 diverse women delegates from all over Afghanistan were ready to attend to make recommendations on each of the topics to be discussed by the official delegates. The women's initiative was supported by civil society in both the United States and Afghanistan and the US government. But the Taliban boycotted the meeting and the United States went forward with the non-conditional withdrawal of troops, effectively ending the peace process.

The four delegates and many more women and men remain engaged, unwilling to simply surrender their country to the Taliban. Women, at great risk to their personal safety, continue to press whenever and however they can for rights. Afghan women are trying to keep pressure on the international community to stand with them, but that is difficult, especially with humanitarian and political attention having moved to Ukraine.

Lessons learned

The UN Peacebuilding Commission was created in 2005 specifically to record and develop best practices of post-conflict reconstruction, and to assist states in transitioning from conflict to peacetime. Laura J. Shepherd has examined the activities of that organization, arguing that peacebuilding activities remain gendered and hierarchical, though not without hope for the future.[41] The need for persistence against the perpetuation of discriminatory practices is key to instituting real change. Groups have worked to develop just such strategies.

Based on 40 cases of peace negotiations from the Broadening Participation Project, several strategies for meaningful participation by women in peace negotiations have been offered.[42] They include: building coalitions using normative and strategic arguments; establishing a credible selection process; creating conditions to make women's voices heard; and keeping power politics – and the public – in mind. When and how to use these strategies, individually and in combination, depends on environmental context, and again how the media shapes the story can be critical. The success and failures of women in Northern Ireland, Liberia, Colombia, and other countries, such as Somalia and Guatemala, offer lessons women and the men who support them can learn from.

In both Northern Ireland and in Somalia – even before the passage of UNSCR 1325 – women built coalitions using broad, non-sectarian normative arguments such as peace and human rights. In Northern Ireland, the Women's Coalition included Catholics and Protestants, loyalists and separatists, thereby earning them a seat at the negotiating table. In Somalia, during the 2002 Peace and Reconciliation Conference, the five clans of the region were represented. Led by Asha Hagi Elmi, a network of women with cross-clan marriages organized themselves into a "Sixth Clan" so that they could participate in the process as well. Asha Hagi Elmi became the first female signatory to a peace agreement in Somalia in 2004. Other parties to the negotiations accepted their input for strategic and political reasons, including bolstering their own legitimacy with the public, though rarely are women's concerns viewed as strategic priorities. If they were, women would more often be included. Further coalitions are important to counter the often-heard complaint that "It is difficult to engage with women [...] because they were not one group."[43]

There are limited seats at any negotiating table if effective work is to be accomplished. Who participates can be decided in several ways – by the mediator, through a formal process, or by the negotiating parties, though if only belligerents select participants, they are unlikely to reach beyond those who echo their positions. Whatever way is selected ought to be transparent. Experience has shown that gender quotas best assure participation by women's groups.

Quotas, however, in any context, also come with issues. Without a quota, there is no guarantee that any women will be included in processes from negotiations to management or board positions. When quotas are included, though, whatever the quota number is, will likely be seen as "enough." Some individuals see no reason for quotas because they believe "merit" will insure equal opportunity. The argument is also made that when quotas are used, an individual's or group's substantive merit may come into question.

While a certain amount of tokenism will undoubtedly prevail, numbers are a prerequisite to inclusivity and so a start, especially if the included women come with knowledge and belief in a UNSCR 1325 gender perspective. Quotas are useful to get women into political processes and organizational positions in critical mass numbers that are requisite for their views not to be snuffed out. Quotas are a tool toward achieving inclusive diversity that must be considered.

The need to create conditions where women's voices are heard, is based on evidence that "when women are present only in small numbers, they are less likely to be able to influence deliberation processes that are based on majority rule."[44] Whether it is one or a few women in a group, or a group of women within a set of larger groups, of mostly men, women are often ignored. If, however, a consensus model for decision-making is used, that can reduce the deficit of authority usually held by the men, and require group behavior that allows, in fact demands, the input of everyone. Beyond direct participation, offering women expert support in drafting memos and reports has been helpful in boosting their input. Additionally, it should be noted that participation in these processes when not part of an official delegation, comes with logistical and financial issues. If international organizations and external supporters want to see women's grassroots organizations represented at meetings, support, including funding, is often required.

Swedish researchers have also recognized that women's political inclusion can be weaponized to legitimize autocratic practices, called "autocratic genderwashing." Autocratic governments sometimes put women – most often women who feel linked to men rather than women for one reason or another – in positions so that they can stress advancing gender equality, while drawing attention away from authoritarian practices.[45] Hence the notion raised in Chapter 2 that feminism does not mean support for any and every woman, as some women choose to work against other women, often for their personal advancement.

Finally, it is important to remember that inclusive processes – peace processes or otherwise – challenge existing power structures and therefore can be expected to meet with friction and/or resistance. How to respond to these challenges to maximize effective input depends on the circumstances: whether it is best to remain outside official talks or to press for inclusion. Further, it cannot be taken for granted that including women in the peace process equates to getting support from the public at large for issues that women will support. The media can and will play an important role in that. In Northern Ireland and in Guatemala, women were involved in the deliberative phase, but faltered in the implementation stage, due to overlooking the need to be directly involved themselves and not recognizing that the public was not fully supportive.

Having women involved in conflict prevention, peace negotiations, and stability building is important, and there are many ways to do that. In the Philippines, a country of 81 provinces, of which 76 are considered conflict-affected areas, women in a special unit of the army, known as "hijab troopers," are playing key roles working with displaced persons in these largely Muslim areas. They are working with women, children, and the elderly, those most affected by the previous conflicts. Not all the hijab troopers are Muslim, but all are trained to assist in psycho-social debriefings to rebuild trust in the government and stability-building programs.

As in other areas of Women, Peace, and Security, for stability-building programs to be effective, time and resources must be devoted to gathering and having available quality, sex-disaggregated metrics to eliminate the approach of making assessments and set goals based on assumptions and partial information. Gender-sensitive programming, achieved by relentlessly asking who will benefit and who will be excluded from programs, is required as part of standard operating procedures. Working with locals and keeping ownership of programs local whenever possible is increasingly recognized as imperative, to leverage the knowledge and experience of grassroots organizations.

Conclusions

Including women in peace processes is certainly no guarantee of success by any definition. Excluding women, however, significantly increases the chances of failure if extended peace is the goal. Women are learning from each other's experiences. Men are slowly coming to appreciate the positive role women can play, but misogyny is still widespread. There remains, however, much learning still to take place.

All countries must recognize that a cessation of fighting may be the first and immediately acceptable goal at peace talks, but there are ways to insert women's views into processes during and after the peace talks, and use their influence to achieve those, toward maximizing the potential for longer-term peace. Mediators who recognize the importance of women's presence, for example, are key. They may be critical to assuring women stay included in political discussions during and, equally important, after peace talks. Perhaps most importantly, those countries with NAPs that commit them to implementation of the WPS framework – and certainly those countries with legislative mandates to do so – should actually do so. That means requiring inclusive negotiating teams and gendered goals.

Notes

1 Marie O'Reilly, Andrea O Suilleabhain, and Thania Paffenholtz, "Reimagining Peacemaking: Women's Roles in Peace Processes," International Peace Institute, June 2016. www.ipinst.org/wp-content/uplo ads/2015/06/IPI-E-pub-Reimagining-Peacemaking.pdf

2 Derek S. Reveron, *Exporting Security*, Georgetown University Press, 2010, p. 19.

3 UN Women, *Women's Participation in Peace Negotiations: Connections between Presence and Influence*, 2012. p. 12.

4 "Evaluation of the Multi-Donor Trust Fund in Sudan," World Bank, December 1, 2012. https://assets. publishing.service.gov.uk/government/uploads/system/uploads/attachment_data/file/311988/Multi-Donor-Trust-Fund-Sudan.pdf

5 O'Reilly, Suilleabhain, and Paffenholz, p. 1.

6 O'Reilly, Suilleabhain, and Paffenholz, p. 9.

7 UN Women, *Women's Participation in Peace Negotiations: Connections between Presence and Influence*, 2012. p. 2. www.unwomen.org/~/media/headquarters/attachments/sections/library/publicati ons/2012/10/wpssourcebook-03a-womenpeacenegotiations-en.pdf

8 UN Women, *Women's Participation in Peace Negotiations: Connections between Presence and Influence*, 2012. p. 8.

9 Author Aisling Swaine Discusses *Conflict-Related Violence against Women: Transforming Transition*, Women's International League for Freedom and Peace, May 11, 2018. https://wilpf.org/author-aisling-swaine-discusses-conflict-related-violence-against-women-transforming-transition/

10 Roohia S. Klein, "The Role of Women in Mediation and Conflict Resolution: Lessons from UN Security Council," *Washington and Lee Journal of Civil Rights and Social Justice,* 277, 2012.

11 Cassandra K. Shepherd, "The Role of Women in International Conflict Resolution," *Hamline University's School of Law's Journal of Public Law and Policy,* 36, no. 2 (2015); citing Klein, 2012, p. 11.

12 Michael D. Matthews, "Hands Up, Don't Shoot," *Psychology Today,* March 8, 2015. www.psycholo gytoday.com/blog/head-strong/201503/hands-don-t-shoot

13 Gordon Adams, "Donald Trump's Military Government," *New York Times,* December 9, 2016. www. nytimes.com/2016/12/09/opinion/donald-trumps-military-government.html

14 Jenna Sapiano and Jacqui True et al., *International Negotiation,* April 2022, pp. 2–3.

15 J. A. Sulka, "Living on Their Nerves: Nervous Debility in Northern Ireland," in *Gender, Health and Illness: The Case of Nerves,* Routledge, 1989, p. 233.

16 Patty Chang, Mayesha Alam, Roselyn Warren, Rukmani Bhatia, and Rebecca Turkington, *Women Leading Peace,* Georgetown Institute for Women, Peace, and Security, 2015, p. 39. https://giwps.geo rgetown.edu/sites/giwps/files/Women%20Leading%20Peace.pdf

17 Niall O'Dowd, "Bill Clinton's Historic Visit to Ireland 20 Years Ago," *Irish Central.com,* November 30, 2015. www.irishcentral.com/opinion/niallodowd/the-peacemaker-bill-clintons-historic-visit-to-irel and-20-years-ago

18 O'Donnell, p. 22.

19 Lynn Carvill, "The Role of Women in Conflict Resolution," *The Role of Women in Conflict Resolution Comparative Study Visit Report: Ireland,* 28 November– 2 December 2013. Democratic Progress Institute. p. 147.

20 Margaret Ward, "Gender, Citizenship and the Future of the Northern Ireland Peace Process," *Eire-Ireland,* Fall/Winter 2005. p. 1.

21 Margaret Ward, "Excluded and silenced: Women in Northern Ireland after the peace process," *50.50 Inclusive Democracy,* June 12, 2013. www.opendemocracy.net/5050/margaret-ward/excluded-and-silenced-women-in-northern-ireland-after-peace-process

22 Ward, 2005, p. 19.

23 Ward, 2005, p. 20.

24 Margaret Ward, "Excluded and Silenced: Women in Northern Ireland after the Peace Process," *50.50 Inclusive Democracy,* June 12, 2013. www.opendemocracy.net/5050/margaret-ward/excluded-and-silenced-women-in-northern-ireland-after-peace-process

25 "Gender Inequality in Northern Ireland: Where Are we in 2020," Women's Resource Development Agency, 2020. https://wrda.net/2020/02/07/gender-inequality-in-northern-ireland-where-are-we-in-2020/

26 Catherine Turner and Aisling Swaine, *At the Nexus of Protection and Participation,* International Peace Institute. June 2021. www.ipinst.org/wp-content/uploads/2021/06/Womens-Participation-Northern-Ireland-2-Final.pdf

27 "Security Council Resolution 1325: Civil Society Monitoring Report," Global Network of Women Peacebuilders, 2011. p. 105. http://peacewomen.org/sites/default/files/GNWP_Monitoring_Liberia.pdf

28 Sara Kuipers Cummings, "Liberia's 'New War': Post-Conflict Strategies for Confronting Rape and Sexual Violence," *Arizona State Law Journal,* March 2011.

29 "How the Women of Liberia Fought for Peace and Won," Tavaana Case Study, https://tavaana.org/en/content/how-women-liberia-fought-peace-and-won

30 Amy Goodman, "Liberian Nobel Peace Prize Laureate Leyman Gbowee: How a Sex Strike Propelled Men to Refuse War," *Democracy Now,* April 27, 2015. www.democracynow.org/2015/4/27/liberian_nobel_peace_prize_laureate_leymah

31 " 'Madame President' Author on 'Street Cred' Economic Power of Ellen Johnson Sirleaf," *NPR,* April 1, 2017.

32 "Citibank Executive on Trial in Liberia," *UPI,* August 23, 1985. www.upi.com/Archives/1985/08/23/Citibank-executive-on-trial-in-Liberia/6574493617600/

33 Helene Cooper, "How Liberian Women Delivered Africa's First Female President," *New York Times,* March 5, 2017.

34 "Praise for the Woman Who Put Liberia Back on Its Feet," *The Economist*, October 5, 2017. www.economist.com/news/leaders/21730015-ellen-johnson-sirleaf-has-not-been-perfect-president-she-has-been-good-enough-praise

35 Bouvier, 2016, p. 7.

36 Bouvier, 2016, p. 13.

37 Bouvier, 2016, p. 19.

38 Roxanne Krystalli and Kimberly Theidon, "Here's How Attention to Gender Affected Colombia's Peace Process," *Washington Post*, October 9, 2016.

39 Krystalli and Theidon, 2016.

40 Krystalli and Theidon, 2016.

41 Laura J. Shepherd, *Gender, UN Peacebuilding, and the Politics of Space*, Oxford University Press, 2017.

42 O'Reilly, Suilleabhain, and Paffenholz, 2015, pp. 26–31.

43 O'Reilly, Suilleabhain, and Paffenholz, 2015, p. 28.

44 O'Reilly, Suilleabhain, and Paffenholz, 2015, p. 29.

45 Elin Bjarnegård and Pär Zetterberg, "How Autocrats Weaponize Women's Rights," *Journal of Democracy*, 33, no. 2 (April 2022). http://uu.diva-portal.org/smash/get/diva2:1686804/FULLTEXT01.pdf

Further reading

Cheldin, Sandra, and Maneshka Eliatamby. *Women Waging War and Peace: International Perspectives of Women's Roles in Conflict and Post-Conflict Resolution*, Bloomsbury Academic, 2011.

Cooper, Helene. *Madame President*, Simon and Schuster, 2017.

Gbowee, Leymah. *Mighty Be Our Powers*, Beast Books, 2013.

Koofi, Fawzia. *The Favored Daughter*, St. Martin's Griffin, 2013.

Leech, Gary. *The FARC*, Zed, 2011.

M'Cormack-Hale, Fredline. *Gender, Peace and Security: Women's Advocacy and Conflict Resolution*, Commonwealth Secretariat, 2012.

Reveron, Derek. *Exporting Security*, Georgetown University Press, 2010.

Shannon, Elizabeth. *I Am of Ireland: The Women of Northern Ireland Speak Out*, University of Massachusetts Press, 1997.

Sullivan, Megan. *Women in Northern Ireland*, University Press of Florida, 1999.

Theobold, Anne. *The Role of Women in Making and Building Peace in Liberia*: *Gender Sensitivity Versus Masculinity*, Columbia University Press, 2012.

10 Women in the military

Women at the front lines

Women have found ways to serve their countries, their cultures, and their causes throughout history. Zenobia, Warrior Queen of the Palmyrene Empire (Syria), fought the Romans in 267. After her eventual capture, she was marched through Rome in golden chains. The Celtic Queen Boudicca also fought and banished the Romans after Nero had her daughters raped and tried to deny them the lands willed to them by her husband and their father, Prasutagus. Trieu Thi Trinh is called the Vietnamese Joan of Arc, cutting a striking figure in bright yellow clothing when riding to battle against the Chinese on a war elephant in the third century. Joan of Arc was a commander in the French army by the age of 17. She was captured, put on trial for heresy and cross-dressing by the English, and burned at the stake in 1430. Nakano Takeko was one of a very few female samurai in Japanese history. She wanted to fight in the Japanese Boshin civil war in the 1860s but was not accepted into the army, so she formed a women's army with her peers. But contrary examples notwithstanding, the role of women in war has been "largely associated with weeping, waiting and working: as wives, mothers and sweethearts."[1]

The WPS framework acknowledges that women are and always have been more than passive agents of security, more than victims, more than weeping, waiting, and working wives, mothers, and sweethearts of those fighting for their beliefs and their countries. The "participation" pillar of the framework specifically speaks to inclusion, for both the direct benefits women bring to the table and to increase the potential for gendered perspectives in plans, policies, and programs. Content analyses conducted on NAPs have shown more women in security forces, broadly defined, is often advocated. Identifying and understanding the root causes of the barriers that women face in militaries is important to abating those barriers.

Band of brothers (and sisters)?

First Lt. Ashley White was killed on October 22, 2011, by an improvised explosive device while on duty in Kandahar Province, Afghanistan. Her story was told in a bestselling 2015 book called *Ashley's War*. The celebratory nature of how Ashley White's story was told allowed the reading audience to see and understand the physical and emotional struggles she faced and overcame, and the emotions of her family in a very powerful way. But the words used in the book also continued "to instrumentalize women's bodies and stories, reenacting many of the misogynistic tropes that contribute to their continued marginalization in in male-dominated space." The language was used to ensure the broad appeal of the book to the American public as the policy change to allow women in combat was coming into effect "and to 'sell' the idea of women in combat."[2]

DOI: 10.4324/9781003413417-11

Ashley White was part of the Cultural Support Team (CST) program, initiated in 2009, of women working with Joint Special Operations Task Units. Though women were banned from serving in ground combat units in 2011, a *need* for skills only women could provide got Ashley and her teammates – all volunteers – *attached* to various units in support roles. Administratively, having them "support" the special operation unit rather than being *assigned* to it circumvented the ground combat ban.

Their primary mission was to engage the female population in areas where contact was deemed inappropriate for male service members and for that, CSTs had to be obviously female by sight. Each CST was also trained to provide support in areas including medical, civic action, search and seizures, and humanitarian assistance. Many of them initially faced resistance from the male special operations units they worked with, the men resentful that they had lost a "shooter" spot in their unit to a woman, though each CST was also a fully trained "shooter." The CSTs were often in the thick of the fighting, on nighttime raids, kicking down doors and being injured and dying with their male colleagues. CSTs tactically assumed positions of subordination in order to achieve their strategic goal of assimilation, and erased their female gender as much as possible to their colleagues, becoming in effect a "third gender" of neither man nor woman.[3]

Even less well known than the CSTs are the members of the covert Female Tactical Platoons (FTP) who also worked alongside special operations teams in Afghanistan. These were Afghan women trained to search and question women and children on high-risk nighttime missions. The program was set up in 2011 and continued until the fall of Kabul in 2021, with FTPs having conducted some 2,000 missions. Some died working for the United States, and 39 were among those evacuated in the chaos that followed the US departure, those women having huge targets on their back. According to a Green Beret who served alongside four FPT platoon members, "They were an affront to everything the Taliban stands for. They were one of the few groups who were kill-on-sight for the Taliban."[4] Again, they performed jobs essential to mission success that men could not do.

Secretary of Defense Ash Carter fully lifted the ground combat restriction in 2015. Today, Ashley White would no longer be structurally banned from serving in the role where she was critically needed. Objections to lifting the ban had come primarily from the US Marine Corps, which raised some concerns when Marine Corps General (ret.) James Mattis was nominated as secretary of defense in 2016. While perhaps the most often heard objection to women in combat focuses on their ability to meet the physical requirements, that was not the case with Mattis. His concerns, voiced in a 2014 speech at the Marines' Memorial Club in San Francisco, focused on mixing "Eros," the Greek god of love, with "the trenches." "The idea of putting women in there is not setting them up for success," he said.

> It would only be someone who never crossed the line of departure into close quarters fighting that would ever even promote such an idea […] Some of us aren't so old that we've forgotten that at times it was like heaven on earth just to hold a certain girl's hand,

he said, to laughter and applause from the audience.[5]

While structural restrictions on women serving in the US military have been removed, women are still fighting for full inclusion. Women assigned as part of a nine-person Stryker combat unit in Afghanistan have said they were often, or at least disproportionately, assigned the last two seats in the vehicle. Those seats are assigned to the unit members who stay in the vehicle rather than disembarking and engaging when the vehicle stops. Whether the seat assignments were made through benevolent sexism or lesser trust in the women's capabilities, it was demoralizing for the women. They just want to do their jobs. Cultural issues are only overcome with the concerted, consistent vigilance of leadership. Unfortunately, too, there are still a considerable number of blind fish in key positions who continue to discriminate against women on active duty and veterans, including the CSTs.

Jaclyn "Jax" Scott was a CST in Afghanistan. When she returned home from consecutive deployments in 2013, she had a brain injury from concussive grenade blasts as well as muscular injuries from heavy falls. But when she sought treatment from an army doctor, he laughed at her account of her trauma being combat related and prescribed her sleep aids for jet lag. Because the CSTs were attached rather than assigned to combat units, the Pentagon had never classified them as combat veterans in their personnel records, important for both medical care and promotions. In 2023, a bipartisan group of military veterans in Congress introduced the Jax Act to require that these women's personnel records be updated to reflect their frontline duties, to remove the burden of proof from the women when seeking medical care. Post-combat discrimination played out in other ways as well.

A Purple Heart woman warrior played a critical role in spurring the Department of Defense to finally drop the ban on women in combat. Air National Guard Major Mary Jennings' medevac helicopter was forced down by Taliban gunfire in 2009. Major Jennings nevertheless managed to land the helicopter safely, thereby saving the lives of her crew and passengers. At the time, the ban on women serving in ground combat was in effect, but not for air combat.

After having landed her helicopter safely and returning Taliban fire during the crew's rescue, Jennings retired from flying. She wanted to become a special tactics officer, a job that supports ground troops by calling in airstrikes. It is a job that requires thinking in 3D terms to give directions to pilots. As Mary Jennings described it,

It's like a different language. You know, we have our own lingo. We have code words that are intended to confuse the enemy if they can pick up our radio transmissions. So it's, you know, purposefully obtuse. So you have to be able to speak pilot. You have to be able to maintain your composure and, you know, when bullets are flying over your head, not escalate your voice.[6]

It was a job for which Mary Jennings was well qualified, but barred from because it was considered ground combat.

As with the CSTs, women were serving in combat roles because they were needed, but not officially assigned to the units to avoid the policy restrictions. They would be attached instead. Mary Jennings saw being attached rather than being assigned as part of the unit as impeding cohesion because the women would not be at the same base with the unit and would not have the opportunity to bond with the men on the team. When the American Civil Liberties Union asked her to file suit against the DOD to change the policy, Jennings was willing, because of a very specific reason.

For me, it wasn't about women's rights. It was about military effectiveness. The reasons that I just told you that we're tying the hands of the commanders in the field and having – making them have to juggle, you know, the name of the status of the woman that they had to put out with the team that they were sending into combat.[7]

The case never reached court because the Pentagon, perhaps anticipating what was coming, changed the rule. Mary Jennings' (now Hegar) story is told in her book *Shoot Like a Girl* (2017).

Discrimination against women wanting to serve their countries in uniform can be overt and cruel. Until 2021, the Indonesian military and police forces conducted abusive virginity tests through vaginal exams on female recruits. Human rights organizations argued that the tests were inconclusive and that women deemed to have failed the test were not necessarily penalized, nullifying any point to the test other than humiliation. The use of virginity tests by security forces in Egypt, India, and Afghanistan has also been documented. These abuses make education regarding the linkage between gender and security an imperative.

Ukraine and Syria

In 2020, there were 31,000 Ukrainian women in the military. As of 2023, that number has nearly doubled. Those numbers effectively make the Ukrainian military one of the most feminized militaries in the region. Women have served, been wounded, been taken prisoner, and died in service to their country.

Some 5,000 women in the military are serving in combat roles, including as paramedics, border guards, and snipers. Lt. Lyubov Plaksyuk was named the first woman to lead an artillery unit in the Ukrainian military. The former history teacher joined the military in 2016, fulfilling a lifelong dream of "protecting the fatherland."[8] As one of two women in her unit, she has stated that she didn't feel that gender has played a role in her job because her male subordinates respect her professionalism. However, 2022 research suggests that headlines touting Ukrainian egalitarianism in the military are misleading.[9]

In 2015, the Ukrainian government decided to move from a partial military mobilization to a full mobilization to be ready if conflicts were to erupt in conjunction with pro-Russian separatists in the eastern region of the country. Partial mobilization, then limited to men, had been hampered by draft dodgers. Consequently, in February 2015 the General Staff declared that it would also be mobilizing women between the ages of 20 and 50 who had registered for and were eligible to be drafted. Mobilization was voluntary for women, though mandatory for men. This gendered difference created a distinction between men's and women's wartime agency and social value; men were afforded less agency than women, but men's service was perceived as having more social value than women's. Women were also afforded exemptions to mobilization unavailable to men if they are mothers, full-time students, or graduate students.

The intent regarding the mobilization of women was to expand the use of women only in certain (traditional) fields, specifically, medical, communications, and logistics. That change acknowledged the need for an expanded talent pool in the military, but also siloed women into culturally acceptable roles. A 2019 UN study found most Ukrainians supportive of gender-based work roles, though men were more supportive (62%) than women (54%). In that study, many Ukrainians were shown to believe that a woman's role is primarily as guardian of the home, children, and husband. For the military, that meant a women could be a nurse or a cook but not a marksman or drone operator. The marked increase in women volunteers that the government was looking for in 2015 did not materialize, indicating that those women most likely to volunteer wanted more than a gender-based work role.

In 2016, the military expanded the roles available to women toward making military service more attractive to them. Still, however, two-thirds of all military positions were off-limits to women, including combat positions. Nonetheless, there were strong indications that job titles often did not match with a combat/non-combat reality, with female office managers and seamstresses sometimes receiving concussions and injuries more aligned with combat. This policy discrepancy denied the women, much like the American CSTs, additional rights within the military and public acknowledgment of their service. It was not until 2018 that all jobs, including combat positions, were opened to women.

The inclusion of women in the 2015 mobilization had consequences for Ukrainian men as well. Specifically, men were being shamed by the women's willingness to fight and the need for their inclusion. Some 75,000 Ukrainian men were mobilized in 2015, with some 60% expected to be conscripted into service. But the target numbers were not reached, though the government imposed a five-year prison penalty for draft dodgers, including through travel abroad. Russia encouraged Ukrainian men to avoid conscription and went so far as to revise its immigration laws to help those who wanted to flee to Russia.

On October 11, 2021, Ukraine's Ministry of Defense issued an order requiring women between the ages of 18 and 60 employed in 100 professions, to register with conscription offices. Those professions included broadly defined medical fields and support staffs for those fields, STEM fields, management, finance, and banking, as well as communications, logistics, postal workers, translators, cooks, butchers, and interpreters. Similar to 2015, however, there was no call or requirement that women serve in combat; in fact, just the opposite. Women were specifically offered the opportunity to serve in places far from the front lines.

As further evidence of Ukrainian views on the role of women in the military prior to the invasion, in 2021 the Ministry of Defense defended a policy decision to require that women in the army train to march Prussian-style in heels for a planned parade. In response to domestic and foreign backlash, the ministry posted pictures on Facebook of women in other military organizations in heels. The ministry backed down only after it was pointed out that the women pictured were not marching, but were in formal dress uniforms. The defense minister promised to look into new, ergonomic footwear.

President Volodymyr Zelensky declared martial law in February 2022 following the Russian invasion. As part of martial law, anyone registered for conscription was banned from leaving the country. With registration mandatory for men and voluntary for women, that inherently affords men less agency to leave, undervalues both the work done by women in communities and that of women in the military, and means that women inherently make up the bulk of refugees fleeing the country. The gendered policies of the Ukrainian government and military initiated since 2015 indicate that while the state wants and needs more individuals in combat roles, gender norms conflict with placing women in those roles. Additionally, the gendered policies make men, as forced combatants, a bigger target for Russian forces. Women like Lyubov Plaksyuk have been able to enter career fields previously unavailable to them, but not because the government encouraged egalitarianism. Her opportunity was afforded through need rather than a government policy supporting equality.

Like women in many other militaries, Ukrainian women in the military function in less than optimal conditions beyond that of being in a war zone. Ukraine has no standard military uniforms for women. They are issued men's jackets, pants, shoes, and even underwear. With women often narrower than men in the shoulders but wider in the hips, jackets can be big in the shoulders or too tight across the chest and pants, if they fit at the hips, too big at the waist, and more often than not too long. Ill-fitting clothing, said to affect over 90% of women fighting for Ukraine, is not a matter of fashion. Ill-fitting clothing can be uncomfortable and restrict movement. Ukrainian women's organizations are trying to address the problem that the government can't in the midst of war. A Ukrainian organization called Arm Women Now has taken on the task of tailoring uniforms for women, and as of 2022, there was a waiting list of several thousand women. The biggest problem regarding clothing for women has been thermal underwear, which needs to fit properly for warmth. But many women have simply gone online and ordered what they need, solving the problem.

In fact, Ukrainian women in the military are not complaining about their clothing, and don't like to be asked about it. Yevhenia Zakrevska, an attorney and human rights activist, joined the military after the Russian invasion, learned to fly drones, and is now doing so as part of the territorial defense of Ukraine's capital, Kiev. She has said she is tired of being asked what it is like to be a woman in the military, about her clothes not fitting, and whether she can get feminine pads. Zakrevska counters, "I don't work as a woman in the army. I work as an aerial reconnaissance officer. And as a woman in the military, I lack shells and artillery."[10] She and others recognize that focusing on "women's problems in the army," disproportionate to army problems in general, can give the impression that women in the military are a problem, not part of a solution. They just want to do their jobs.

In Syria, the Kurdish Women's Protection Units (YPJ) provide a different model of women's military service. Syria has been ravaged by war since 2011, peaking between 2012 and 2017 when the Islamic State of Iraq and the Levant (ISIL, or Daesh) took over much of Syria's northeastern territory. Territorial governance of Syria in 2023 is divided among several groups, most prominently Syrian Arab Republic led by the repressive regime of Bashar al-Assad, various rebel forces, and the Kurdish Syrian Democratic Forces (SDF) in the northeast. The YPJ played a key role in expelling ISIS from that region, and continue to play a key role in holding it.

YPJ is the all-female brigade of the People's Protection Units (YPG), the armed forces of the region of Kurdistan known as Rojava, or western Kurdistan (which is northeastern Syria). The YPJ was formed in 2013 mainly of ethnic Kurds, to fight alongside the male YPG of the SDF, which was then part of the US-led campaign against ISIS. The Kurds are an Iranian ethnic group living in contiguous areas of Iraq, Iran, Syria, and Turkey and have long sought a state of their own. Women have been involved in Syrian resistance fighting since 2011, then as part of mixed-sex units, with the YPJ formed and expanded in 2013 after allegations that the need for fighters was such that the YPG was recruiting child soldiers. There were approximately 5,000 YPJ fighters at the height of the fight against ISIL, and the same number today, which many observers see as an indication that the YPJ message is attractive to women and useful to the SDF, now concerned about a potential Turkish invasion of its territory.

The YPJ is politically aligned to the Syrian Democratic Union Party. Party philosophy is based the writings of Abjullah Öcalan, a Kurdish ideologue imprisoned in Turkey, with the concept of Jineology ("science of women" in Kurdish) foundational to those writings. Jineology advocates gender equality and that women's liberation is necessary for Kurdish liberation. According to Öcalan, "A country can't be free unless women are free,"[11] and has emphasized that the level of women's freedom determines the level of freedom in society at large. In support of this philosophy, in 2015 when areas of Syria were liberated from ISIS, sharia was abandoned and centers where women could learn about female emancipation were set up and schools opened for children. Those centers, called Mala Jinê (Women's House) are shelters of a sort where all staff and members are mothers, and a place women can go to talk about issues like GBV and find potential support systems. Mala Jinê centers often work in conjunction with other area women's committees. Acceptance of gender equality, however, can be a hard sell in traditional Muslim societies, sometimes even among women.

For example, religious conservative women were key in re-electing conservative, authoritarian Turkish president Erdoğan in 2023. Erdogan successfully tapped into the women's desire to maintain a conservative Muslim view of female roles in Turkish society, first as mothers and wives, but also secondarily to be members of the workforce. The women view the latter, allowed and supported by Erdoğan, as a relaxation of previous societal restrictions and therefore see Erdoğan as their protector. The women's conservative societal views mesh with his as well.

Upon joining the YPJ, women must spend at least a month practicing military tactics and studying the writings of Öcalan. According to one recruit, "I decided to join to fight the Daesh not just for me, but for every woman in the region."[12] Married women are not accepted into the

YPJ and members are discouraged, though not banned, from dating and using cell phones while they are in the YPJ. They are encouraged instead to focus on comradeship with other women in their daily lives. In any communal decision regarding either the YPJ or the YPG, there is a requirement that no less than 40% of the participants are women and every YPJ unit is led by a woman.

The group has garnered support and praise from groups internationally for confronting and redefining gender roles in the region. The YPJ was recognized as instrumental in the battle to take back control of the region and the city of Kobani from ISIL in 2014, with that battle seen as a turning point in the war against ISIL. The YPJ also played a critical role in rescuing and providing security for Yazadis trapped on Mount Sinjar in Iraq in 2014, including a large population of women. ISIL viewed Yazadis as a community of devil worshipers and regularly used captured Yazadi women as sex slaves.

YPJ combatants understand they are feared by opponents such as ISIS/ISIL fighters because those opponents believe being killed in battle by a woman is a disgrace and dishonor that will prohibit them from entering paradise. But YPJ members also understand that if they are captured, they will be raped and brutally killed, making it imperative that they succeed or become a suicide warrior to avoid capture. During a 2019 Turkish offensive into Kurdish-held areas of Syria, Turkish-backed Free Syrian Army fighters killed and mutilated the body of a YPJ fighter known by her nom de guerre "Kobane." They "played with her corpse"[13] while cameras rolled, generating significant anger among Kurds when it was shown on social media. YPJ members regularly use one or more aliases because they know they are being targeted. A YPJ commander credited with having saved American lives in the war against ISIS, was killed by a Turkish drone strike in July 2022. Forty-two-year-old Salwa Yusuk, also known as Ciyan Afrin and Gian Tolhildan, was killed with two other YPJ fighters. She had been with the military for about ten years, had a reputation for courage on the battlefield and astute military planning, and was a founder and leader in the YPJ. She, and other martyred YPJ members are not forgotten, with public remembrances common in cities and their own villages.

When warriors go home

A 1999 *New York Times* article described battlefield experiences of a second-generation woman Eritrean soldier, and her expectations for when the fighting stopped.

> Hiwet Yonanes, 21, said she had noticed one major difference: women rarely take prisoners. "Women are very bad," she said. "They don't capture at all. Most of the Ethiopians know that." But she also said the Ethiopians, who do not have women in combat, treat the female Eritrean soldiers differently than the men. On the second day of a huge battle at Tsorona in March, she said, five Ethiopian soldiers tried to take her prisoner – but without drawing their guns. "They thought it would be easy to capture me," she said. "It was very stupid of them. I didn't see them but my friends did and shot them right before they got to me." Ms. Tekeste, whose mother was a soldier, said that when the war is over she will think about getting married and starting a career. But the fact that she fought, she said, is still not enough to make her, or any woman, equal. It is only a start, she said.[14]

The struggle for equality among Eritrean women continues. Not only did the empowerment that women experience as soldiers largely evaporate in civilian society, but they often faced additional prejudice, claiming they had "lost their womanly qualities."[15]

Women Eritrean ex-fighters – sometimes born into families of fighters – were largely unprepared to integrate or reintegrate into society, lacking resources, skills, or job prospects. Further, the very skills that made them strong fighters stigmatized them as wives and potential wives. Some husbands divorced them in favor of a "civilian" wife. Former women fighters had experienced independence, sexual freedom, and equality with men. When the fighting stopped, though, they found their morality suspect, their femininity doubted, and their ability and willingness to act as obedient wives questioned.

Gender equality was achieved during the years of fighting by eliminating the domestic sphere and the feminine identity. There were no separate spindle and spear domains, only spear. During the civil war, men and women were working toward liberation. There was a single goal for all Eritreans. However, after independence, women were again marginalized because that single focus was lost when the country began to center its attention on national development. Competition during development creates winners and losers within a formerly united society. Competitors can easily eliminate a group of competitors by returning to the traditional marginalization of women.

Other African women freedom fighters are or have been, in similar situations. In South Africa, Mozambique, and South Sudan, women found that whereas men are celebrated as liberators, "the female fighter is not often celebrated"[16] after peace is won. Women FARC fighters in Colombia faced similar situations as well.

Through disarmament, demobilization, and reintegration (DDR) programs between 2002 and 2012, the size of the FARC shrunk from 20,000 to 8,000, with women comprising 40% of FARC numbers. Part of the problem with reintegration and including women into DDR efforts stems from the "gray areas" of conflict where women are most often involved.

> The roles, statuses, and experiences of female combatants are often quite different than those of their male counterparts. These differences not only shape women's experiences during conflict, but often linger long afterward. During conflict they may serve as bush-wives, cooks, spies, and frontline fighters; they are responsible for establishing camps or carrying weapons. Quite often their role is to collect weapons and hold them in a cache until the fighting ceases, a function that is often overlooked, but critically important when planning for disarmament. Qualifications for entry into DDR programs often require combatants to bring in a certain number of a type of weapon, and sometimes require the women to demonstrate a working knowledge of these weapons. Women and girls may be responsible for establishing weapons caches, but due to their low status they often cannot meet DDR requirements.[17]

The Colombian Reintegration Agency (CRA) was created to guide former fighters back into civilian life. At least initially, they were more successful with men. Women complained they were largely offered training in low-paying fields like cooking and tailoring, and not provided the child care often necessary to attend training classes or get jobs. Gender analysis was integrated into CRA programming in 2013 regarding job opportunities. Nevertheless, cultural issues persisted.

The Colombian government launched a public service campaign in 2012 designed to look like a lipstick ad. "Guerrillera," it says, "feel like a woman again. Demobilize." It featured lipstick colors with names like "freedom," "love," "happiness," and "tranquility," and promised women that they could "smile and become the mother [they've] always dreamed of being."[18] Further, the director of the CRA stated in 2016 that female former combatants have sometimes lost their "feminine features" by doing the same work as men and want to get them back. "We put a strong focus on accompanying them and helping them again reconstruct those feminine features that they want to construct."[19]

While women may indeed want to reconstruct the feminine features he refers to, they are also focused on supporting themselves and their families.

Other issues come into play as well for former fighters, including cultural stigmatization and concerns about physical security. Women not wanting to be identified as former FARC fighters in a conservative country like Colombia – with their morality suspect and femininity doubted in the same way as Eritrean women – is not surprising. The relatively low numbers of women processed through the CRA indicate that many women opted not to identify themselves as former guerrillas and instead try to reintegrate on their own. But that leaves them without government financial allowances, psychological support, and job training.

Both men and women former fighters have feared reprisals regarding personal violence from parts of Colombian society as well, with women the more vulnerable. Therefore, in some cases they are reluctant to self-identify. The challenges women ex-fighters have faced in Colombia are likely to be much the same as those in other countries: against marginalization and stigmatization. It also makes inclusive diversity and gendered perspective in relief and recovery all the more important.

Progressive militaries?

The military offers many women opportunities and career training unavailable elsewhere while they proudly serve their countries. Israel, Norway, Canada, and the United States are among the countries that have asserted success at integrating women into the military. That assertion is largely based on women being allowed to serve in combat. But to be clear, just as no country treats its women the same as it treats its men, no military does either.

In Israel, both men and women perform compulsory military service, and women began being integrated into combat positions in 1995. Canada opened most military occupations to women in 1989, and all occupations with the integration of submarine service in 2000. Norway was the first country to allow women to serve on submarines, in 1985. But integration has not been easy, nor is it yet complete. Each country has its unique issues, and all have intraservice sexual assault rates above what would be expected within organizations that claim camaraderie and honor as part of their ethos. In most cases, structural barriers within these countries have been removed, but cultural barriers remain in place regarding women's entry into and progression in certain fields, and full acceptance as a comrade in arms.

Israel is the only country in the world with mandatory two-year conscription for women and calls its army a "people's army." Israel considers its threat level such that all adult citizens must contribute to security. Additionally, compulsory military service is considered to further the Israeli goal of creating an integrated society. That is, the Israeli Defense Force (IDF) has been a melting pot allowing immigrants and minority groups to share a joint rite of passage into Israeli society.

Women served alongside men in paramilitary groups predating Israeli independence in 1948, typical of instances where groups are fighting for independence or against invasion. After independence, though, women in the military were largely relegated to administrative jobs, and to being medical assistants and trainers, except during times such as the 1973 Yom Kippur War when Israel was actively engaged in fighting. Women's largely support status was challenged in 1995 when Alice Miller petitioned the Israeli Supreme Court for access to pilot training after having been rejected on the basis of sex. The Court's ruling in Miller's favor had a profound effect on women being able gain access to previously male military domains.

Most famously, the Israeli Caracal unit was formed in 2004, a coed battalion named for a desert cat whose gender can be difficult to determine. The battalion is comprised of approximately 70% women and its job is to patrol Israel's often dangerous border with Egypt's Sinai Peninsula. While the Caracal unit is often cited as proof of women's effectiveness in combat, the requirement for "proof" – which can erode confidence – has been an issue. A female Caracal member explained in 2013:

> There's a lot of pressure on the women to be just as good as the men because we have a lot to prove. There's always a question of could they shut down the unit if we don't do as well. You don't see them threatening to shut down the paratroopers.[20]

Over time, the women have proven their value to the country. Caracal Captain Michal-Lee Eliel said in 2022 that she believes that women "no longer have to prove anything to society."[21] Whether full acceptance by male colleagues holds true or not is more tenuous.

In 2014, the IDF initiated another mixed-gender, light infantry battalion called the Lions of Jordan, followed in 2015, by the creation of the Bardalas (cheetah) mixed-gender unit. In both cases, the reason for the creation of the units was need. Mandatory IDF service for men was cut from three full years to two years and eight months in 2015, creating a "manning" gap to be filled. That forced the army to be more amenable to opening more jobs to women rather than it indicating a shift in gender attitudes. Many of the remaining obstacles to women in the IDF are cultural, not obstacles in terms of a woman's ability.

Zeev Lerer of Tel Aviv University's Peres Academic Center Gender Studies Department and a retired IDF lieutenant colonel, has pointed out that "pictures of women with guns have a lot of PR value, but that is not a sign of integration."[22] The ramifications of women being excluded from some exclusive units extend beyond their military service. Women, for example, rarely serve in the elite high-tech army units often considered a fast track into post-service lucrative positions in Israel's high-tech industry. It wasn't until 2022 that an IDF/business collaboration was formed to help women enter into still highly male-dominant high-tech fields, including cyber.

The influence of religion on the IDF is also a consideration. In the past, much of the Orthodox Israeli community opted for national service – volunteering in hospitals, educational and social-welfare institutions – rather than military service to fulfill the Israeli universal conscription requirement. Since 2015, however, there has been an increase in young religious women joining the IDF, many to escape the confines of conservative religious life. Prominent rabbis have spoken out against women serving in the military in the past and in conjunction with the rise in Orthodox women's enlistment. Their reasoning put forth in a 2016 editorial appears a mix of seeking to perpetuate the spindle/spear dichotomy and nationalism:

> In our view, the military framework is not appropriate for women in general and for religious women in particular. We are talking about an aggressive, combative system with numerous modesty-related problems that run counter to the lifestyle of the religious woman. There are all kinds of organizations that are using the army to promote their egalitarian viewpoints. They are even trying to advance women to [more] combat positions. These are outrageous notions that are trying to change us into an egalitarian army instead of a winning army.[23]

The assumption in the last part of the rabbis' argument appears to be that an army of men will win, but adding women threatens their ability to do so; women "spoil" the army. Their argument has persisted and gotten louder since 2016.

Finally, the IDF, like many other military organizations, has a serious problem with sexual assault. Data for 2020 included 1,542 sexual assault cases, including 26 cases of rape, 391 obscene acts, and 92 cases of disturbing photos and videos. By comparison, there were 1,239 complaints filed in 2019, and 514 complaints filed in 2012. A 2021 report stated that a third of women IDF soldiers experience sexual harassment during their mandatory service, though less than half file complaints. Of those who do, 44% said their complaints were not handled properly, and 26% said their complaints were not handled at all.[24] When women don't trust the system they work in, egalitarianism is not part of that system.

Like Israeli women, Norwegian women also made significant contributions to the World War II effort, yet found offers for their post-fighting services less accepted, or overtly rebuked. In 1953, the Norwegian Parliament debated and rejected allowing women to serve in the military. That decision was reconsidered in 1976, when Parliament decided to allow women to volunteer for non-combatant military positions. Finally, in 1984 Parliament bestowed on women the same opportunities and rights as men, on a voluntary basis, throughout the organization. But Norway has struggled to claim that the Norwegian Armed Forces (NorAF) have successfully integrated even though Norway became the first European country to make national service compulsory gender neutral in 2015 and brought the percentage of women serving to 33% in 2020.

Norway is generally considered one of the most gender-balanced countries in the world and is consistently ranked among the top three or four countries on most gender equality indexes. But Norway also has a highly gender-segregated labor market, which is something of a paradox. Women choose traditional careers in health, education, and care by a significant margin, with men dominating construction, transportation, and information technology. Within NorAf, increasing the number of women provides diversified labor but not necessarily in all fields. With conscription, joining the military became highly competitive. While both men and women must register for the military, only about 13% are actually called upon to serve, most often those with both the strongest motivation and the skills. While most women serve in non-combat-related fields, for some women, joining the military has offered them the chance of a lifetime.

In 2014, Norway began recruiting for a new special forces unit called Jegertroppen (Hunter Troop) and for the world's first-ever all-female military training program. The rationale, as with CSTs, was operational need.

> In Afghanistan, one of our big challenges was that we would enter houses and not be able to speak to the women," explained Captain Ole Vidar Krogsaeter, an officer with Norway's Special Forces Operations. "In urban warfare, you have to be able to interact with women as well. Adding female soldiers was an operational need."[25]

There were no women in Norwegian special forces prior to 2014. Selection for Jegertroppen is highly selective and rigorous, as is training, which takes a year and includes modules in Arctic survival, counterterrorism, urban warfare, long-range patrols, and airborne operations.

The majority of women selected for NorAf service stay only for the mandatory two years. A primary reason for leaving is sexual harassment and bullying. Norway has been able to boast an overall slight decrease in harassment in recent years, but not among the age group where it is most prevalent, young women. In 2020, 63% of women under 30 said they had been harassed, clearly indicating a culture-based problem. The Norwegian military has come under fire for using sexist memory aids in training, such as calling a standing formation "C*** in the ass" or staff teaching conscripts the phrase: into the panties, up the P***y in order to remember a compass rule. Another memory aid described a compass setting: 3/4ths – "just as drunk as a woman should be when you take her home from the club."[26]

Given the egalitarian reputation of Norway, social scientists have spent considerable time and effort exploring the sexist culture too often found in militaries, including their own.

A 2007 Norwegian study presents a summary of the academic literature on the relationship between militarism and masculinity, beginning with a quote from British sociologist John Hopton.

Historically, there is a reciprocal relationship between militarism and masculinity. On the one hand, politicians have utilized ideologies of idealized masculinity that valorize the notion of strong active males collectively risking their personal safety for the greater good of their wider community, gaining support for the state's use of violence, such as wars in the international arena and aggressive policing in the domestic situation. On the other hand, militarism feeds into ideologies of masculinity through the eroticization of stoicism, risk taking and even lethal violence. [27]

The environment that is created is referred to as hegemonic masculinity, where practices are normalized by consent to legitimize men's dominance and justify the subordination of women and other marginalized and feminized ways of being a man.[28] Consequently, the argument is, the military does not seek just any kind of male, but rather one characterized by a propensity toward violence, aggression, and a sense of invulnerability. This propensity is supported by standard language used in officer evaluations, which encourages more masculine attributes.

It has also been suggested, however, that a multiplicity of masculinities exist within the military – members of the infantry, for example, potentially being very different than cyber warriors whose battlefield is a computer screen – thereby questioning the notion of hegemonic masculinity. Intersectionality has been used to consider these multiplicities, suggesting male vulnerabilities in some situations, though not without some feminist scholars questioning the application of intersectionality for use with dominant groups such as military men.[29]

Norwegian sociologists released a report on Norway's military in 2014 titled *The Army: The Vanguard, Rear Guard and Battlefield of Equality.* One of the report's findings was considered particularly noteworthy: that unisex dorms in the Norwegian army were associated with a decline in sexual assault.

Unisex dorms eroded gender divisiveness, which was replaced by a shared status as soldiers [...] The success of the unisex dorms indicates that hegemonic masculinity can be superseded through direct contact with women in close quarters [...] unity around camaraderie becomes more important than divisiveness around gender.[30]

The authors also suggested that other factors, including strong leadership, common goals, and equal positions, likely factored into the success of the unisex dorms.

A 2021 study included an experiment to consider whether broader prejudices in a dominant group could be changed for the better if the group was exposed to members of a minority group. They found that male soldiers in a mixed-gender group had far more positive attitudes about their female colleagues after boot camp than those who had only trained with other males.

However, six months after the end of the experiment, male attitudes had changed again, and there was no longer a difference in attitudes between the groups.[31]

Finally, it should be noted that, in the course of studying how culture affects women in non-traditional careers such as the military, Norwegian researchers also found how their culture works negatively against men. Women entering nontraditional careers are largely supported by friends, family, and mentors for trying to break gender barriers. But men who choose to go into, for example, "care" career fields can face negative backlash. The experience of a Norwegian male training to be a nurse provides an example.

> I face prejudices all the time. "Are you gay or are you here to pick up girls?" Is the standard reaction. And that is not only from those who do not know better. I have also heard it from lecturers and student councilors.[32]

Hence, changing cultural career norms will benefit both men and women, and society.

As in Norway, structural barriers to Canadian women soldiers serving in combat roles were removed well over a decade ago. Though originally traditionalist – in the 1950s, the only roles women could serve in in the military were nurse, dietitian, or administrator – Canadians began considering allowing women in combat in 1970. The Canadian military was against integration and, according to Lt. Col. Shirley Robinson, who served as deputy director of women personnel at the time, stalled by initiating a series of trials to see what combat roles women might be suited for. "Those trials should never have happened," she said. "Women had already been out there in harm's way."[33] As has happened before, change eventually came through a legal challenge.

Canada passed the Charter of Rights and Freedoms – the Canadian Bill of Rights – in 1982. Soon thereafter, a discrimination complaint against the Canadian Armed Forces (CAF) was filed with the Canadian Human Rights Tribunal. Following the discrimination complaint, the Tribunal instructed the CAF to fully integrate women into the military within ten years. By 1989, all restrictions on women were gone. Combat roles were then voluntary for both men and women in the Canadian military. With structural barriers removed, cultural barriers still had to be addressed.

The Canadian government commissioned a study in 2003 to identify cultural issues related to assimilation and integration within the military and provide suggestions for addressing those challenges.

> Based on the women's perceptions of effective leadership, the findings from this study suggest that both integration and assimilation are currently in force in the Canadian combat arms. In terms of integration, participants spoke of the importance of both feminine and masculine characteristics in defining effective leadership; most leaders in this study did not feel that they must adopt a masculine leadership style in order to be seen as effective; and all eight leaders in this study described their own leadership style in integrative terms, even emphasizing the importance of their feminine attributes to effective leadership. In terms of assimilation, many participants perceived negative implications in relation to a female exhibiting feminine leadership characteristics. Furthermore, nearly one-half of followers felt that women leaders must become more masculine in order to be perceived as effective. Thus, the current situation regarding women, leadership, and gender integration in the Canadian combat arms is complex and contradictory, with both integrative and assimilative forces in operation.[34]

Once again, feminine traits were not perceived as detrimental to leadership, but were seen as potentially detrimental to assimilation. Regarding recommendations, the study pointed to leadership attitudes and practices as key: not singling out women, having positive attitudes toward women in combat, and setting the example. While Canada has gone a long way toward integration, it is still plagued with sexual assault and harassment issues, extending to the highest levels of the military.

In March 2015, the *External Review into Sexual Misconduct and Sexual Harassment in the Canadian Armed Forces*[35] was released. The report found that the Canadian military is plagued with "an underlying sexualized culture." As a cultural issue, while policies and structure can play a role in abating problems, the report again pointed to the need for the direct and sustained attention of military leadership to abate issues. Canada's Chief of Defense Staff General Jonathan Vance initiated a program called Operation Honour in response, calling sexual assault and harassment a threat to the institution. Shortly thereafter, the media began reporting on the internal response. "Some recruits at the Royal Military College, as well as other Canadian Forces personnel including individuals at National Defence headquarters in Ottawa, dubbed Op Honour as 'Hop On Her' – a play on words suggesting sexual aggression or even assault."[36] With sexist attitudes blatantly displayed apparently without fear of reprisal, it is not surprising that 25% of women serving in the Canadian military have said that they were sexually assaulted while serving, and the government has had to set aside $800 million to settle class action lawsuits.

Not long after Vance retired in 2021, he became steeped in scandal himself when it was revealed that Vance had carried on a long-time affair with a female army subordinate and fathered two children with her. He subsequently pleaded guilty to obstruction of justice in trying to get the subordinate to lie to investigators. Other top Canadian military officers, including a navy admiral and a human resources officer whose responsibilities involved eliminating sexual harassment, have similarly been under investigation or charged. A 2022 report to the Canadian government headed by Louise Arbour, a former Canadian Supreme Court justice and UN High Commissioner for Human Rights, made 48 recommendations for institutionally addressing the problem, including the hiring of an external monitor, an overhaul of the military's educational institutions and service academies as "from a different era, with an outdated and problematic leadership model,"[37] and regular reports to the public. Recruiting and retention have become a problem given the lack of public trust in Canadian military leadership.

The US Congress passed the Armed Forces Integration Act in 1948, allowing women to serve as regular, permanent members of the military. Air Force General Wilma Vaught, one of the early women to reach flag rank, recalled some of the considerations behind the legislation in a 2011 interview. The congressional committees, for example, "thought about the age that women would be when they would be considered for admiral or general, they would be going through menopause. And if they were, they might make irrational decisions."[38] Perhaps ironically, more recent studies have found that men who take supplemental testosterone – with prescriptions rising from 1.3 million to 2.3 million in just a four-year period, often for no medical reason – were likely to make impulsive and faulty decisions.[39] Yet it has been women's potential for irrational decision-making that has consistently concerned (largely male) decision makers.

Women were originally only allowed to reach a certain rank, and their numbers restricted to no more than 2% of their overall force. Further, pregnancy meant immediate discharge. Women were not allowed to serve in combat or command men. In fact, Vaught said that when she went to basic training in the 1950s, her basic training focused more on how to sit properly and apply makeup, rather than on physicality. It was more charm school than military training.

During World War II, American women served the defense effort in multiple ways, perhaps most famously as Rosie the Riveter, but also in jobs such as Women Air Force Service Pilots (WASPs). With pilots in short supply in 1942, the program was started so that male pilots could be detailed to combat. Women would be trained to fly cargo planes, though initially Army Air Corps General Henry "Hap" Arnold wondered if "a slip of girl could handle the controls of a B-17 in heavy weather."[40] They proved they could. In fact, beginning in 1944, over 1,100 women flew almost every type of military aircraft, including B-26 and B-29 bombers. They ferried aircraft across the country, towed targets behind their planes to allow male gunners target practice (with live ammunition), tested repaired aircraft, and performed any other flying jobs they were asked to do. Their safety records were comparable to and sometimes better than those of their male counterparts. In service to their country, 38 WASPs lost their lives, though they were not considered part of the military.

The women, led by pioneer aviator Jacqueline Cochran, hoped that having demonstrated both their competence and value, the WASPs would become part of the military and endure past the war years. That did not happen. In fact, by 1944 the program was in jeopardy. The end of the war was in sight and flight training programs were slowing down. Male civilian instructor jobs were at risk, as instructors were no longer needed in large numbers. Rather than chance being drafted as ground troops, the civilian instructors lobbied for the WASP jobs, and got them. Arnold shut down the WASPs. The women were sent home.

In 1976, the air force announced that it was going to admit women to its flying program, saying, "it's the first time that the Air Force has allowed women to fly their aircraft."[41] That gross misstatement motivated the WASPs to action. They lobbied Congress for military status and found an ally in Senator Barry Goldwater, who had also ferried aircraft during the war. In 1977, the WASPs were finally granted military status, through legislation. It was not until legislation in 2016, however, that a WASP was allowed interred at Arlington National Cemetery. The secretary of the army, responsible for the cemetery, had previously refused WASP requests to be buried there based on a technicality relating to the 1977 legislation.[42] They had served their country, but had to fight every step of the way to get their country to acknowledge their service.

Then, when the need for support personnel in Vietnam reached critical levels, military policy was changed to allow women in combat zones. Additionally, in 1967 the military lifted the cap on the number of women who could serve and removed the women's ceiling on rank. In 1980, Vaught was promoted to brigadier general. When she retired five years later, she was one of only seven females serving as a flag officer in the military. Vaught has repeatedly made the point that women in the military have made breakthroughs through legislation and lawsuits, especially in the 1970s. "They sued over women being forced to leave the service on the day they were diagnosed as being pregnant," Vaught said. "They sued over the principle that if women had children in their household, they had to get out [of the service]."[43] As an unmarried woman with no children, Vaught was personally largely unaffected by those policy changes, but was acutely aware that others were, and of women gradually being granted greater opportunities. Opportunity, however, is different from equal treatment and inclusivity.

US service academies first admitted women in 1976. Over 300 women enrolled at the US Military Academy at West Point, New York, the US Naval Academy at Annapolis, Maryland, the US Air Force Academy in Colorado Springs, Colorado, and the US Coast Guard Academy in New London, Connecticut. The first women graduated from the academies in 1980. In those first coeducational classes, 66% of the women graduated, compared to 70% of the men. The men's attrition rate due to academic failure was, however, twice that of the women.

In 1994, the Government Accounting Office (GAO) conducted a study titled *Military Academy: Gender and Racial Disparities*. The summary indicates somewhat different academy experiences and perceptions between men and women, and a continually higher attrition rate for women.

> Women consistently received offers of admission at higher rates than men, but also consistently experienced higher attrition than men. Women's academic grades were lower than men's, particularly during freshman and sophomore years, despite generally higher academic predictor scores. In contrast, women's physical education grades were somewhat higher despite lower predictor scores in this area. Although reviewed more frequently for Honor Code violations and for failure to meet academic standards, women were recommended for separation less often […] A GAO survey of cadets, staff, and faculty revealed perceptions that women and minorities were generally treated the same as men and whites. Some male cadets, however, viewed women as receiving better treatment in some areas. To a somewhat lesser degree, minorities were also viewed as receiving better treatment. [44]

Attrition rates have continued to be a point of comparison, given the investment made in the men and women who attend the academies. Differences between service academy rates of attrition and the reasons behind attrition are therefore of particular interest.

At West Point, attrition rates between men and women in the 1990s were proportionally the same. Women left less for academic reasons and more for medical and personal reasons. Men left for conduct, military and academic deficiencies, and honor code violations. Most often, men and women left West Point for reasons of "motivation."[45]

During the same period, women's attrition at the Air Force Academy was noted as double that of West Point. Academy officials and others wondered if there was a connection between 25% of women leaving the Academy in the early 1990s and a high number of sexual harassment complaints there.[46] Sexual assault issues have swirled around all the military academies since women began being admitted. Congress has investigated, the DOD has investigated, and the academies have conducted internal investigations of the persistent problems. The hypermasculine environment of military academies and a reporting and correction system that often provides the perpetrator impunity and leaves the victim tagged "the problem," are commonly found issues. Those issues are not unique to the service academies, but extend to the military services in general.

Rape is an occupational hazard for many women in the military. In a 2011 article, political scientist Rebecca Hannagan and psychologist Holly Arrow posit reasons behind the problem.

> underpinnings of tensions among heterosexual males, among heterosexual females and between males and females and how these tensions have played out in the strongly gendered context of warrior culture. In the absence of cultural intervention that take into account deep-seated conceptions of women in the military as unwelcome intruders, sexual resources for military mean, or both, military women operate in an environment in which sexual assault may be deployed to enact and defend traditional military structures.[47]

Again, leadership is required for successful "cultural intervention."

Lack of hard data is a problem in addressing military gender integration just as it is in other areas of gender integration and equality. As in many organizations, women in the military do not see it in their interests to report information. They expect male leadership to circle the wagons around the accused, fear getting transferred, or worse, being tagged as the problem. There is also a general lack of transparency when it comes to the release of data from the military. For example, curiously, researcher requests for information about faculty diversity in Professional

Military Education have in some instances been rejected as "need to know," meaning restricted due to sensitivity. Most other academic institutions readily release, even boast about, their diversity statistics.

Being in the minority, the conundrum women face in reporting incidents of abuse is significant. Two women who fought in Iraq describe the issues they encountered:

Says Bethany Kibler, 27, a noncommissioned officer in the Army reserves who spent a year in Iraq, women must fight doubly hard against stereotypes like the idea that they wield their sexuality to win special treatment or get pregnant to avoid service. This leads to "a sort of female hate." To overcome this, most women in the military act tough and tend to be judgmental of each other. Many women feel compelled to keep up with the men, to act like their sisters. But in such permissive stressful circumstances, that armor is easily breached.

Kayla Williams, who wrote proudly about her Iraq experience in *Love My Rifle More Than You: Young and Female in the US Army*, says that between the six-and eighth-month mark of her 2003 deployment "there was a general breakdown in military bearing and professionalism" among her team in the field. Fellow soldiers started flipping out, other got their kicks from telling rape jokes. Williams didn't care much when she was called a "bitch" in a heated moment, but she lost it when a fellow soldier tried to force her hand onto his penis in the dark. She reported the incident and he was transferred. But the damage was lasting. "I felt somehow betrayed, she admits and, conversely, "like I had somehow led [...] to this situation." She worried that because she had tried to be a pal, she may have sent the wrong signals. She eventually succumbed to being "the bitch" rather than "the slut." The dichotomy women say is the male code. "It was difficult and lonely."[48]

While tensions in war zones exacerbate misogynistic attitudes, they persist more broadly as well.

In March 2017, a scandal erupted involving a private Facebook group of some 30,000 men, called Marines United, a forum intended as a way for active-duty and veteran marines to form and maintain a sense of community, considered important for esprit de corps and mental health. But it was also being used to share or promote the sharing of nude images of female service members, what some individuals called "revenge porn."[49] Upon investigation, the scandal spread, with members of other branches of the military found involved in similar activities. Just as the Navy Tailhook scandal in 1991 brought women forward to testify to the prevalence of sexual harassment, so too has the Marines United scandal. One female Marine told of "investing in spray paint that I carried with me when I was on the FOB [Forward Operating Base]. I needed it to cover increasingly detailed and explicit drawings of me that decorated every porta john on Fallujah."[50] Another woman told of taking a weapon with her to the showers because of the "ubiquitous fear of sexual assault."[51] As in other cases of violence against women, an underlying struggle for power exists, and followers model behavior on leaders and what they perceive leaders will tolerate.

According to the Department of Defense, in 2021, 33% of women serving in the military reported sexual assault. Many more women chose not to report incidents as well as they do not trust the system, with good reason. Sixty-two percent of women who filed complaints said they had faced retaliation as a consequence, and less than 5% of complaints filed result in a criminal conviction. It is important as well to acknowledge that there is a culture of disbelief regarding male sexual assault victims, making it even more difficult for men to file complaints.[52] Both men and women appear penalty-free targets in the military.

Canadian political scientist Megan MacKenzie, posits in her book *Beyond the Band of Brothers: The US Military and the Myth That Women Can't Fight* (2015), that the US exclusion of women in combat was always about protecting the military's identity as a male-only "band of brothers." Her argument is twofold: that the combat exclusion was an evolving set of guidelines and rules designed to keep the all-male combat units elite, essential, and exceptional, and that the exclusion was not based on any research or evidence related to women and war, but rather was created and sustained through stories, myths, and emotional arguments, such as that delivered by General Mattis in 2014.

Regardless of objections, women have been in combat zones and roles for many years, as evidenced by women being wounded and held as prisoners of war. Necessity drove interest in integrating women into the military during the George W. Bush administration. "The decision to invade Iraq in 2003, the miscalculation of the subsequent insurgency and civil war, and the desire to wage a global terror war […] made it impossible for the all-volunteer force to function without women in combat roles."[53] Reality took over. Of the approximately 300,000 women deployed to Afghanistan or Iraq, roughly 500 received the Purple Heart, awarded to those military members wounded or killed while serving.

Lori Piestewa was the first woman killed in Iraq when her supply truck was ambushed in 2003. Her best friend, Jessica Lynch, was severely injured and taken prisoner in that same attack, her wounds cared for in an Iraqi hospital. Lynch's highly publicized rescue by US Special Forces shortly thereafter became the subject of a later congressional investigation. The investigation focused on "mythmaking" and whether Private Lynch was used by the army as a political prop and as a show of patriotism and courage by her rescuers – brave men rescuing a hapless woman – allegations supported by Lynch herself.

Other military women rose to prominence during the Iraq War, though not always in a positive way. Lt. Col. Diane Beaver says she will forever be known as "the torture lady" for penning a memo subsequently used to justify the use of torture at Guantanamo Bay. Beaver was an army lawyer tasked by her superiors to define interrogation techniques that could be used on detainees. The methods she penned became Department of Defense policy. Beaver later said she "tried to consult experts and superiors on the content of the opinion prior to issuing it, but received no feedback" and "fully expected that it would be carefully reviewed by legal and policy experts at the highest levels before a decision was reached. I did not expect that my opinion, as a Lieutenant Colonel in the Army Judge Advocate General's Corp, would become the final work on interrogation policies and practices within the Department of Defense."[54] Nevertheless, she took full responsibility for its contents. While it was later suggested that she had the option of resigning or speaking out publicly against what she was being asked to do, for women having to constantly prove themselves to "the boys," that is a difficult option.

Army Reserve Brigadier General Janis Karpinski was the highest-ranking officer to be punished (demoted to colonel) for the Abu Ghraib prisoner abuse scandal, as she was the commanding officer at the prison. She and her unit, 3,400 soldiers under the eight hundredth Military Police Brigade, were deployed to Iraq in 2003 to conduct the prisoner of war mission. That mission, like so many others, was extended and changed once in Iraq. Karpinski was put in charge of three large jails, and her reservists became responsible for handling suspected terrorists for interrogation, though none were trained for that mission. General Geoffrey Miller, who outranked Karpinski, initiated that mission change. Miller came from Guantanamo, bringing prisoner interrogation techniques already being used there with him. According to Karpinski in an interview, the military intelligence people working with Miller "removed Abu Ghraib from my command, yes, and turned it over to the command of military intelligence,"[55] thereby limiting her involvement and opportunity for oversight. Like Beaver, she takes responsibility for her complicity regarding prisoner abuse at Abu Ghraib, but says she believed everything going on there was with the implicit and explicit approval of her superiors, including Secretary of Defense Donald Rumsfeld.

Perhaps not surprisingly, when initially appointed to her position in Iraq, Karpinski's womanhood was the subject of a number of positive media stories, often portraying her as "caring" and "loves her soldiers."[56] After the scandal broke, though, the media angle changed significantly, with those who questioned her innocence or limited involvement often doing so in very gendered terms. Karpinski was suddenly characterized as tough, masculine, even inhuman. Her sexual preference was questioned, including referring to her as a "dyke" and "bull dyke," though without any evidence of her sexual orientation. Analysis suggests, however, that her sexual preference was not really the point of the changed portrayal. Rather, it was to suggest that Karpinski had deviated from traditional gender roles, so she must be sexually dysfunctional.[57] Karpinski has maintained that she was a scapegoat, partly because she is a woman. "They made me a pox on our history."[58] She has also questioned why she received no support from feminist organizations.

Globally, women both during their active military service and afterward often face challenges involving healthcare, veterans benefits, and recognition as a veteran, even in countries with very large militaries like the United States. A 2020 study by the Defense Health Board (DHB) found that the Pentagon still uses a one-size-fits-all (men) healthcare system that often fails to provide proper medical care to women. The study suggested that consequently, the Pentagon is wasting money, hurting readiness, and negatively impacting retention.

In the United States, some military services have taken steps to better accommodate women's needs, such as offering refrigerators for women to store breast milk and finding better ways for women pilots to relieve themselves in-flight. However, women still find themselves challenged regarding care for musculoskeletal injuries, reproductive and genitourinary issues, and mental health issues. The 2020 DHB report documents that many problems faced by women in the military stem from improper clothing and equipment.

The DHB report also found that access to contraception varies between services and affects the rate of unintended pregnancies. Unquestionably, too, increasing rollbacks in women's reproductive rights in the United States will have multiple negative effects on military retention and readiness. Screening protocols for eating disorders, more prevalent in women than men, also vary, leading to "stark differences" in the reported prevalence of diagnoses that can affect both care and retention.[59] It is not a stretch to conclude that the prevalence of these issues in the US military, which has the funding to fix them if it were a priority, infers that the same and more issues are prevalent in other militaries as well.

Conclusion

Structural barriers to women in military occupations are slowly being removed in many countries. In 2017, for example, the Indian army announced it would allow women in combat. But the mixed successes of Israel's gender integration efforts, the paradox of the Norwegian experience with gender integration in the military, Operation Honour issues in Canada, and the Marines United scandal in the United States evidence that cultural barriers to inclusivity within the military ranks remain. Recent data from the Veterans Administration says suicide rates for female veterans in the United States has skyrocketed in the past decade, twice that of their male counterparts and two to five times more likely than in the civilian population. Progress is evidenced in some areas though.

Among the success stories of work associated with the WPS framework has been increasing the numbers of women in militaries around the world, toward more inclusive diversity and gendered perspectives. But it is important to remember that doors have been opened for women not because of changes in attitudes toward gender stereotyping, but because of need. Raising entry-level numbers in only particular fields isn't enough. Integration means equal access to opportunities and equal access to success that will only be possible when cultural issues are addressed and individuals held accountable for providing a safe environment within which women can play their part in serving their country.

Notes

1 "The She-Soldiers of World War One," http://ww1centenary.oucs.ox.ac.uk/unconventionalsoldiers/the-she-soldiers-of-world-war-one/

2 Major Lauren Ward, USMA, "Military Masculinities, Tactical Femininities, and the 'Third Gender' in *Ashley's War*, presentation at the WPS Symposium in Newport, RI, April 27, 2023.

3 Ward, 2023.

4 Amanda Ripley, "The Untold Story of the Afghan Women Who Hunted the Taliban," *Politico*, April 8, 2022. www.politico.com/interactives/2022/afghan-women-soldiers-taliban-us-refugees/

5 Rebecca Kheel, "Mattis' Views on Women in Combat Takes Center Stage," *The Hill*, January 12, 2017. http://thehill.com/policy/defense/313871-mattis-to-face-questions-over-women-in-combat-and-lgbt-troops-at-confirmation

6 Terry Gross interviewing Mary Jennings (Heger). "A Purple Heart Warrior Takes Aim at Military Inequality in 'Shoot Like a Girl,'" NPR. March 2, 2017. www.npr.org/templates/transcript/transcript.php?storyId=517944956

7 NPR, March 2, 2017.

8 Aleksandar Palikot, "Women at War: Ukraine's Female Soldiers Dream of Freedom, Fight for Survival," *Radio Free Europe*, January 26, 2023. www.rferl.org/a/ukraine-war-women-soldiers-female-freedom-survival/32240805.html

9 Jessica Trisko Darden, "Ukrainian Wartime Policy and the Construction of Women's Combatant Status," *Women's Studies International Forum*, January–February 2023. www.sciencedirect.com/science/article/pii/S0277539522001066

10 Victoria Guerra, "Ukrainian Women at the Front: Don't Ask Us about Pads, We're Short on Weapons," *Worldcrunch*, February 4, 2023. https://worldcrunch.com/focus/ukraine-female-soldiers

11 Benedetta Argentieri, "One Group Battling Islamic State Has a Secret Weapon – Female Fighters," Reuters, February 3, 2015. https://web.archive.org/web/20150203191806/http://blogs.reuters.com/great-debate/2015/02/03/the-pro-woman-ideology-battling-islamic-state/

12 Argentieri, 2015.

13 "Syrian Kurdish Forces Say Fighter Mutilated by Turkish-Backed Rebels," Reuters, February 2, 2018. www.reuters.com/article/us-mideast-crisis-syria-afrin/syrian-kurdish-forces-say-fighter-mutilated-by-turkey-backed-rebels-idUSKBN1FM2LX

14 Ian Fisher, "Like Mother, Like Daughter, Eritrean Women Wage War," *New York Times*, August 26, 1999. www.nytimes.com/1999/08/26/world/like-mother-like-daughter-eritrean-women-wage-war.html

15 Marthe Van Der Wolf, "Africa's Female Fighters: They Bled and Died on the Battlefields of Freedom and Were Forgotten after Victory," *Mail & Guardian Africa*, September 25, 2014.

16 Van Der Wolf, 2014.

17 Sahana Dharmapuri, "Just Add Women and Stir?" *Parameters*, Spring 2011, p. 62.

18 Megan Alpert, "To Be a Guerrilla, and a Woman, in Colombia," *The Atlantic*, September 28, 2016. www.theatlantic.com/international/archive/2016/09/farc-deal-female-fighters/501644/

19 Alpert, 2016.

20 Jodi Rudoren, "Looking to Israel for Clues on Women in Combat," *New York Times*, January 25, 2013.

21 "How Does the Caracal Battalion Work, the Combat Unit of the Israeli Army Where Women Are in the Majority," April 2022. www.infobae.com/en/2022/04/17/how-does-the-caracal-battalion-work-the-combat-unit-of-the-israeli-army-where-women-are-in-the-majority/

22 Judith Sudilovsky, "Despite Some Progress, Most Combat Roles Are Closed to Women in the IDF," *Jerusalem Post*, August 13, 2015.

23 Mordechai Goldman, "Rabbis Speak Out against Women's Enlistment in IDF," *Al-Monitor*, November 27, 2016. www.al-monitor.com/pulse/originals/2016/11/israel-girls-enlisting-national-religious-movement-rabbis.html

24 Zina Rakhamilova, "The IDF Has a Problem with Female Soldiers," *Jerusalem Post*, January 3, 2023. www.jpost.com/opinion/article-726466

25 Elizabeth Braw, "Norway's 'Hunter Troops,'" *Foreign Affairs*, February 8, 2016.

26 "A Look at Norway's Approach to Gender-Neutral Conscription," SecurityWomen, October 22, 2021. www.securitywomen.org/post/a-look-at-norways-approach-to-gender-neutral-conscription

27 Inger Skjelsbaek, *Gender Aspects of International Military Interventions: National and International Perspectives*, Report to the Norwegian Ministry of Defense, International Peace Research Institute, 2007. p. 13.

28 Rachel Jewkes et al., "Hegemonic Masculinity: Combining Theory and Practice in Gender Interventions," *Culture, Health and Sexuality*, October 2015, pp. 96–111.

29 Marsha Henry, "Problematizing Military Masculinity, Intersentionality and Male Vulnerability in Feminist Critical Military Studies," *Critical Military Studies*, 3 (2017).

30 Leah Ruppanner, "Why Norway Says No Way to Gender Segregation in the Military," *The Conversation*, August 13, 2014.

31 Siw Ellen Jakobsen, "Researchers Conducted a Gender Equality Experiment on 500 Recruits, *ScienceNorway*, June 2, 2021. https://sciencenorway.no/gender-and-society/researchers-conducted-a-gender-equality-experiment-on-500-recruits/1869059

32 Björn Lindhal, "Nordic Men Face Different Challenges from Women in Non-traditional Jobs," *Nordic Labour Journal*, October 28, 2022.

33 Ian Austen, "Armed Forces in Canada Resolved Issue Long Ago," *New York Times*, January 24, 2013.

34 Angela Febbraro, *Women, Leadership and Gender Integration in the Canadian Combat Arms: A Qualitative Study*, Defence R&D Canada, December 2003. http://cradpdf.drdc-rddc.gc.ca/PDFS/unc31/p521088.pdf

35 www.forces.gc.ca/en/caf-community-support-services/external-review-sexual-mh-2015/summary.page

36 David Pugliese, "Operation Honour Dubbed 'Hop on Her' by Soldiers Mocking Military Plan to Crack Down on Sexual Misconduct," *National Post*, October 26, 2015. http://news.nationalpost.com/news/canada/operation-honour-dubbed-hop-on-her-by-soldiers-mocking-militarys-plan-to-crack-down-on-sexual-misconduct

37 Ian Austin, "Canada's Military, Where Sexual Misconduct Went to the Top, Looks for a New Path, *New York Times*, May 30, 2022. www.nytimes.com/2022/05/30/canada-military-sexual-misconduct.html

38 Renee Montage, "General Remembers Her 'Different' Military Days," *NPR*, February 23, 2011. www.npr.org/templates/transcript/transcript.php?storyId=133966767

39 Therese Huston, "Men Can Be So Hormonal," *New York Times*, June 24, 2017. www.nytimes.com/2017/06/24/opinion/sunday/men-testosterone-hormones.html

40 Susan Stamberg, "Female WWII Pilots: The Original Fly Girls," NPR, March 9, 2010. www.npr.org/2010/03/09/123773525/female-wwii-pilots-the-original-fly-girls

41 Stamberg, 2010.

42 Katherine Sharp Landdeck, "A Woman Pilot Receives the Military Funeral the Army Denied Her," *The Atlantic*, September 2016.

43 Karen Parrish, "Women's Military History 'A Revolution' General Says," *DOD News*, March 3, 2016. www.defense.gov/News/Article/Article/685650/womens-military-history-a-revolution-general-says

44 NSIAD 94-95, March 17, 1994.

45 Billie Mitchell, "The Creation of Army Officers and the Gender Lie," in *It's Our Military, Too! Women and the US Military*, Judith Stiehm, ed. Temple University Press, 1996.

46 Tom Bowman, "Air Force Dropout Rate Double That of Other Academies," *Baltimore Sun*, May 22, 1994. http://articles.baltimoresun.com/1994-05-22/news/1994142026_1_force-academy-military-academy-female-cadets

47 Rebecca J. Hannagan and Holly Arrow, "Reengineered Gender Relations in Modern Militaries," *Journal of Trauma and Dissociation*, 12, no. 3, p. 305.

48 Vlahos, 2008.

49 Jared Keller, "The Rise and Fall (and Rise) of 'Marines United,'" *Task and Purpose*, March 16, 2017, https://taskandpurpose.com/rise-fall-rise-marines-united/

50 Thomas, 2017.

51 Rachel Gotbaum, "A Female Former Marine Speaks Out about Nude Photos of Servicewomen," Public Radio International, March 8, 2017. www.pri.org/stories/2017-03-08/former-female-marine-speaks-out-about-facebook-page-shared-nude-photos

52 Heather Mongilio, "Latest Military Sexual Assault Report Shows 'Tragic Rise' in Cases, Pentagon Officials Say," *USNI News*, September 1, 2022. https://news.usni.org/2022/09/01/latest-military-sexual-assault-report-shows-tragic-rise-in-cases-pentagon-officials-say#:~:text=And%20that%20stigma%20plays%20out,percent%20of%20female%20service%20ones.

53 Vlahos, 2008.

54 Statement of Diane E. Beavers before the Senate Armed Service Committee, June 17, 2008.

55 "Col. Janis Karpinski, the Former Head of Abu Ghraib, Admits She Broke the Geneva Conventions But Says the Blame 'Goes all the Way to the Top,'" *Democracy Now,* October 26, 2005.

56 Susan Taylor Martin, "Her Job: Lock Up Iraq's Bad Guys," *St. Petersburg Times,* December 14, 2003, p. A8.

57 Laura Sjoberg and Caron Gentry, "Reduced to Bad Sex: Narratives of Violent Women from the Bible to the War on Terror," *International Relations*, 22, no. 1(2008), p. 15.

58 Vlahos, 2008.

59 Jared Serbu, "After 70 years of integration, Military Health System Still Isn't Addressing Issues," November 16, 2020. *Federal News Network*, https://federalnewsnetwork.com/dod-reporters-notebook-jared-serbu/2020/11/after-70-years-of-integration-military-health-system-still-isnt-addressing-womens-needs/

Further reading

Block, Peter. *Community: The Structure of Belonging*, Berrett-Koehler, 2009.

Browne, Kingsley. *Co-Ed Combat: New Evidence That Women Shouldn't Fight the Nation's Wars*, Sentinel HC, 2007.

D'Amico, Francine, and Laurie Weinstein. *Gender Camouflage*, New York University Press, 1999.

Hegar, Mary Jennings. *Shoot Like a Girl*, Berkley, 2017.

Holmstedt, Kristin. *Band of Sisters*, Stackpole Books, 2008.

Lemmon, Gayle Tzemach, *Ashley's War*, Harper Perennial, 2017.

Lowry, Donna. *Women Vietnam Veterans: Our Untold Stories*, AuthorHouse, reprint ed., 2015.

MacKenzie, Megan. *Beyond the Band of Brothers*, Cambridge University Press, 2015.

Mattis, James, and Kori Schake (eds.), *Warriors and Citizens: American Views of Our Military*, Hoover Institute Press, 2016.

Myers, Sarah Parry. Earning Their Wings: The WASPs of WWII and the Fight for Veteran Recognition, University of North Carolina Press, 2023.

Norman, Elizabeth. *We Band of Angels*, Random House, 2013.

Williams, Kayla. *Love My Rifle More Than You: Young and Female in the US Army*, W.W. Norton, 2006.

11 Women political leaders

Why women?

Research indicates that women often consider politics differently than men, regarding electoral and non-electoral participation, political interests, and agenda setting. Women raise issues that men overlook, initiate and support bills in areas specific to women and children, and seek to end abuses and break molds that otherwise would often go unrecognized or unchallenged. It was Chilean president Michelle Bachelet, for example, who pushed and succeeded in allowing women into the traditionally male-only Chilean navy in 2018. Whether in domestic or international conflict management, women tend to be more collaborative and compromising, rather than competitive and focused on winning, with greater collaboration often producing more constructive, goal-focused outcomes for disputing parties, and better, lasting relationships.

Empirical studies have demonstrated a direct relationship between women's involvement in peace and conflict issues, and the likelihood of war erupting. Greater numbers of women in parliament have been related to a reduced risk of civil war. A 5% increase in the percentage of women in parliament has been correlated with a state being five times less likely to use violence when faced with an international crisis.[1] And as previously discussed, women can play an essential role in preventing and countering violent extremism, often by urging and implementing effective nonviolent approaches based on cooperation, trust, and women's unique access to communities.

But getting more women into political positions where they can influence security questions has been and continues to be a considerable challenge. Senator Elizabeth Warren explained the situation at a 2013 hearing on Capitol Hill. "Washington works for those who have power. And no one gives up power easily, no one [...] Nobody's just going to say 'women have arrived and let's just move over.'"[2] To be a participant in the political process required, first, that women have the right to vote. It is important to recall that that right was only relatively recently granted, and not without a struggle.

Spindle/Spear and suffrage

In 1776, Abigail Adams wrote to her husband, American founding father John Adams, asking him to "remember the ladies" as men wrote the laws of our new nation. He laughed at her "saucy" letter and responded with words that still resonate with some individuals: "We know better than to repeal our masculine systems."[3] That correspondence serves as a reminder that early democracies of the twenty-first century did not originally embrace the idea of women's empowerment. The spindle/spear divide between women/men firmly held. Being granted voting

DOI: 10.4324/9781003413417-12

rights, a fundamental step toward empowerment, was a hard-fought battle that lasted well into the twentieth century.

A young Winston Churchill dissented from a bill in Parliament to grant women suffrage in 1897 and provided his rationale for doing so:

> on the grounds that it is contrary to natural law and the practice of civilized states; that no necessity is shown; that only the most undesirable class of women are eager for the right; that those women who discharge their duty to the state viz marrying and giving birth to children are adequately represented by their husbands; that those who are unmarried can only claim a vote on the ground of property, which claim on democratic principles is inadmissible.[4]

Churchill's view reflected those of most British people at the time, including many women, who considered politics a dirty, often alcohol-fueled pastime in which they wanted no part. Churchill later changed his views, due largely to seeing the important roles that women played in the 1914–1918 war years.

The evolution of voting rights dates back to Athens, the cradle of democracy. In ancient Athens, only adult male citizen landowners were granted the right to vote, substantially narrowing those qualified from among the general population. In later centuries, Europe was ruled largely through monarchies, though occasionally certain men could vote for parliaments of one variety or the other. Movement toward universal suffrage began only during the interwar years.

New Zealand was the first country to grant universal suffrage in 1893. Canada granted women the right to vote in 1917, followed by Britain in 1918, and the United States in 1920 with the passage of the 19th Amendment, but only after 52 years of relentless effort. One 1915 New York referendum alone involved 10,300 meetings, 7.5 million leaflets, and a parade of 20,000 people, and the women still lost. Two years later when another effort was made for women's suffrage in New York, the *New York Times* argued that the country was at war and so "strong men must make the decisions that control policies."[5] Suffragette Elizabeth Cady Stanton once remarked that the long slog of the movement "now gets on everybody's nerves."[6] Suffrage movements elsewhere were able to gain momentum from the successes of women in Britain and the United States. Between 1931 and 1952, Spain, France, Italy, and Greece followed suit in granting women the right to vote, joined by Switzerland and other European countries, as well as the majority of Latin American countries.

When American women finally won the right to vote in 1920, suffragists expected a national transformation of politics. They thought that with women voting, there would be less government corruption, better and more education and housing bills, and a number of improvements in the lives of families. Initially, it looked like they might have been right. Congress passed the Sheppard-Towner Maternity and Infancy Protection Act of 1921, a program to educate poor women about child care and establish clinics in impoverished rural areas to bring down infant mortality rates, which were much higher in the United States than in other industrialized nations. Soon thereafter, though, Utah senator William H. King argued on behalf of the Act's opponents, including physicians who felt their livelihood was being threatened, and anti-suffragist women's groups, that the bill was being championed by "neurotic women [...] social workers who obtained pathological satisfaction in interfering with the affairs of other people [...] and Bolsheviks who did not care for family and its perpetuity."[7] Fears of socialism and misogyny won the day and the bill was repealed in 1929.

Marriage was still the ultimate goal of the vast majority of American (and other) women at the time, making their fate strongly linked to their husbands, so most women were voting much like their husbands, by ethnicity, economic class, and geographical location. It was not until the

1980s that pollsters began seeing women voting on domestic programs and social safety nets independent of their husbands. Also significant regarding changes in women's voting behavior in the 1980s was the rise in the numbers of single women and women as head of households.

Though Adams' and Churchill's overt concerns have been muted over time, the spindle/spear divide continues to manifest itself in more indirect ways across different cultural contexts. At the individual level, women with generally the same qualifications as men often talk themselves out of running for political office based on the lack of self-assurance, Imposture Syndrome issues discussed in Chapter 4. Researchers have found American women twice as likely as men to see themselves as "not at all qualified to run for office" even when their credentials were equivalent. Men also see themselves as likely or very likely winners in political races, far more than women. Additionally, some women do not want to get involved with what they see as corrupt male politics. Kyrgyzstan activist Nurgel Djanaeva, explained: "The only way for me to feed my family, while working in government, is to be corrupt, so I'd rather work for an NGO and have a living wage."[8] In places like Cambodia and Rwanda, NGO's have begun equipping women with the confidence and skills to run for office through grassroots programs.

At the institutional level, many global political bodies like parties and legislatures continue to be unwelcoming to female colleagues, either overtly or passively. Even after passage of the 19th Amendment to the US Constitution granting women the right to vote, some states barred women from running for office. Oklahoma did not allow women to run for all state offices until 1942. More furtively, the French constitution was amended in 1999 and the electoral law in 2000, mandating that political parties nominate an equal percentage of male and female national legislative candidates. Initially, the law was vague about its implementation requirements and so politicians were able to sidestep any real change; female legislative representation barely rose, from 11% in 1997 to 18% in 2007. Closing loopholes in the system, however, resulted in the rate of women's representation rising to 38% in 2023.

In Brazil, between 1996 and 2000 quotas were imposed to increase the number of women in its national legislative bodies, starting at 20% and reaching 30%. At the same time, however, another regulation was passed allowing parties to present 50% more candidates than seats available. That provision provided a crucial "escape clause" for quota implementation. Consequently, the number of women in the legislature actually decreased for a time. Women still hold only 18% of legislative seats as of 2023. In many cases there is a patina of legislative change, but with little or no actual change without active intervention and accountability to assure the intent is achieved.

At the sociocultural level, elite and media scrutiny of husbands and children, physical attractiveness, and largely unsubstantiated concerns about qualifications are more pervasive for female political aspirants.[9] These issues have fed into individual considerations. Shauna Shames' book *Out of the Running* (2017) considered why relatively few millennials, especially women, have wanted to run for office in the United States. Many women found both the fundraising required, up to 70% of a candidate's time, and the media scrutiny off-putting. They expected to face discrimination in what is seen as still very much a man's world. "They think they won't get a fair show and so many don't try."[10] Since 2016, however, more American women from both parties have become willing to run for office, many spurred by the current polarized state of American politics. Unfortunately, they still face more and more personalized challenges than their male counterparts.

Maryland lieutenant governor Kathleen Kennedy Townsend addressed the question "What Should a Powerful Woman Look Like?" in a 2016 *New York Times* editorial. She discussed receiving unending commentary on her hairstyle, being expected to wear stockings in 95-degree heat, not wearing blush, wearing flats, and wearing "too many bracelets." She also considered the dilemma of walking the line between being referenced as the "unglamorous Kennedy" and overhearing an animated conversation in the Fox News green room about "Sarah Palin's positions" – and not on policy. It has only been recently that some American male politicians have received anywhere near the personal scrutiny of women, specifically former New Jersey governor Chris Christie on his weight and Donald Trump on his hair, tan, weight, gesticulations, and language.

Leadership qualifications

Just as with the question of what qualifications are needed for a woman to succeed in the military – whether brawn is always a prerequisite – the question of what voters consider important qualifications for a political leader is being asked as well, in the United States and elsewhere. Exit polls taken by both CNN and Fox News found that Hillary Clinton was considered more qualified than Donald Trump on questions of both who would be a better commander in chief (49%–46%) and who would better handle foreign policy (53%–42%). Male candidates can garner credibility simply by being male, while experience and credibility can work against women candidates.

In 2016, blatant sexism rose its ugly head in Italy, with one male candidate for mayor of Rome telling the media that a pregnant female candidate should withdraw and concentrate on breastfeeding her baby, and a female mayoral candidate in Milan being taunted for her looks, called "ugly, obese," and a "housewife" who should stay home. As a candidate, Philippine president Rodrigo Duterte joked about the gang rape of an Australian missionary and pledged to shoot criminals, hang them using fishing line, or drown them in Manila Bay. Openly advocating misogyny and violence is not off limits for candidates, or even elected officials.

In July 2020, a reporter witnessed a brief but fiery incident between Alexandria Ocasio-Cortez and Florida Republican representative Ted Yoho on the steps of the Capitol. Yoho approached Ocasio-Cortez and called her "disgusting." She walked away but Yoho offered a parting remark, "Fucking bitch." He later denied the last comment, using the "I'm married and have daughters" defense that men often invoke when trying to hide their bad behavior behind women. Instead, he expressed regret for his abruptness and professed to have been driven by patriotism. Ocasio-Cortez rejected his I'm-more-patriotic-than-you defense and Yoho's non-apology on the House floor, reminding her colleagues that she is somebody's daughter too.

Suggesting violence against women as appropriate has now been normalized to the extent that, when presented with an oversized gavel like that used by the House Speaker at a Republican dinner in 2021, House Minority Leader Kevin McCarthy felt comfortable "joking" that if he were Speaker it would be hard not to hit Nancy Pelosi with it. "Joking" about hitting an 81-year-old woman with a gavel should be considered inappropriate under any circumstances.

Why voters cast their ballots for individuals has created more than a cottage industry of analysts. A 2019 analysis of capabilities that differentiate excellent leaders from average or poor leaders conducted by leadership development specialists Zenger Folkman revealed women rated higher on 17 of the 19 capabilities. Among 1) takes initiative, 2) possesses resilience, 3) practices self-development, 4) drives for results, 5) displays high integrity and honesty, 6) develops others, 7) inspires and motivates others, 8) bold leadership, 9) builds relationships, 10) champions change, 11) establishes stretch goals, 12) collaboration and teamwork, 13) connects to the outside world, 14) communicates powerfully and prolifically, 15) solves problems and analyzes issues, 16) shows leadership speed, 17) innovates, 18) possesses technical and professional expertise, and 19) develops a strategic perspective, men outscored women only on the last two, and by only one percentile. The European Academy for Executive Leadership synthesized key global leadership traits into four "threshold" traits: integrity, humility, curiosity, and resilience.

Women leaders around the world have adapted different leadership "styles" according to circumstances and their own personality traits. Israel's Golda Meir, Indira Gandhi in India, and the United Kingdom's Margaret Thatcher are all known for the same type of "masculine" qualities as many of their male peers, and they were not known for pushing an egalitarian social agenda. Conversely, Chilean president Michelle Bachelet appointed an equal number of men and women to her cabinet and has been quoted as saying, "I took a gamble to exercise leadership without losing my feminine nature."[11] Some women are overt feminists, like Hillary Clinton, while others are more ambiguous. Angela Merkel stated in 2019 that "parity (for women) in all areas seems logical to me. I don't need to constantly mention it specifically."[12]

New Zealand's Jacinda Ardern became globally known as the model for a new generation of progressive women leaders, using both masculine and feminine traits according to the needs of specific situations. Besides multitasking as a national leader, partner, and new mother, during her tenure she led one of the most successful Covid-19 "elimination" strategies during the global pandemic and acted with both empathy and tough resolve to outlaw military style semiautomatic weapons after a tragic mass shooting at two New Zealand mosques by a White supremacist.

Similarly, Nordic prime ministers Sanna Marin from Finland, Mette Fredericksen from Denmark, and Katrín Jakobsdóttir from Iceland are also considered to have taken a more humanistic approach to governing. Being trailblazers, however, attracts skeptics and draws scrutiny. A leaked video of 36-year-old Sanna Marin dancing and drinking with friends at a 2022 private event while she was prime minister resulted in an official investigation, which ultimately cleared her of unlawful conduct in the performance of her duties. Marin lost her bid for re-election in 2023, primarily due to voter concerns about the Finnish economy.

Italian women have divided feelings about a populist, far-right woman serving as Italy's first female prime minister. Giorgia Meloni was elected in 2022 on a platform of "God, homeland and family." She touted her sex while running for office, in terms of breaking a glass ceiling, but didn't particularly court women's votes given her support for potentially regressive women's rights. She drew the ire of many Italian women after retweeting a video of a woman being raped in the street, by an immigrant, as an anti-immigration statement. Especially as numbers grow, there will be as many leadership styles exhibited and issues surrounding women political leaders as there are for men.

Women's access to political power

There are three sets of factors that play into women's access to political positions. First is structure. Most women who have held top political offices – president, prime minister, or chancellor – are from dual executive systems, where they share power with another executive. Consequently, women more often serve in systems where executive authority is more dispersed, as opposed to in those systems with more unified executive structures. In many of these cases, women are in positions of weaker authority. Women presidents elected by the public, for example, may hold relatively nominal positions, serving primarily as figureheads. As such, they may have very little substantive power as compared to prime ministers. Women fare better in reaching positions of power when they can bypass the public.

There are also numerous examples of weak female prime ministers operating under much stronger presidents. This is often the situation for women in Africa, who are sometimes unilaterally appointed by the president and subsequently subject to dismissal at his will. The same is true of several female leaders in Eastern Europe, though Eastern Europe also ranks high among regions with a large number of women in top elected positions. Not all national leadership posts are created equal, requiring a close look at who actually wields power.

Second, social and economic factors also play into women's ability to access political power. In many countries, women do not have access to the same levels and types of education that most often lead to being considered "qualified" for political office. As prior examples have shown, men are often considered qualified simply by their gender. Women, however, are more often held to a different, higher standard.

And finally, cultural factors also play into women's role in politics. In some countries, religion and culture may place prohibitions on women's political activity by forbidding women to speak in front of men, seek political office, or attend political meetings. In countries where women are bought through bride prices or sold through dowries, their voices are deliberately stifled. Where gender stereotypes prevail, women's opportunities for political participation can be limited.

In the 1990s, gender quotas began being recognized and utilized by many countries as the most effective way of "fast-tracking" women's increased political participation. In 1995, delegates to the United Nations Fourth World Conference on Women unanimously signed the Beijing Platform for Action. Part of that platform involved setting 30% as the target for women in decision-making, as (as already stated) 30% is considered the critical mass required for women as a group to be able to exert a meaningful influence in legislative assemblies. As of 2021, 132 countries had adopted constitutional, electoral, or political party quotas. The United Nations has pushed for the representation of women and minorities in all new constitutions, and gender quotas are often included in post-conflict constitutions or laws, with different approaches available.

The three general types of quotas are reserved seats, legislative candidate quotas, and voluntary party quotas. Reserved seats are the most common type of quota, where there is a legal mandate to set aside a certain percentage of seats for women (or minorities). Legislative candidate quotas require political parties to have women as a certain portion of their nominees. While this requirement pushes parties to find and even nurture suitable women candidates, it does not guarantee they will be seated. Voluntary party quotas range from recommendations to mandatory rules regarding the addition of women candidates and how they are presented, including a so-called "zipper provision" that men's and women's names be alternated on the ballot.

While quotas have been considered a significant factor in the rising number of women in many countries' governments, not all countries are supportive. Ironically, the countries found most resistant are liberal democracies, including the United States, where conservative political views advocate "gender blindness." In Afghanistan, rather than supporting quotas, the US government offered indirect support of Afghan women through the implementation of more than 200 projects aimed helping Afghan women.[13] In 2004, however, the Afghan government passed a law putting a quota in place for parliamentary seats. Yet, "the State Department cites the presence of a gender quota in the Constitutional Loya Jirga (CLJ) as an illustration of its commitment to Afghani women."[14]

Steps forward can quickly be countered with steps backward. Even before the Taliban resumed power in Afghanistan in 2021, commitment to women's representation in the CLJ was tenuous. In 2013, the lower house of the Afghan parliament cut the quota for women's seats from 25% to 20%, and election to parliament was dangerous for women. In 2014, former Afghani parliamentarian Noor Zia Atmar ended up in a battered women's shelter and then fleeing the country. Her husband did not share her egalitarian views and began beating her. The situation worsened when she asked for a divorce, which he and his family felt would bring shame to his family.

Subsequently, she began fearing for her life, and with good reason. The same year another female parliamentarian, Rooh Gul, was riddled by gunfire as she traveled through Ghazni province. She survived. Her eight-year-old daughter did not.

Parliamentary systems have offered women more roads to leadership. Margaret Thatcher served as the prime minister of the United Kingdom from 1979 to 1990. Indira Gandhi served as prime minister of India from 1966 to1977 and then again from 1980 until her assassination in 1984. Benazir Bhutto was prime minister of Pakistan from 1988 to 1990 and then again from 1993 to 1996. Angela Merkel served as chancellor of Germany between 2005 and 2021. Theresa May served as prime minister of the United Kingdom from 2016 to 2019. Jacinda Ardern served as prime minister of New Zealand from 2017 to 2023. Britain, India, Pakistan, Germany, and New Zealand have parliamentary rather than direct election presidential systems of government, with leaders rising to power through party promotions rather than general elections where gender bias can more easily be a factor. In parliamentary systems, collaboration is fundamental, with the ability to collaborate and negotiate typically considered more feminine. In direct election presidential systems, however, leaders act independently of the legislature and are expected to lead in a quick and decisive manner, traits more often associated with men. Iceland boasts being the first country to directly elect a female president, single-mother Vigdís Finnbogadóttir, who served from 1980 to 1996.

Traditionally, kinship has been a well-used route to political power for both men and women. Indira Gandhi was the daughter of India's first prime minister, Jawaharlal Nehru. After her assassination, her son Rajiv Gandhi served as prime minister from 1984 to 1989, her daughter-in-law Sonia Gandhi led the Congress Party, and her grandson Rahul Gandhi remains in Parliament in 2023. Argentina's Christina Fernandez de Kirchner succeeded her husband, Carlos, as president. She had held national office before assuming the presidency while he had not. Benazir Bhutto, another daughter of a former prime minister, served as Pakistani prime minister and then chair of the Pakistan People's Party until her assassination in 2007, when her husband, Asif Zardari, assumed command of the party and became president. The Kennedy and Bush political dynasties in the United States have seen mostly males politically benefiting from family names. Having recognizable family names can help, or hurt, male or female candidates, as both Hillary Clinton and Jeb Bush learned in 2016.

Researchers have studied under what circumstances women in political dynasties rise to power. In some cases, for example, a woman may be seen as not as independently politically ambitious as a man and therefore is supported by status quo advocates who assume her malleable. The aging politicians who initially supported Indira Gandhi assumed her a *gungi gudiya*, Hindi for "dumb doll," which turned out to be far from the case. Or, since women are considered the unifiers of the family, they can be called upon to heal and unite a country after a period of conflict, as was the case with Liberia's Ellen Johnson Sirleaf. Sometimes as well, women rise to power in times of crises. An initially business-focused study by University of Exeter researchers found that in male-led companies facing crises, study subjects preferred that a woman take over to calm the waters. Also, in times of crises, the chance of failure is high. The "glass cliff" theory that evolved from that study holds that women are often placed in positions of power when the situation is dire, with men uninterested because the likelihood of success is low and they don't want to be tagged as failures.

It may be no coincidence that after 26 years of male leaders, Theresa May got the nod as Britain's prime minister in 2016 (in a race with another woman, Andrea Leadsom) and was left to deal with the British departure from the European Union, known as Brexit. Decided on a 51% to 48% vote to leave, many Brits opposed the idea, and many supporters had unrealistic expectations regarding what would be achieved for Britain after exiting, given a campaign powered by vague slogans and dubious promises. Exeter researcher Michelle Ryan described Brexit as "really a lose-lose situation for the prime minister. Whatever she negotiates, no one will be happy."[15] Even when women leaders have not been thrust onto on a glass cliff, the seemingly stable ground they are standing on may quickly fall away.

The harder they fall

In Chapter 4, it was pointed out that women are judged more personally than men, as they are expected to be nice, and "likable." It has now been found, too, that women are more likely to be blamed when things go wrong than are men, even when data shows women sometimes to be more competent overall. A 2017 study of surgeons found that "patients of female surgeons were 4% less likely to die, be readmitted or experience complications 30 days after their surgery compared to patients of male surgeons."[16] Yet, another 2017 study found that doctors judge female surgeons more harshly when patients die than they do male surgeons. Referrals to female surgeons drop by over 50% when a patient dies at the hands of a female surgeon, with only a small slowing of referrals for male surgeons who lose a patient.[17] Surgeons are not the only women to experience professional backlash more fiercely than their male counterparts.

Women politicians also face stereotype-based social costs. When women are perceived as power-seeking, voters react not just negatively but often with feelings of moral outrage. "Because power and power-seeking are central to the way masculinity is socially constructed and communality is central to the construction of femininity, intentionally seeking power is broadly seen as anti-communal and inconsistent with the societal rules for women's behavior."[18] Women are expected to be "nice" and to work for the communal good. Women are penalized for exhibiting the same traits of political leadership that are expected of men. Women politicians also face swift, fierce, and more long-lasting political backlash than men.

In 2011, Dilma Rousseff became president of Brazil, Christina Kirchner began a second term as president in Argentina, and Michelle Bachelet had an approval rating of more than 80% after completing her first presidential term in Chile. In 2016, Kirchner had been indicted, Rousseff was impeached, and Bachelet's approval rating had plunged to below 30%. Crises and corruption are more or less staples of Latin American politics, leading analysts to ask what is behind the more-than-normal outrage against these politicians. Gender played a role.

> Several officials from Mrs. Kirchner's administration, including her former vice president Amado Boudou, have been tarnished by corruption cases. But she [Kirchner] received the brunt of the public's anger on Friday after a judge indicted her on allegations related to a financial scandal that she denies, and a prosecutor sought to extend a money-laundering investigation. In Brazil, public outrage over a sprawling graft scandal at the national oil company has coalesced around Mrs. Rousseff and helped drive impeachment proceedings, even though she was not directly named in the investigation. In Chile, recent accusations of corruption have embarrassed many business executives and politicians, but a case involving Ms. Bachelet's daughter-in-law has in large part caused Ms. Bachelet's approval rating to plummet.[19]

The Latin "machismo" culture resulted in strong backlash against women politicians perceived to have let the populace down, and swiftly boomeranged voters back to traditional role expectations. During Rousseff's impeachment proceedings, conservative politician Jaufran Siqueira posted a picture of a house engulfed in flames on Facebook with the caption, "this is what will happen to feminists when Jaufran is elected."[20] He later said it was "a joke."

Rousseff's, Kirchner's, and Bachelet's successors all reflected a cultural shift back to more traditionally acceptable, machismo politicians. Rousseff's former vice-president, Michel Temer, succeeded her. The cover of the Brazilian magazine *Piaui* portrayed the cultural shift, depicting "the 1950's-style suburban idyll" in which the gray-haired 75-year-old president is greeted by his spouse, Marcela, a soft-spoken former beauty pageant contestant 42 years younger.[21] Temer appointed a cabinet devoid of women. Ironically, by May 2017 Temer too was under investigation for corruption and obstruction of justice and did not run for re-election. He was succeeded by the openly misogynistic Jair Bolsonaro. Earlier, as a member of the Brazilian legislature, Bolsonaro had dedicated his vote to impeach Rousseff, who had been tortured as a political prisoner in the 1970s, to one of her torturers. Kirschner's successor in Argentina was Mauricio Macri, who served as President from 2015 to 2019. His third wife, fashion designer Juliana Awada, is 15 years his junior. Macri proudly told a television reporter that she was "insatiable" in bed.[22] Chilean billionaire business executive Sebastian Pinera followed Bachelet as president, having already served as president from 2010 to 2014. During that tenure he was censured by women's groups for "joking" on a state visit to Mexico, that when a woman says "no" it means "maybe," when a woman a woman says "maybe" it means "yes," and when she says "yes" she's not a lady.

Latin America is not the only region where a woman leader has been ousted recently. South Korean president Park Geun-hye was impeached and convicted of corruption in 2017. Corruption in South Korea is many-faceted, and has a long history. Investigations by prosecutors have been described as "lackadaisical." Bribery is common practice, including of the judiciary. And media internal censorship, depending on organizational interests, is not uncommon.[23] It is within this stew of corruption that Park, South Korea's first woman president, lost office.

Park Geun-hye comes from a South Korean political dynasty, as the daughter of popular former dictator Park Chung-hee. The public's reaction to daughter Park Geun-hye stems in part from many South Koreans seeing her as a modern version of her charismatic father.

> A widely shared Twitter post last year summed up the challenges Ms. Park has faced in the shadow of her father's legacy and with the cultural misgivings over female leaders: "When President Park Geun-hye does well, she wears the clothes of Park Chung-hee. But when she does badly, she becomes a woman."[24]

Park was not been a champion of women's rights, either as a legislator or as president. She rose to power through the support of her father's remaining elderly, conservative cohorts. According to the leader of the Korean Women's Association United, Kim Young-soon, gender inequality has gotten worse under the Park administration, with sex crimes increasing and a growing wealth gap that took a harder toll on women.[25]

A general backlash against women politicians quickly followed in South Korea, and a significant rise in misogyny overall. There were online attacks against Park using an old Korean tirade against assertive women: "If a hen crows, the household collapses." Koreans have focused on Ms. Choi's lack of experience in government or policymaking, which she was accused of interfering with, calling her an *ajumma* (homemaker) "from Gangnam" (a district of Seoul associated with affluence and moral weakness). South Korean women's groups reacted with dismay. According to one feminist group: "President Park is taken as evidence that women are not qualified for politics."[26]

Women politicians are neither saintly nor uncomplicated. But public tolerance of women politicians' faults seems as thin and unforgiving as the "culture of humiliation" experienced by women caught in illicit relationships with men. The men are forgiven and the women are endlessly shamed. When women politicians are seen to fail and a cultural boomerang back to traditional proclivities occurs, rollbacks in women's empowerment can be swift and deep.

Making a global difference

The United Nations has worked tirelessly to facilitate structural changes in elections toward increasing women's political participation, through a variety of means. In Kenya, for example, UN Women supported a five-year civil society campaign as Kenya's new constitution was being drafted. The focus was on

> enshrinement of key rights, including a ban on all forms of violence against women and girls, the right to own land, and equality in marriage. The campaign also included the right to political representation, in the form of a rule stating that no more than two-thirds of elected seats could be held by persons of either gender.[27]

Kenyans overwhelmingly endorsed the new constitution in 2010, as a big political win for women.

In 2012, UN Women went back to work, establishing a team of prominent Kenyan women's rights advocates, who met with the Independent Electoral and Boundaries Commission and with political parties to make sure that candidate nomination lists included the required number of women. Then UN Women worked with partners to train and support women candidates, and instituted a major campaign intended to encourage voters to consider electing women. The campaign featured advertising on television, radio, and in major newspapers, all in local languages. When elections were held in 2013, women were elected to 87 of the 416 seats in the newly established National Assembly and Senate chambers, up from 22 women in the old 222-seat one-chamber Parliament. While the good news was that the percentage of women representatives nearly doubled, not all the election news was good.

Most of the electoral gains in the legislature were due to reserved seats rather than success at the ballot box. Miriam Kamunyu was the lead author of *Key Gains and Challenges: A Gender Audit of Kenya's 2013 Election Process*, a report on how women fared in the polls. The media reported on her report presentation:

> The results disappointed backers of the new constitution. In the national assembly, women won just six percent of directly elected constituency seats, down from eight percent in 2007. Not a single woman was elected to the powerful position of governor or senator for the 47 newly created counties.
>
> Kamunyu, presenting the report on Wednesday, accused virtually all the bodies involved of failing to uphold women's rights – the electoral commission, the political parties, the police and the registrar for political parties.
>
> At the launch of the election campaign, women candidates said their supporters were beaten, they were slandered and their billboards were defaced, without redress.[28]

The report concluded that the political parties remained the bastion of the traditional patriarchy and the subjugation of women. It was the parties that were keeping women from being nominated for key positions.

As of 2022, things remained much the same in Kenya. Of some 16,000 political candidates running in various elections, only approximately 2,000 were women. Kenya has the lowest rate of women parliamentarians in East Africa at 23%. In 2018, male politicians avoided a parliamentary vote intended to guarantee women one in three seats in the National Assembly and have ignored court orders to implement the gender quota. Changing culture remains harder than changing structure.

In Pakistan, UN Women supported a 2012 women's voter registration drive, resulting in adding 40 million women to the National Database and Registration Authority. Part of the effort involved the issuance of Computerized National Identity Cards, which are important in many instances simply by providing women with legal identification. Further, supported by UN Women and the UNDP, the Pakistani election commission put a system in place to collect voter turnout data by sex, toward pinpointing barriers to women's civic rights. Consequently, in 2013 elections there was a national voter turnout of 55%, up from the past, with voter turnout for women an unprecedented 40% of all votes.[29] As of 2018, despite gains from the past, Pakistan still ranked last in the world for female turnout in elections.

At local, state, and national levels, having women in politics can make a difference in policy and actions. In areas of India where women lead the panchayats (local councils), the number of drinking water projects was 62% higher than in those with men-led councils. In Norway, a direct causal relationship was found between the presence of women in municipal councils and child care coverage. Yet whether structural or cultural, or both, there are still a significant number of barriers to be overcome by women in politics.

The American experience

Dating back to George Washington, the US president is considered first and foremost the commander in chief, a frame of reference more difficult for women to realize. According to Laura Liswood, secretary general of the United Nations Foundation's Council of Women World Leaders,

> America is still considered as the policeman of the world, the guardian of the world and we still have a very gendered version of what leadership means. Not only do we have to be liked, we also have to be tough.[30]

It is important to note, however, that the United States doesn't actually elect a president by popular vote. Had that been the case, Hillary Clinton would have become president rather than Donald Trump as she won the popular vote 48% to 46%. Presidents are elected by the Electoral College, a system set up by the founding fathers in the eighteenth century to protect small states, but that in the twenty-first century allows for minority rule.

Gender was a prevalent theme in the 2016 US election, perhaps most glaringly when candidate Trump called Clinton a "such a nasty woman."[31] But experts caution that generalizing about American voters' views on women candidates based on their attitudes toward Hillary Clinton could be misleading, because she is "such a special case and a unique figure, having been around for so long. Did people vote against her because she was a woman or because her name is Clinton? Of course, it could be both."[32]

A 2018 Pew survey conducted in the United States found that seven in ten Americans view certain leadership traits of higher value to men than women. Being assertive, decisive, and ambitious helped men more than women seeking high political office. Being approachable, physically attractive, and compassionate helped women more than men. And while women were expected to be compassionate, showing emotions hurt women candidates more than men. Various studies over the years have found that almost any trait can hurt women politicians, again putting them in the Madonna-Whore-like impossible situations discussed in Chapter 4.

Producer Rory Kennedy's 2014 documentary *Makers: Women in Politics* traces the modern political history of American women in politics. Even after obtaining the vote in 1920, women for many years remained in the political background, campaigning for men candidates or, in a few exceptional cases, gaining access to office through "the widow's route" when their husbands died in office. Most often, though, the widows merely carried out their husband's policies and voted the party line. Republican Senator Margaret Chase Smith was the first to break that tradition and was in fact the first senator to speak out in 1950 against Joe McCarthy, at time when it was politically risky to do so. Republican Representative Liz Cheney similarly put country above party in her willingness to hold then President Donald Trump responsible for the January 6, 2020, attack on the US Capitol, though doing so meant losing her seat in Congress.

It was not until the 1970s, with the women's liberation and the anti-Vietnam War movement, that more women began independently to work their way into Congress. Shirley Chisholm, the first Black women elected to Congress, and Patricia Schroeder were among those who broke into what has been called the "most exclusive boys club in the world." In *Makers*, Schroeder tells the story of being vetoed from a position on the Armed Services Committee by the chair and having the veto overridden by the other members. But when she arrived for her first committee meeting with the other new member, African American Ron Dellums, the peevish chair had arranged for only one seat to be at the dais for the two of them. Schroeder also later found out that the FBI had been tracking her and her staff during her campaign, including recruiting her husband's barber as an informant regarding her anti-war views.

For many years, low numbers of women in Congress resulted in them largely being ignored. Consequently, in 1977, 13 women in Congress decided to form a bipartisan Women's Caucus, with the aim of increasing their power.[33] As issues concerning women, especially single women, women in the workforce, and women head of households, began to come to the forefront of politics throughout the 1980s, women voters began to vote differently than men, leaning increasingly Democratic. The Caucus began to develop a voice of their own and support legislation that focused on women's concerns. The 1993 Family and Medical Leave Act was the first piece of legislation passed from the Women's Caucus.[34]

The importance of women's votes became apparent in 1984 when Democratic presidential candidate Walter Mondale selected Congresswoman Geraldine Ferraro as his vice-presidential running mate. Ronald Reagan won the election against Mondale, but women had taken another step forward toward political inclusivity. The symbolism was significant. There would not be another woman at the top of the Democratic or Republican ticket until John McCain selected Sarah Palin as his running mate in 2008. Whether Palin helped or hurt the ticket due to her "hockey mom/pitbull" style that created significant divisiveness among women voters, and her tendency to "go rogue" in the campaign, she did become the role model for many future conservative women candidates.

There were a number of obstacles for women seeking office throughout the 1980s. One was money. Men did not want to support women candidates. EMILY's List is an organization founded in 1985 to fund pro-choice Democratic women. The name "EMILY's List" is an acronym for "Early Money Is Like Yeast" (i.e., it makes the dough rise). The yeast reference is an axiom of political fundraising that says receiving major donations early in a race is helpful in attracting other, later donors. Subsequently, women's political action committees, such as the nonpartisan Women's Campaign Fund, and partisan organizations like EMILY's List exist specifically to boost women candidates in fundraising. While women candidates anticipate that they will have more difficulties than men in fundraising, research now shows near parity in the ability to raise funds in many cases.

Other obstacles faced by women in the 1980s still persist. While it seems unlikely that Hillary Clinton and Sarah Palin might have much in common, as women politicians they both faced significant personal scrutiny regarding their looks, their dress, their energy, their competence, and their family life. Clinton was criticized for her handling of her husband's extramarital affairs, while Palin was questioned about how much time she would have for her national duties given that she is the mother of five children, including a special needs child. These are personal issues male politicians are rarely asked to address. When Clinton choked up during the 2008 New Hampshire primary, she was portrayed as being too emotional and having "broken down." *New York Times* columnist Maureen Dowd asked if Clinton could "cry her way to the White House."[35] Conversely, in 2016 she was accused of having the personality of a robot.[36] The media portrayed Palin, who embraced motherhood and being a tough "hockey mom," as sexy, stupid, and conniving. Women politicians are judged differently, and more personally, than their male colleagues.

In the United States, women have not been asked to run for office at the same rates as men. Jean Sinzdak, from the nonpartisan Rutgers University Center for American Women and Politics, has said:

> men are recruited for political office at higher rates than women at every level of government. And given that women have been likely to step forward only when they have the right degree, a ready support network, and the backing of seasoned professionals, that recruitment is essential.[37]

Women candidates can also suffer from what is called "pragmatic bias." That is, voters will withhold support for candidates they perceive as having a low chance of success. However, in comparable races (e.g., not a "safe seat" district where one party dominates), when voters believe that women both want and will support women candidates, they are elected at the same ratios as men.

As of 2023, there are a total of 150 women serving in the US Congress. On the Senate side, there are 25 in total: 15 Democrats, 9 Republicans, and 1 Independent. On the House side, there are 125 in total: 92 Democrats and 33 Republicans. While the majority of women in Congress are still Democrats, largely sparked in reaction to the election of Trump, Republican women recently made significant gains in their numbers from the past. Part of the reason the United States is ranked 27 in the 2022 Global Gender Gap Index, and 44 in the Gender Inequality Index is the relatively low level of women's political participation. However, as of 2023, women hold almost 28% of national legislative seats, an all-time high, indicative of an upward trend.

The highest level of elected political office that a woman has held is Speaker of the House, third in line for the presidency. Nancy Pelosi, a Democrat from California, held that office from 2007 to 2011, and then again from 2019 to 2023. First elected to the House in 1987, she worked her way up through party positions to be Speaker. Pelosi has been called "the strongest and most effect speaker of modern times" and has been "the most successful non-presidential political fundraiser in US history."[38] Nevertheless, Democratic colleagues have challenged her leadership position more than once, and the Republican Party has consistently used her as a lightning rod to attract voters away from Democratic candidates. Prior to the 2010 midterm elections, the National Republican Congressional Committee featured her in 70% of its ads, and more often than then-President Barack Obama in the 2012 and 2016 elections.[39] Though competitiveness and confidence are acceptable, even desirable qualities of male leaders, for women they are "inconsistent with prescriptive female stereotypes of warmth and communality [...] the mere indication that a female leader is successful in her position leads to increased rating of her self-ishness, deceitfulness, and coldness."[40] Pelosi was in a no-win position, even with her party peers. "The more successful Pelosi is, outmaneuvering and dominating her male adversaries, the more threatening she becomes."[41]

The importance of women's leadership was perhaps most vividly demonstrated during the 16-day government shutdown in 2013 after neither a budget nor a continuing resolution could be agreed upon in an increasingly partisan Congress. According to Republican Senator John McCain and other male politicians interviewed in *Makers*, it was through the leadership of congressional women, working together on a bipartisan basis, that a compromise was reached and the shutdown finally ended. According to the women involved, they were more committed to problem-solving than self-aggrandizement, power building, and getting credit. Their focus on solving the problem relates back to collaboration and innovativeness being traits more associated with women and that true leaders, men and women, are interested in moving forward regardless of whether or not they will get credit.

However, the 2013 bipartisan triumph may have been a one-off, possible because both parties get blamed when the government shuts down. When partisan issues are involved, though, agency comes strongly into play. Legislatively, their differing views on agency mean that, for example, while liberals will see reproductive health as a group issue and support legislation to require employers and insurance companies to cover contraception costs as part of healthcare, conservatives, including conservative women, will more likely see cost coverage as a personal responsibility and vote against government intervention. In areas related to women in the work-force, views on agency can also intercede, evidenced in a 2020 fight in California over "gig work" at companies like Uber and Lyft. Whereas liberal women there supported efforts to man-date that "gig work" pay benefits that help women as a group long term, conservative women argued against such efforts as hindering individual women's near-term opportunities to earn – flexible gig work often being attractive to women – if businesses pay workers less due to having to pay benefits.

Intersectionality has long recognized differences among women. As already discussed, the views of one woman do not necessarily represent the views of another based on factors including views of agency, linked fate theory, and considerations and attributes that contribute to individual privilege and discrimination. Consequently, the willingness and ability of women in Congress, particularly in the House of Representatives where members run for re-election every two years, to reach across the aisle has not fared well. The Lugar Center–McCourt School Bipartisan Index provides scores and rankings for members of Congress, based on objective measures regarding how well members of opposite parties work with one another based on bill sponsorship and co-sponsorship data. Looking at the data from 2021, of the 435 members of Congress in total, 24% had a positive bipartisan score, with women making up only 26% of that number.

Navigating voter and partisan constraints on agency has been an issue for women in both political parties. Republican women lawmakers and 2022 candidates, for example, found repro-ductive rights a difficult minefield to navigate after the Republican-supported 2022 Supreme Court reversal of *Roe v. Wade* and the subsequent landslide win for reproductive rights in Kansas. The American majority views on reproductive rights were affirmed again in Wisconsin in 2023, on a vote for a judgeship on the Wisconsin Supreme Court, with the winning judge vowing to reverse the state's ban on abortion imposed by the state legislature. On the Democratic side, progressive women have found themselves at odds with their more conservative party leadership, which is largely motivated by a drive for party consensus, thereby inhibiting their agency.[42]

Violence, deepfakes, and disinformation

Women's global political activism has, unfortunately but not surprisingly, engendered significant backlash. Marielle Franco rose from poverty to gain prominence as a Black, lesbian, human rights activist and Rio City Council member before being assassinated in 2018. Franco had been outspoken against the kinds of selective law enforcement, police brutality, and extrajudicial killings that make women penalty-free targets of abuse and violence. Two ex-policemen were arrested in 2019 for her murder, and a third suspect was shot dead by police in 2020 when he resisted arrest. Some Franco supporters suspect he was killed because he had information the police did not want revealed.

Jo Cox, a member of the British Parliament, was 41 years old when she died in June 2016 after having been shot and stabbed multiple times by a White supremacist. Cox was married with two children and had formerly worked in international humanitarian aid through the organization Oxfam. Her attacker claimed she was a traitor to White people and portrayed himself a martyr at trial, saying his actions were "for Britain."

Women politicians across the globe have been targeted for violence. A 2016 study by the Inter-Parliamentary Union found that nearly 82% of women members of parliament have suffered some form of psychological intimidation, and nearly half of them have received threats or been the target of rape, beatings, or abductions during parliamentary terms, including threats to kidnap or kill their children. Forcing women out of elections can come in other ways as well.

Diane Rwigara was a 2017 presidential hopeful in Rwanda and a women's rights activist. She was a strong critic of Rwandan president Paul Kagame, and the sole female challenger in the race. Seventy-two hours after she announced her intention to run, she found manufactured nude photos of herself posted on the Internet. The attempt to humiliate and intimidate her did not deter her, but eventually she was arrested and jailed on charges of forgery and tax evasion. After almost a year in jail, she was acquitted. Meanwhile, Kagame was re-elected.

Deepfakes, where artificial intelligence is used to transpose a face or body onto someone else to create a new, manufactured fake image, has received attention in conjunction with high-level officials. There has been considerable public concern regarding the damage to national security that could be done with, for example, a fake video of President Joe Biden supposedly saying he intended to carry out a nuclear strike on a particular country. More probable, however, are deepfakes being used against women politicians and public figures in the attempt to silence their voices. It is already being done and increasingly frequently. Ninety-six percent of all deepfakes depict fictitious, non-consensual pornography, and 99% of those were made of women. Online websites advertise "the largest collection of Alexandria Ocasio-Cortez deepfake porn videos." Other derogatory or negative deepfake imagery is also used besides porn. Manipulated imagery purporting to show Jacinda Ardern smoking crack went viral on Facebook in 2021, resulting in commentary such as "what else is she partaking of behind closed doors, is she really fit to run this country" and "I actually think it might be true. Her boyfriend is a dealer."[43]

Beyond politicians, Indian journalist Rana Ayyub spoke out against the Indian government's response to the rape of an eight-year-old girl and found herself the target of a deepfake video created as part of a coordinated online hate campaign. Australian Noelle Martin advocated against image-based sexual abuse and found herself the subject of manufactured images and deepfake video. Helen Mort, a UK poet and broadcaster, discovered deepfakes of herself online.[44]

In the United States, a 2022 study by the Center for Democracy and Technology found that women politicians of color are particularly targeted for abuse:

In a press interview, former Vermont state house representative Kiah Morris said she reported at least 26 incidents to the local police where she and her family felt threatened between 2016 and 2018. The severity of the targeted abuse both on and offline ultimately led Rep. Morris to a premature resignation three months before the end of her second term in office in 2018. In the same story, U.S. Rep. Nikema Williams expressed the view that the onslaught of mis- and disinformation and abuse seemed to be designed to intimidate women of color out of government: "Early on, when we were getting the list of credible threats coming in for members of Congress, they were centered around members of color and there are only 25 black women that serve in the United States […] there's not that many of us […] which I think is part of the whole thing of people trying to scare people [black women] into silence."[45]

The implications of this targeting of women of color are especially important given that their representative numbers are already low, at only 10% of candidates who ran for Congress in 2020.

Disinformation/misinformation campaigns against women generally are increasingly frequent, many of them coordinated rather than random. The Wilson Center, a nonpartisan think tank, conducted a 2020 study on how gender, sex, and lies are weaponized against women online, specifically women politicians. The report concluded that online gendered abuse and disinformation is a national security threat, as many of the bad actors responsible are associated with Russia, Iran, and China, and that the threat has been largely ignored. They further concluded that gendered and sexualized disinformation is distinctly different from broad-based gendered abuse. It is often conducted through "malign creativity," or coded language, context-based visual and textual themes, and other tactics to avoid detection on social media platforms, and so extremely challenging to address.

The study focused on words and visuals used to imply or spread disinformation on selected social media platforms (platforms selected based primarily on researcher access to data) in conjunction with 13 women politicians: Jacinda Ardern (New Zealand), Priti Patel (UK), Chrystia Freeland (Canada), and from the United States, Susan Collins, Kirsten Gillibrand, Kamala Harris, Jaime Herrera Beutler, Alexandria Ocasio-Cortez, Ilhan Omar, Elissa Slotkin, Elise Stefanik, Lauren Underwood, and Gretchen Whitmer. The study found gendered abuse and disinformation widespread. Twelve of the 13 subjects were affected by gendered abuse and 9 of the 13 were targeted with gendered disinformation narratives of a racist, transphobic, or sexual nature. The overwhelming majority of keywords relating to abuse and disinformation were directed at Kamala Harris on Twitter, at 78% of the total number of recorded instances.

Sexual narratives about the women were the most common, accounting for 31% of the total data collected, again primarily targeted at Kamala Harris. Transphobic and racist narratives accounted for only 1.6% and 0.8% of the findings, respectively. To be clear, the transphobic narratives implied that the target was *actually a man*. Though the numbers are low, they were relatively widespread, thereby affecting a number of different research subjects. Apparently originating through QAnon, a photo of Kamala Harris was circulated next to her supposed former male identity, Kamal Aroush, complete with a backstory. A video of Jacinda Ardern showing a pleat in her dress, was interpreted and circulated as evidence of Ardern having male genitalia. Gretchen Whitmer's facial features were compared to transgender celebrity Caitlyn Jenner, with targeters asserting that her similar bone structure was "proof" of Whitmer's male identity. Alexandria Ocasio-Cortez has been targeted online through the frequent use of words like "tranny" or "transsexual." Online gendered abuse and disinformation is often intersectional in nature, with abusers frequently engaging in both sex and race narratives, compounding the threat for women of color.

Women politicians that abusers did not choose to sexualize were generally older politicians: Chrystia Freeland, Kirsten Gillibrand, Susan Collins, and Priti Patel.

Though often associated with controversial policies, Priti Patel was also the only high-profile politician against whom coordinated disinformation campaigns were not found. Online abusers appeared to target her through more traditional misogynistic abuse, using words like "bitch," "fat," and "witch."

Violence against women politicians and candidates has emerged as a major deterrent to women's political participation. Some women candidates have been forced to hire personal security for themselves and their families, at their own expense. The brutal hammer attack on Nancy Pelosi's 82-year-old husband, Paul, in October 2022 by a QAnon conspiracy theorist evidences the danger families of women politicians increasingly face. The multitude of challenges, and threats, faced by women candidates and politicians, has created a chilling effect on some, but for others it has just made them more determined not to be left out.

Conclusion

Suffrage was an important step toward political inclusiveness but only a first step. Women still face considerable uphill battles when running for offices, starting with simply not being seen as "having what it takes" in terms of decisiveness and an ability to face tough challenges, especially in security-related areas. They are further faced with a very different, personalized type of scrutiny as candidates that inhibits many women from running for office. When in office, they offer different types of leadership and decision-making skills and styles than men, often thereby opening opportunities for action not otherwise possible. Sometimes, those new opportunities are simply not welcome, as they shake an often stale and corrupt status quo. If politics are corrupt, then so too will be society. If society is corrupt, stability and hence security will be tenuous at best.

The Women, Peace, and Security framework advocates inclusive diversity toward more gendered perspectives, policies, and programs. But to be clear and restate a key premise, gender expertise is an analytical competence, not a physiological trait. Male allies who support gender equality are needed and wanted. But having more women leaders is also part of reaching gender parity as they offer differing styles and more policy options for conflict settlement, bring often otherwise ignored issues to the decision-making table, and are generally additive to good policymaking and implementation. Their voices need to be heard.

Notes

1 Mary Caprioli and Mark Boyer, "Gender, Vilence and International Crisis," *Journal of Conflict Resolution*, August 2001, pp. 503–518. Cited in Marie O'Reilly, *Why Women: Inclusive Security and Peaceful Societies*, Inclusive Security, 2015, p. 4. www.inclusivesecurity.org/wp-content/uploads/2017/06/Why-Women-Report-2017.pdf

2 www.msnbc.com/msnbc/elizabeth-warren-we-have-chance-we-have-fight-it

3 https://history.hanover.edu/courses/excerpts/165adams-rtl.html

4 Richard Langworth, *The Churchill Documents*, vol. 2, Hillsdale College Press, 2006, p. 765.

5 Gail Collins, "The Glass Ceiling Holds," *New York Times*, November 11, 2016.

6 Collins, 2016.

7 "The National Relief Society and the US Sheppard-Towner Act, *Utah History Quarterly*, 50, no. 2, 1982. https://issuu.com/utah10/docs/uhq_volume50_1982_number3/s/133940

8 Swanee Hunt, "Let Women Rule," *Foreign Affairs*, May/June 2007, 86, no. 3.

9 www.ndi.org/what-we-do/gender-women-and-democracy

10 Katrin Bennhold and Rick Gladstone, "Over 70 Nations Have Been Led by Women. So Why Not the US?" *New York Times*, November 10, 2016.

11 "Michelle Bachelet Quotes," *101Sharequotes.com.* 2016. http://101sharequotes.com/quote/michelle_bachelet-i-took-a-gamble-to-exercise-lead-64826.

12 Jill Petzinger, "Did Angela Merkel Matter For Women?" *Foreign Policy*, December 13, 2021. https://foreignpolicy.com/2021/12/13/did-angela-merkel-matter-for-women/

13 Mona Lena Krook, Diana Z. O'Brien, and Krista M. Swip, "Military Invasion and Women's Political Representation," *International Feminist Journal of Politics*, February 10, 2010, p. 69. http://mlkrook.org/pdf/krook_obrien_swip_10.pdf

14 Krook, O'Brien, and Swip, p. 69.

15 Katrin Bennhold, "Glass Cliff, Not Just Ceiling, Often Impedes Women Rising in Politics, *New York Times*, October 5, 2016. www.nytimes.com/2016/10/05/world/europe/glass-cliff-uk-women-politics.html

16 Christopher Wallis, Bheeshma Ravi, Natalie Coburn, Robert Kam, Allan Detsky, and Raj Satkunaswam, "Comparison of Postoperative Outcomes among Patients Treated by Male and Female Surgeons," *BMJ*, October 17, 2017. www.bmj.com/content/bmj/359/bmj.j4366.full.pdf

17 Heather Sarsons, "Interpreting Signals in the Labor Market: Evidence From Medical Referrals," October 31, 2017. https://scholar.harvard.edu/files/sarsons/files/sarsons_jmp_01.pdf;
    Julia Belluz, "Women Surgeons Are Punished More Than Men for the Exact Same Mistakes, Study Finds," *Vox,* October 23, 2017. www.vox.com/science-and-health/2017/11/23/16686532/surgeon-mistakes-gender-wage-gap

18 *Personality and Social Psychology Bulletin*, 36, no. 7 (2010), p. 923.

19 Jonathan Gilbert, "South America's Powerful Women Are Embattled. Is Gender a Factor?" *New York Times*, May 4, 2016.

20 Simon Romero and Anna Jean Kaiser, "Some See Anti-Women Backlash in Ouster of Brazil's President," *New York Times*, September 7, 2016.

21 Romero and Kaiser, 2016.

22 Alejandro Rebossio, "Juliana Awada, Fashion Mogul and Future First Lady of Argentina," *El Pais*, November 25, 2015. http://elpais.com/elpais/2015/11/25/inenglish/1448466351_432980.html

23 Justin Fendos, "The History of a Scandal: How South Korea's President Was Impeached," *The Diplomat*, January 24, 2017.

24 Choe Sang-hun, "Gender Colors Outrage over Scandal Involving South Korea's President," *New York Times*, November 21, 2016. www.nytimes.com/2016/11/22/world/asia/south-korea-park-geun-hye-women.html

25 Sang-hun, 2016.

26 Sang-hun, 2016.

27 "Women Elected to One-Fifth of Seats during Kenyan Elections," UN Women, March 28, 2013. www.unwomen.org/ru/news/stories/2013/3/women-elected-to-one-fifth-of-seats-in-kenya

28 Katy Migiro, "New Laws Ignored, So Women Trailed in Kenya 2013 Election," *Reuters*, December 5, 2013. http://news.trust.org//item/20131205145820-u5bql/

29 "Sharp Increase of Women Voters in Pakistan's Recent Elections," UN Women, August 21, 2013. www.unwomen.org/en/news/stories/2013/8/pakistan-elections-feature

30 Katrin Bennhold and Rick Gladstone, "Over 70 Nations Have Been Led by Women. So Why Not the US?" *New York Times*, November 10, 2016.

31 Jannell Ross, "Trump's 'Such a Nasty Woman' Comment Has Sparked Something," *Washington Post*, October 20, 2016. www.washingtonpost.com/news/the-fix/wp/2016/10/20/trumps-such-a-nasty-woman-comment-has-sparked-something/?utm_term=.d19ad6f30fa1

32 Bennhold and Gladstone, 2016.

33 www.womenspolicy.org/our-work/the-womens-caucus/caucus-history/

34 "Celebration of 20 Years of the Women's Caucus," *Congressional Record*, 143, no. 142, October 21, 1997. www.gpo.gov/fdsys/pkg/CREC-1997-10-21/html/CREC-1997-10-21-pt1-PgH8840-3.htm

35 Maureen Dowd, "Can Hillary Cry Her Way Back to the White House?" *New York Times*, January 9, 2008. www.nytimes.com/2008/01/09/opinion/08dowd.html
36 Windsor Mann, "Hillary Clinton Personality: Robot," *National Review*, October 8, 2015. www.nationalreview.com/article/425233/hillary-i-went-shopping-once-windsor-mann
37 Christina Cauterucci, "How Do You Inspire Women to Run for Office?" Elect Trump," *Slate*, January 16, 2017. www.slate.com/articles/news_and_politics/cover_story/2017/01/when_women_run_they_win_and_trump_s_election_is_inspiring_a_surge_of_new.html
38 Peter Beinart, "The Nancy Pelosi Problem," *The Atlantic*, April 2018, p. 11.
39 Beinart, p. 11.
40 Victoria Brescoll and Tyler Okimoto, "The Price of Power: Power Seeking and Backlash against Female Politicians," *Personality and Social Psychology Bulletin*, June 2, 2010.
41 Beinart, p. 12.
42 Joan Johnson-Freese and Alexandra Nicole Islas, "Will More Women in Congress Mean More Bipartisanship?" WIIS Blog, March 16, 2023. https://wiisglobal.org/will-more-women-in-congress-mean-more-bipartisanship/
43 "Fact Check-Clip of Jacinda Ardern Smoking Cannabis Is a Deepfake," *Reuters*, November 16, 2021. www.reuters.com/article/factcheck-newzealand-ardern/fact-check-clip-of-jacinda-ardern-smoking-cannabis-is-a-deepfake-idUSL1N2S71BZ
44 Suzie Dunn, "Women, Not Politicians, Are Targeted Most Often by Deepfake Videos," Centre for International Governance Innovation, March 3, 2021. www.cigionline.org/articles/women-not-politicians-are-targeted-most-often-deepfake-videos/
45 Thakur, Dhanaraj, and DeVan Hankerson Madrigal, "An Unrepresentative Democracy: How Disinformation and Online Abuse Hinder Women of Color Political Candidates in the United States," October 27, 2022. https://cdt.org/insights/an-unrepresentative-democracy-how-disinformation-and-online-abuse-hinder-women-of-color-political-candidates-in-the-united-states/

Further reading

Allen, Jonathan, and Jamie Parnes. *Shattered: Inside Hillary Clinton's Doomed Campaign*, Crown Publishing, 2017.
Berevoescu, Ionica, and Julie Ballington. *Working Paper: Women's Representation in Local Government, A Global Analysis*, UN Women, December 2021.
Bjarngård, Elin, and Pär Zetterberg (eds.). *Gender and Violence Against Political Actors*, Temple University Press, 2023.
Boorstin, Julia. *When Women Lead: What They Achieve, Why They Succeed, and What We Can Learn from Them,* Simon and Schuster, 2022.
Campus, Donatella. *Women Political Leaders and the Media*, Palgrave Macmillan, 2013.
Cunningham, Anne C. *Women as Political Leaders*, Enslow, 2017.
Genovese, Michael A., and Janie S. Steckenrider. *Women as Political Leaders: Studies in Gender and Governance*, Routledge, 2013.
Lockhart, Michele, and Kathleen Mollick (eds.). *Global Women Leaders: Studies in Feminist Political Rhetoric*, Lexington Books, 2014.
Lockhart, Michele, Kathleen Mollick, and Diane M. Blair (eds.). *Political Women: Language and Leadership*, Lexington Books, 2013.
Shames, Shauna. *Out of the Running*: *Why Millennials Reject Political Careers and Why it Matters*, NYU Press, 2017.
Traister, Rebecca. *All the Single Ladies: Unmarried Women and the Rise of the Independent Nation.* Marysue Rucci Books, 2016.
Traister, Rebecca. *Big Girls Don't Cry: The Election That Changed Everything*, Free Press, 2010.

12 Women, peace, and security in security organizations

Too much talk, not enough action

International organizations provide a stage upon which WPS initiatives and challenges play out with dramatic effect. In a world where climate change and resource competition result in increasing disasters and human conflict, international organizations serve a critical role in advancing strategic and operational priorities for their signatories. The twentieth anniversary of UNSCR 1325 (2000) marked a singular moment for reflective research on the headway of the WPS agenda and the continued barriers to its most effective implementation. Though not comprehensive, the research indicates that, despite the disparate impacts inflicted by disasters and conflict on women and girls on all continents, representation in preventing, resolving, and recovery remains ad hoc. This chapter reviews some of the key efforts made by regional, security-related international organizations to enact the WPS agenda, highlighting new initiatives, areas of progress, and the struggle to gain measurable success.

For the purposes of this chapter, security-related organizations are broadly defined. As has been pointed out throughout this text, security goes beyond military troops and missions and relates to development, economics, and all elements of human security as well. Therefore, consideration of whether and how WPS is handled in the North Atlantic Treaty Organization (NATO), the African Union (AU), the Association of Southeast Asian Nations (ASEAN), the Organization of American States (OAS), and the European Union (EU) offers the opportunity to consider just how "mainstream" WPS has become in a variety of organizations in the more than two decades since its passage. Most importantly, organizations are comprised of countries, the views of which are all shaped by separate cultures and national interests.

UNSCR 1325 reflects the recognition that international and non-international armed conflict has a gendered impact and those most impacted often have the least influence. As discussed throughout the book, the WPS agenda has four pillars, Participation, Protection, Prevention, and Relief and Recovery. These pillars are part of a continuum and are often prioritized differently given the culture and foreign policy priorities of the enacting state or states, as is the case with regional organizations.

After 20 years, the more critical research suggests that WPS on the international stage is siloed by the "militarized security approach" of international and non-international armed conflict, and that it too often ignores more localized violence against women and girls because it has fallen prey to "pinkwashing," meaning the deliberate appropriation of gender equality movements for the sake of public relations, but actually often supporting regressive political ends and check-the-box rhetoric.[1] While tangible action and significant change have been slow to be realized, there are examples of regional initiatives and state-led plans that recognize the

DOI: 10.4324/9781003413417-13

role of women in promoting peace and security which are slowly moving the proverbial ball down the court toward a new normal.

North Atlantic Treaty Organization (NATO)

NATO is a collective security alliance established during the Cold War to prevent Soviet forces from overrunning Europe. Collective security binds members together through a commitment to protect each other and presents a united front against aggression. NATO has evolved over time, not without some struggle, to establish its post-Cold War mission. The years of struggle were most intense immediately after the fall of the Soviet Union when it was thought, hoped, that Russia would democratize and westernize. But that didn't happen. Now, with many former Soviet satellites integrated into NATO, the mission is largely to contain Russia.

WPS efforts within NATO have been challenged by the slow movement of internal gendered structures and the external pressures of the Russian invasion of Ukraine and the European migrant crisis. The importance of status quo-oriented, internal gendered structures cannot be overstated regarding the slow-rolling of mainstreaming efforts. After the 2000 passage of UNSCR 1325, NATO took immediate steps to adopt its first Action Plan, toward mainstreaming the WPS pillars into NATO-led Operations and Missions, and in 2012 to establish and appoint women to key positions like the Special Representative for Women, Peace, and Security.

NATO took additional efforts to support implementation through the task force and committee creation, and perhaps most notably, the establishment of gender adviser positions to provide operational support to military commanders during NATO-led operations. The first NATO GENADs were deployed in 2009, well before any individual states, to the two NATO strategic commands and to the International Security Assistance Force in Afghanistan, replaced in 2015 by the Resolute Support Mission that operated until September 2021. As with all GENAD positions, success has and continues to depend on personal commitment and knowledge, resources and access, and leadership.

In October 2021, NATO adopted a new WPS Action Plan focused on NATO's partnerships with third countries, international organizations, and civil society. This Action Plan highlighted innovation, climate change, resilience, and new technology as filters through which the WPS agenda can be further promoted. The attempted operationalization of WPS by NATO has yielded policies, strategies, training, and education across the Alliance with a global training program heralded by the Nordic Center for Gender in Military Operations. The Nordic Center for Gender in Military Operations helps NATO "manage[s] the training needs of personnel from member and partner nations to provide tailored training solutions to satisfy all NATO requirements."[2]

However, the advancement of WPS on the organizational level and within the member states has in many instances fallen short of expectations. Though representational indicators are a simplistic measure of success without political or tactical context, it is worth noting that of the 31 NATO members in 2023, five have women as their heads of state and 28 out of 31 have or have had WPS NAPs. Yet the challenge continues for NATO and its member states, to go beyond policy creation and surface-level assessments of achievement. In 2022, NATO unveiled a new Strategic Concept document, outlining NATO's priorities, core tasks, and approaches for the next decade. The 2022 Strategic Concept describes the security environment facing the Alliance, reaffirms its values, and spells out NATO's key purpose of ensuring collective defense for its allies. It further sets out NATO's three core tasks of deterrence and defense; crisis prevention and management; and cooperative security. While it also recognizes the continuing impact of conflict-based violence on women, the three references to the WPS framework only reiterate talking points rather than highlighting new areas for direct engagement.[3]

NATO stepped out early with plans, policy, and educational requirements and opportunities for mainstreaming WPS, indeed ahead of many country efforts, including the United States.[4] Since then, however, actual implementation has arguably floundered. The special adviser position remains open, and there are new efforts to gain traction in the operational environment, but many of the traditional internal structures remain intact, funding is insufficient, and new regional threats, like the Russian invasion of Ukraine and the migrant crisis, are bringing to light NATO's WPS shortcomings. The Russian invasion of Ukraine could and should be an opportunity for NATO to revisit previous efforts at Participation, Protection, Prevention, Relief, and Recovery, and initiate new ones in an environment where women and girls were thrust into conflict overnight. There has considerable commentary on NATO's perceived decision to remain silent when Russia's invasion represents "a war fought not just in terms of territory but also represents a fundamental attack on democracy and NATO values including individual liberty, human rights, and the rule of law."[5]

In the face of reports of sexual violence against Ukrainian women in violation of the law of armed conflict, NATO has not acted despite WPS being adopted as part of NATO's Strategic Concept, Ukraine's signature on NATO's WPS policy, and the longtime involvement of NATO in helping Ukraine develop its own WPS plan. It has been argued that the Russian invasion of Ukraine is exactly the situation envisioned by UNSCR 1325, calling for the renewed use of GENADs and the activation of WPS principles in diplomatic engagements.[6] The failure to reassert the importance of the WPS agenda during this conflict has led some scholars to argue that NATO's external efforts are more rhetoric than substance, with WPS providing a "safe issue" and "good news story" for NATO's leadership without substantive changes to on-ground realities.[7]

Recent research and discussions have also exposed two other issues that are impeding the mainstreaming of WPS within NATO, one essentially bureaucratic, the other relating to human nature. The first relates to lack a lack of consensus with NATO regarding the place of Women, Peace, and Security in relation to NATO's focus on human security as a means to action, rather than a conceptual framework for action. At the June 2022 Madrid Summit, human security was highlighted, specifically, the "centrality of Human Security and [...] ensuring that Human Security principles are integrated into our three core tasks." Human security is a way to understand global vulnerabilities as stemming from human, individual people-centered threats, rather than traditional national security threats that suggest a military solution. As a conceptual framework, it predates Women, Peace, and Security, but does not conflict with it, especially because it focuses on cross-cutting topics just as Women, Peace, and Security does. However, when there are two organizational offices fighting for resources and relevance, there is the potential for bureaucratic in-fighting, where everyone loses. Analyst Samantha Turner has pointed out that "without consensus, compromise, and collective action, Women Peace and Security and Human Security risk being sidelined in NATO's mission set."[8]

The second issue relates to why NATO has done better with plans and policies relating to WPS than it has with actual operationalization in the field. One suggested answer to that question is a lack of WPS-related doctrine, which is an issue for all militaries, not just NATO. Doctrine is defined as the fundamental principles by which military forces or elements thereof guide their actions. As explained in relation to the US Army, for example:

It is a body of thought on how Army forces intend to operate as part of a joint force and a statement of how the Army intends to fight. It establishes a common frame of reference including intellectual tools that Army leaders use to solve military problems. It is supposed to focus on how to think – not what to think.[9]

Perhaps most importantly, military forces train based on doctrine. In conflicts, soldiers resort to their lowest level of training; without written doctrine, the means that lead to ways to get things done can't be created; hence, doctrine appears essential for the true operationalization of WPS principles to occur.

Early on, efforts toward the mainstreaming of WPS within NATO were promising. More recently, though, rhetorical support has not been matched with follow-up action. That, unfortunately, will be a recurring theme in this chapter.

African Union (AU)

The AU was created in 2002 and states its mission as to "Defend the sovereignty, territorial integrity and independence of its Member States; Accelerate the political and socio-economic integration of the continent; Promote and defend African common positions on issues of interest to the continent and its peoples; Encourage international cooperation." Since 2003, the AU has also authorized several peacekeeping missions, including in Burundi, Sudan, Somalia, and operations against non-state armed groups, specifically the Lord's Resistance Army, Boko Haram, and the Sahel Region Jihadists, with mixed success, primarily due to funding challenges and logistical inadequacies. Nevertheless, peacekeeping has presented the AU with opportunities to enhance its capabilities in conflict prevention, management, and resolution. Women serve in the AU's peacekeeping forces, though their numbers are low. The AU has set a target goal of 5% female military peacekeepers and 15% of civilian force by 2030.

Much as in NATO, the AU provides an important WPS injection point to the international community. Since 2003, the AU has adopted multiple WPS-related policies and imperatives: the African Charter on Human and People's Rights on the Rights of Women in Africa (Maputo Protocol adopted in 2003), the Solemn Declaration of Gender Equality in Africa (2004), the AU Gender Policy (2008), the Framework for Post Conflict Reconstruction and Development (2006), the Policy Framework for Security Sector Reform (2011), and AGENDA 2063 (2015). The AU also created a Peace and Security Council in 2002, charged with the prevention, management, and resolution of conflicts. It is intended to facilitate timely and efficient responses to conflict and crisis situations in Africa, including through peacekeeping missions where women serve as peacekeepers.

Despite the declarations and charters in place, the WPS effort in Africa fluctuates with the rights and educational opportunities afforded to women and girls across the 55 member states. The Global Study on the Implementation of UNSCR 1325 alleges that these policies have not resulted in a meaningful difference in the daily lives of women in conflict, nor have they sufficiently increased the participation of women in the peace process. As is the case with many of the WPS global efforts to date, there is a growing concern that the AU's policies, along with the

> myriad of monitoring and evaluation templates being produced must not be an end in themselves or be seen as the panacea for effective implementation, i.e., spending most of the resources and energy on developing quick end products in tick-box exercises, rather than on figuring out ways to move beyond the hurdles currently delaying implementation.[10]

While AU commitments have also been adopted in regional instruments and policy frameworks that emphasize women's participation in decision-making and conflict resolution, the commitment by the member states to go beyond policy is difficult to see. Many of the WPS resources in the AU that support operational efforts on the ground are externally funded and related to GBV, with training and support insufficient for implementation. The criticism lies in the "easy button" approach of the effort. The narrow, templated focus on including women in efforts to prevent and respond to GBV enables the existing power structure and gender-based roles to continue,[11] but does little to promote fundamental structural change. Additionally, the effort to monitor the impacts of ground-level efforts remains sparse.

Twenty-eight of the 55 member states of the African Union have NAPs, and the AU continues to promote and facilitate the development and adoption of more. Additionally, four regional organizations within Africa have adopted NAPs: the Economic Community of West African States (2020), the South African Development Community (2020–2024), the Great Lakes Region (2020–2024), and the Economic Community of Central African States (2020–2024). Having plans is only a first step, though, with follow-through essential and often lacking.

One of the greatest potentials of the WPS agenda in the African Union lies in the inclusion of women during the peacemaking process. Madame Bineta Diop was appointed as the AU special envoy on Women, Peace, and Security in 2014. She has worked tirelessly since, advocating for women, often working the Network of African Women in Conflict Prevention and Mediation, commonly known as FemWise-Africa, to promote and professionalize the role of African women in mediation processes, conflict prevention, and peacemaking efforts. But the AU bureaucracy, like the UN, is large and cumbersome.

The WPS principles did gain significant legitimacy through the contributions of women during the peace negotiations in Liberia and South Sudan. The role of South Sudanese women in ending a 30-year dictatorship and participating in the transitional government structure was made possible by a 35% quota represented in the development of the 2018 peace agreement, known as the Revitalized Agreement on the Resolution of the Conflict in the Republic of South Sudan. While the signatures on the Agreement are all those of men, 7 of the 17 civil society signatories were women, a success for meaningful influence in getting to the table and affecting the text of the agreement.[12] Even this small step matters because

> [w]omen at the negotiating table raise issues that are vital for sustainable peace, expanding peace process agendas. They also more often advocate for excluded groups and the need to address underlying causes of conflict, such as development and human rights issues.[13]

Unfortunately, the inclusion of women in peace negotiations is still not the rule but a goal. At a 2023 event marking International Women's Day, Leyman Gboowee, recipient of the 2011 Nobel Peace Prize for her work mobilizing the women of Liberia in conjunction with ending that country's long civil war, spoke out for inclusion.

> It has been proven time and again that men do make war but are unable to make peace themselves. Sadly, the conversation is the same in 2023. How do we discuss the issue of peace and security and leave out fifty percent of the population?

She went on the call NAPs tools "for politicians and political actors to window-dress women peace and security issues as they cover up for the failure" to actually advance women's rights. She said it was essential to include women in all peace missions, referring to them as "custodians of their communities," and concluded, "we will continue to search for peace in vain in our world unless we bring women to the table."[14] The violence that still too often permeates through Africa shrinks the civic space for women's organizations and activists to operate, making progress toward gender equality difficult at best.

While UNSCR 1325 policies to promote gender equality and inclusivity are in place, the desired outcomes have not been broadly realized. Researchers contend that the current peace processes are "largely designed to settle disputes between men with the ability to do harm" and that the invitation to women to join can legitimize the flawed process.[15] Yet, many of the more regional WPS movements on the continent are trying to dismantle the patriarchal nature of peacebuilding. The AU 2020 report highlights new efforts to recognize gender issues arising during the conflict through the Continental Early Warning System. The Continental Early Warning System identified civil society organizations that could promote information sharing on a common platform related to potential, ongoing, and post-conflict situations. Ideally, this initiative will better enable states and the AU to anticipate areas where specific action under the NAPs is needed.

Association of Southeast Asian Nations (ASEAN)

Initially formed in 1967 to fight communism in the region, ASEAN has since evolved to promote economic and security cooperation among its ten member states: Brunei, Cambodia, Indonesia, Laos, Malaysia, Myanmar, the Philippines, Singapore, Thailand, and Vietnam. ASEAN works under a construct that has become known as "the ASEAN way," meaning by painstaking consensus and nonintervention, and often offered as an excuse for regional and organizational inaction. The bloc's impotence regarding security-related issues generally is said to be reflected in its inability to develop a unified approach toward China's expansionist intentions in the South China Sea and in responding to Myanmar's civil war. Consequently, the WPS agenda within ASEAN has been and continues to be fraught with competing power demands, resistance to cultural norms, and resource-based conflicts within its area of responsibility.[16]

A Regional Plan of Action (RPA) was only recently adopted by ASEAN leaders during the fortieth and forty-first summits in November 2022. Only Timor-Leste, the Philippines, and Indonesia have adopted state NAPs, and the slow implementation in this region is attributed to restrictions, backsliding, and sexist practices that impose barriers to women's entry into different branches of the national security apparatus.[17] Notably, the development of the regional plan came after significant international attention on ASEAN and the geographical region due to prior inaction regarding UNSCR 1325. Indeed, Southeast Asian nations separately and collectively have been implicitly and explicitly criticized for "lagging behind" and "underachieving" in the support and promotion of WPS principles.[18]

Analysts have argued that the failure to adopt a WPS agenda earlier is not due to the cultural aspects of "consensus and nonintervention," but rather an elite mindset that continues to frame women as not only separate from political concerns but as fundamentally "apolitical."[19] As the result of the regional stronghold on gendered stereotypes – spindle/spear – there is considerable hesitancy on the part of regional political leaders to increase quotas for women and mainstream acceptance of women as political actors with inherent contributive value. Thus, while women's political participation in the region is improving, with several states enacting quotas and despite ASEAN's recently developed RPA, the efforts to normalize participation in the military and security sectors continue to lag.

It is also important to note that strong regional proclivities in support of the male-dominant status quo means that NAPs and other standards used to measure gender equality or to judge countries against each other can quickly become problematic. While that is true everywhere, it is perhaps especially true in Southeast Asia given its consensus, nonintervention mantra, and the strong Asian "saving face/losing face" version of honor. "Face" is a combination of social standing, reputation, influence, dignity, and honor. Causing someone to lose face lowers their standing in all those areas in the eyes of their peers. Consequently, in Asia individual and organizational mistakes and shortcomings are often ignored in the interest of allowing individuals and organizations to "save face." Given that cultural propensity within the context of the poor regional attitudes toward gender equality leaves WPS implementation as largely aspirational in many countries.

The case of Myanmar, a member state of ASEAN, reflects the challenges of the WPS agenda in the Southeast Asia region. Aung San Suu Kyi became the de facto leader of Myanmar in 2016, having been a national symbol of democracy before she was appointed state counsellor. Her father, Aung San, was an independence activist and revolutionary. As in Indonesia, India, Pakistan, and other countries, women leaders rise to power as daughters of the "founding fathers" of their nations, making it difficult to determine whether they are the result of evolving attitudes or "symbols of their husbands, brothers, and fathers."[20] Perhaps indicative of the answer, the military takeover in Myanmar in 2021 provided a "stark reminder that having a woman head of state is not necessarily a precursor to greater gender diversity in political institutions, particularly where gains in women's political participation have not been formalized."[21]

Aung San Sui Kyi, often called The Lady, was under house arrest when she received the 1991 Noble Peace Prize for her work trying to bring democracy to then military-ruled Myanmar (also known as Burma). While she fell from grace internationally after failing to support the Rohingya population before she was ousted, she remains wildly popular among the Buddhist majority population. The situation in Myanmar illustrates that the role of women in peace and security cannot be achieved through a single woman leader, but instead through the comprehensive inclusion of women at all levels of decision-making.

The ASEAN RPA lists some initial implementation priorities, which include determining anticipated technical and financial needs; defining roles and responsibilities within their institution and of partners; creating timelines and milestones, with clear benchmarks and deliverables; and proposing measures of effectiveness and methods of assessment that, at minimum, detail their involvement both pre- and post-intervention.[22] To meet these objectives, ASEAN may look to the Philippines, which has earned recognition for the inclusion of women in formal peace processes. In 2014, a historic peace agreement was brokered between the Philippine government and the Moro Islamic Liberation Front, an armed insurgent group. Women's civil service organizations were consulted throughout the negotiations with women representing 22% of the negotiators and 27% of the signatories. Miriam Coronel-Ferrer, the government's principal negotiator during the Bangsamoro negotiations, was the first woman in history to sign a major peace settlement with an insurgent group while acting as chief negotiator.[23]

That is not to say, however, that the Philippines has been a bastion of gender-equality enlightenment. Under right-wing populist president Rodrigo Duterte, who served from 2016 to 2022, women generally and women politicians specifically were targeted with not just harassment but also violence. Duterte told his soldiers in 2017 that they could each rape up to three women on the island of Mindanao where he had declared martial law, with impunity, and followed that in 2018 with directions to soldiers to shoot female rebels "in the vagina" to render them useless. In many ways, Duterte more represents regional attitudes toward women than the experience of the women negotiators in 2014.

Commentary on the adoption of the WPS agenda by ASEAN notes the challenges of implementing a more liberal agenda set by the UN into a world that is not as "liberal" as the West, where the agenda was established.[24] Acknowledging that the WPS framework, in many ways, challenges the norms of many ASEAN member states, the next five years will be an important test to see how adaptable aspects of the agenda might be. The implementation efforts of ASEAN's RPA will also provide a new act on the international stage that explores the underlying role of cultural norms and the intersection with gender-based conflict management.

Organization of American States (OAS)

The OAS states its mission as strengthening peace and security in the Western hemisphere; promoting representative democracy; ensuring the peaceful settlement of disputes among members; providing for common action in the event of aggression; and promoting economic, social, and cultural development. The notion of a united Latin America in the southern hemisphere dates back to liberators José de San Martin in the south and Simón Bolivar in the north of the South American continent. The creation of the OAS was strongly supported and bolstered by the United States and key US officials, including Franklin Roosevelt in the 1930s and George Marshall post-World War II, to increase regional security, fight communism in the Western Hemisphere, and support commercial development. The OAS charter was signed by 21 countries, including the United States, in 1948 and went into effect in 1951, and today includes 51 countries. Its headquarters are in Washington, DC, and US inclusion has been both a boost and a hindrance for the organization, as it has at times been viewed as a puppet of the US government. Also, Latin America is riddled with regional organizations that cross-cut each other, sometimes making focused efforts on particular topics difficult.

A 2022 OAS-sponsored study, titled *A Pathway to Peace and Security Forged by Women: An Agenda for the Americas*, begins by bluntly stating,

> for those of us working in the Americas it has been a challenge to foster the appropriation and application of this agenda, in particular in regional political and normative forums such as the Inter-American Commission of Women and the Organization of American States.[25]

Difficulties in implementation reflect the full spectrum of WPS challenges and initiatives.

Most work on gender equality in Latin America remains at the national level due to different interpretations of the WPS principles, to different views on the Western origin of the principles, to cultures, and to political and economic capabilities. As of 2023, there are nine WPS National Action Plans in Latin America – Argentina (2015), Brazil (2017), Chile (2015), El Salvador (2017), Guatemala, (2017), Paraguay (2015), Mexico (2021), Peru (2021), and Uruguay (2021). No Caribbean country has yet adopted a NAP. While Latin America is one of the most underrepresented regions in terms of NAP adoption, Mexico, Chile, and Colombia have adopted an FFP, reflecting varying views among countries regarding the utility and desirability of a NAP, as discussed in Chapter 1 Mexico and Chile have both a NAP and support for FFP.

Although there is no detailed work plan on, for example, Mexico's new FFP, Mexico states its FFP aims as: (1) integrate a gender perspective and a feminist agenda into all aspects of Mexico's foreign policy; (2) achieve gender parity in the Secretariat of Foreign Affairs and conducting organizational reforms in support of gender equality in the workplace; (3) fight all forms of gender-based violence; (4) ensure that feminist leadership and the contributions of women – especially women from Indigenous groups, Afro-descendants and other historically excluded groups – to Mexico's foreign policy development are visible, and (5) pursue an intersectional feminist approach in all foreign policy actions.[26] However, Mexico's NAP and the new FFP do not include official dialogue mechanisms for the monitoring and evaluation of its policies and principles. There is also considerable criticism for the misalignment between Mexico's NAP, FFP, and domestic politics,[27] especially given Mexico's track record regarding GBV. Some international scholars see Mexico's efforts largely as a strategic narrative whereby Mexico can project a "positive image on the international arena, help achieving their objectives, and persuade others to follow suit."[28]

Within areas of high internal conflict and gender-based violence, the principles of UNSCR 1325 have been widely adopted by women's movements in civil society, including in Guatemala, El Salvador, Colombia, and Honduras, but until recently, have garnered limited state attention.[29] In contrast with the low level of civil society engagement evidenced in Mexico on NAP and FFP development, the NAPs of El Salvador and Guatemala stand out for the inclusion of local women's organizations in their development. In Guatemala, the government received technical and logistical support from UN Women and NGOs. Although it was approved only in 2017, the first draft of the Guatemalan NAP went through a long process of consultations with civil society organizations, beginning in 2013. Adopting a more inward-focused approach, Guatemala's NAP relies on the WPS Agenda to navigate the country's postwar situation. It importantly highlights the links between aggression in wartime and the violence perpetrated against women after the conflict. The general objectives of the NAP involve incorporating gender equality and women's rights into the full social and political spectrum of Guatemala, and the continued involvement of women in addressing conflict-related violence within local communities.

A 2022 analysis of Latin American NAPs by a Brazilian think tank provided a comparative mapping of the region in terms of WPS implementation, concluding that "the content and scope of the NAPs can and should be adapted to suit particularities of each country and region."[30] On a narrower basis, a US group developed an analytic tool for assessing the status of women's participation in security forces in Latin America and the Caribbean.[31] While both are valuable tools for those seeking to advance WPS principles, they can also create scorecards that generate resentment and resistance internally among countries.

While there is no regional RPA nor much mention of UNSCR 1325 on an organizational level, OAS has several resolutions on gender equality and the empowering of women as well as a focused committee, the Inter-American Committee of Women. The Inter-American Committee of Women has promoted the political rights of women and has effectively pushed for greater parity in political leadership and decision-making, but there are major differences in the Americas in the level of WPS agenda recognition or implementation.

Within the OAS, the Inter-American Defense Board (IADB), which is part of the OAS' Secretary General, hired a gender adviser for the first time in 2022. The IADB also sponsors a yearly WPS seminar to bring together individuals interested in the topic. While the OAS has done little in terms of operationalizing WPS in practice, it does provide one of several venues through which the US military's Southern Command has been able to work multiple WPS boots-on-the-ground programs over the years, particularly in encouraging and training more women into regional militaries.

While the OAS remains formative in its efforts to advance WPS principles within Latin America, member countries have clearly taken it upon themselves – or not – to advance their individual plans. The orientation of Latin American NAPs, that is, whether the plan adopts an "inward"- or "outward"-looking policy orientation, thus varies from country to country. The general trend in South America is to adopt outward-facing NAPs, which are mostly concerned with their international engagement and foreign policy strategies, thereby avoiding having to deal with internal gender imbalances. However, many of the countries that have suffered military repression and dictatorships have successfully made progress in designing and implementing NAPs which are intended to enable democratic transitions. This diversity reflects the adaptability of the WPS agenda, which can and should be adjusted to meet local needs and priorities. Yet, considering the alarming levels of insecurity and vulnerability that affect women and girls in the region, the lack of convergence and commitment on these issues indicates that coordinated and synergistic efforts to tackle these issues remain to be seen. In this regard, the silence on common gendered insecurities, such as disarmament, drug and human trafficking, persecution of women, human rights, and environmental defenders, as well as forced migration is particularly striking.[32]

European Union (EU)

The EU was created in 1993 to enhance European political and economic integration through the creation and adoption of a single currency (the euro), a unified foreign and security policy, and common citizenship rights, and through the advancement of cooperation regarding immigration and asylum policies, and judicial affairs. As of 2023, it is comprised of 27 members. The United Kingdom was a founding member but left in 2020.

The EU has several initiatives for promoting the implementation of UNSCR 1325 and is externally committed to mainstreaming a gender perspective in all its internal and external actions. In 2008, the EU adopted the Comprehensive Approach to the EU implementation of UN Security Council Resolutions 1325 and 1820 on WPS; in 2018, it adopted the EU Strategic Approach to Women, Peace, and Security, which was followed a year later by the EU Action Plan on WPS in 2019 and the Gender Action Plan in 2020 (known as the "GAP III"). As the third of its kind, the GAP III is considered a "more comprehensive approach" that integrates the priorities of the EU's external-facing efforts and "proposes a three-pronged approach and progressive principles, namely endorsing a transformational, intersectional and human rights-based approach to promote gender equality."[33] Despite the multiple iterations, GAP III and the intersection with the WPS Agenda have not been fully realized and the EU is looking for ways to meet emerging WPS demands while also serving as a leader on the global stage. Within the EU member states, a lack of accountability remains a challenging obstacle. As has been noted,

> Indeed, due to its intergovernmental nature, EU foreign and security policy has no hard incentives to compel relevant actors to fulfill the WPS demands [and] there are no EU mechanisms in place to monitor progress or setbacks on the ground.[34]

The European migrant crisis, resulting from the ongoing conflict external to the member states, represents a major area of criticism for the EU's (and NATO's) lack of action in a WPS-dominant domain. With an emphasis on implementation committees and high-level, in-house expertise, the international community expected more of the EU in incorporating the WPS priorities into the ongoing response to the refugees who are forced to relocate into the EU geographical area. Policy analysts argue that conflict-affected women seeking asylum in Europe are not the focus of the security-based response efforts.[35] When global threats to peace and security arise, WPS often fades into the background as counterterrorism and nationalist agendas take the spotlight. Thus, the response to conflict-generated migration has become a challenge for the WPS framework in the EU, with observers questioning the EU's efforts to account for the experience of women and girls forced to leave their homes and the disparate impacts and violence they face.

Many European NAPs make explicit mention of refugees, mostly related to those within their territory, with some expanding on the basic commitments. Part of the issue is "the idea that women from EU partner countries are (subconsciously) seen as 'beneficiaries' of EU conflict prevention while the expertise and perspective they bring to the table are overlooked or not taken seriously."[36] This reflects a lot of the dynamic in the EU between those inside and those outside; "middle-class, European women, often those who serve in masculine, hard-security roles, disregard women from other parts of the world."[37]

Like many other organizations charged with implementation of WPS principles, the EU has been criticized for not paying enough attention to its own gendered internal norms and practices, which then inhibit the effective execution of external goals. In terms of mediation and peace-making, for example, it has been argued that the EU is burdened with "the practices that produce and reproduce gender even through the process of implementing a gender sensitive or gender-aware security framework."[38] Lack of self-awareness, bureaucratic inertia, and outright resistance can make it easier to want to "fix" others than to address internal issues first.

Conclusions

This chapter was included to remind readers that WPS is a security agenda being addressed within security-related organizations and that political institutions structure human interactions. Consequently, it is important to understand why those organizations are or are not effective in achieving their stated goals. Indeed, the culture of an organization and the people within it exert considerable influence on their goal setting and the prioritization of what is followed up on and what people are held accountable for.

That is not to say that there isn't good work being done regarding Women, Peace, and Security within each of the five exemplary organizations considered here. Quite the contrary. There are many hard-working individuals in each striving to make a positive difference within their organizational confines. Getting organizations to take a hard, critical look within is always a difficult task though, one that requires leadership, commitment, follow-through, and a willingness to compromise and think inclusively. There is a matrix of positive small and large WPS-related activities that go on within and among countries and organizations. Small steps forward must be celebrated as ones to build on.

Notes

1 Chinkin and Reese, 2019; Sowa, T. "In My View: Are Feminist Foreign Policies Translating to Real Action?", in *Development Co-operation Report 2023*: *Debating the Aid System*, Paris: OECD, 2023. https://doi.org/10.1787/337d6469-en: Luke Kelly, Emerging Trends within the Women, Peace and Security (WPS) Agenda, 2022. https://opendocs.ids.ac.uk/opendocs/bitstream/handle/20.500.12413/17202/EIR_49_Women_peace_and_security.pdf?sequence=1&isAllowed=y; Diana Morais, S. Turner, and K. A. Wright, "The Future of Women, Peace, and Security at NATO," 2022. http://turkishpolicy.com/article/1146/the-future-of-women-peace-and-security-at-nato

2 www.act.nato.int/gender-advisor

3 www.nato.int/nato_static_fl2014/assets/pdf/2022/6/pdf/290622-strategic-concept.pdf

4 Joan Johnson-Freese and Andrea Goldstein, "How the Pentagon Can Build on NATO's Success with Women, Peace and Security," *The Strategy Bridge,* May 13, 2019. https://thestrategybridge.org/the-bridge/2019/5/13/how-the-pentagon-can-build-on-natos-success-with-women-peace-amp-security

5 Morais, Turner, and Wright, 2022.

6 Katherine Wright, "Where Is Women, Peace, and Security? NATO's Response to the Russia–Ukraine War," *European Journal of Politics and Gender*, 5 May 2022, pp. 1–3.

7 Wright, 2022.

8 Samantha Turner, "Forward Together: Women, Peace & Security & Human Security at NATO," Stimson Center Issue Brief, February 24, 2023. www.stimson.org/2023/forward-together-women-peace-security-human-security-at-nato/

9 John Spencer, "What Is Army Doctrine?" *Modern War Institute*, March 21, 2016. https://mwi.usma.edu/what-is-army-doctrine/

10 Cheryl Hendricks, "Progress and Challenges in Implementing the Women, Peace and Security Agenda in the African Union's Peace and Security Architecture," *Africa Development*, 42, no. 3(2017), pp. 73–98.

11 Toni Haastrup, "Women, Peace and Security—the African Experience," *Political Insight*, 10, no. 1(2019), pp. 9–11.

12 Sarah Pelham. "Born to Lead: Recommendations on Increasing Women's Participation in South Sudan's Peace Processes," Oxfam, January 30, 2020. https://policy-practice.oxfam.org/resources/born-to-lead-recommendations-on-increasing-womens-participation-in-south-sudans-620934/

13 Marie O'Reilly, "Why Women? Inclusive Security and Peaceful Societies," *Inclusive Security*, 2015. www.inclusivesecurity.org/wp-content/uploads/2017/06/Why-Women-Report-2017.pdf, p. 8.

14 Edith M. Lederer, "Governments Criticized for Keeping Women from Peace Talks," *Associated Press*, March 7, 2023. https://apnews.com/article/women-peace-negotiations-sexual-violence-exclusion-bb4583012fd18c7b2231e270d12a69ec

15 Hendricks, 2017.

16 Mathew Davies, "Women and Development, Not Gender and Politics: Explaining ASEAN's Failure to Engage with the Women, Peace and Security Agenda," *Contemporary Southeast Asia*, pp. 106–127.

17 Jennifer Howe, "Progress and Challenges to Implementing Women, Peace and Security in Southeast Asia," Pacific Forum, 2022. https://pacforum.org/wp-content/uploads/2022/01/issuesinsights_Vol22 WP1-Jan2022-Jennifer-Howe.pdf

18 Maria Tanyan, "Feminist Peace and Security the *Other* ASEAN Way," Pacific Forum, Vol. 2, WP 3, January 2022. https://pacforum.org/wp-content/uploads/2022/01/issuesinsights_Vol22WP3-MARIA-TANYAG.pdf

19 Davies, 2016.

20 Jacqui True, S. Niner, S. Parashar, and N. George, "Women's Political Participation in Asia and the Pacific," In SSRC Conflict Prevention and Peace Forum. 2012.

21 Howe, 2022.

22 https://asean.org/wp-content/uploads/2022/11/32-ASEAN-Regional-Plan-of-Action-on-Women-Peace-and-Security.pdf

23 www.cfr.org/womens-participation-in-peace-processes/Philippines

24 Sandra Brink, "The Women, Peace, and Security (WPS) Agenda: A Normative Investigation of the Agenda in Southeast Asian Countries," 2022. www.diva-portal.org/smash/record.jsf?pid= diva2%3A1670621&dswid=-4860

25 Alejandra Mora, H. Anderson, A. I. Garita, and A. Kielhold, "Pathways to Peace and Security Forged by Women: An Agenda for the Americas," CIM. 2022. www.oas.org/es/cim/docs/NotaConceptual-LanzamientoInformeMPS-EN%20(1).pdf

26 www.gob.mx/sre/prensa/mexico-adopts-feminist-foreign-policy?idiom=en

27 Ekatherina Zhukova, M. R. Sundström, and O. Elgström, "Feminist Foreign Policies (FFPs) as Strategic Narratives: Norm Translation in Sweden, Canada, France, and Mexico," *Review of International Studies*, 48, no. 1(2022), pp. 195–216.

28 Zhukova et al., 2022.

29 Mora et al., 2022.

30 Paula Drumond et al., "Mapping the Women, Peace and Security Agenda in Latin America," BRICS, 2022. https://bricspolicycenter.org/wp-content/uploads/2022/10/BPC_PB_v12_n4_MPS_AmLat_G SUM.pdf

31 Chantal de Jonge Oudraat et al., Enhancing Security, WIIS, 2022, www.wiisglobal.org/wp-content/ uploads/2021/01/REV.2-Enhancing-Security-Report-Jan-22-21.pdf

32 Paula Drumond, and T. Rebelo. "Global Pathways or Local Spins? National Action Plans in South America," *International Feminist Journal of Politics*, 22, no. 4, (2020), pp. 462–484.

33 Sophie Desmidt, "How the Women, Peace and Security Agenda Is Integrated into the EU's Gender Action Plan." ECDPM Briefing Note 141. Maastricht: ECDPM. October 25, 2021.

34 Jessica Almqvist, "Rekindling the Agenda on Women, Peace and Security: Can the EU Lead by Example?" ElCano Royal Institute. March 2021.

35 Aiko Holvikivi and A. Reeves, "The WPS Agenda and the 'Refugee Crisis': Missing Connections and Missed Opportunities in Europe," Working paper. 2017. www.researchgate.net/publication/318318 631_The_WPS_agenda_and_The_'Refugee_Crisis'_Missing_Connections_and_Missed_Opportun ities_in_Europe/link/596375e9aca2728c111fbce4/download
36 Nina Bernarding and K. Lunz. "A Feminist Foreign Policy for the European Union," Centre for Feminist Foreign Policy. June 2020. https://centreforfeministforeignpolicy.org/wordpress/wp-content/uploads/2023/01/Study-Feminist-Foreign-Policy-for-the-European-Union.pdf
37 Laura Davis, "Kissing the Frog: Gender Equality in the EU Conflict Prevention and Other Fairy Tales," EU-CIVCAP, 2018, quoted in Bernarding and Lutz, 2020.
38 Toni Haastrup, "Creating Cinderella? The Unintended Consequences of the Women, Peace and Security Agenda for EU's Mediation Architecture," *International Negotiation*, 23(2018) p. 221.

Further reading

Aduda, Levke, and Johanna Liesch. (2022) "Women at the Table: Identifying Factors through which Women Have the Opportunity to Influence Peace Agreement Design." *Journal of Global Security Studies*, 7(1).
AUC. (2023). *Report on the Implementation of Women, Peace and Security Agenda in Africa 2020*. African Union (au.int).
Bellou, Fontini, and Kalliope Chainoglou. (2022) "The WPS Agenda in the Eastern Mediterranean: The Cases of Greece, the Republic of Cyprus and Turkey." *Interdisciplinary Political Studies*, 8(1), pp. 57–80.
Davies, Sara E., Kimberly Nackers, and Sarah Teitt. (2014). "Women, Peace and Security as an ASEAN Priority." *Australian Journal of International Affairs*, 68(3), pp. 333–355.
Davies, Sara E., and Jacqui True. (2022) "Follow the Money: Assessing Women, Peace, and Security through Financing for Gender-Inclusive Peace." *Review of International Studies*, 48(4), pp. 668–688.
Didaoui, Yasmine. "The European Union's Strategic Approach to Women, Peace and Security: A Real Change?" 2021. www.diva-portal.org/smash/record.jsf?pid=diva2%3A1612174&dswid=6606
Nhengu, Dudziro. "Feminisms, WPS Agenda and Women's Peacebuilding and Peacemaking Networks in Africa: Solution or Quandary?" July 23, 2022. https://zenodo.org/record/6891071#.ZD_yLezMLAM
O'Sullivan, Mila, and Katerina Krulišová. "Women, Peace and Security in Central Europe: In between the Western Agenda and Russian Imperialism." *International Affairs*, March 2023.
Sánchez, Carolina Jiménez. (2022) "Caliphate Women Limbo and the Action of the European Union." *Journal of Regional Security*, 17(1), pp. 65–82.
Thomson, Jennifer, and Sophie Whiting. (2022). "Women, Peace and Security National Action Plans in anti-gender governments: The Cases of Brazil and Poland." *European Journal of International Security*, 7(4), pp. 531–550.
True, Jacqui, and Antje Wiener. (2019). "Everyone Wants (a) Peace: The Dynamics of Rhetoric and Practice on 'Women, Peace and Security.'" *International Affairs*, 95(3), pp. 553–574.
von Hlatky, Stéfanie. *Deploying Feminism: The Role of Gender in NATO Operations*, Oxford University Press, 2022.

13 Moving forward

The Women, Peace, and Security framework created by UNSCR 1325 in 2000 has evolved and continues to evolve as the global security environment evolves. NAPs are becoming less standardized to Western expectations and more tailored to regional and national cultures and needs, and appropriately so. WPS principles are even more pertinent and needed today for sustainable peace in every nation than they were originally, given the intervening geopolitical, economic, climate-related, and pandemic-related events that have occurred, creating new problems and simultaneously setting back gender equality efforts. Additionally, with a correlation between democracy and gender equality now clearly evident, it appeared in 2000 that democracy was on the rise. Currently, however, support for authoritarian, right-wing populist factions has emerged even in what were thought the staunchest democracies. The consequent rollbacks in gender equality where right-wing populist factions have taken hold are alarming.

The Ukrainian fight to push the Russians out of Ukrainian territory presents questions relevant to the future of both international relations and gender equality, because a threat to democracy somewhere is a threat to democracy everywhere. Will the future be one where borders and sovereignty are respected, or will it be one where autocrats are allowed to invade other countries at will, take land, and get away with it? If the latter is the case, it won't stop with Ukraine. Further, as Erica Chenoweth and Zoe Marks pointed out in their 2022 *Foreign Affairs* article "Revenge of the Patriarchs: Why Autocrats Hate Women," misogyny and authoritarianism often go hand in hand, and in fact reinforce each other. While strong-arm authoritarianism/fascism is difficult to maintain over time, the rollbacks on women's issues that accompany authoritarian rule can be brutal. What autocrats fail to realize is that it is women who stabilize societies. It is women who make the difference between a temporary, fragile peace that must be held together by constant fear and force, and an enduring, positive peace.

Fortunately, once the relationship between gender equality and positive peace – true security – is recognized, it can't be unseen. Once seen, affirmations of the linkage between gender and security, positive and negative, that are in the news daily are no longer perceived as unique events but as part of a bigger picture. Decision-makers truly interested in enduring peace begin to understand and act on gender equality as being as key to peace as economic growth and a strong defense. Military leaders who understand Women, Peace, and Security begin to recognize that its principles provide a war-fighting advantage. Therefore, it is imperative that recognition of the gender equality/security linkage be expanded, as intended through National Action Plans, and in the United States, the 2017 Women, Peace, and Security Act. It is also important to remember that NAPs and the Women, Peace, and Security Act have both internal and external components and executing one without the other is self-defeating. And finally, there has been too much rhetoric and performative declarations, and not enough action. Expanded knowledge

DOI: 10.4324/9781003413417-14

through education, focusing on both internal and external WPS components, and moving beyond box-checking are fundamental to moving forward.

Education

Education is key to expanding knowledge of the relationship between gender equality and security generally, and the Women, Peace, and Security framework specifically. Knowledge must be mainstreamed into all types of education. The reality of that statement, however, is that the first step is to teach the teachers. That won't be easy, though it should be easier in some institutions than others.

For government employees, including military members, attendance at training and educational programs is a requirement for career advancement in most countries. In educational institutions sponsored and administered by government organizations – like NATO, militaries, foreign affairs institutions, and so on – there is often more organizational control over faculty work requirements and curriculum than in civilian academic institutions. Also, the more senior government schools tend to think of themselves as delivering professional education akin to that of law schools and business schools, rather than as liberal arts institutions. That being the case, it is fairly standard practice that professions like law, accounting, medicine, and so on require continuing education of their practitioners as part of their professional licensing. It would therefore not be unreasonable to require continuing education of faculty at government-run educational institutions as well.

For example, faculty could be required to complete a 12-hour (which would be enough to cover the basics) Women, Peace, and Security faculty development course offered at various times over the course of a year or two, and then offered intermittently for new faculty until deemed no longer needed. Faculty would then have the requisite knowledge to integrate gender considerations into the core curriculum. This seems especially reasonable given that in the United States, for example, it is the Department of Defense, the Department of State, USAID, and the Department of Homeland Security that are charged, by law, with WPS implementation. While there have been several stand-alone events on WPS within PME, sometimes including publications,[1] mainstreaming WPS into core curricular materials is required to assure that future leaders are knowledgeable, and to effectively integrate WPS principles into military doctrine so it does not fall to the wayside during crises.

Resistance to mainstreaming WPS into core curricula at some government schools often relies on variations of the same stale arguments that have hindered implementation of WPS generally. In the US Department of Defense, for example, there has been a drumbeat argument that there are so many important Pentagon-required subjects to be covered within PME, that there is simply no room for anything else without taking something out. That argument smacks of seeing WPS as a nice thing to do, but expendable. It also reflects a fundamental misunderstanding of gender equality as a stand-alone topic rather than an integral part of other topics and more generally, still seeing security as a "male" field. The latter is reflected in a variety of ways including low numbers of women faculty and low representation of women in PME curricular readings.

PME institutions, at least in the United States, often disingenuously bemoan that there that there aren't women in the field to hire as faculty or women-authored articles to include in the security-focused curriculum. Yet according to Data USA, women were awarded 56% of graduate degrees in International Relations and Security Studies in 2020, a number fairly consistent at least since 2012. Regarding readings, based on two in-house surveys of authored core curricular articles used in PME curriculum, one at the Naval War College and the other at the Joint Forces Staff College, women authored or coauthored about 10% of what the students read.

Yet a quick review of articles in *Foreign Affairs*, a premier international relations and security affairs journal, published between May/June 2022 and May/June 2023 shows women authoring or coauthoring approximately 37%, so there are women-authored articles available. Similarly, 55% of articles and editorials published by the *Harvard International Review* from April 2022 to April 2023 were authored by female scholars. Not surprisingly, organizational culture plays a role in hiring, promotion, and retention practices for women and minorities[2] and in them being seen as valuable contributors to national security through indicators such as publications.

Another excuse against mainstreaming WPS into PME is that for it to happen, WPS would have to be designated a "special area of emphasis (SAE)" by the Pentagon. Different SAEs are designated annually or thereabouts. For academic year 2020–21, for example, the SAEs were: Great Power Competition; Globally Integrated Operations in the Information Environment; Strategic Deterrence; Modem Electromagnetic Spectrum Battlefield; Space as a Warfighting Domain; Ability to Write Clear and Concise Military Advice Recommendations. That argument is moot, though, given that within the DOD WPS Implementation Strategy there is a requirement to assure that "WPS principles are appropriately reflected in relevant DoD policies, plans, doctrine, training, *education,* operations, resource planning, and exercises" (italics added). In actuality, resistance stems from a total lack of, or misunderstanding of, the WPS framework by a largely, retired-military, male faculty and administration. It is seen as actually more DEI (gender justice rather than security studies) and overall "not relevant to me." Some navy personnel, for example, have even suggested that while WPS might be relevant to other military services, it is not relevant to the navy because the navy operates at sea rather than on land. While a baffling argument generally, it is also ignores that the navy was onshore in Iraq, and Afghanistan, and will be again in the future.

In civilian academia at large, the obstacles are in some ways even greater. Faculty are specialized in their often-narrow fields, proudly and defiantly autonomous, and unlikely to welcome intrusions into the development and execution of their course material by administrators. However, I make it a practice to encourage my WPS students, who have "seen" the significance of gender equality to IR course material, to ask questions pertaining to the relevance of gender in courses where it is omitted, and to (strongly) suggest the future inclusion of such on course evaluations. Enough student comments on course evaluations can perhaps encourage gender and gendered inclusion of subject matter from faculty, but resistance will be strong. Civilian academia is an elitist culture made up of subject matter experts who bristle at challenges to their expertise. Overall, a critical mass of teachers at all levels who are cognizant of the role of gender equality in international relations must be developed.

Until gender equality considerations are mainstreamed, opportunities critical to small advantages that create big wins in geopolitical, strategic competition may well be missed. Are, for example, gender considerations being fully integrated into intelligence assessments? Are gendered plans being implemented in crises and relief and recovery, or forgotten in favor of standard operating procedures, thereby missing opportunities to make real change in gender structures? Are gender inequalities keeping women from filling critical-need roles in areas like cyber and AI? Are women being assigned – not attached – to Special Forces units so that they are considered a full part of the team, thereby maximizing their input into operations? Are feminine as well as masculine approaches to negotiations being used? Are women routinely included in negotiations? As is often heard in WPS circles, though they play an important role there, you don't need women just to win battles, you need women to win wars and keep the peace.

Again too – and this can't be repeated too often – gender expertise is an analytic competence, not a physiological trait. Some of the strongest proponents of WPS from my WPS classes have been men. There are an increasing number of male advocates at conferences, workshops, and symposia too, many of them former military or foreign service types who have witnessed the benefits of gender considerations. That is important because the reality is, the more male allies there are speaking up for implementation of WPS, the more skeptics will be persuaded. I have often seen it be the case that (mostly male) skeptics will accept the importance of the WPS principles if recommended by another man rather than a woman. A WPS panel was included at a 2022 convocation-related event at the Naval War College. The first speaker was Lt. General (ret.) Daniel "Fig" Leaf, the former president of the Asia Pacific Center for Security Studies and a strong WPS ally. He spoke eloquently and substantively about WPS before the other three women on the panel (including myself) spoke, but most of all he conveyed the message of "this is important, listen up" to the audience of warfighters interested primarily in warfighting tactics.

Internal and external components

The need to convince skeptics and to broadly expand the WPS support spectrum ties in with the second necessary step to move WPS implementation forward. Organizations charged with implementing WPS principles within countries must acknowledge and act on the premise that those principles apply internally as well as externally. It has been noted that many NAPs focus on either externally related plans and programs, or on internally increasing the number of women in security forces. For those countries seeking to increase the number of women in the military, for example, they would do well to assess their own practices, policies, and institutions. As was the case in Ukraine before the full mobilization, women were not interested in joining the military under conditions that limited their opportunities, and within a notably misogynistic culture (which rapidly changed when the women became needed) to serve national security needs. Whether Ukraine will resort back to its misogynistic ways after the fighting stops, as has happened in so many other countries, remains to the seen.

Rates of sexual assault in militaries around the world strongly indicate that WPS principles are not fully integrated into militaries. Women too often remain penalty-free targets of mistreatment and GBV, even at the hands of those who they are expected to trust their lives to and who claim honor as part of their ethos. The report on Ft. Hood after the murder investigation of 20-year-old Vanessa Guillén by another soldier called sexual assault an "insider threat." A 2022 US Department of Defense sexual assault report stated that one in ten female sailors in the US Navy experienced sexual assault in 2021, though the US Marine Corps had the highest percentage of assaults at 13.4% of females serving. The numbers were called "disappointing" and "tragic." What they were was reflective of institutions where "real man" masculinities prevail, are encouraged, and where the dangers of which largely go unheeded, undiscussed, and unaddressed. Those dangers affect not only the women they serve with, but the countries they are serving or have served. The potential negative consequences of that reality were shown in the United States, for example, on January 6, 2021, in the United States.

In January 2023, three active-duty Marines were charged with participating in the January 6, 2021, riots at the US Capitol. One of them, Micah Coomer, an intelligence, surveillance, and reconnaissance system engineer at Camp Pendleton, CA, posted on his social media page, "Glad to be part of history … I'm waiting for the boogaloo" (Civil War 2). Two other active-duty military members have been charged with crimes related to January 6 as of April 2023. A disproportionate 20% of the defendants in the Capitol riot cases served in the military, while only about 7% of American adults are veterans. This includes a veteran and member of the Oath Keepers convicted of seditious conspiracy (a plan or effort to overthrow the government), and recent indictments of members of the Proud Boys for sedition made up primarily of military veterans. The military has a problem that affects not only the women who serve, but also national security overall given that, as pointed out in Chapter 1, national security is predicated on the ability of the government to identify and mitigate all threats to the safety, security, and functioning of the United States, great and small, domestic and foreign. Women should not have to serve at their peril, nor should the nation have to wonder if its defenders support democracy.

Finally, it has been over 20 years since UNSCR 1325 was passed and implementation is still in the very formative phase. Unfortunately, that delay is at least partially attributable to security institutions often paying little attention to civil society initiatives. That gap must be bridged, and education will play a part in that. There are also many well-intentioned, informed, and industrious individuals in civil society organizations and government institutions working to implement WPS globally. Unfortunately, there are more blind fish and skeptics who see the effort as superfluous, outright resisters who see gender equality as against their interests, and those who see gender equality as a nice-thing-to-do-when-convenient but an expendable bargaining chip when realpolitik rears its head.

Retired US Army Colonel and APCSS WPS Chair James Minnich has pointed out that security organizations are not boys' clubs that women wish to join. Perpetuating that view is itself a security threat as global threats today create problems for which every country needs the best and brightest to address them, regardless of gender, race, religion, sexual orientation, age, and so on. To date, there has been a considerable degree of incorporation of women into security systems, at least in some countries, but that has meant that women have had to adapt to the system, thereby losing much of what they have to contribute by simply adding to the status quo. Minnich suggests that the better alternative is inclusion, whereby the system adapts to women, thereby gaining from their additive value. Within the context of requiring women to adapt, culture is an instrument of group control.[3]

The reality is that men can introduce neutrality into gender allyship. As allies, or supporters, men can point out that changes to gender-inequality norms have value to all people that women cannot point out without the suggested changes sounding merely self-serving. Being an ally, however, can come with risk and social costs to men, specifically the risk of being shunned by the in-group. Leadership shapes culture and can negate or minimize those costs. If leaders are committed, they can create feelings of belonging, as an emotion born in security and support.[4] Inclusion and feelings of belonging are what it will take to truly achieve the Women, Peace, and Security goals.

Women play a big role in negating gender stereotypes, too, not only regarding working on their own competence and confidence, but going back to the first political order, the home. Women, it was recently pointed out at a US military-sponsored WPS conference by a senior woman military officer from a patriarchal country, must raise sons who support and respect women. There isn't a religion in the world that dictates that men mistreat women. We all have a role to play in making real change happen. Unfortunately, there has been too much performative allyship and not enough real commitment to date.

Moving beyond performance

There is too much performative allyship of gender equality going on – individuals, organizations, or countries merely professing to be supporters – and not enough meaningful action. It is time to do more naming and shaming. Performative allyship examples abound, perhaps most glaring through President Donald Trump signing the Women, Peace and Security Act in 2017 while simultaneously gutting international funding for women's reproductive care, blocking laws supportive of equal pay in the workplace for women, asking the Center for Disease Control to omit certain words from its budget – including evidenced-based, transgender, and diversity – and disbanding the White House Council on Women and Girls. Performative allyship, pinkwashing, has also been used to divide and conquer vulnerable communities. Companies have been called out for pinkwashing, in areas such as trying to convey support of LGBTQ+ communities by use of a pride flag on corporate logos in advertising. Daimler Benz did that 2021, but chose not to run the ad featuring the pride flag-colored logo in the Middle East so as not to offend potential consumers there, evidencing thin commitment to professed principles.

It was only after international actors drew attention to a lack of WPS action in Southeast Asia that ASEAN stepped up and took a positive step forward in the development of a Regional Action Plan. But national and regional action plans are only as meaningful as the actions that follow. While it is true that change takes time, time sometimes needs a nudge. There are carrots and sticks that can be used to "encourage" meaningful action. In the United Nations, for example, nations that provide individuals to serve in peacekeeping forces – relatively lucrative jobs for many individuals – had to be "encouraged" to send more women in non-administrative roles like policing and military operations. Previously, some country administrators had claimed there simply weren't women in their countries trained and available for those roles. When provision of women for those roles was tied to UN staff support for country administrators at headquarters, though, there were suddenly women available. Such "encouragement" would be useful in other instances of slow implementation of WPS principles as well.

Politicians and groups have also voiced rhetorical support for one group as a means to attack another. Marine Le Pen, representing a political party known for its anti-feminist, homophobic views, appointed gay advisers during her 2017 presidential bid in France, to distance herself from her party's traditional homophobic platform. But the feminist movement and the LGBTQ+ movement are not mutually exclusive. In fact, they strongly intersect at considerations of gender. Cooperation between those groups offers the best chance of success for all marginalized communities, including as well with the FFP supporters. Keeping alert to attempts to divide and conquer will be key in building broader communities of support for both movements.

There has also been consideration regarding whether or not countries should be required to commit a certain amount of spending to a NAP as an indicator of real commitment. Then, however, the question becomes how much? And if the NAP doesn't have a budget, what are the consequences? Is the country left out of WPS conversations? Those may be exactly the countries that need to be in conversations. There are also instances of low-income countries making strides in ways not requiring funding as much as leadership commitment to inclusiveness. In 2022, Jamaica, one of the poorest countries in North America, became the first country in the world to have a woman as chief of staff of the military, Rear Admiral Antonette Wemyss Gorman.

Learning from and using best practices can make what is an inherently complex process of gender integration smoother. CDR Ella van den Heuvel from the Netherlands Armed Forces has worked as a gender adviser in many capacities for more than ten years. She has assembled a very pragmatic set of suggestions for advancing gender integration in military organizations, which she presented at a May 2023 Gender Integration Seminar in Jordan, that are applicable more broadly as well.

- Develop a Gender Action Plan with concrete actions that are clearly explained
- Ensure full commitment of leadership (at the highest level) for gender integration and the execution of the Gender Action Plan
- Hold the leadership accountable for the achievement of the goals of the Gender Action Plan
- Ensure that the Lead Gender Adviser (a gender expert with practical experience) has direct access to the leadership

- Ensure a sufficient budget for the Gender Unit, to execute the Gender Action Plan
- Ensure sufficient gender capacity, gender expertise, and skills to execute the actions at head-quarters level and to provide guidance and support to the Gender Advisers/Gender Focal Points at the unit level
- Provide training to Gender Focal Points and colleagues who are supporting gender integration
- Put continuous effort into raising gender awareness within the organization by organizing gender courses/workshops/training/briefings/seminars at every level
- Give practical examples and use scenarios in order to make it clearer what the effect is of applying a gender lens
- Emphasize that gender integration is enhancing operational effectiveness
- Work closely together with your DEI colleagues, but keep WPS as a separate pillar in order not to lose focus on the UNSCR 1325 on WPS
- Collaborate with external partners (other ministries, international organizations, NGOs, women's organizations, and so on) to learn from each other and (on occasion) organize sessions together
- Go for small steps forward – be pragmatic and realistic in what you can achieve; Put lots of effort into "doing" things. Implementation means: taking action
- Find your allies/pick your battles/believe in what you are doing: implementing 1325 is needed!
- Create moments for reflection!

Inclusive diversity and the incorporation of gendered perspectives will not happen "naturally" as it goes against the grain of a very power-motivated status quo. But it can happen.

Conclusion

A wider coalition of support for the Women, Peace, and Security platform is needed and will be a key component in mainstreaming its principles. WPS is relevant to and can be conveyed via the financial world, city planning, health, and so on, and even the arts. In many countries, for example, singing and dancing is an acceptable way for women to express themselves, including at political rallies.[5] Part of that expansion will be broadening the WPS knowledge base generally and beyond civil society groups where it originated. Most likely, in many cases that expansion will require more data-driven evidence of the linkage between gender equality and long-term security.

A student in my WPS class once expressed frustration and indignation that "proof" is often required to convince skeptics that women play a role in security. While I share her feelings, needing data is the reality of where we are. If achieving the desired goal requires adopting means that would not be adopted in a "fair" world, then that's what needs to be done. Strategic communication is all about achieving a goal: sending the right message to the right audience through the right medium at the right time. If it takes data to convince decision-makers that gender equality is important to national security, then data must be part of the message conveyed. The world is far from fair. More and better gender-differentiated data remains key.

In the meantime as well, every person can contribute to furthering the principles of Women, Peace, and Security. It is not just the right but the responsibility of all individuals, for example, to vote. Democracy is under siege and assuming that others will step up and protect it from authoritarianism, with rollbacks in gender equality certain to follow, is a recipe for disaster. Also, for those who have "seen" the value of gender equality to national security, talk about it – within families, classrooms, and organizations. Offer to give or arrange a presentation or lead a discussion to raise awareness among those men and women who might simply be blind fish. I've been amazed and gratified by the variety of ways students who have taken my WPS course have proactively stepped up to spread the word. The cover of this book was created by a former student, depicting an acid-attack survivor who had been a guest speaker in the class. The artist has created a full portfolio of drawings depicting violence against women, shown in galleries and distributed as bookmarks and postcards through her own efforts. Others have started women's focused financial funds, created an organization to empower girls and young women, funded women's projects, written articles within their own professional fields, created mentorship programs within their professional organizations, gone on to teach courses elsewhere, and much, much more. WPS practitioner and advocate Stephenie Foster created a how-to book, *Take Action: Fighting for Girls and Women* (2021), for individuals wanting to do more. There is something everyone can do.

The WPS framework will continue to evolve as the world evolves. Remember, development and execution of strategy is not a linear process but a circular one that requires constant maintenance to avoid misalignment of the component parts. The goal of this book has been to provide students with the situational awareness of gender equality in the security-related environment requisite to build successful strategies, micro and macro, to move forward.

Notes

1 Laura MacKenzie and Dana Perkins (eds.), *Women, Peace & Security in Professional Military Education*, Marine Corps University, 2022.
2 Joan Johnson-Freese, Ellen Haring, and Marybeth Ulrich, "The Counterproductive Sea of Sameness in PME," *Joint Force Quarterly*, July 2014. https://ndupress.ndu.edu/JFQ/Joint-Force-Quarterly-74/Article/577529/the-counterproductive-sea-of-sameness-in-pme/
3 James M. Minnich, "Politics of Belonging: Men as Allies in the Meaningful Inclusion of Women in the Security Sector" in *Women, Peace, and Security in a Fragile World: Perspectives on Warfighting, Crisis Management, and Post-Conflict Transitions*, ed. Saira Yamin, Naval War College Press, forthcoming.
4 Minnich.
5 Marilyn Rockefeller and Joan Johnson-Freese, "Dancing for Democracy: Understanding Malawi's First Female President," *Orbis*, Spring 2013, pp. 268–281.

Index